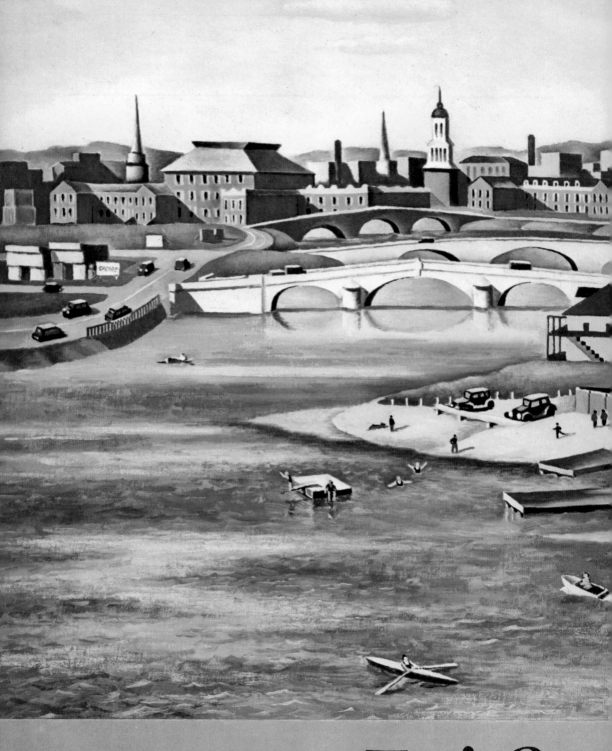

Life

Oil painting by Yvonne Twining Humber

in America

America is not anything if it consists of each of us. It is something only if it consists of all of us; and it can consist of all of us only as our spirits are banded together in a common enterprise. That common enterprise is the enterprise of liberty and justice and right.

WOODROW WILSON, 1916

by

MARSHALL B. DAVIDSON

Life *in* America

IN TWO VOLUMES: VOL. II

Published in Association with the Metropolitan Museum of Art

HOUGHTON MIFFLIN COMPANY BOSTON

The Riverside Press Cambridge

1951

CONTENTS

CONTENTS

VI

AMERICA

AT LEISURE

AMERICA AT LEISURE

INTRODUCTION

To SUCH a representative Puritan as Samuel Sewall the April Fool's Day pranks of Boston children were not naughty or a nuisance, but "an abuse of precious time . . . a profanation!" It was God's time they wasted, a gift from heaven that should be improved on earth, not frittered away. Frequently and meticulously the early New England colonists legislated against idleness and the "mis-spending" of time. Tireless industry assured salvation, if not necessarily from Old Nick, at least from the threat of starvation or privation in a land that was raw and that could be cruel. A pioneer society could not support drones if New Zion were to be built in the wilderness. In an effort to explain those conditions of American life to his European correspondents Benjamin Franklin delighted to write them that in this country everyone worked. There was no idle class, rich or otherwise. Of all living creatures, he wrote, quoting the Negro legend, only the hog didn't work. "He eat, he drink, he walk about, he go to sleep when he please, *he* live like a gempleman."

For several generations after the Revolution leisure was still not a conspicuous feature of American life. Strangers to American ways commented with surprise on the everlasting busy-ness of people in the States. "It is well known," wrote James Silk Bucking-ham, "that they are among the most constantly occupied and busiest people in the world." Human activity seemed geared to a driving necessity, in the home as in the shop and the field. American housewives, complained Mrs. Basil Hall, an English visitor, in 1829, "are so constantly at work with real business, that they have no time to think of little minor things that constitute refinement." At every call her hostesses—the governor's wife included—kept her waiting while they tidied-up from some menial task they were obliged to help with if housework were to proceed apace. Their husbands, in turn, were so concerned with workaday cares that they found neither time nor interest for the pursuits of leisure—little enough of either, indeed, to pay proper attention to their wives.

Man, woman, and child alike knew that work was never finished on the farm. "There is no greater defect in educating children," counseled an early agricultural magazine, "than neglecting to accustom them to work." Those who remained on the soil, a large part of the population until a late date, could expect little else in life. Not that recreation was denied at any time. Playfulness could always find an approved outlet in productive social activities—in house-raisings, bees, militia musters, and similar purposeful get-togethers—and beyond the frontier of urban influence long continued to do so in an old, accustomed manner. "The Americans seldom do any thing without having [a frolic]," wrote a traveler in early Illinois. "Thus they have husking, reaping, rolling frolics, etc., etc. Among the females, they have picking, sewing, and quilting frolics. Reaping frolics, are parties to reap the whole growth of wheat, etc. in one day. Rolling frolics, are clearing woodland, when many trees are cut down, and into lengths, to roll them up together, so as to burn them, and to pile up the brush-wood and roots on the trees. . . . Picking cotton, sewing, and quilting frolics, are meetings to pick cotton from the seeds, make clothes, or quilt quilts; in the latter, the American women pride themselves. Whiskey is here too in request, and they generally conclude with a dance."

The gospel of work maintained its authority long after the social needs it expressed had disappeared. The American's passion for incessant industry, concluded a French visitor in the 1830's, was a matter of inheritance and training as well as of circumstance. Even those far removed from any threat of hardship continued to work from a grim inner compulsion that consumed most of their time and energies. "Who that has travelled in Europe is not familiar with the type of the broken-down American business-man, sent abroad to recruit his collapsed nervous system?" observed the *Nation* in 1873; "With his harried, hungry mien, unfitted by life-long habit for taking any pleasures in passive contemplation."

That recreation could be a good thing in itself, no less a necessary thing, was only slowly acknowledged. The need was first felt in the cities as they filled up with people suddenly divorced from old rural habits and caught in a novel routine that lacked the informal diversions of country life. The growing urban democracy, assertive and prosperous as it was, demanded amusements befitting its peculiar needs, and was willing to pay for them. People who paid for their food instead of growing it, who bought their clothes instead of making them, who paid rent instead of building their homes, learned to pay for their entertainment instead of creating it. When the city populace, unwashed mechanic, weary housemaid, and all the rest, took over the patronage of the theater during the early years of the nineteenth century, promise was given of the enormous commerce in recreation which would follow. By mid-century it already appeared that a good part of the American population was willing, if not eager, to get their recreation vicariously and at a price.

A new attitude toward leisure and recreation came about inevitably, although the adjustment was accomplished against the opposition of time-worn moral strictures. From an early date, numbers of the wealthier class had discovered the pleasures of play and had evolved or imported pastimes for their own special benefit. One by one these were usurped by the masses, as they found the time, and were made their own. With the steamboat and the railroad offering cheap excursions, even travel was possible for the common man. Dancing had long since overcome early Puritan disapproval and ceased to be a fashionable vice. By 1839 it was reported that the waltz, a daring innovation, was "fast absorbing the favorite old dances." Five years later it was the polka, another startling novelty, that threatened to "overrun the world" with its popularity. Soon, wise and important men like Emerson and Holmes were urging Everyman to get out and play, to build his muscles, freshen his spirit, and enjoy the leisure he earned in his working hours. One wonders how they would view the special "Sports Bay" in the Cathedral of Saint John the Divine in New York.

By the opening years of the twentieth century Americans were taking their recreation in dead earnest. Step by step the working hours of most people had grown fewer, their leisure greater, and their hunt for amusement more intense. Having fun, according to one critic, had become the crowning ritual of American life. Billions of dollars were involved in the business of supplying it through moving pictures, automobiles, radio, professional sporting events, sporting equipment for amateurs, vacation equipment and facilities, and endless other means.

As has been pointed out, if Americans were to return to the concepts of their Puritan forefathers and shun amusement as an evil, the country's entire economy would be seriously dislocated.

PLAYING BALL.

The Metropolitan Museum of Art
PLAYING BALL, EARLY 19TH CENTURY. Engraving from an award of merit.

AMERICA LEARNS TO PLAY

Games played with a ball may, as Thomas Jefferson observed, stamp no character on the mind but, in one form or another, they have provided an immemorial pastime for American children, men, and occasionally, even women.

"Let any one visit Washington Parade, or indeed any of the fields in that neighborhood," reported the New York *Evening Post* in 1828, "and he will find large groups of men and boys playing ball and filling the air with their shouts and yells . . . the annoyance has become absolutely intolerable . . . and ought to be put an end to without delay." The complaint could have been written almost any time in any American community; the end is not yet in sight.

In spite of its danger to health ("by sudden and alternate heats and cold"), to limbs, and to the propriety of gentlemen scholars, college students played their games with sticks and balls on most early campuses and commons. Cricket enjoyed popularity where English influence lingered. But the time required to complete a game, two days on an average, was a handicap to American participants. Leisure in the new republic was not yet so abundant nor, according to high opin-

ion, without a serious menace to the morals.

Off campus and on, in the fall of the year, football of one sort or another was popular by the end of the eighteenth century. "Before winter comes on the Foot Ball," wrote William Bentley, the noted Salem divine and diarist, in 1791, "which is differently pursued in different places. In Marblehead, even heads of families engage in it, & all the fishermen while at home at this season. The bruising of shins has rendered it rather disgraceful to those of better education." The game was, he added, "unfriendly to clothes, as well as safety."

The ball used might have been a leather-covered bladder or a bag filled with sawdust. The game itself was highly informal and unsystematized and attracted few spectators. It was, and remained for long years, purely a participant's sport. President Timothy Dwight of Yale College who, allegedly, is shown in the illustration opposite watching his students play football in tall hats and swallowtail coats, hardly constituted a cheering section. In 1822, as a matter of fact, the college prohibited the game in its buildings or yard under pain of a fine "not exceeding fifty cents."

6

The Metropolitan Museum of Art

CRICKET ON THE DARTMOUTH CAMPUS, 1793. Engraving by Samuel Hill after a drawing by J. Dunham from the *Massachusetts Magazine.*

The Yale University Library

FOOTBALL AT YALE COLLEGE, 1807. Engraving by Amos Doolittle.

7

THE GAME OF GOLF, 1782. A political satire from *Het Nieuwe Nederlandsche, Fransche, Americanische, en Engelesche Kolfspel*; Amsterdam, 1782.

A BATHING PARTY IN NEW YORK, 1810. Painting by William P. Chappel. Courtesy of the Museum of the City of New York.

Golf, in one form or another, seems to have been a pastime of New Yorkers from the seventeenth century. The inventory of Governor Burnet in 1729 mentions "Nine Gouff Clubs, one iron ditto and seven dozen balls." This may possibly have referred to a form of midget golf more closely related to hockey than modern golf, as illustrated in the political satire shown opposite; a game played with a crooked club, a small ball, and holes in the turf of an enclosure. Fifty years later the *Royal Gazette* of New York carried an advertisement for what was probably a more familiar version of the game: "To the Golf Players. The season for this pleasant and healthy Exercise now advancing, Gentlemen may be furnished with excellent Clubs and the veritable Caledonian Balls, by enquiring at the Printers'." After the Revolution, the game was for a while played in other colonies as well, although interest then lapsed for almost a century.

During the hot seasons people of all rank sought refreshment in and by the water. As ever, men and boys took their dips with complete informality, at the risk of "exposing themselves to the walks of gentlemen and ladies." Ladies were more circumspect but no less eager for the plunge. At New Lebanon in 1792, Mary Palmer Tyler recalled: "Several of my companions . . . would swim like mermaids. . . . The swimmers would dive off the platform and after sporting around like a bevy of boys skip up the stairs and dress themselves, telling me I was foolish not to share so great a luxury."

Most early cities had provisions for public bathing in the form of highly popular floating baths with showers, attendants, and other conveniences. In such places the proprieties were more strictly regarded. "We saw the females," wrote William Bentley in his diary for 1819, "not uncovered, enjoying the water of the cove." He probably meant they were completely clothed. A swimming school started in Boston in 1827 won immediate success, attracting such patrons as Audubon and John Quincy Adams who, at sixty-one, took occasional dives from its six-foot springboard.

9

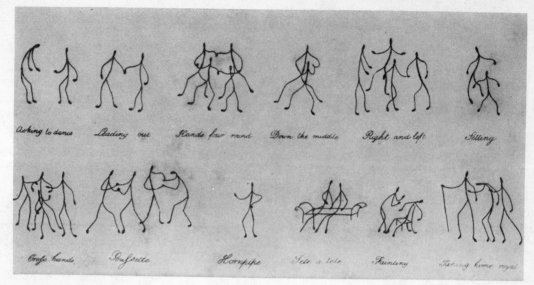

Asking to dance   Leading out   Hands four round   Down the middle   Right and left   Sitting

Cross hands   Poussette   Hornpipe   Tete a tete   Fainting   Taking home royal

The New-York Historical Society

THE SQUARE DANCE. From the *Port Folio*, Philadelphia, 1817.

The Worcester Art Museum, Goodspeed Collection
THE WALTZ. Engraving by Alexander Anderson. An imported novelty that won its way to popularity in American ballrooms during thé 1830's and '40's.

Of all leisure-time pursuits dancing enjoyed the greatest popularity with both sexes in country and city alike. The Reverend Andrew Burnaby, an early British critic of American ways, had complained that the dancing he saw in the country districts of Virginia before the Revolution was "without method or regularity." "A gentleman and lady stand up," he wrote, "and dance about the room, one of them retiring, the other pursuing, then perhaps meeting, in an irregular fantastical manner. After some time, another lady gets up, and then the first lady must sit down, she being, as they term it, cut out: the second lady acts the same part which the first did, till somebody cuts her out. The gentlemen perform in the same manner."

New steps introduced into the cities spread rapidly even into rural and inland regions. Reactionaries who protested against "the abomination of permitting a man who was neither your lover nor your husband to encircle you with his arms, and slightly press the contour of your waist," were powerless to discourage such exciting new diversions as the polka and the waltz.

THE POLKA. Lithograph by Pinkerton, Wagner & McGiugan. From the *Ladies' National Magazine*, 1844.

The Metropolitan Museum of Art
PRIMPING FOR THE BALL. Lithograph by Hervieu from Mrs. Trollope, *Domestic Manners of the Americans*, London, 1832.

The public rooms of such magnificent new establishments as the Tremont House in Boston, the first "modern" hotel of America, provided large, novel arenas for those who must dance. While the elders frowned at this fresh invitation to popular, public amusement, dancing provided rare and irresistible occasions for the sexes to mix in their recreation. At a public ball in Cincinnati Mrs. Trollope was surprised to find "a large room filled with extremely well-dressed company, among whom were many very beautiful girls. . . . I had not yet been long enough in Western America," she added, "not to feel startled at recognizing in almost every full-dressed *beau* that passed me, the master or shopman that I had been used to see behind the counter, or lolling at the door of every shop in the city."

In the still farther West dancing could be a riotous revel that attracted people from many miles about and that lasted through the night if not through the entire week. On the distant frontier Indian squaws substituted for their white sisters on the dance floor and, from some reports, went through their steps with quite as much grace.

DANCING THE QUADRILLE AT TREMONT HOUSE, BOSTON, ABOUT 1840. Lithograph by B. W. Thayer and Company.
The American Antiquarian Society

WALL STREET FROM BROADWAY, 1834. Lithograph by P. Maverick, Jr., after a drawing by Hugh Reinagle (?). Photograph courtesy of the Museum of the City of New York.

Sleighing was another popular diversion which, in season, permitted the mingling of the sexes and often served as a prelude to or an aftermath of a dancing frolic. Private vehicles vied with larger public sleighs that could be rented in most northern cities. Five dollars an hour was not an unusual rate for the hire of a big many-seated sleigh. Public and private vehicles were often handsomely designed and brightly decorated; the harness and other trappings of the horses were as gay as the rest of the equipage.

"Broadway exhibits the gayest scenes you can conceive," wrote Adam Hodgson in 1821. "Painted sleighs with scarlet cloth and buffalo skins are dashing along in all directions at a prodigious speed; some with two horses abreast, some harnessed as tandems and others with four in hand. Everybody seems to make the most of the snow while it lasts, and night does not put an end to its festivity. The horses have a string of bells around their necks, and in these fine moon light nights I hear them dashing away long after midnight."

The fact that a sleighing frolic was one of the rare sports in which young ladies could join with the men probably accounts for the reports that these otherwise fragile creatures seemed so tireless and that they could defy the grimmest weather to the music of jingling bells. According to several travelers, women invariably spoke of sleighing with rapture. Warmly covered with buffalo robes or bear skins and further protected with foot stoves and bags of hot sand, they and their escorts often sang their way through the winter nights to their destination.

13

THE DELPHIAN CLUB OF BALTIMORE CELEBRATING ITS FIRST ANNIVERSARY, ABOUT 1816. Drawing by "Kennuk-kofritz," a club member.

ROBERT GILMOR EN ROUTE TO EUROPE, 1829–1830. Drawing from his sketch book.

HIGHROCK-IODINE AND EMPIRE SPRINGS AT SARATOGA, NEW YORK, 1848. Lithograph by Deroy after a drawing by August Köllner.

Gentlemen of standing ever had their clubs where they could retire from prying female eyes, the hurly-burly of business, and the bumptiousness of democracy. Philip Hone reported that New York's Union Club, founded in 1836, immediately became "a great resource for bachelors, and 'men about town' . . . an excellent lounging place for young and old beaux, each of whom would fain be thought what the other is."

In a country where there was virtually no hereditary wealth, gentlemen of leisure were few and they were furtive about their leisure. Whatever the easy state of a man's affairs, he felt obligated by public opinion to spend his time in some sort of public or private business. "He would think himself in bad repute," wrote Tocqueville "if he employed his life solely in living. It is for the purpose of escaping this obligation to work that so many rich Americans come to Europe, where they find some scattered remains of aristo-cratic society, among whom idleness is still held in honor."

Until leisure attained a more respectable status, those who could afford it in conspicuous fashion, if they didn't flee the country, disguised their indulgence at "health" resorts that profited by the trade in valetudinarianism, real or affected and, in any case, costly. "The worthy, fashionable, dashing, good-for-nothing people of every state . . . flock to the Springs," remarked the *Salmagundi Papers* in 1807, ". . . to exhibit their equipages and wardrobes, and to excite the admiration, or . . . the envy of their fashionable competitors. . . . The lady of a Southern planter will lay out the whole . . . produce of a rice plantation in silver and gold muslins, lace veils, and new liveries; carry a hogshead of tobacco on her head . . . while a lady of Boston or Salem will wrap herself up in the net proceeds of a cargo of whale oil, and tie on her hat with a quintal of codfish."

A SCENE FROM *The Contrast* BY ROYALL TYLER, 1787. Engraving by Peter Maverick after William Dunlap.

In 1774 the Continental Congress had recommended that the colonists "discountenance and discourage all horse racing and all kinds of gaming, cock fighting, exhibitions of shows, plays and other expensive diversions and entertainments." That injunction was part of a policy of austerity to meet the demands of crisis. But for years after the Revolution, as in the colonial period, the theater faced opposition on the grounds of impiety, immorality, expensiveness, and its distraction from industry. Play-going, warned Timothy Dwight, representing a solid bloc of public opinion, endangered "that most valuable treasure the immortal soul."

The South had always been more hospitable to the theater, and the church there was more tolerant. In Charleston even a minister was known to have written a play. The conspicuous patronage of one Southern gentleman, George Washington, lent the drama a certain propriety everywhere, although his appearance in the President's box of the old John Street theater in New York in 1789 was more frequent than many citizens could approve of.

"DESIGN OF A BUILDING PROPOSED TO BE ERECTED AT RICHMOND IN VIRGINIA TO CONTAIN A THEATRE, ASSEMBLY-ROOMS, AND A HOTEL," 1797–1798. Architect's drawing by Benjamin Henry Latrobe.

EXTERIOR OF THE CHESTNUT STREET THEATRE IN PHILADELPHIA, DESIGNED BY LATROBE AND OPENED IN 1794. Aquatint by M. Marigot from Charles William Janson, *The Stranger in America*, London, 1807.

An occasional colonist had turned his hand to play writing, notably Thomas Godfrey, whose *The Prince of Parthia* was played by a professional English troupe at the old Southwark Theater in Philadelphia in 1767. In 1787 *The Contrast*, by Royall Tyler, Harvard alumnus and war veteran, was played professionally in New York and later in Philadelphia and Baltimore. The play was aimed at a native audience and introduced a character, Jonathan, who stands at the head of a long file of stage Yankees. Appealing to patriots everywhere the comedy, in its closing lines, concludes "that probity, virtue, honour, though they should not have received the polish of Europe, will secure to an honest American the good graces of his fair countrywomen, and . . . the applause of the Public."

People of wealth and fashion in numerous cities, including Boston, gradually gave the theater the standing and support it needed to overcome lingering prejudice. When the Chestnut Street Theater opened in Philadelphia after a long controversy—its boxes "lined with a pink colored paper, with small dark spots, and supported by pillars representing bundles of reeds (gilt) bound with red fillets . . . festoons of crimson curtains, with tassels intervening, and a profusion of glass chandeliers"—that city became the drama capital of the country, a distinction it retained for a generation. The handsome new theater, "immediately became a place of fashionable resort, to the great emolument of the performers" according to Charles Janson from whose book of travels the above illustration is taken.

"I saw a great crowd of folks going into a long entry that had lanterns over the door,"

17

INTERIOR OF THE PARK THEATER, NEW YORK, 1822. Water color by John Searle. Charles Mathews and Miss Johnson are playing a scene from Moncrieffs's farce *Monsieur Tonson*. Many prominent New Yorkers are portrayed in the audience.

remarked Jonathan in Tyler's play back in 1787, describing his first visit to the theater. "So I went right in, and they showed me a way, clean up to the garret, just like a meeting-house gallery. And so I saw a power of topping folks, all sitting around in little cabins, just like father's corn cribs; and there was such a squeaking with the fiddlers, and such a tarnel blaze with the lights, my head was near turned." As the nineteenth century progressed and the theater reached out to an ever-wider audience, the masses gradually replaced the "topping folks" as the drama's main support. The second Park Street Theater that opened in New York in 1821 seated 2500 persons and it was soon reckoned small compared to the Bowery and Broadway of succeeding years.

Antagonism to the theater as an un-American activity, both too aristocratic and too British for republicans, fell away as American playwrights provided more American themes for native actors to perform, and as prices of seats were reduced to a 75c or 50c top with ample room in the gallery at 12½c to 37½c. Shakespeare was ever a favorite but the serious performances, like today's movies, were usually interlarded with popular "shorts," not excluding trained-animal shows, to broaden the appeal to larger and less fastidious audiences.

For Mrs. Trollope the motley audience that crowded the theater during her days in America quite spoiled the show. "Men came into the lower tier of boxes," she wrote, "without their coats; and I have seen shirt

A SCENE FROM THE DRAMATIZATION OF JAMES FENIMORE COOPER'S POPULAR HISTORICAL NOVEL, *The Spy*, 1823. Painting by William Dunlap. The scene is that in which Harry Wharton, a Loyalist, being unable to deceive Captain Lawton of the Virginia Horse by a crude disguise, takes off his wig and eye patch, which he holds in his hands. Dunlap was a distinguished playwright as well as a painter.

The New York State Historical Association

The American Antiquarian Society

YOUNG DEMOCRACY AT THE THEATER. THE STAGE IN 1852 FROM THE PIT. Lithograph from *The Old Soldier.* "Illustrated by his Son John."

sleeves tucked up to the shoulder; the spitting was incessant, and the mixed smell of onions and whiskey was enough to make one feel even the Drakes' acting dearly bought by . . . enduring its accompaniments. The bearing and attitudes of the men are perfectly indescribable; the heels thrown higher than the head, the entire rear of the person presented to the audience, the whole length supported on the benches, are among the varieties that these exquisite posture-masters exhibit. The noises, too, were perpetual, and of the most unpleasant kind; the applause is expressed by cries and thumping with the feet, instead of clapping; and when a patriotic fit seized them, and 'Yankee Doodle' was called for, every man seemed to think his reputation as a citizen depended on the noise he made." The new urban democracy was taking the theater for its own and in its own way.

Even Walt Whitman, loud champion of democracy, felt that the theater had become, at least in New York, a scene of vulgarity and coarseness on both sides of the footlights. But the drama, from Shakespeare to variety, widened its appeal to all classes in all sections of the country. In the rôle of "Mose," the rough and ready fire laddy whose legendary exploits in and about New York's Bowery are mentioned in another chapter, Francis S. Chanfrau played to almost every theatrical town in the country. In *Mose in California* and *Mose in China,* produced in 1849 and 1850, the popular stage hero developed into quite a cosmopolitan character.

Actors who played the early western circuit with local stock, with supers often drawn hastily from the populace, and with improvised props, if any, brought entertainment to frontier communities in a heroic manner. At Columbus, Georgia, in 1832, a group of Creek Indians was hired at fifty cents and a glass of whiskey each, paid in

DANCING FOR EELS.

A SCENE FROM *New York as it Is*, STARRING FRANCIS S. CHANFRAU AS "MOSE." THE FIRE LADDY, 1848. Lithograph by E. & J. Brown after a drawing by James Brown.

advance, to impersonate the Peruvian army in *Pizarro,* a popular stock play. The exuberant redskins used their cues to stage a realistic Creek war dance, scalping King Ataliba (by removing his wig), demolishing the High Priest's altar, burning the sun, and frightening the sacerdotal virgins of the cast off into their dressing rooms. At Pittsburgh before an audience of keelboat men and foundry workers the "virgins" were impersonated by an old Irish cleaning woman and the property man, draped in cotton gowns and gauze veils—a deception which did not convince the pit. Under any circumstances frontier audiences were likely to be unrestrainedly enthusiastic in their criticisms, pro and con.

A SCENE FROM SHERIDAN'S *Pizarro*. After drawings by A. R. Waud. From Sol. Smith, *Theatrical Management in the West and South for Thirty Years,* New York, 1868.

The American Antiquarian Society

A FREE-FOR-ALL IN THE WEST. Engraving from *The Crockett Almanac,* 1841.

The rough-and-tumble, eye-gouging, ear-and-nose-biting fights of frontier regions attracted an excited audience that needed no tickets. British visitors, particularly, developed a morbid interest in such brutal outbursts, probably through some atavistic streak since this form of "sport" was an old English custom imported into the brave new world. In any case they repeatedly cited the maimed survivors without ears, eyes or nose whom they met in their travels. "Very few rounds had taken place," wrote Thomas Ashe of a fight he witnessed in 1806 between a Kentuckian and a Virginian, "before the Virginian contracted his whole form, drew up his arms to his face, with his hands closed in a concave, by the fingers being bent to the full extension of the flexors, and summoning up all his energy . . . pitched himself into the bosom of his opponent . . . [and] brought him instantly to the ground. The Virginian never lost his hold; fixing his claws in his hair and his thumbs on his eyes, gave them an instantaneous start from their sockets . . . and made one further effort and fastening on the under lip of his mutilator tore it over the chin. The Kentuckian at length gave out, on which the people carried off the victor . . . as the first rough and tumbler."

The American Antiquarian Society

A STREET FIGHT. Also from *The Crockett Almanac,* 1841.

In areas where loneliness was sometimes a desperate thing and the need of some form of companionship correspondingly intense, any get-together under whatever auspices took on a phenomenal importance. The interminable church services of early New England had their social as well as their religious aspects, and years later the camp-meeting revival, typical of the West but by no means peculiar to it, was a form of holy social entertainment. It brought together people of pent-up spirits and joined them in a concerted discharge of emotion. Occasionally such mass meetings reached an unforgettable sublimity. The immense crowds of fervent spirits gathered in a clearing of the thick forest, their earnest faces gleaming from the mingled rays of the moon and the numerous altar fires, joining their voices in a solemn chorus, presented a scene of woodland worship that impressed even the most unsympathetic witness.

At other times and more notoriously, the meeting gave way to a mass-hysteria whose violence was terrifying. "The noise was like the roar of Niagara," wrote one witness of the meeting at which he was converted. "The vast sea of human beings seemed to be agitated as if by a storm. . . . Some of the people were singing, others praying, some crying for mercy in the most piteous accents, while others were shouting most vociferously. . . . At one time I saw at least five hundred swept down in a moment, as if a battery of a thousand guns had been opened upon them, and then immediately followed shrieks and shouts that rent the very heavens."

At such frontier meetings the antics of the penitent and of those of doubtful heart —the paroxysms (the "jerks"), the barks ("to tree the devil"), the rolling, laughing, and running exercises, the anguished and ecstatic wailing and the shrieking and the not infrequent transfer of emotion from religion to sex—represented to cool, sensitive witnesses a demoniacal orgy of utter barbarism. But this was a turbulent world and the turbulence of such demonstrations went far to channel emotions that might otherwise have had less picturesque consequences. Even at its unrestrained worst the revival meeting helped to unite and tame a harsh, unruly wilderness.

A CAMP MEETING, 1830–35. Lithograph by Kennedy & Lucas after a painting by A. Rider.
The New-York Historical Society

Court time at the county seat provided a different reason for close and distant neighbors to gather together and make the most of an infrequent occasion. Judge, jury, litigants, and spectators were often all known to one another and, while trials were usually conducted in orderly fashion, the traditional ceremonies were few and the atmosphere informal and generally personal. "Whilst causes of considerable interest were under trial," wrote John Palmer of a session he attended in 1817, "the pleaders and clerks not absolutely employed were reading newspapers, or whispering to some acquaintance; and I several times saw a large can of cyder brought in from a neighboring tavern, and handed around amongst the jury. . . ."

The manners of the people at the town he visited, wrote Palmer, "were convivial. It was *court time,* and with Americans that implies frolicking time. All the time that could be spared from the sessions-house was spent in playing at quoits, ten-pins, horse-racing, and betting on the weight of their horses. . . . [The judges] are under no restraint but dine at the ordinary with the other inmates of the tavern, and mix in common with them, smoking their segars, and cracking jokes indifferently with all."

Raising the heavy, mortised frame of an early house was the sort of job that called for more manpower than an unaided family could ordinarily provide. The difficulty was usually solved by means of a neighborly get-together in which the work was speeded by the prospect of the frolic that invariably followed and by the strong drink that as invariably flowed.

The economic advantage of thus joining forces with neighbors more or less remote, to do the job quickly, had developed into an institution of colonial life, one that long persisted in the hinterland. Bees—for log-rolling, house-raising, husking, quilting,

A RURAL COURT SCENE, 1849. Painting by A. Wighe.

The Rhode Island School of Design, Museum of Art

Collection of Colonel and Mrs. Edgar W. Garbisch

FLAX-SCUTCHING, 1847. Painting by Linton Park.

flax-scutching, or whatever the job—brought people together in the name of essential work and provided them with a rare chance to be sociable. The excitement of reunion made play of toil and perpetuated a spirit of voluntary association which became an integral part of the democratic faith.

"Americans of all ages, all conditions, and all dispositions constantly form associations," wrote Tocqueville in the 1830's, ". . . to give entertainments, to found seminaries, to build inns, to construct churches, to diffuse books, to send missionaries to the antipodes. . . . I met with several kinds . . . of which I confess I had no previous notion." The periodic musters of volunteer firemen, sometimes bringing together companies from a wide area, were pageants in which the water-pumping contests of the members provided excitement and entertainment for large gatherings. It was a purely indigenous institution that partially disguised the spirit of match-play, discouraged in other forms as wasteful of time and conducive to gambling. (See the next two pages.)

Collection of Edward W. C. Arnold
RAISING A HOUSE, NEW YORK, 1810. Detail of a painting by William P. Chappel. Photograph courtesy of The Museum of the City of New York.

FIREMAN'S MUSTER, MERRIMACK SQUARE, MANCHESTER, N. H., 1859. Lithograph by Endicott.

The earnest purposefulness that kept Americans so tirelessly busy at their work and that also was the excuse for much of their play, at times made it hard for commercial entertainers in search of an audience. Even in the cities where the communal excitements of bees and other productive diversions had no place, the public could find serious uses for their leisure. The mid-years of the last century witnessed a temporary but astonishing phenomenon when ordinary workmen and factory girls rushed from their jobs to crowded lecture halls to improve their minds after hours with an avidity that was "a matter of wonderment" to foreign visitors. In 1841 Philip Hone reported that the theaters of New York were all but deserted while the Lyceum was hard put to find lecturers enough to satisfy the crowds who came to listen.

During those same years the lecturers most successful competition came from the burnt-cork comedians whose minstrel shows played to packed houses over a score of seasons. As many as ten groups were playing at one time in New York, and the Christy and Woods minstrels, performing in a theater that seated twenty-five hundred "in spite of crinoline," found it difficult to accommodate the nightly crowds that came to laugh

The American Antiquarian Society

THE ETHIOPIAN SERENADERS, 1847. Lithograph by Firth and Hall.

The Pleasure Railway at Hoboken, N. J., about 1830. Lithograph by D. W. Kellogg & Co.

and applaud the antics of the Ethiopians.

The minstrel show was an indigenous form of entertainment, a folk art that cut through all manner of sophistication and found a response at every level. Humor and music were directed at the man in the street who, as planned, saw the joke and felt the melodic charms of "Massa's in de Cold, Cold Ground," "My Old Kentucky Home," and other favorites. "Dixie" was a minstrel tune before it became the battle song of the Confederacy. Less than a year before he became President, Lincoln shouted for an encore of it from his box at a performance. Even England applauded the buffoonery of "Jim Crow."

More varied diversion was offered to New York's rank and file across the Hudson River in Hoboken's "Elysian Fields." Here, of a Sunday, they could wander through the wooded park, row in bright colored boats,

swing in a huge yellow gondola, and otherwise disport themselves in carefree holiday fashion. "I never was so forcibly struck with the prosperity and happiness of the lower orders of society in this country," wrote Fanny Kemble in 1835, "as yesterday returning from Hoboken. The walks along the river and through the woods, the steamers crossing from the city, were absolutely thronged with a cheerful, well-dressed population abroad, merely for the purpose of pleasure and exercise. Journeymen, labourers, handicraftsmen, tradespeople, with their families, bearing all in their dress and looks evident signs of well-being and contentment. . . ."

At least here, she felt, one saw a counterbalance to the curse of incessant toil and "the debasing pursuit of wealth" which had marked every urban American male she met with a melancholy character.

29

In spite of Miss Kemble's pleasant observations it was growing increasingly difficult for the ordinary city dweller to find the right place and time to indulge in outdoor sports and other active leisure-time pursuits. To those with a country background, and they were many, such limitations canceled out much of the advantage of urban life. "The physical deterioration of the Americans, as a people," dolefully commented *Harper's Weekly*, "is remarked upon by almost every traveler who comes among us. . . . The employments of American women, especially of those resident in cities, are so entirely sedentary, that they do continual violence to the laws of nature." In 1832

The New-York Historical Society
FEMALE CALISTHENICS. Engraving from *Atkinson's Casket*, 1832.

A BILLIARD PARLOR, ABOUT 1830. Lithograph by C. G. Childs after a drawing by Edward W. Clay.
The Historical Society of Pennsylvania

BOWLING AT THE KNICKERBOCKER SALOON, BROADWAY, NEW YORK, 1847. Lithograph by Martin & Beals.

Atkinson's Casket recommended to city-bound females the calisthenic exercises illustrated on the opposite page which were "calculated to give strength, not only to the arms and shoulders, but also to the back."

The portrait of the urban male, as drawn by *The People's Magazine* in 1835, was even more grim. "How often do we see a young man with an intelligent but very pale countenance," the periodical asked, "whose legs have hardly strength to support the weight of his bent and emaciated body? He once probably was a strong and active boy, but he came to the city, shut himself up in an office, took no exercise because he was not obliged to take any, grew nervous and bilious . . . and may probably linger out a few years of wretched existence, when death will be welcomed as his best friend."

Some Americans felt with John Adams that the bloom of life was lost indoors at the billiard table. To play the ancient game well

was a clear sign of ill-spent youth. But the game had its many devotees over the years, including one woman who wrote to *The Ladies' Billiard Messenger* (a periodical "Devoted to Literature and Billiards") that the game made her forget all her troubles, and that she could play it confident that she was not sacrificing health to a morbid appetite for amusement.

A sport criticized along with billiards was pin bowling, of which the first recorded match in America was held at the Knickerbocker Saloon, Broadway, New York—"the largest bowling saloon in the world," it was reported—in 1840, although bowling on the green was an old sport. The air of dissipation that hung heavy over the alleys made them a public nuisance, the press remarked. The game was prohibited in several places and popular interest did not develop elsewhere on a large scale until late in the century.

ROPER'S GYMNASIUM IN PHILADELPHIA, ABOUT 1830. Lithograph by Childs and Inman.

A quarter of a century after the complaints of invalidism registered in *Atkinson's Casket* and *The People's Magazine,* the situation had apparently worsened. "I am satisfied," wrote Oliver Wendell Holmes in an *Atlantic Monthly* of 1858, "that such a set of black-coated, stiff-jointed, soft-muscled, paste-complexioned youth as we can boast in our Atlantic cities never before sprang from loins of Anglo-Saxon lineage . . . and as for any great athletic feat performed by a gentleman in these latitudes, society would drop a man who should run round the Common in five minutes."

Another writer in the same magazine commented on the current belief that physical vigor and spiritual sanctity were incompatible. In a sporting match the best preacher would be chosen last since athletic capacity was in inverse ratio to spiritual accomplishment. There were clergymen, however, who recognized the importance of a sound constitution if their work in improving humanity was to be successful and who lent both their approval and attendance to gymnasiums. The strengthening of the flesh, it was hoped, might encourage more "willingness of the spirit."

The first gymnasium in the United States was opened at the Round Hill School in Northampton, Massachusetts, by Dr. Karl Beck, a German refugee, in 1825. In the years immediately following, first-class establishments were set up in the larger cities and enjoyed the patronage of the best people. Supporting the cause, the New York *Evening Post* advised its readers in 1830 that it could "be assumed that a physically healthy population is likewise a moral one and vice versa. Morality being thus closely linked with and dependent upon health, and a dense population unfavorable to the latter, it ought to be a popular sentiment in all our large cities to establish and support institutions intended to develop our physical power and give health and vigor to the human frame." The instructor at the New York gymnasium was a well-known English pugilist who taught boxing as a gymnastic art and manly science, not to be confused with the brutal sport of prize fighting.

An instructor in Boston had proposed to teach the art of boxing as early as 1798. It was, said a slightly later teacher, a gentleman's necessary defense against the ungovernable passions of ruffians. As practised professionally, however, the sport was more offensive, in every sense of that word, than defensive. Fighting with bare knuckles and with few rules stated or observed fell little short of the mayhem of frontier fighting. Death or disfiguration was not unusual. It remained popular largely as a spectator's sport, although much of the press railed against it as a brutal, uncivilized importation from England, all of which it was.

In 1835 the New York *Mirror* printed an alarm stating that "the detestable practise of prize-fighting threatens to take root within the soil of our native land." Twenty-four years later *Leslie's Illustrated Newspaper* identified the sport with the "lowest vice of our cities" but played safe by sending a special correspondent and an artist to London to cover the famous international bout between John C. Heenan, America's favorite "Benicia Boy," and Tom Sayers, the English champion in 1860. The bout was a draw, but *Leslie's* gave it full coverage.

Laws prohibiting fights in America were numerous, but a growing public found the excitement it craved in watching or even more often in reading about such contests. In 1849 when Yankee Sullivan fought Tom Hyer, the bout was held in the backwoods of Maryland to escape the law, but by 1860 when the champion, Heenan, held an exhibition at Jones Wood outside New York, the crowd had grown to thirty thousand spectators.

THE GREAT FIGHT BETWEEN TOM HYER AND YANKEE SULLIVAN (FOR $10,000), MARYLAND, FEBRUARY 7, 1849. Lithograph by James Baillie.

The Yale University Art Gallery, Whitney Collection of Sporting Art

Collection of Edward W. C. Arnold

PEYTONA AND FASHION'S GREAT MATCH FOR A $20,000 PURSE, UNION COURSE, LONG ISLAND, MAY 13, 1845. Lithograph by H. R. Robinson after a drawing by C. Severin. Photograph courtesy of the Museum of the City of New York.

There has hardly ever been a time when horse racing was not popular in America, particularly in the South. When Diomed, a famous racer, died in 1808 the mourning in the Old Dominion was almost as great in some circles, it is said, as when the Father of His Country had died nine years before. With the nineteenth century the sport had developed from more or less impromptu or informal contests to highly organized and advertised attractions that drew huge throngs of spectators from neighboring cities and involved large sums of money. Boats sailing from New York advertised accommodations for those planning to attend the races at Charleston, S. C., the oldest and best-known track in the country at the time. The great race between the southern horse, Sir Henry, and the northern horse, American Eclipse, held at the Union Course on Long Island in 1823, was witnessed by a crowd of about one hundred thousand, many of whom had come from long distances by stage or steamboat. When Eclipse won the purse of $20,000, decided by winning two out of three four-mile heats from the best blood and bottom of southern horseflesh, the South suffered almost mortal anguish. Twenty-two years later when Peytona met Fashion at the same course the traffic jam en route was so bad it seemed that many would never get near the course. Those who successfully made the trip complained of the number of gamblers, touts, and fancy gentlemen who thronged the way. But there were other people of all stripes. Hone noted in his diary that Wall Street was entirely deserted on the day of the race.

During the next twenty years horse racing won greater importance and popularity than it had ever enjoyed before. Even Boston finally capitulated and staged a well-attended affair in 1862. William Dean Howells, revisiting his adopted home, Boston, was bewildered at such happenings in New England and fearfully hoped there was "nothing

34

GOING TO THE TROT, 1869. Lithograph by Currier and Ives.

wicked in so much apparent enjoyment."

Trotting matches had long since been accepted as a national sport in Boston as everywhere else. It was New England, in fact, that made this distinctively American contribution to the pursuit of pleasure. By the 1870's it had grown to "mammoth proportions" and won "a far greater share of public attention than any other of the public pastimes which contribute to the enjoyment of the people." There were few towns with a population of more than five thousand that did not claim some facilities for light-harness racing.

Its easy and early acceptance was partly due to the fact that the pleasure of trotting might be justified in terms of utility. To improve the speed and stamina of light-harness horses would better the strain of driving and draught horses generally. Hence the "agrikultural hosstrots" that came to grace virtually every state and county fair in the country. Trotting also avoided the taint of excessive commercialism that frightened the pure of heart when they contemplated the enormous bets placed at the race track.

In the early days of the sport the race course was often an open road. As roads and turnpikes improved and as light carriages and wagons were perfected, an informal brush with a fellow traveler became a tempting excitement, an element of enjoyment that could be added to the ordinary problem of transportation. The gentry made quite a fashion of it and took special pride in their speed on the highway. In 1825 a number of gentlemen in and about New York organized a Trotting Club to improve the pace of their road horses; and in subsequent years the well-to-do in other cities followed suit. Special races were staged and the names of the fastest trotters were soon household words among all classes of society. Still, it might be claimed, the trotting turf, for all the sporting interest it aroused, was a helpful refinement of road driving.

Cockfighting was another ancient sport that flourished in America, under cover in New England, openly in the South, and according to the sectional derivation of the people in western communities. Enthusiasm and partisanship at the cockpit were as intense as at the race track and among very much the same wide variety of spectators, from the most respectable to "the fancy"—the disreputable element that bred on gambling.

The sport and its followers had changed very little in character since Samuel Pepys had gone to his first cockfight at a pit in Shoe Lane, London, in 1663, "being directed by sight of bills upon walls . . . but, Lord! to see the strange variety of people from Parliament man . . . to the poorest 'prentices, bakers, brewers, butchers, draymen, and what not; and all those fellows one with another in swearing, cursing, and betting."

A century and a half later the same sort of performance was attracting the same sort of mixed audiences of restless *fans* through the same sort of ads in America. "My favorite chicken, Mad Anthony," a Virginian with intersectional ambitions for his champion advertised in the New York *Evening Post* in 1822, "can, on the second Saturday in May next whip any fowl of his weight in the United States for any amount—fight agreeable to the rules of cocking."

It took a hardened sophist to contend that these gory spectacles served the material purpose of breeding a tough race of fowls whose eggs had superior flavor, but the theory had its advocates among the spectators.

As in sport, so in other entertainment, cold cash in large amounts became an ever more vital factor. When P. T. Barnum brought Jenny Lind, "the Swedish Nightingale," to sing for American audiences in

NEARING THE ISSUE AT THE COCKPIT, 1870. Painting by Horace Bonham.

The Corcoran Gallery of Art

JENNY LIND'S FIRST APPEARANCE IN AMERICA, SEPTEMBER 11, 1850. Lithograph by N. Currier.

1850, he guaranteed one thousand dollars each for one hundred and fifty concerts, all expenses paid. Her début at Castle Garden in New York was one of the most spectacular events ever held in that venerable building. Top price paid for a seat was two hundred and twenty-five dollars and the total sales for the first concert amounted to almost eighteen thousand dollars, her share of which the artist gave to New York charities. The concerts took their place along with the fugitive-slave law and the spirit rappings of the Fox sisters as a leading topic in newspapers all over the country.

"It is amazing what heaps of money they have here," Jenny wrote home to Sweden. In their different ways both the singer and her entrepreneur captured the American public; the one by her "unrivalled voice . . . and the intelligence and sensibility of which it is the organ"; the other by his showmanship that so shrewdly tapped the purses of crowds eager and waiting to be entertained. Barnum took in over seven hundred thousand dollars from the singer's tour. As a museum director, impresario, circus manager, and as a supreme showman he made the public pay handsomely for its pleasures. He also led the way to popular entertainment until the American city provided a variety of fare for its swarming amusement lovers that was unmatched in Europe.

'SELLING' THE PUBLIC, 1850. Lithograph by W. Schaus.

37

THE COUNTRY-WIDE SCENE

At the rate the public, most obviously the fast-growing urban population, was, by the middle of the last century, flocking after professional entertainers, two legged, four-legged, and winged, it seemed possible that a large part of the nation might degenerate into spectators. "The good folk as well as the bad," wrote Philip Hone from the midst of the New York scene, "must be amused . . . they must have some way of passing their evenings besides poking the fire and playing with their children."

By Hone's day the need for recreation, especially of those cut off from the work-play habits of country life, was slowly winning serious recognition. Perhaps, as Oliver Wendell Holmes observed a few years later, Americans had not yet learned how to play; but they had more time than their ancestors to study the problem. Good and bad, rich and poor, urban and rural, eastern and western folk, were casting about for the enjoyments that best suited the conditions of their life.

Conditions varied enormously and changed constantly throughout the nation. Almost until the present generation change was less apparent in the country than elsewhere. Until the widespread use of agricultural machinery, the telephone, and the automobile—until the outbreak of World War I—the American farm remained the stronghold of traditional values. Those who remained on it found much of their pleasure in an accustomed, independent manner, relying largely on their own resources and the amusements coincident with constructive activity.

Those who were drawn to the cities found a world where opportunities for recreation, like everything else, were all too often by-products of chaotic growth. Wealth concentrated in cities, however, and leisure too, and that combination inevitably led to the organization of amusements that would kill time, for better or for worse, in a systematized manner.

In the cow towns and mining camps of the West, it was noted, two agents of civilization pressed their claim for men's spare moments, the church and the gambling joint. At Leadville, Colorado, in typical manner, one of the few city blocks had little else but saloons and dance halls that were filled night and day by men who drank, gambled, and who, for fifty cents, had "the privilege of dancing with a worn and haggard creature." But one by one these turbulent little centers quieted down to a more balanced program, or disappeared altogether.

The immigrant brought with him his own traditional ways of meeting the "problem of leisure," grafting onto the American scene the mature habits of Old World society. Here the contribution of the Germans was conspicuous. In the larger cities their convivial and musical habits on Sundays met head-on with the old Sabbatarian traditions of America. On the other hand, in his travels to the Texas frontier Frederick Law Olmsted was delightfully surprised by German pioneers playing Beethoven symphonies on grand pianos in their log huts. German music festivals where choral societies competed for a prize became an annual, national event at Cincinnati.

Wherever the way was open and the season right, hunting and fishing never failed to tempt men away from home and the cares of business. However, Americans, according to the English-born sportsman Frank Forrester, were inclined to practise such pleasures too informally and with little deference to established custom.

All in all, in neighboring city streets as in widely separated sections of the country, America was a land of contrasting habits that fitted no easy formula.

Mrs. Sarah Griswold Morse and Mrs. Edward Lind, Wife and Daughter of the Artist S. F. B. Morse, Playing Chess on the Lawn at "Locust Grove," Poughkeepsie, New York. Daguerreotype by Morse, taken after 1848. Morse had met Daguerre in Paris and had been trying to take portraits by his process as early as 1839.

Kennedy & Co.

THE GEM SALOON, CORNER OF BROADWAY AND WORTH STREET, NEW YORK, 1854. Lithograph by A. Fay.

How many American man-hours of leisure have been spent in conviviality will never be totaled. The tippling habits of the metropolis with its mahogany, gilt, and cut-glass barrooms—and its dives—have never been much less than notorious. Even in many smaller communities one dispensary for every hundred inhabitants seemed the average to travelers of the 1850's. The hard-working, monotonous routine of most people, their generally salty diet, the excessive heat of American summers, and a widespread feeling that cold spring water was dangerous to drink, have all been advanced as reasons for this native bent. In the country, Horace Greeley recalled from his childhood days, "there was no merrymaking, there was no entertainment of relatives or friends, there was scarcely a casual gathering of two or three neighbors for an evening's social chat, without strong drink." House raisings, he went on to say, dances, militia training, elec-

tions, and even funerals were regarded as inadequately celebrated without spirituous enlivenment or consolation.

From an early date in colonial history militia training days were occasions for general celebration. Long ago Cotton Mather had ruefully observed that on such days the path from the drill field to the tavern was short and easy. In later times when there was less need for serious training, muster day developed into a periodic carnival of racing, wrestling, dancing, and trading that brought people from miles around, the bibulous without fail. The popularity of the militia as an institution is indicated by the alacrity with which immigrant Germans organized companies, as they formed German Odd Fellow lodges and tribes of German Red Men.

The militia inevitably lent its glittering presence to the celebration of the Fourth of July. Throughout the land people in every

40

station and circumstance seized on that anniversary as an occasion for toil-forgetting merry-making. The day traditionally provided rich diversion of every sort, from "the tall, the graceful, the majestic, the beautiful giraffe and the elegant display of beautiful women" that graced the occasion in New York in 1838 to the buffalo hunts and catfish fries that attracted barefoot prairie folk from a hundred miles distance during the next generation. But in the end it was something more than an annual frolic. The same depth of emotion that inspired the camp meeting went into the formal ceremonies. In 1831 Tocqueville, perhaps America's most understanding critic, considered the reading of the Declaration of Independence which he heard at Albany one of the more thrilling experiences of his thoughtful life. The oration was a ritual of profound, symbolic significance to Americans, old and new. Amid all the jubilation the day was one of rededication.

The Chicago Historical Society
A MISSOURI GERMAN ARTILLERYMAN; A FRENCH CARICATURE OF THE AMERICAN MILITIA, ABOUT 1865. Lithograph after a drawing by Jules Draner.

"THE DAY WE CELEBRATE," THE FOURTH OF JULY, 1875. Lithograph by John C. McRae after a painting by F. A. Chapman.

The Yale University Art Gallery, Mabel Brady Garvan Collection

A NEW ENGLAND PICNIC, ABOUT 1855. Painting by Jeremiah Pearson Hardy.

In settled parts of the country Americans were no longer struggling with the wilderness. The population of the larger cities indeed, had almost forgotten it. They may, perhaps, have inherited that "unconquerable aversion to trees" bred in their ancestors by their long conflict with the forest. But those who understood the changes that were taking place in American life urged their countrymen to mend their habits and their point of view. To a people whose working routine was becoming increasingly sedentary, their daily lives cooped up in lath and plaster, out of-door recreation was not only harmless, it was necessary for health and happiness and for the vitality of the race.

Emerson urged his readers to look beyond their city walls and workaday concerns. Cities had not room enough for the human senses. The mechanics of life in a shop and in an office were restricting and artificial. Man needed nature—a sight of the fields and the stars and the distant horizon—as he needed food and drink. Nature was medicinal and healing. Nature, he wrote, was "the circumstance which dwarfs every other circumstance, and judges like a god all men that come to her. We have crept out of our close and crowded houses into the night and morning, and we see what majestic beauties daily wrap us in their bosoms. How willingly we would escape the barriers which render them comparatively impotent, escape the sophistication and second thought, and suffer nature to entrance us."

Thoreau, writing in a day when America's resources still seemed endless, warned his countrymen to preserve the natural beauty of their land before it was altogether despoiled by the plundering advances of civilization—before they might lose what they had not yet learned to appreciate.

Those words from such high sources, and from others, were not wasted. "We find a fascination in carrying back our civilization

SKATING IN CENTRAL PARK, NEW YORK, 1860. Painting by Winslow Homer.

to the wilderness," jubilantly proclaimed *Appleton's Journal* just after the Civil War. "The eagerness with which we enter upon picnics," the periodical continued, "the keenness with which we relish them, are proof of the supremacy of the out of doors. Nature is still dear to us, notwithstanding all the veneering of civilization; and it is pleasant to reflect how, at this moment, on the sides of innumerable hills, on mountain tops, in wooded valleys, by many a lake and rivulet, on little wooded islands, in the far off prairies, in southern savannas, are countless picnic parties, all of which, let us hope, are finding full realization of the true ideal of a picnic." The ideal was to eat, drink, lie, sit, walk, or talk "with something of the unconstraint of primitive life." It was a social device to snatch a brief spell of freedom from the binding conventions of urban life.

In the next decade half a dozen popular magazines devoted their pages to nothing but out-of-door activities. "America's playhouse is all-out-of-doors," declared one of them.

Skating had always been a popular outdoor recreation in the northern states and some prominent Americans, among them the artists Benjamin West and Charles Willson Peale, were celebrated for their talents on the ice. But when Thomas Wentworth Higginson, the famous Boston abolitionist and writer who was also an ardent apostle of "manly outdoor exercises," in the mid-nineteenth century enthusiastically pointed out the benefits of the sport, the renewed interest he excited was known as "Higginson's revival." Lakes, rinks, and other frozen bodies of water soon carried huge crowds of gliding devotees. Special excursion trains ran to outlying points from Boston with as many as fifteen hundred skaters aboard. Crowds as large as fifty thousand tried their runners on the ponds in New York's Central Park.

DUCK SHOOTING. Painting by Arthur Fitzwilliam Tait.

From colonial days down to the present, hunting and fishing have been leading outdoor activities in America. Both had the initial virtue of combining profit with pleasure, which was virtue enough to keep the sports innocent in the eyes of the strictest moralists. Captain John Smith was quick to point that out in his first report on New England. What more pleasure could the future Yankees have, he asked, than "to recreate themselves before their owne doores, in their owne boates . . . where man, woman and childe, with a small hooke and line, by angling, may take divers sorts of excellent fish, at their pleasures? And is it not a pretty sport, to pull up two pence, six pence, and twelve pence, as fast as you can haule and veare a line?"

Time so spent was not "mis-spent." Even the venerable Cotton Mather fished, apparently unbothered by his conscience for the pleasure he might have found in hooking his next meal, and he was followed by generations of angling dignitaries. Daniel Webster, it is said, prepared his finest orations before the trout in his basket and claimed that he earned his robust constitution by his innumerable vigorous hunting excursions.

America was long a paradise for hunters, be the game water fowl or grizzly bears. As early as 1795, the growing scarcity of game in some sections had led to laws proclaiming closed seasons for hunting. However, it was a large land and in most places you did not have to go far to find game always in season or, in some circumstances, to have it find you. In America, recalled one Englishman, who had visited the country early in the nineteenth century, "were no game laws to tax the pocket and principles. . . . You could take your rod or gun, jump over a gate and wing or hook your victim before the door of a mansion without the trouble of inquiring to whom it belonged. Here was no eternal 'Trespassers beware,' or 'Spring

44

guns' to warn the reader that a rabbit's legs were of more value than a man's. The benevolent Americans forgave every man his trespasses, and pointed their guns only at the enemies of their country."

For a long period the gun was the staff of life for a good portion of the American population and the skill of native riflemen all but legendary, but that the legend was based on fact was clearly demonstrated before an international audience at Bunker Hill and a generation later at New Orleans. Along the frontier William Tell would have been just another marksman, not as good as many.

"The men have shooting matches all to themselves in the autumn," wrote Thomas L. Nichols, "when turkeys are fat, and Thanksgiving is coming. Turkeys are put up to be shot at so many rods' distance, at so much a shot. Of course the poor shots pay for the turkeys which the good ones carry home. . . . These riflemen, who killed their game without injuring their skins, barked squirrels off the trees, and shot wild turkeys in the head, would hold candles in the night for each other to snuff with a bullet

Collection of the late Harry T. Peters
STRIPED-BASS FISHING. Painting by Tait.

without extinguishing the light, drive a nail into a tree with a ball without bending it, or split a bullet into two equal halves on a knife-blade. The fathers or grandfathers of those men had fought with the Indians, and carried their rifles into the field to their work, and to church on Sundays, that the war-whoop might never surprise them unarmed. Marksmanship always seemed to me an instinct, and hereditary."

TURKEY SHOOT, 1879. Painting by John Whetton Ehninger.
The Museum of Fine Arts, Boston, M. & M. Karolik Collection

In early rural America, life was all of a piece. To the farmer nature was not a retreat from the worries and strains of business. It was his shop and his office. How to spend his leisure was no problem—he had none. Recreation had to be found in close association with the daily round of his work. The bees and frolics that celebrated such seasonal chores as reaping, husking, and picking and such speed-up programs as log rolling, house or barn raising, sewing and quilting parties, were the business as well as the play of life. To be constantly employed was the normal condition of existence. To be idle seemed an aberration of natural law and even when circumstances made it possible to relax from toil the typical Yankee, at least, preferred to keep up the appearance of industry.

"Whittling . . . ," wrote Captain Marryat, "is a habit, arising from the natural restlessness of the American when he is not employed, of cutting a piece of stick, or anything else, with his knife. Some are so wedded to it from long custom, that if they have not a piece of stick to cut, they will whittle the backs of the chairs, or anything within their reach. A Yankee shown into a room to await the arrival of another, has been known to whittle away nearly the whole of the mantel-piece. Lawyers in court whittle away at the table before them; and the judges will cut through their own bench. In some courts they put sticks before noted whittlers to

Corn Husking, 1860. Painting by Eastman Johnson.

save the furniture. The Down Easters, as the Yankees are termed generally, whittle when they are making a bargain, as it fills up the pauses, gives them time for reflection, and moreover prevents any examination of the countenance—for in bargaining, like in the game of brag, the countenance is carefully watched, as an index to the wishes."

A back-country wedding offered occasion for celebration (see the next two pages) that was often improved upon with rare abandon. The charivari, or "shivaree," that followed consisted of every conceivable manner of noise making until the bride and groom bought off the celebrants with food, drink, and any other treat that could be commanded. "A few evenings since," re-ported an early Nebraska newspaper, "an unearthly noise, caused by beating tin pans, empty oyster cans, ringing cow bells, shooting fire crackers, playing on the 'Pigaree' and such like instruments was heard in our quiet city. The cause was soon ascertained. Billy Hoblitzell, some weeks ago, concluded that it was 'not good to be alone'—especially as cold weather was approaching—took to himself a 'better half'—has been staying 'out home'—maybe to fool the boys until they would forget—fixed his house in town this week—moved in—boys wide awake—after him — 'trotted him out,' as above described. Finale, oyster-treat at Hugh Baker's Saloon." The shivaree was over and the bride and groom were left in peace.

Coming to the Point, 1854. Painting by William Sidney Mount.

The New York Public Library

WEDDING IN THE BIG SMOKY MOUNTAINS, 1872. Painting by John Stokes.

THE BUFFALO HUNT, 1861. Painting by Tait.

Slaughtering game—particularly the buffalo—on the prairies and Plains, beyond being a means of livelihood and a lucrative business for professional hunters, was a sport that attracted amateurs from the East and Europe. The Grand Duke Alexis of Russia was but one of the notables who enjoyed a buffalo chase, a chase arranged especially for him and his large entourage

ROPING A GRAY WOLF IN WYOMING, 1879. Photograph by Grabill.

on the plains of western Kansas by Buffalo Bill, General Custer, and General Sheridan. Emigrants, merchants, and any odd traveler joined in the major sport until the land seemed at times a stinking waste where countless carcasses were left to rot when the shooting was over.

"The first flight of the buffalo," wrote one hunter, "is comparatively slow, but when pressed by the huntsman, the rapidity with which these apparently unwieldly animals get over the ground, is amazing. Alex F. and myself having the fleetest horses, each of us singled out a victim. . . . We were shortly alongside, and our double barrels told with deadly effect, the huge beasts rolling on the ground in death, within a hundred yards of each other." It was a familiar story. Early travelers on the Plains had reported that it sometimes took them a week to pass by a single herd of buffalo. Their innumerable hordes had blackened the landscape as far as the eye could reach. When the carnage

COWBOYS COMING TO TOWN. From *Harper's Weekly*, 1889, after Frederic Remington.

was over the buffalo was all but extinct.

For the cowboy hunting game might be sport to break the monotony of long hours in the saddle, practice in using his lariat or six-shooter, and protection of the stock in his charge. Roping a buffalo for sheer excitement could be perilous fun. "I remember on one of those buffalo-roping stunts," wrote one Westerner, "a cowboy roped a big bull around the neck. It wasn't long before his horse played out. When he tried to stop the animal it made a run at his horse. Knowing that it would eventually kill the horse, and maybe the rider, I shot him before he had done any such damage." Before he could get his rope off such dangerous beasts the cowboy always had to kill them.

If wolves menaced the herds of cattle all hands joined in an organized hunt, sometimes aided by greyhounds kept at the ranch for that purpose. But all too few diversions broke the tedium of life on the ranch during the winter months. In the ceiling of one

bunkhouse a visitor counted 3620 bullet holes made by bored cowboys who had killed time and quieted their restlessness by shooting at flies. Carefully memorizing all the type on tin-can labels and reciting them in a rapid singsong delivery was another contrived amusement that consumed otherwise wearisome hours.

After the boredom of the ranch and the loneliness and rigor of the range the cowboy's rare day in town was usually a riotous celebration, as told in another chapter. The shanty towns of the wilder West, the mining camps as well as the cow towns, were little else than centers of entertainment, made up largely of saloons and dance halls for the rough and ever ready characters who drifted in from the Plains and mountains determined to have their fun at any price they could pay. One cowman, to compensate for months of austerity, ordered a champagne bath that drained the supply of the entire town at five dollars a bottle.

The Museum of the City of New York, J. Clarence Davies Collection

FASHIONABLE TURNOUTS IN CENTRAL PARK, 1869. Lithograph by Currier and Ives after a drawing by Thomas Worth.

In the older and thickly settled communities of the East the dissipation of leisure took more organized forms. Here, where wealth was a somewhat less novel feature of society and where work was theoretically concentrated in the business hours of the day, idleness had lost much of the taint attached to it in earlier, rural America. In some precincts, indeed, idleness was made conspicuous as a measure of success in the world: Leisure had become identified with display, as it traditionally was in most established societies.

Nothing was more striking, more brilliant, or more vivid, reported *Appleton's Journal* in 1869, "than the appearance of the grand drive at the Central Park, on a fair day, in the fashionable season. . . . Probably nothing more fully exhibits the wealth, luxury, and taste of New York City than its fancy 'turnouts' and private carriages. . . . At least fifty new carriages a day [are produced by New York manufacturers]. The

fashionable styles are: the Clarence (large family or state carriage); landau (opening on the top); landaulet (opening on the top, with appliances to remove the front section if desired); coupé (for fair weather or fresh air); pony-phaeton (riding *al fresco*); and a four-in-hand drag, which, within a few years, has become one of the most conspicuous features of the Central Park drives."

On the other hand, Sabbatarians and custodians of the established order were increasingly disturbed by the way the least fashionable of the cities' population was spending its Sundays, its one day of leisure in the week. New attitudes were developing to contradict the traditional American conception of the Lord's Day. Immigrants—Germans, Irish, Jews, and others—who little knew or cared how sternly Puritans may have felt towards the Sabbath, found the day fit for their own customary recreations. "Where is the city in which the Sabbath day is not losing ground?" it was earnestly inquired. "To the mass of workingmen Sunday . . . is a day for labor meetings, for excursions, for saloons, beer-gardens, baseball games and carousels." To toilers of any faith it became a day of release from the pressures of city life, although as was pointed out to them by pious critics, the divine law had not yet been repealed. A sympathetic portion of the press, however, recognized that the less favored city-dwellers had their "peculiar wants." The greatest of these wants, it reported, "is liberty, and for that reason the public insist that Sunday shall be a day of social freedom." Several states with large urban populations seriously modified their Sunday blue laws during the 1880's.

Whatever their status Americans must learn the art of relaxation, urged the *Nation*. That it was better to wear out than to rust out, as an overused proverb claimed, was not even a half-truth "but an invention of Sabbathless and unvacationed Satan."

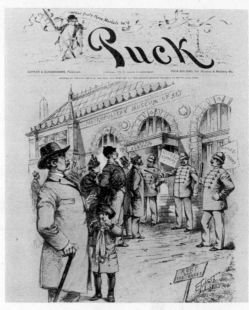

The New-York Historical Society
"How the Workingman Enjoys the [Metropolitan] Museum on His Only Day of Liberty." A satirical commentary from *Puck* in 1889.

Sunday "Social Freedom" in the Bowery, 1874. Engraving from the *Illustrated Christian Weekly*.
The New-York Historical Society

The New-York Historical Society, Bella C. Landauer Collection

EXCURSION ADVERTISEMENT. Lithograph by Chas. Hart.

A BRIDAL PARTY AT PROSPECT POINT, NIAGARA FALLS, IN THE 1870's.

To get out of the city altogether for a breath of fresh air was one freedom made possible even for slender budgets by steamboats and railroads that offered cheap Sunday and holiday excursions, there and back within the day. On a summer day in 1845 one editor reflected that so many vacationists were quitting New York for the cool delights of the country that the city, it seemed, would soon "be abandoned to the dog-killers, cabmen, and police justices at the Tombs." For a growing class of people a longer retreat during the summer was becoming feasible and popular. After the Civil War Newport, Long Branch, Nahant, the White Mountains, and other places as far south as Florida and as far west as the Rockies were attracting seasonal crowds of vacationists that increased by the year.

This voluntary and approved flight from incessant work, on such a scale at least, was a novel development in American life, hailed by progressives.

"Twenty-five years ago," observed the *Nation* in 1873, "clerks and young employees hardly ever expected a holiday, except as a matter of particular favor. Now a fortnight of freedom in the year is getting to be regularly understood as a part of their contract. A fortnight is but half enough. . . . The fact is that every man who possibly can should force himself to a holiday of a full month in the year, whether he feels like taking it or not. . . . An employer of labor should see to it." The ceaseless scheming for the future, habitual with Americans, said the magazine, had undermined all sense of reality in the present—as in the case of the law student who took his books to Niagara Falls on his honeymoon.

THE RISE OF SPORTS

Except in the upper reaches of society so much outdoor recreation was informal and unsystematized that it was easy to underestimate the amount of sporting activity that actually went on in America. Nothing in rural recreation resembled organized sport as an Englishman, let us say, would have recognized it. Within urban limits as well, a passing traveler would have seen little to persuade him that Americans were a sports-loving people, that they engaged in sport, that is, for its own sake. Rapid urbanization was robbing a still growing part of the population of traditional outlets for their physical energies and few of the substitute excitements of city life called on a single muscle, save those of the paid performers. "To roll balls in a ten pin alley by gaslight or to drive a fast trotting horse in a light wagon along a very bad and a very dusty road," observed an English visitor in 1855, "seems the Alpha and Omega of sport in the United States."

About mid-century, however, a sharp observer might have noted the beginnings of a phenomenal change. First in the cities, then virtually everywhere, Americans were awakening to the pleasures and possibilities of systematic and deliberate play. Baseball already had rules and formal regulations and was attracting a widening public interest. In the decades that followed, a bewildering succession of other games and pastimes swept in and out of popular favor. What Emerson had called the invalidism in American life was threatened by one athletic craze after another. Each one took on some of the fervor of an old-time revival.

In an article entitled "Muscular Christianity by a Christian Muscleman," the *Overland Monthly* voiced the prevailing enthusiasm: "We presume to introduce the

The New York Public Library

BASEBALL AS IT WAS PLAYED IN THE 1860's. Lithograph by S. Van Campen from *Base ball as viewed by a Muffin*. New Bedford, Mass., 1867.

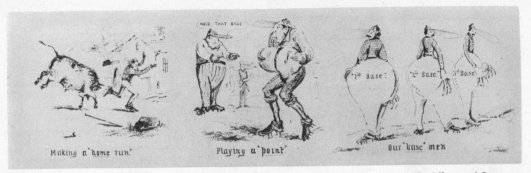

"A Comprehensive View of Base Ball," 1859. Details of a lithograph by William T. Crane.

oar, the bat, the foil, the gloves, the dumb-bell, and the Indian Club, as most efficient helps to virtue and most potent means of grace. While to those most earnest in the swift pursuit of health fast-flying or already fled, we intimate that the new wheel-footed biped—the velocipede—may help them the sooner to overtake the chase."

By the end of the century the earlier picture was reversed. Baseball, croquet, skating, tennis, bicycling, golf, and swimming had become widely popular diversions, or were fast becoming so. In almost every case the new pastime had first been introduced as a fashionable indulgence of the genteel. Even baseball was initiated as an exclusive amusement. But in sports as in clothing, fashion propagated itself downard, to paraphrase Bishop Alonzo Potter. One after the other the public took them over and made them its own. Gentility retreated from sport to sport until only polo, coaching, yachting, and a few other expensive pursuits remained beyond reach of the masses of people.

The evolution of American baseball out of the earlier bat-and-ball base-circulating games was clearly marked with the organization of the Knickerbocker Club by a group of New York business and professional men in 1845, and with the formulation of a code of rules that outlined the modern game. From its beginnings baseball was both a spectator's and a participant's sport, attracting growing audiences and at the same time widespread popularity as an active pastime.

A tendency to keep the game at a certain social level beyond reach of hoi polloi quickly broke down. (The Knickerbockers took to the field in straw hats, blue trousers, and white shirts.) Before the Civil War delegates from more than fifty clubs, composed of enthusiasts from all ranks, attended the convention of the National Association of Base Ball Players.

The pitcher used an underhand delivery; no one wore a glove; the outfielder caught fly balls in his cap; and the umpire, in full top-hatted dignity, ignored any distinction between strikes and balls. But even before the war, it was reported, one match attracted fifteen thousand spectators. Baseball was already clearly recognizable as America's National Game. The pressure on players of outstanding teams by gamblers and a rabidly interested public was mounting too high for it to remain a purely amateur sport. With competitive interest at such a pitch there was already a suggestion of professionalism. "They make batting a business," reported the *Galaxy* of the touring clubs, "and depend for money on the receipts from spectators."

A widening interest in the new game was fostered by the informal contests behind the lines during the Civil war. Albert G. Spalding was one of the many who learned the attraction of the sport from returned soldiers. It was he who pitched an unknown team from Rockford, Illinois, to a victory over a heralded Washington club in 1867.

UNION ARMY PRISONERS PLAYING BASEBALL AT SALISBURY, NORTH CAROLINA, 1863. Lithograph by Sarony, Major and Knapp after a drawing by Major Otto Botticher.

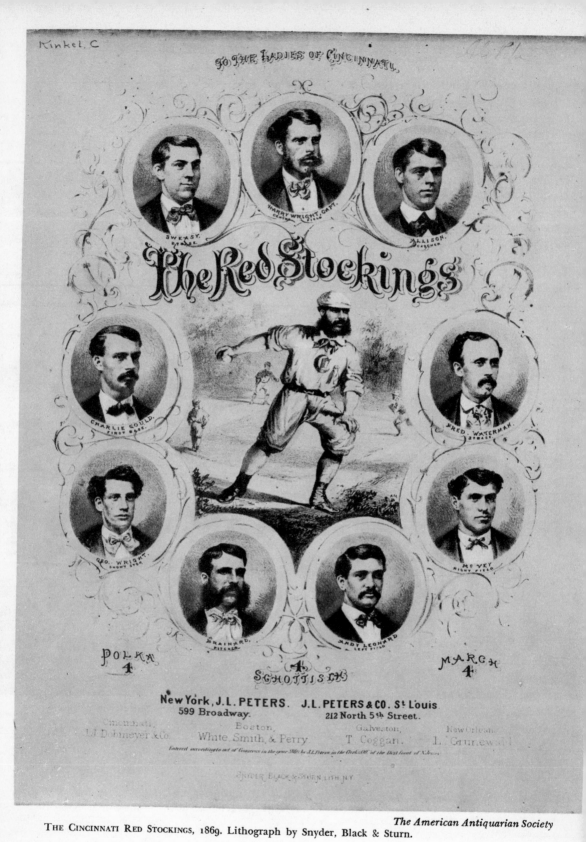

THE CINCINNATI RED STOCKINGS, 1869. Lithograph by Snyder, Black & Sturn.

"It is a mania," reported *Galaxy* in 1868. "Hundreds of clubs do nothing but play, all summer and autumn. What pleasant days are not devoted to matches are spent in practice. When the 'nine' are not contending with visitors, they themselves are traveling over the country, from Bangor to St. Louis. . . . Since the war, it has run like wildfire. Young soldiers, full of vigor, and longing for comradeship and manly exercise, found them in this game. . . ."

In 1869 when the Cincinnati Red Stockings were openly paid for their services and won every game in a country-wide tour, baseball started its professional history. Seven years later its National League of Professional Baseball Clubs put the professional sport on a stable, businesslike basis.

By the 1880's professional baseball was a big business attracting during a season, among the major teams alone, hundreds of thousands of spectators of all ages and conditions and of both sexes. Strikes and balls were called, gloves and other equipment

The Rhode Island School of Design, Museum of Art
BASEBALL PLAYERS. Water color by Thomas Eakins, 1875.

were introduced, rules for pitching were improved, and a good ball was developed. For several years post-season "world series" games were played between the National League and a short-lived American Association. The championship series between Detroit and St. Louis in 1887 attracted a paid attendance of over fifty-one thousand.

PROFESSIONAL BASEBALL, 1887. Lithograph by the New York Lithographic Co.

The Library of Congress

Collection of R. W. G. Vail

A Sand Lot Game of the 1870's, at the West Branch School, Geneva, New York. Photograph by James Gardiner Vail.

Attendance at the big professional games was small compared to the untold millions of bystanders and rooters who watched amateur and pick-up games on sand lots and playgrounds all over the country. And the paid performers were few compared to the tireless enthusiasts of all ranks and ages who played for nothing but their own pleasure.

During these same years following the Civil War, a croquet craze swept the nation in whirlwind fashion. From one end of the land to the other few lawns were left unmarked by the universally popular game. Sets with candle sockets atop the wickets and posts enabled enthusiasts to play into the dark of night. Beyond the Mississippi people came from miles away to play with a neighbor's set, if they had none of their own. Croquet parties tested the merits of the players of a town and championship matches were held with teams from other towns. "Of all the epidemics that have swept over our land, the swiftest and most infectious is croquet," reported the *Nation* in 1866.

"One prime feature of the new game," a playing manual pointed out, "is that it is an outdoor sport in which ladies and gentlemen may alike engage. Hitherto, while men and boys have had their healthful means of recreation in the open air, the women and girls have been restricted to the less exhilarating sports of indoor life. . . . Grace in holding and using the mallet, easy and pleasing attitudes in playing, promptness in taking your turn, and gentlemanly and ladylike manners generally throughout the game, are points which it is unnecessary for us to enlarge on. . . . Young ladies are proverbially fond of cheating at this game; but they only do it because . . . they think that men like it."

The social consequences of the pastime were immediately apparent. As a boon to courtship the game was celebrated. "But the mallets and balls unheeded lay," ran the song illustrated at the right, "And the maid and the youth! side by side sat they, And I thought to myself is that Croquet?"

The American Antiquarian Society
THE SOCIAL ASPECTS OF CROQUET, 1866. Lithograph by F. H. Carter, after a drawing by S. S. Frizzell, from a music sheet cover.

CROQUET, 1866. Painting by Winslow Homer.

The Art Institute of Chicago

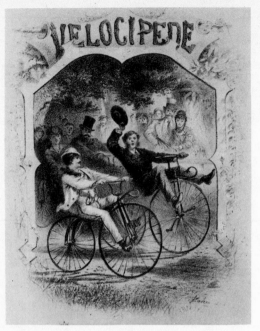

THE VELOCIPEDE, 1869. Lithograph published by
Koppitz, Prüfer & Co.

America was behaving like a pleasure-
starved nation in the zest it showed for new
sports. Croquet was hardly launched before
the velocipede was introduced and adopted
with a still greater furor. Its almost immediate popularity rivaled even that of baseball.
The girl of fashion took to wheels in a costume of divided skirts "not unlike the trousers of a Zouave." The Odd Fellows' Hall in
Iola, Kansas, the local press reported in
1869, was crowded with young bloods who
were bound to "ride her or die," but who
only suffered sprains and contusions. The
early "bone shaker," with wooden frame
and iron-shod wheels, jarred its rider out of
all complacency. The fad subsided very
quickly but while it raged it seemed to
Henry Ward Beecher that the "coming
man" was coming on a velocipede.

The "wheel-footed biped" was back in the
running again a decade later when high-
wheeled bicycles were imported from England. Perched high in the air, editorialized
the *Wheelman* in its first number, in 1882,
the rider feels that "he is making a consider-

able spectacle of himself and needlessly
eliciting public remark; both of which sensations are not agreeable to men of tender
sensibilities. But those feelings soon wear
off." They must have, for in that same year
20,000 of the new machines were in use. To
the urban pedestrian the bicycle offered
release from the city during his leisure, a
relatively speedy way of getting into the
country for communion with green and
growing things, without the pandemonium
and jostling of a train ride.

The introduction of new "safety" models
with wheels of equal size and pneumatic
tires gave bicycling a fresh, spectacular
popularity. Special machines with dropped
frames and others built for two riders were
designed to encourage women to take to the
road along with the men. This they did with
an enthusiasm that brought down a shower
of controversy about the proprieties, female
health, and women's rights. By 1893 a million "bikes" were in use and the number was
increasing rapidly. No form of outdoor exer-

Now drinking crystal dew of summer skies
From out some lily cup above his head.

COMMUNING WITH NATURE VIA THE BICYCLE, 1882.
From the *Wheelman*.

CYCLING ON RIVERSIDE DRIVE, 1895. From *Harper's Weekly*, after a drawing by W. A. Rogers.

cise had ever won such an enormous and enthusiastic following in American history. The bicycle provided fun, exercise, convenience, and speed for those who craved it and would work for it. Cycling, said one journal, drove away dyspepsia, headaches, insomnia, sciatica, and imparted "a vigorous tone to the whole system." It was an ideal corrective for national invalidism.

But the "Christian Muscleman" had not spoken for all his brethren. There were still those among the pious who looked askance at such conspicuous enjoyment and waste of time—especially on the Sabbath, the only day many people were free to play. It was a delicate point, nicely argued. "Whether bicycle riding on Sunday be sinful, or not," wrote the *Wheelman* in 1882, "depends entirely on the spirit in which it is taken and the associations of the ride. A man may truly serve God in taking an invigorating spin, if his heart is attuned to what is right." Combining the exercise with light and foolish conversation or exhibitions of fancy riding, on the other hand, was patently degrading and debilitating and not to be countenanced as a Sabbath pastime. "You cannot serve God and skylark on a bicycle," pronounced a clergyman. "Better bicycle ten minutes than a cycle in a sleigh!" retorted *Puck*. To either viewpoint it was an important topic.

During the score of years that the sport maintained its great popularity it did more than anything else to bring a free, wholesome companionship to men and women. It played a large part in liberating women from the bondage of Victorian fashions in clothes and behavior. To bicycle a woman admittedly must have legs, an attribute not admitted by earlier standards of etiquette. And, as contemporary fiction and anecdote were quick to suggest, the bicycle, especially the one built for two, was built for romance. At the turn of the century the census bureau declared that "few articles ever used by man have created so great a revolution in social conditions as the bicycle."

TOURING IN THE COUNTRY, 1896. From *Harper's Weekly*, after a drawing by A. B. Frost.

LAWN TENNIS, 1887. Aquarelle print by L. Prang & Co.

GOLF, 1897. From *Scribner's Magazine*, after a drawing by A. B. Frost.

Lawn tennis came into sudden favor as an "elegant and pleasant pastime" during the late 1870's. Until vigorous and expert tournament play showed the possibilities of the game, it remained too "polite" for common entertainment and was generally considered a sport for the classes. It was a game which almost from the beginning the ladies played. Indeed, as early played, it was adapted to their heavy-skirted limitations and the considerate returns of their flannel-trousered and blazered escorts. It was, in short, "sissy."

The popularization of golf in the nineteenth century was delayed by the common notion that it, too, was a rich man's pastime. To build and maintain links of any size did require a considerable capital investment and to play the game over a good-sized course demanded leisure that was only becoming common at the turn of the century. By the 1890's, however, the well-enough-to-do had established a number of clubs with layouts of from six to eighteen holes where even pioneer women players might practice the game. In 1914, with country clubs springing up in every suburb, golf was already considered one of the favorite outdoor pastimes of America, although the popular vogue of the sport had barely begun. Crowded municipal links of recent years, all over the country, tell their own story of mass leisure and a changed attitude towards the game.

By the 1880's a thoroughly American version of football had been developed and systematized. The game was to a large extent an intercollegiate sport and, since it had its greatest early success in the exclusive eastern colleges, it enjoyed the close attention of fans with social rank. However, it rapidly won a far wider audience than could be listed in the Social Register. Fifty thousand spectators watched the Princeton-Yale game of 1893.

The passion for watching and reading about athletic contests was developing in every level at a mounting rate. "It has now grown to vast proportions," wrote James Bryce in 1905. "It occupies the minds not only of the youth at the universities, but also of their parents and of the general public. Baseball and football matches excite an interest greater than any other public events except the Presidential election, and that comes only once in four years." That same year the President of the United States called a conference in the White House to discuss the roughness, professionalism, and overemphasis that threatened the sport of intercollegiate football.

FOOTBALL, ROCHESTER *vs.* CORNELL, OCT. 19, 1889. Photograph by S. R. Stoddard, Glen Falls, N. Y.
The Library of Congress

With increasing means and leisure at its disposal the general public, the enormous middle class of American democracy, continued to appropriate one "exclusive" sport after another. Rowing races which in the 1830's and 1840's had been sponsored by clubs of "young men of the highest respectability" had not only become common intercollegiate events, but the business of professionals whose names were on everyone's tongues.

So with virtually every other form of recreation first introduced by the better-to-do. The wealthier fringe of society was obliged to retreat to other recreations, imported from the aristocracy abroad if need be, requiring paraphernalia that removed their pleasures beyond popular imitation—yachting, polo, fox hunting, coaching, and other costly diversions.

The interest in yachting, a sport which had been practiced by a few since 1812, had been fired by the startling victory of the *America* at the Cowes regatta in 1851 and was renewed when the English challenger, *Cambria,* crossed the Atlantic in an attempt to recover the trophy in 1870. In the painting reproduced opposite, the successful defender, the American yacht *Magic,* is shown rounding the Sandy Hook lightship followed by three other American schooners.

The fashion of four-in-hand driving in custom-built coaches introduced an extravagant hobby safely beyond mass imitation. The meticulous pageantry of the annual Parades and the regularly scheduled runs of a few road coaches into the country and return with guards winding their horns in orthodox "olden" English style, to the wonder of the countryside, provided highly exclusive amusement as long as it lasted—from the establishment of the Coaching Club in 1875 until the expensive new automobiles, at the turn of the century, suggested more novel entertainment to those who could afford it.

JOHN BIGLEN. Water color by Thomas Eakins, 1873.

The Metropolitan Museum of Art

THE DEFENSE OF AMERICA'S CUP, 1870. Painting by James E. Buttersworth.

COACHING THROUGH NEW JERSEY, 1903. Water color by Max Klepper.

A TROLLEY-CAR EXCURSION, 1896. From *Harper's Weekly,* after a painting by F. Cresson Schell.

The millions, meanwhile, found their own pleasure wagon in the trolley car. By 1895 ten thousand miles of electric transit lines were in operation in the nation. Cheap to operate and cheap to illuminate with the still relatively new incandescent light bulbs, the trolley car was a novel and irresistible vehicle for an inexpensive joy ride. Carnival excursions to outlying amusement parks, promoted by the traction companies, rapidly became an enormously popular diversion for city people—wherever the lines were operated, wherever people longed for a brief, inexpensive "breather" away from familiar surroundings. Trolleys brightly decorated with colored electric lights, in tandem and with a band of musicians aboard, provided a glittering, melodious caravan to joy for anyone with a few cents in his pocket of a week-end evening in summer. Every city with electric traction went through a brief period of "trolley excite-

ment" during the last decade of the nineteenth century.

Sunday was becoming the workingman's holiday, although it was no day of rest for those who ran the cars and manned the amusement stalls or for the public who taxed those facilities in their pursuit of happiness.

Before the century closed the amusement resorts and trolley parks at the outskirts of most cities, large and small, had become a vital part in the recreational life of the otherwise city-bound worker. The commercialized development of all the likely sites within easy range of the Sunday crowds was as unplanned and chaotic as the growth of the city itself. But, such as they were, recreational facilities were open to all and within reach of most of the people. The mingling of pleasure-bent multitudes frequently from areas where the population was most polyglot and restricted was a unifying force where it was most needed.

Coney Island, 1896. Photographs by Byron.

The last quarter of the nineteenth century saw the circus flower in its full glory, attracting all classes, all ages, all colors, in all sections of the land to its seasonal performances. It reached places too remote and obscure to attract electric cars. It was the unforgettable event of rural life.

"From the time the 'advance man' flung his highly colored posters over the fence till the coming of the glorious day we thought of little else," wrote Hamlin Garland of his prairie childhood. "It was India and Arabia and the jungle to us. History and the magic and pomp of chivalry mingled in the parade of the morning, and the crowds, the clanging band, the haughty and alien beauty of the women, the gold embroidered housings, the stark majesty of the acrobats subdued us into silent worship. . . . To rob me of my

memories of the circus would leave me as poor as those to whom life was a drab and hopeless round of toil. It was our brief season of imaginative life. In one day—in a part of one day—we gained a thousand new conceptions of the world and of human nature. It was an embodiment of all that was skillful and beautiful in manly action. It was a compendium of biologic research but more important still, it brought to our ears the latest band pieces and taught us the most popular songs. It furnished us with jokes. It relieved our dullness. It gave us something to talk about.

"We always went home wearied with excitement, and dusty and fretful—but content. We had seen it. . . . Next day as we resumed work in the field the memory of its splendors went with us like a golden cloud."

CALLIOPE! THE WONDERFUL OPERONICON OR STEAM CAR OF THE MUSES.
AS IT APPEARS IN THE GORGEOUS STREET PAGENT OF THE GREAT
EUROPEAN ZOOLOGICAL ASSOCIATION!
BRITISH MUSEUM. ROYAL COLISEUM. GALLERY OF ART. WORLD'S CONGRESS AND GIGANTIC CIRCUS! 12 Tents! 900 Men and Horses! One Ticket Admits to All!

The Library of Congress

A CIRCUS ATTRACTION. "CALLIOPE! THE WONDERFUL OPERONICON OR STEAM CAR OF THE MUSES."

"The Circus is Coming." 1871. Painting by Charles Caleb Ward.

THE CIRCUS PARADE, 1900. From the *Ladies' Home Journal*, after a drawing by A. B. Frost.

THE BUSINESS OF PLAY

The moral obligation to save time which had been such a strong influence in early colonial days has remained a sovereign force in American life. Time once saved in the name of Christian virtue has come to be saved in the name of simple efficiency, but the urgency to save it has hardly diminished. That efficiency, in turn, has piled up more leisure for more people than has ever been known elsewhere in history. It happened quickly, within a few short generations, and to a nation with a recent pioneer tradition of unmitigated hard work—a nation trained to believe that killing time was a crime—it was bewildering. What to do with leisure now that we had it became a major problem of our civilization.

Until the end of the last century the great labor-saving machines of industry had produced few devices to improve the leisure

they were creating. Then, as the century turned, came the industrial revolution of recreation. With the movie, the auto, the radio, and lately television, commerce and recreation became inseparable. To keep the wheels of the new industries turning America had to be sold on play—on the latest film and its stars, the newest car and the most beguiling trip to take in it, the most remarkable radio or television set and its sponsored delights—as inexorably as it was sold the national brands of anything else. Within a few decades the country's pleasure and its business became completely interdependent. The commerce in playthings was an important part of the national economy. "To profit by the potential market offered by increasing leisure," it was officially reported to President Hoover, "many forms of amusement or recreation have been

A KINETOSCOPE ARCADE IN SAN FRANCISCO, LATE NINETEENTH CENTURY.
The Museum of Modern Art Film Library

provided on a commercial basis, as for instance, moving pictures, automobile touring, travel, radio, boxing, tennis, golf, baseball, football, dancing, and 'resorts.' On these and similar recreations in the late 1920's our experts show that we spent 10 to 12 billion dollars a year!" With so much at stake the nation could hardly afford not to play, watch, or listen to its games and other amusements. To have fun was not only the great tribal ceremony of America as an English writer suggested, it had become almost an economic necessity.

Many of the diversions that were contrived to dissipate the new leisure made more immediate demands on the purse of an individual than on his active sportfulness. Guardians of human welfare, self-appointed and entrusted, lamented the growing "recline" in American recreation that was encouraged by the entertaining efforts of large commercial interests. "No previous generation had made such progress in the art of being amused," observed historians of the post World War I era. "None had been so incapable of amusing itself." Even the creative joy of tinkering with imperfect mechanisms was vanishing before the technical advances of industry. Few people "got out and got under" their cars as they commonly had in the second decade of the century nor did many dare, wish, or have reason to anatomize their more modern, sleekly cased radios. "How does the American adult spend his leisure time?" asked a writer in the *Atlantic Monthly* in 1937. "The chances are eight to ten that he will drive his car along Route 168, watch a 'moom' picture, listen to the Itty Bitty Kiddie Hour, or else enjoy a few inches in the bleachers while someone on the field plays for him."

The strange magic of moving pictures was first housed in the nickel slot machines of Edison's invention. Such little peep shows were a side business of penny arcades and billiard parlors and the modest and very brief amusement of the public whose pleasures came cheap. When the moving images were released onto a screen visible to many people no one could guess the consequences. "May not small towns see city shows by the Vitascope?" asked one newspaper. "May not actresses, who realize how fleeting youth is, preserve themselves in their prime? Indeed to what use may not the Vitascope be put?"

The movies won an early success as a substitute for the lantern slide in illustrated talks. Among the pioneer exhibitors was the lecturer, Lyman H. Howe, who used the new device in the best Lyceum tradition. From the outset, observed one authority, "his aim . . . was to make every presentation as educational as it was entertaining, to instruct his audiences subtly yet surely while amusing them." Over the years that followed millions flocked to his "pictorial excursions" into a wide world miraculously brought within four walls. "The desire for this kind of entertainment is essentially American, reported the *Moving Picture World*. "The American mind is laudably an acquisitive one."

The Library of Congress
ADVERTISEMENT FOR HOWE'S "TRAVEL FESTIVAL," 1898.

NO, IT IS NOT A MAGIC LANTERN SHOW

NOT TO BE COMPARED. IT IS A MOST ADVANCED, INSTRUCTIVE AND ENTERTAINING STUDY.

The Pioneer Limited
LIGHTNING
⚙ EXPRESS

YOU WILL not be disappointed if you come with your mind made up to enjoy an evening of continuous fun and laughter because we guarantee to kill the blues. Don't fail to come. Tell your friends to come. Bring the wife and children. If you don't like our performance tell the manager and get your money back.

21 NIGHTS
IN CHURCHES OF ST. LOUIS.
27 NIGHTS IN CINCINNATI.
25 NIGHTS IN KANSAS CITY

FIVE DIFFERENT TIMES OVER
UNITED STATES AND CANADA

WASHINGTON, D. C.--Rev. W. F. Crafts:
"I was delighted with an entertainment by these gentlemen at one of our Chautauquas."

ST. LOUIS, MO.--Rev. E. C. Cole, First Baptist Church:
"Unquestionably the best ever given in our church."

BARRE, VERMONT.--Rev. Thos. H. Mitchell, First Presbyterian Church: "Our highest anticipations were realized."

Read the Testimonials

We have a treat for you
this season
come and see for yourself

Laing Bros. Moving Pictures

South Royalton, Vt.--Rev. E. E. Wells, Pastor M. E. Church: We had a crowded house. The views presented were first class. "They were fine" was the verdict of young and old.

Washington, D. C.--Rev. Wilbur F. Crafts: I was delighted with an entertainment by these gentlemen at one of our Chautauquas, and have pleasure in commending them.

Northfield, Vt.--Rev. H. S. Hazen, Congregational Church: It was eminently satisfactory here--very interesting and instructive.

Fort Edward, N. Y.--Mr. Laing.--Dear Sir:--Your program of Moving Pictures and the receipts at the door were both satisfactory. We want to get you to come again a little later in the season.--M. G. Cole, Pastor 1st M. E. Church.

Williamstown, Vt.--Rev. D. H. Strong, Congregational Church: We were more than entertained by the Laing Bros. They gave us the solid cream of good things, undiluted by the cheap trashy stuff often thrown in. Everything was clean and high class.

Saranac Lake, N. Y.--Warren Ward, President Epworth League, M. E. Church: It was high class and very pleasing. Receipts, $125.

Ferrisburg, Vt.--Rev. Geo. H. Bailey, Congregational Church: I was more than pleased. I was highly delighted, and the audience shared in my appreciation and pronounced it wonderful.

St. Louis, Mo.--Dr. E. C. Cole, First Baptist Church: The fine moving pictures in this exhibition were unquestionably the best ever given in our church.

The New-York Historical Society

MOVING PICTURE ADVERTISEMENT, ABOUT 1900.

At the start no one was particularly concerned with the subject matter of the films. It was enough that railroad trains, fire engines, and galloping horses seemed to move, that the roaring surf at Dover threatened to break right over the front rows of the audience (thereby causing a panic at one early showing). Here was a dynamic new language which, even in its stuttering beginnings, spoke directly to the man in the street, or rather the man who drifted into the penny arcades from the street.

When it was discovered that moving pictures on a screen could tell a connected story, any sort of a story, and tell it vividly, eloquently, and with fresh conviction, the new art became a social force of incalculable power for good or evil. Like the democratized theater that Mrs. Trollope had complained of years before, the early flicker dramas pursued and captured a wide public.

But there was a difference. Like most popular amusements the theater was a class entertainment that had been gradually taken over by the masses. The new "Nickel Madness," reversing a time-honored progression, was a popular excitement from the start. In time it occasionally attempted to provide more sophisticated entertainment but even then, as in the legitimate drama of the 1840's that interlarded Shakespeare with acrobatic performances, the "serious stuff" of the movies was balanced with variety fare to level the program to a low common denominator.

The immense appeal of the pictures and their pervasive influence at the broad base of humanity made the sort of story they did tell a matter of deep concern to the protectors and leaders of society. The issue of censorship so early raised never has been satisfactorily settled.

A SCENE FROM *Cripple Creek Barroom,* AN EDISON FILM, 1898.

The Museum of Modern Art Film Library

"Between 1906 and 1908," reads the *Independent* for February 6, 1908, "moving picture theatres . . . have opened in nearly every town and village in the country . . . every city from the Klondike to Florida and from Maine to California supports from two to three to several hundred." At the rate of several million a day people were already acquiring the movie habit. Many men, it was claimed, were even neglecting the saloon for this novel form of "madness." "In almost every case," reported the New York *Herald,* "a long, narrow room formerly used for legitimate business purposes, has been made over into what is popularly known as a 'nickelodeon.' At the rear a stage is raised. Across it is swung a white curtain. Before the curtain is placed a piano, which does service for an orchestra. Packed into the room as closely as they can be placed are chairs for the spectators, who number from one to four hundred and fifty."

That widespread popularity was sharply increased by the perfection of new techniques, most of them developed by D. W

Griffith. In Griffith's hands "the struggling art of the common people," became in truth an art, the only art which men still living have witnessed from its beginnings and for most Americans today, of all the arts the one most vitally alive and most generally appreciated. By the use of such innovations as the fade-in and fade-out, the close-up and long shot, high- and low-angle shots, and by his novel experiments in cutting and editing his films, Griffith gave the movies a range, a flexibility, and a dramatic force that won new audiences at almost every level.

With such films as *The Birth of a Nation* the screen carried its message and its entertainment into circles that had seen only cheap vulgarity in the offerings of the nickelodeon. The picture was shown at the White House for President Wilson, his Cabinet, and their families, an epochal achievement since no film had ever before been permitted inside those doors. The power of the medium in such hands as Griffith's was vividly revealed by the violent controversies and demonstrations that greet-

AN EARLY MOVIE HOUSE, 1914.

The Museum of Modern Art Film Library

ed the first public showings of this epic. (Griffith's family had been ruined by the fall of the Confederacy and by the Reconstruction Period and his story was decidedly biased.)

Even in lesser pictures the movies afforded better daily entertainment than had been available to the mass of the people before their advent. Attendance figures showed with utter certainty that nothing so appealing had ever served for human diversion.

The movies' hold over its growing audience was further secured by the "stars" of first magnitude that rose to outshine any hero or heroine the stage had ever produced. Vast masses of people who were completely unfamilar with the names and achievements of the greatest figures in history or literature, current or past, quickly came to know every antic, every familiar gesture, every curl and dimple of the screen's newborn great. In serials, the silent, glamorous, endlessly resourceful celebrities held the nation breathless with suspense and expectation from one week to the next.

The Museum of Modern Art Film Library
CHARLIE CHAPLIN IN *The Tramp*, 1915.

BATTLE SCENE FROM D. W. GRIFFITH'S *The Birth of a Nation*, 1915.

The Museum of Modern Art Film Library

An Electric Automobile, Boston, 1902. Water color by W. L. Taylor.

During the first decades of the movies' growth one other mechanical marvel was forging adamantine claims on public favor—the automobile. In the more othodox fashion of amusements, and in the beginning it was almost exclusively so considered, the automobile first won attention in the upper reaches of the social scale, although its descent to the popular level was meteoric. In 1901 *Life* ran a bit of doggerel that gave a light touch to the exclusiveness of the new cars:

> *"A man who would now*
> *Win the parvenu's bow*
> *Must belong to the automobility."*

Five years later the association of the automobile with ostentation and privilege was still so strong that Woodrow Wilson asserted that "nothing has spread socialistic feeling in this country more than the use of the automobile . . . to the countryman they are a picture of the arrogance of wealth, with all its independence and carelessness." To have a "limousine face" was at one time a reliable signal of economic well-being; on the open road linen dusters, firmly knotted veils, goggles, and the rest of the paraphernalia recommended for tourists remained for a while the regalia of a class.

But within a decade Wilson's complaint was as obsolete as the horseless carriages he had complained about. The improving car was rapidly endearing itself to the rank and file of Americans. It had the speed of the railroad trains their fathers had developed and the ranging freedom of their grandfathers' ox-carts; the country was magnificently large and inviting; and its people enjoyed increasing well-being and leisure. The era of endless tinkering before, during, and after a day's drive had proved the nation's ingenuity and tested, at least, its sense of humor. The ubiquity the inexpensiveness and the dependability of the standard car — notably the Ford — evolved so fast it could hardly be considered seriously. Ford, they said was going to deliver his "rattling good little cars" by mail; he was going to paint them yellow so that dealers could hang them in branches and retail them like bananas; and so on, endlessly.

A TOURIST AT THE GRAND CANYON, 1902.

The Library of Congress

AL. JOLSON'S TERRIFIC HIT!

HE'D HAVE TO GET UNDER-
GET OUT AND GET UNDER
(TO FIX UP HIS AUTOMOBILE)

WORDS BY
GRANT CLARKE &
EDGAR LESLIE
MUSIC BY
MAURICE ABRAHAMS

MAURICE ABRAHAMS MUSIC CO.

The Library of Congress

A POPULAR SONG OF 1913.

For Everyman the auto had become "the symbol of freedom, the badge of equality, and the vehicle of opportunity"—and he took to the road by the million, often as not for the simple pleasure of going someplace else effortlessly and cheaply.

Like the movies and the auto, the radio began as a mechanical plaything. But with more dramatic swiftness than either of the others it fixed itself on the public as an almost universal and necessary habit. Only a very few years separated the first broadcast from KDKA, Pittsburgh, in 1920, the development of the chain system of broadcasting in 1926, and the estimated ten million receiving sets in use in 1928.

Radio offered cheaper and easier entertainment to more people than any other arrangement yet devised. It offered more than that, of course; it was a vital means of communication with almost unimaginably wide range and variety of expression. The

A SUNDAY ON THE ROAD IN THE 1930's.

The Portland Cement Association

A RADIO BROADCAST OF THE MID-NINETEEN-TWENTIES.

small voice of reason or the blatant trumpet-ings of doom could with equal ease be heard in every corner of the earth. What usually filled the airwaves from American stations was something safely within those limits. Programs subsidized by commercial inter-ests mainly concerned with selling a product of almost any nature chose entertainment—heavily punctuated by special pleading—as the most effective agency for this purpose. If the spellbinders were right and their broad-casts provided a fair index of what the aver-age American mind and taste wanted or would endure, then the critics of society had cause to lament. On the other hand, if the air waves were a medium to be conscien-tiously used for the public benefit, then, as Secretary of Commerce Herbert Hoover observed, it was "inconceivable that we should allow so great a service, for news, for entertainment, for educational and for vital commercial purposes to be drowned by advertising chatter."

When you're alone with your set and feeling at ease, you can make it work wonders; but when company is present you get "dial fright," and everything seems thoroughly hopeless.

LISTENING TO THE BROADCAST, 1928. From the *Radio News*.

It was more alarming to some that in their passion for watching and listening to entertainment the vast majority of Americans were altogether losing their desire and ability to create or participate in amusements. "Tonight in the United States of America in the year 1928," wrote Stuart Chase, "thirty million people are in their homes listening to sounds coming out of a small polished box. Wrapt and motionless they sit. Anon someone turns a knob and the rhythm of the sound changes, but its eternal monotonousness never changes. . . . Then somebody turns another knob and the timeless chant goes on. . . . We are not playing ourselves. We are being played to—and at three removes from the original source."

Back in the relatively decorous days of the turkey-trot Mr. and Mrs. Vernon Castle remarked that, at long last, America had begun to take is place among the nations that enjoy life. The Jazz Age, come and gone in a kaleidoscopic procession of excitements, seemed to leave little doubt of it.

The New-York Historical Society
HAVING FUN IN THE 1920's. Cartoon by John Held, Jr., from Life, February 18, 1926.

America had apparently discovered an uninhibited capacity for amusement and time to indulge it. Play was the thing.

Far and away the best and most active players of the era, however, were those who played for a serious purpose—usually a purse —before their sedentary fellow citizens. The modern gladiators who performed in arenas and before crowds larger than their Roman prototypes became well-known heroes of American life, rivaling in popular interest the highest statesmen and the brightest stars of the screen. If heroes are created by popular demand the public got what it wanted. To make sure the public wanted what it got, prodigious sums were invested in the ballyhoo of athletes, amateur and professional, whose names never left the headlines. Parson Weems never did more for George Washington than commercial promoters of sporting spectacles, along with the press, radio, and movies, did for such champions as Babe Ruth, Jack Dempsey, Red Grange, Bobby Jones, and others.

In his glory Red Grange was carried two miles on the shoulders of his fellow students, his football jersey was framed and displayed, he was suggested for Congress, he was offered a huge salary by a real estate firm, and he ultimately accepted a movie contract for $300,000. Babe Ruth packed the huge new Yankee Stadium week after week by swatting innumerable home runs beyond the limits of its well-cared-for field. In three years Gene Tunney received one and three quarter millions of dollars in the ring, most of it by twice defeating the hitherto unconquerable Jack Dempsey. In 1927 145,000 people paid about $2,600,000 to see the second Tunney-Dempsey fight in Chicago, although at the conclusion of the bout two thirds of the distant customers in the outermost seats did not know who had won.

During the 1920's and 1930's college football presented an autumnal pageant that dwarfed anything Lord Bryce had seen and remarked upon a generation earlier. "Every fall," reported one sports writer in 1937, "forty million Americans . . . pay an average

Press Association, Inc.
HAROLD E. ("RED") GRANGE,
THE "GALLOPING GHOST."

Brown Brothers
"BABE" RUTH, THE "SULTAN OF SWAT."

JACK DEMPSEY, THE "MANASSAS MAULER."
Acme Photo

A FOOTBALL GAME IN THE SUGAR BOWL, 1941. Photograph by Gabriel Benzue.

Life Magazine

A COMMENTARY ON COLLEGIATE FOOTBALL. Drawing by Rollin Kirby, 1930.

customers—by commercial promoters—and with good management attracted bigger crowds than either professional baseball or intercollegiate football. It was, to be sure, a game actively played by more youths of both sexes than any other sport. But the spectacle of a frenzied crowd of men and women trying to follow a capacity audience of more than eighteen thousand people (at two dollars and a quarter each) into Madison Square Garden on a snowy March night in 1937, to watch a game between obscure college teams imported from the Midwest to entertain the city populace, had the character of a Roman circus in the eyes of one reporter. The public could afford to pay for both its bread and its circuses. But, reflected a sports writer, were we becoming a nation of paying spectators with a small corps of paid talent to provide the circus?

of forty million dollars to watch twenty-two boys kick each other and a leather ball around a field." One of the distinct advantages of going to college, or having gone, was a preferred seat in one of the "lunar craters" that pocked the land from Boston to Berkeley and that once a week in season were filled with overflowing crowds of undergraduates, alumni, and, largely, the general public. Those who could not squeeze into the giant stadiums of an autumn Saturday afternoon to enjoy the outdoor pageantry of a big game might, with less effort and more comfort, listen to Graham McNamee describe the game over the air. The resemblance of this amateur sport to a very large commercial amusement business was too obvious to escape frequent and heated mention. During the relatively few weeks of the football season in 1927— from late September to about Thanksgiving Day—thirty million spectators paid about fifty million dollars to watch games played throughout the nation.

Basketball, America's only indigenous popular sport, was also tapped for cash

BASKETBALL DRAWS THE CROWDS. Photograph by Sheinheimer.

GOING TO THE MOVIES, 1945. Photograph by Herbert Gehr.

Life Magazine

Columbia Broadcasting System

TELEVISION, 1945.

The habit of passively sitting and watching and listening became for a great many people almost synonymous with leisure. No one knows exactly how many billions of people have attended the movies over the years. Even during the depression of the 1930's, apparently, the figures climbed ever higher. (In May, 1948, Audience Research, Inc., estimated that the average weekly attendance was sixty-seven million.) It was obvious years ago that the spirit, the language, the dress, the gadgetry, the behavior, and even the physical appearance of a wide public was being conditioned by Hollywood standards. The effects were apparent far beyond the American border in all directions. In many parts of the world Hollywood's picture of American habits and manners has served as the main version of life in the United States.

Whatever the effects in this country more than elsewhere, the "movie habit" laid claim to an enormous public. Good, bad, and indifferent, the moving picture had developed into a recognizable, popular art form— an art in more vital touch with the mass of people than the more exalted forms had achieved for at least a century past. "If all the lyrical poets, painters and sculptors now living were forced by law to stop writing poetry or producing art," wrote one distinguished critic, "a very small fraction of the . . . public would become aware of this fact, and a still smaller fraction would seriously regret it. But if the same thing should happen with the movies there would be the most gruesome of revolutions within a week."

At the middle of the twentieth century, television threatens to encourage the reclining tendencies of the leisurely more broadly than even the movies or radio had done and at about the same level of entertainment.

Mt. Rainier National Park.

The evil in America's recent recreational history has often been blazoned in the headlines, or heralded by highly articulate critics. The good is oft interred in government statistics; as an anonymous, daily activity it made less exciting copy. Yet the automobile which made sedentary gear shifters out of so many people who used to ride bicycles or play croquet in their leisure, also carried into the open country for a day of vigorous sport just as many who earlier had rarely left their seat at the burlesque or their stance at the corner beer parlor.

The travel industry and tourist trade grew to enormous proportions. Overnight cabins and trailer camps dotted the roadsides to accommodate the "tin-can" nomads who often just kept going on the road during their vacation days. The pursuit of happiness, as someone has said, had become the happiness of pursuit. For the swarms of newcomers who swelled the population of Cali-

Jones Beach, Long Island, New York, 1941.

Fairchild Aerial Surveys, Inc.

fornia, Florida, and other places previously considered somewhat remote from the large eastern centers, the automobile had discovered the land of sunshine. In a very real way America — scenic, historic, romantic America — was being rediscovered. "See America First" expressed the benign nationalism that played its part in tourism.

Reliable cars and better roads brought virtually the entire country within reach of the serious vacationist. In 1939 well over a score of national parks, reserved "as a pleasuring ground for the benefit and enjoyment of the people," attracted sixteen million visitors, practically all of whom motored there. A decade later the annual visitors numbered almost twice as many. After several generations of frenzied city building man seemed to have rediscovered an ancestral need for the wilderness as a revitalizing force in life. As part of a government-sponsored recreation program the national parks offered an

The Public Roads Administration
U.S. ROUTE #1, NEAR ALEXANDRIA, VIRGINIA, 1942. Photograph by J. R. Hillers.

increasingly popular retreat from what Theodore Roosevelt had called the menace of overcivilization.

To many Americans nothing brought home the reality of war in another hemisphere more intimately than gas rationing and the loss of their automobility in 1942.

TRAILER CAMP, MIAMI, FLORIDA. Photograph by Al Burgert.

Life Magazine

By the second quarter of the present century America had traveled almost one hundred and eighty degrees of the circle from its starting point three hundred years before when New England magistrates (and Virginia "Cavaliers") had legislated against the evils of idleness and the perils of giddy amusements. No people ever had more time to spend and more varied ways to spend it than Americans of recent years. To explore the deeper values of leisure was as possible as to skate the surface. The radio brought Bach and Beethoven as well as boogie-woogie to the most remote and humble room in the land, the movies offered the Abbey Players as well as Abbott and Costello to audiences numbering many millions a week. Attendance figures at museums, libraries, and universities were in their measure as impressive as Hooper ratings and Hollywood statistics.

The opportunity for recreation in almost any sense was no longer considered a beckon from the devil or a gap in society's inner defense; it was considered neither the privilege of a few nor the right of many. It was the need of all—a need as basic as education, police and fire protection, and other elementary services of government

From the late 1800's the major cities of the country, those whose remarkable growth had robbed their humbler citizens of open air and recreational facilities, had been extending their parks and playgrounds. By 1915 more than four hundred cities had opened playgrounds for children; between 1930 and 1940 alone the acreage of city parks grew from three hundred thousand to nearly half a million. Through funds from the Works Progress Administration the movement had a big boom during the Great Depression when swimming pools, tennis courts, golf courses, and supervised sports programs—as well as drama, music, and dance projects—all became the concern of government. Society encouraging play was a far cry from Governor William Bradford's scathing disapproval of the "dancing and frisking togither, (like so many fairies, or furies rather)" that he saw at Merry Mount in the early days of the Plymouth colony.

"BACH AND BEETHOVEN AS WELL AS BOOGIE-WOOGIE." A radio broadcast.

The National Broadcasting Company

A SWIMMING POOL IN A CITY-SUPERVISED PLAY CENTER, BROOKLYN, N. Y., 1942. Photograph by Arthur Rothstein for the Farm Security Administration.

"DANCING AND FRISKING TOGETHER" ON THE MALL, CENTRAL PARK, NEW YORK CITY.

VII
THE URBAN
WORLD

THE URBAN WORLD

INTRODUCTION

THE URBAN WORLD

DURING the years when all America seemed to be moving to the West, more people were actually moving into the cities of the land at every point of the compass. "We cannot all live in cities," exclaimed Horace Greeley as he watched the mounting tide of humanity that swept into New York, "yet nearly all seemed determined to do so." The urban movement, especially after 1850, became the greatest of all migrations. It did not capture the imagination as did the slow march of covered wagons into the West, but it involved more people and had consequences that were quite as vital in the making of the nation.

Not only in America, but all over the civilized world, people were leaving their farms, their flocks, and their herds and heading for urban areas. In Europe, many used the city merely as a transfer point in their progress to better farming lands in America—to the great dominion of fresh soil whose increasing bounty when thrown on the European market drove them from their own hard-worked plots of earth. On the other hand the diet of those without the means or initiative to cross the Atlantic—those who swelled the laboring classes of European cities—was supplemented with cheap and abundant food out of the great American breadbasket. That flow of produce from the New World in the latter part of the nineteenth century caused an economic revolution in the Old World hardly less disruptive than that caused by the flood of American gold and silver in the sixteenth century.

In America the constant improvement of farm machinery and methods progressively reduced the proportion of the population needed on the farm to feed the rest. Between 1800 and 1860 the rural population of this country quadrupled, but the number of townspeople increased twenty-four times. Such a major shift of activity would have been impossible if farm production methods had remained as static as they were over past millennia. Or, it might as truly be said, if teeming city populations had not clamored for more production from each working farmer, the advances in agricultural techniques would not have been so constant and rapid. The mammoth invasion of the city by the countryside would also have been impossible if the bigger communities had not developed mechanical means and social techniques to function on a scale suddenly grown so large.

People who massed together in cities faced problems that never concerned the farmer and the frontiersman, or that were for the latter private, not social, matters; problems that, with minor variations, were common to city life everywhere and whose solution lay far beyond the reach of any single individual. The freedom of the pioneer had to be tempered in the city where every individual act had possible bearing on the lives of others and on the general welfare. Conditions of urban life called for a sense of social responsibility and a capacity for collective effort that had to develop along with the physical attributes of the community.

In the beginning much that was later recognized as a basic function of civic administration was left to private initiative. New York's privately operated Tea-Water Pump long stood as a picturesque but pathetic reminder that the city was fast outgrowing its provisions for good water. Years of the nineteenth century passed before any American city was served by a professional, municipally operated fire department. The scavenger pigs that long roamed the streets of so many American cities constituted a notorious example of haphazard street cleaning and refuse removal. They were so numerous in Cincinnati in the 1850's that whenever they numbered six thousand they were rounded up and sold at auction. They were only then disappearing from the streets of New York.

Urban growth was so rapid, both in Europe and in America, that the solution to many novel problems had to be provided by improvisation until a considered plan could be evolved. Between 1800 and 1860 the population of greater London leaped from a million, more or less, to over three million, of Paris from something more than a half million to almost two million. In the next half-century their rate of increase continued, Berlin's population soared from less than a million to nearly four million, and other Old World cities grew in proportion. But in America the process was even more rapid and it was pushed to further extremes, the mischief along with the good.

The quick rise of New York from a quiet harbor town to an enormous cosmopolis in a matter of decades, and the meteoric progress of Chicago from a remote prairie hamlet to the greatest railroad center, grain market, livestock market, and meat-packing center in the world in an equally brief span of time, were highlights of an unparalleled social evolution. On a reduced, but still impressive, scale those achievements were repeated throughout the nation. Village outposts of one generation were the flourishing cities of the next. The absentee of ten years returned to find that Cincinnati, Pittsburgh, Nashville, and scores of other communities had mushroomed beyond all recognition.

Still farther west as the railroads fingered their way through the prairies and over the mountains to the Pacific, cities sprang up from nothing in a few months' time. At the magic touch of iron rails Omaha, Kansas City, Duluth, Oakland, Portland, Seattle, Tacoma, and again others were born and almost immediately matured to a booming life. With the opening of the Cherokee Strip, Guthrie and Oklahoma City evolved within hours from inconspicuous town sites to tented cities with thousands of inhabitants.

As wondering visitors from abroad pointed out, the new towns that were rising so fast in America could not be compared with European towns of the same population. In Buffalo and Cleveland, wrote Captain Marryat in 1839, "are stores better furnished, and handsomer, than any shops in Norwich, in England; and you will find, in either of them, articles for which, at Norwich, you would be obliged to send to London. It is the same thing at almost every town in America with which communication is easy." In this country there was no single city that was the political, economic, and social center of the nation. "The size of the country, its federal constitution," wrote another English observer, "would, either of them alone, be enough to hinder any city from becoming the one real national centre, like a great European capital. No city can be a real national centre to people who live three thousand miles off. Even if it could be so for political purposes, it could not be so for social purposes." Meanwhile, however, each pioneer American city promised itself the most distinguished future as a metropolis. Increase in size and growth of population and importance were matters of intense local pride with cities in every corner of the nation.

Nothing, apparently, could stop their persistent growth. One after another was visited by fire, flood, or other disaster, and each in turn, with hasty beginnings wiped out, rose from destruction quickly and confidently to a fresh start in the race for prominence. Even the ghost towns, the abandoned shells of false starts, emphasized the lusty hope of people ever ready to build a bigger city elsewhere.

The process quickened in the later years of the century, with the larger cities growing faster than the smaller ones. Key urban centers not only drained the countryside but received the dispossessed and the ambitious of Europe at a rate that, within decades, transformed the nation. In 1790 the urban population of America was barely five per cent of the total. In 1850 it was fifteen per cent, in 1900 thirty-nine, and in 1940 fifty-six per cent of the total. The country had literally gone to town.

THE CITIES THAT WERE

At the time of Washington's inauguration the United States boasted only a handful of cities worthy of the name—Boston, New York, Philadelphia, Baltimore, and Charleston. The population of New York, the first capital under the Constitution and the largest city, numbered barely 33,000—fewer people than enter a large modern office building in the course of a day. Philadelphia, the succeeding capital, was somewhat smaller without its suburbs; Boston, Baltimore, and Charleston considerably smaller. Within a decade Washington took incipient form as the permanent capital of the nation and in 1803 New Orleans, already over eighty years old and with a colorful history under two other flags, became a city of the Union.

Visitors tried to liken those American communities to one or another European city. But the analogies were superficial, if handy. Each of the little "cities in the wilderness" had been born of widely different circumstances and, excepting Washington, each had been shaped differently by its separate colonial experience. Each entered the Union with its distinct inheritance marked in its physical appearance, the character of its people, and the nature of its enterprise.

THE HEART OF PHILADELPHIA, SECOND AND MARKET STREETS, 1799. Engraving by W. Birch & Son. Distances from the city to other places were measured from this intersection. The Court House, built in William Penn's time, is shown at the left standing in the middle of Market Street. To the north can be seen the steeple of Christ Church.

PHILADELPHIA, 1797. Etching by Gilbert Fox after a drawing by John Joseph Holland.

Philadelphia

John Adams, leaving for home "in a very great rain" at the conclusion of the First Continental Congress, had bidden a regretful adieu to "the happy, the peaceful, the elegant, the hospitable, and polite city of Philadelphia." William Penn's "green town" was then, and remained for a number of years following the Revolution, the metropolis of the country. Few if any cities in history had grown to such size and importance so rapidly and so gracefully. None in America could boast of so many houses, people, and streets, such an array of public buildings, or such renown for civic achievements as greater Philadelphia.

In 1790, barely a century after its settlement, Philadelphia with its contiguous suburbs claimed a population of 42,520 people. It remained for a while the most important financial and commercial center in the New World. As in colonial days it was the home of many distinguished men of science and letters and a mecca for foreign visitors, some of whom called it "the London of America."

It was to Philadelphia that Moreau de Saint-Méry fled from the Terror in 1793. And it was there that he met those other celebrated fugitives from the ax, Talleyrand, the Duke of Orleans (the future Louis Philippe), the Duke of Rochefoucauld-Liancourt, and the Count of Noailles, all of whom, like so many humbler immigrants before them, found the city a haven from the discords of Europe.

Penn's original checkerboard plan had served the growing needs of the city well. That regularity continued to impress foreign visitors, as did the fact that some of the streets were numbered and others bore the names of forest trees. Saint-Méry was intrigued by the singular custom of numbering the houses with even addresses on one side of the street and odd on the other, an idea he took back with him and put into practice in Europe. The monotony of the houses, still apparent to visitors entering Philadelphia by train, was more than made up for, according to some early travelers, by their remarkable cleanliness, inside and out.

"The houses [of Philadelphia] are well built, chiefly of red brick, and in general three stories high," reported Charles Janson of the city in 1799. "In some of the new streets uniformity is observed . . . which may vie with those of the fashionable parts of London. A great number of private houses have marble steps to the street door, and in other respects are finished in a style of elegance.

"The streets are paved with large pebble-stones in the carriage-road, and the foot-pavements, which are raised ten or twelve inches higher, with brick. They are tolerably well lighted and guarded in the night; the watchman calling the hours as in London. Many of the new streets have of late been planted with rows of poplars, whose rapid growth, and spiral form, peculiarly adapt them to shade the avenues of the city in the sultry season of the year."

In its fondness for worldly diversion the Quaker City had long since outgrown Penn's sober precepts. Its cock fights, its exclusive fishing parties on the Schuylkill, and its dancing assemblies and concerts that had provided excitement in colonial days were hardly interrupted by the Revolutionary War. "Indeed," wrote a traveler from Germany in 1783, "the long sojourn of many foreigners, military men and others, has

HIGH STREET, PHILADELPHIA, 1799. Aquatint by M. Marigot. From Charles William Janson, *The Stranger in America,* 1807.

The Metropolitan Museum of Art

greatly changed manners, tastes, and ideas, widening and increasing a disposition for all pleasures." The temper of the city was aristocratic and when it served as capital of the nation from 1790 to 1800 the "republican court" at Philadelphia put on a better show than Washington, D.C., would be able to stage for long years to come. Rochefoucauld-Liancourt observed that he had attended balls in Philadelphia "where the splendor of the rooms and the variety and richness of the dresses did not suffer in comparison with Europe." During its capital days, overcoming stern resistance from the legions of decency, Philadelphia built the Chestnut Street Theatre, at that time the most elaborate playhouse in the country.

For all its high life Philadelphia owed much of its character to the lasting influence of the Quakers. Long since outnumbered by more worldly people and constantly losing members to more stylish sects, the Society of Friends had relinquished its old ascendancy in matters of government. But, as one visitor remarked in 1812, the Friends had given "a tone to the manners of the people different from what is to be found in most other places." The Russian Svinin, who was in Philadelphia at the same time, wrote that on Sundays, "one meets in the streets of Philadelphia only gloomy faces, the faces of people sunk in meditation, and one does not see a single smile—it is as though the city were in mourning." Speaking of Quakeresses, he remarked that their bonnets lent "their snowy languid faces ... a kind of melancholy which heightens the seductive charm of their blue eyes and fair tresses." They had, he added, "fine figures and small feet." Beyond such picturesque contributions the Quakers had endowed their city with a spirit of religious liberty and tolerance and provided it with medical and penal codes that were models of enlightenment for cities elsewhere in the new nation. Indeed, the colossal statue of Penn which today crowns the City Hall is a symbol of the lasting influence of the Quakers in much that is best in Philadelphia's civic life.

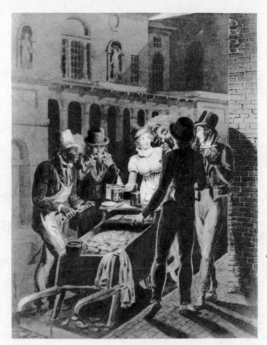

The Metropolitan Museum of Art
NIGHT LIFE IN PHILADELPHIA; AN OYSTER BARROW IN FRONT OF THE CHESTNUT STREET THEATRE, 1811-1812. Water color by Paul Svinin.

The Metropolitan Museum of Art
SUNDAY MORNING IN FRONT OF THE ARCH STREET MEETING HOUSE, PHILADELPHIA, 1811–1812. Water color by Paul Svinin.

THE TONTINE COFFEE HOUSE, CORNER OF WALL AND WATER STREETS, NEW YORK, ABOUT 1798. Painting by Francis Guy.

New York

If eighteenth-century Philadelphia was the London of America, New York was its Liverpool. If the prevailing temper of Philadelphia was aristocratic, that of New York was commercial. Not for a generation after independence was secured did the city fully enter upon its destiny as one of the world's greatest seaports and "the great commercial emporium of America." But even in the 1790's, during the boom caused by European wars, shipping in and out of New York increased by giant strides. The capital of the country moved away to Philadelphia, the capital of the state to Albany, but the registered tonnage of New York harbor doubled in five years, trebled in fifteen. The city enjoyed "the most eligible situation for commerce in the United States," and by 1797 was already handling a larger volume of foreign trade than Philadelphia.

The Tontine Coffee House, where every ship's arrival and clearance was registered, was long one of the most active and important spots in the city. It housed the stock-exchange and insurance offices and here, from eleven to two o'clock each day, merchants, brokers, and others met to do business "in a large way" and to discuss the booming progress of the city.

Few cities in the world have so completely obliterated the traces of their past history as New York has done in the name of progress. There is far less left of the New Amsterdam of Peter Stuyvesant than there is of the Athens of Pericles. The lower tip of Manhattan Island, once so thoroughly Dutch in appearance, had been radically changed even before the eighteenth century was over. Much of the older city, it is true, had burned to the ground during the Revolution; but the rest was systematically razed in the years following. When James Fenimore Cooper visited the city in 1828 he was told there were not five hundred buildings standing that dated further back than the peace of 1783. "A few old Dutch dwellings yet remain," he reported, "and can easily be distinguished by their little bricks, their gables to the street, and those steps on their battlement walls . . ."

Brooklyn did not become a part of New York city until 1898 and even since then it has retained a separate character as the "city of houses and churches," with its own accent and its own major-league baseball team. But from an early date the rivalry between the larger cities led New York to count Brooklyn's population in with its own, as Philadelphia claimed the citizens of Northern Liberties and Southwark to swell its figures.

The New York Public Library, Stokes Collection
A VIEW OF BROAD AND WALL STREETS, NEW YORK, 1797. Drawing by John Joseph Holland. Dwellings still stood with "their gables to the street and . . . steps on their battlement walls."

BROOKLYN, NEW YORK, 1817–1820. Painting by Francis Guy.

The Brooklyn Museum

A VIEW OF BOSTON ABOUT 1810. Bulfinch's new State House is shown in the dead center of the print. Aquatint by J. L. Boqueta de Woiseri.

Boston

In the game of counting heads and in the race for size Boston continued to fall behind the other leading cities in the years following the Revolution. But it was ever the capital of New England, a region, claimed one of the Cabots in 1804, where there was among the people "more wisdom and virtues than in any other part of the world."

As always, it seemed to be a city where new, expectant visions freely mingled with old traditional practices. At the opening of the nineteenth century the "modern" state house recently completed by the self-taught architect Charles Bulfinch almost threw a shadow on its venerable predecessor, although it would never overshadow it in public regard. But despite Bulfinch's modern touches Janson saw in Boston "a considerable resemblance to an old city in England." It was seen at its best advantage, he thought, when approached from the sea, and its Long Wharf, rather than either of its state houses, seemed to that visitor the city's most famous monument.

Deep water was one of the training schools of the city. Half the youths of Boston expect-ed to go to sea before they settled back into a counting house. "There were curious things to me about the Boston of those days," remembered one of the citizens in 1864. "Miles away there was the smell of the salt-water; nearer, there was the pungent odour of bituminous coal imported from Liverpool. . . . Long ranges of molasses casks, with their bungs out [were stored] on Central Wharf, by the West Indian traders. Every boy who came along had the unquestioned privilege of putting his pine-stick into the bunghole of these casks, and licking off the molasses or treacle and sugar that adhered to it. Some was thin, sour, and fermenting; some thick, sweet, and, to the unsophisticated taste of boyhood, delicious. It was easy to tell the best casks; they were covered with the drippings of our predecessors. The juveniles heeded not the stories of negroes' toes, said to be sometimes barrelled up by accident in Jamaica, or even young negroes entire, who had the misfortune to fall into the vats. . . . Taste was stronger than imagination, and we licked the molasses and smeared our clothes and faces."

STATE STREET AND THE OLD STATE HOUSE, BOSTON, 1801. Painting by James B. Marston.

BOSTON HARBOR; LONG AND CENTRAL WHARVES, 1832. Painting by Robert W. Salmon.

BALTIMORE, 1803. Painting by Francis Guy.

Baltimore

Baltimore, the youngest of the principal cities, was by 1800 already more populous than Boston. The manner in which such full-blown centers of population suddenly flowered in the American wilderness never ceased to astonish European visitors. "It is hardly thirty years since the town was established," wrote the German traveler,

The Maryland Historical Society
THE ROMAN CATHOLIC CATHEDRAL, BALTIMORE. Water color by the architect, Benjamin Henry Latrobe, about 1805.

Johannes Schoepf, in 1783, "and already it may be counted among the larger and richer American cities. It numbers almost 2000 houses, for the most part built of brick . . . and this number is very nearly equal to that of all the houses in the remainder of the province of Maryland. . . . Baltimore has already drawn to itself the whole trade of southern Pennsylvania. . . ."

When Saint-Méry visited the city a decade later he was astonished at the number and enterprise of its merchants. Also he counted there the churches of ten different denominations and marveled at "this liberty of religion, this respect for conscience!" A generation still later the highly critical Mrs. Trollope thought that Baltimore was "one of the handsomest cities to approach in the Union." From a distance the visitor saw the domes of the Catholic Cathedral, designed by Benjamin Henry Latrobe and, after its completion in 1821, one of the most impressive buildings in the new nation. It was a fair reminder that Maryland had been the first colony in America to offer refuge to Roman Catholics.

Washington

The Federal City of Washington, conceived as a political compromise, was erected on virgin soil ceded to the new nation by Virginia and Maryland. George Washington himself, with three other commissioners, chose the actual site on the Potomac River; and under Washington's supervision a plan for the future city was prepared by Major Pierre L'Enfant, a French volunteer who had served in the Revolutionary Army. The cornerstone of the city was laid in 1791, the first lots then sold, and the government buildings commenced within the next few years; but a century passed before the city seriously began to resemble L'Enfant's vision.

Mrs. John Adams, the first First Lady to preside at the White House, wrote to her daughter in 1800: "The house is on a grand and superb scale, requiring about thirty servants to attend and keep the apartments in proper order, and perform the ordinary business of the house and stables . . . lighting the apartments, from the kitchen to parlours and chambers, is a tax indeed, and the fires

A PLAN OF THE CITY OF WASHINGTON, D. C., 1792. Engraving by Thackara and Vallance.

we are obliged to keep to secure us from daily agues is another very cheering comfort. To assist us in this great castle, and render less attendance necessary, bells are wholly wanting, not one single one being hung through the whole house, and promises are all you can obtain. . . . The house is made habitable, but there is not a single apartment finished. . . . We have not the least fence, yard, or other convenience, without, and the great unfinished audience-room I make a drying-room of, to hang up the clothes in . . . [but] it is a beautiful spot, capable of every improvement, and the more I view it, the more I am delighted with it." Hardly had the President's House been completed than it was destroyed by the British.

The cornerstone of the Capitol building was laid in the autumn of 1793 and Congress first sat in the building in 1800. But only in 1824, after a succession of architects had modified the original plan of Dr. William Thornton, and after the building had been reconstructed following its burning at the hands of the British in 1814, was it considered complete. Its present appearance was not approximated until the new dome and far-spreading wings were added during the Civil War. Mrs. Trollope and her party, however, were "struck with admiration and surprise" to find such a structure rising out of the landscape of the raw, young city.

For long years the Federal City continued to seem a "City of Magnificent Intentions"— "a little village in the midst of the woods"— "a capital without a city." Unpretentious private and boarding houses and shops, some no more than shanties, offered "an awful contrast" to the few public buildings. Pennsylvania Avenue for decades remained a stretch of yellow, sticky mud or deep, fine dust, according to the season and the weather. Even in 1842 Dickens compared it to a London slum suburb—"put green blinds outside all the private houses . . . plough up all the roads . . . erect three handsome buildings in stone and marble, anywhere, but the more entirely out of everybody's way the better . . . make it scorching hot in the morning and freezing cold in the afternoon, with an occasional tornado of wind and dust; leave a brick-field without the bricks, in all central places where a street may naturally be expected: and that's Washington."

The Library of Congress

THE EAST FRONT OF THE PRESIDENT'S HOUSE, WITH THE ADDITION OF THE NORTH AND SOUTH PORTICOS, 1807. Water color by Benjamin Henry Latrobe.

THE UNITED STATES CAPITOL, 1824. Water color by Charles Burton.

E STREET, WASHINGTON, D. C., 1817. Water color by the Baroness Hyde de Neuville.

CHARLESTON, 1831. Painting by S. Barnard.

Charleston

Charleston retained its earlier character, and still does, more faithfully than any other of the larger cities that had grown out of the colonial wilderness. It grew, too, but less quickly and the old pattern of life was intensified rather than changed as it was in northern cities. Vessels increasingly crowded its wharves, bringing necessities and luxuries from Europe and the North in exchange for rice and cotton. From the outlying plantations where large crews of slaves grew those staples, Charleston still offered a gay and carefree retreat for the planters during the seasons of "country fever." To facilitate passage between country and city the Santee Canal was dug in 1802 as an all-weather highway connecting the Santee River and Charleston, a distance of twenty-two miles.

A regular packet equipped with "16 mahogany sleeping places and some conveniences in the English taste" ran between the southern city and New York, accommodating Charleston aristocrats off to a cool vacation in the North and visitors from the North who came to enjoy the special delights of the town. "In no part of America," wrote Morse in his *American Geography*, "are the social blessings enjoyed more rationally and liberally than in Charleston." Here, too, Northern visitors were delighted by the veranda'd city mansions covered with stucco in gay colors and standing within little gardens of orange trees, palmettos, and magnolias—an exotic spectacle more resembling southern Europe than the New World.

The Carolina Art Association,
Gibbes Art Gallery, Charleston
"A BASON AND STOREHOUSE BELONGING TO THE SANTEE CANAL," 1803. Water color by Charles Fraser.

UNDER MY WINGS EVERY THING PROSPERS

Kennedy and Company

NEW ORLEANS, 1803. Water color by J. L. Boqueta de Woiseri.

New Orleans

In New Orleans the United States received by purchase from Napoleon in 1803 a city ready-made in the European mold. Fifteen years earlier much of the old, wooden French town had burned down and over the ashes was built a brick and plaster city. But Mrs. Trollope thought it still resembled "a French Ville de Provence" when she landed there in 1828. Then as now, in any case, New Orleans offered the most colorful and enchanting variant of urban life in America.

The inhabitants of the old city must have shuddered at the thought of dominion by Americans whom they knew largely as the coarse and boisterous rivermen who for some years past had descended upon them out of the northern wilderness with their miscellaneous freight. Until the canals and railroads diverted much of the traffic, New Orleans remained the gateway for the vast inland trade of a continent. In the first six months of 1803, it was reported to Jefferson, one hundred and seventy-three ships of all nations had entered the Mississippi with cargoes valued in the millions of dollars.

It was at New Orleans during the war of 1812 that Jean Laffite, the last of the great freebooters to work the Louisiana coast, offered his services to Andrew Jackson in defense of the city against the British. Jackson, recognizing a character cut to his own heroic pattern, accepted the bid.

The Louisiana State Museum
JEAN LAFFITE (HOLDING UP HIS NOGGIN), PIERRE LAFFITE (STANDING), DOMINIQUE YOU (SMOKING A PIPE), AND AN UNIDENTIFIED COMPANION, ABOUT 1810–1820.

PHOENIX, AMERICA

The enormous faith and vitality, the purposefulness and the dreaming, that went into city building in the nineteenth century was nowhere more evident than in the American West. As examples, Pittsburgh, Chicago, and San Francisco, at the crossroads and terminals of transcontinental traffic shot up out of the earth, burned almost level at least once, and immediately rose up again with increased vigor and optimism. Their hasty first growth, largely of timber construction, marked them for disaster. But disaster served as a stimulus. Never had urban development seemed so full of promise.

Pittsburgh

The first flood of emigrants who were to use Pittsburgh as the Gateway to the West had barely begun at the close of the Revolution. In 1790 it was a hamlet of a few hundred people and a military garrison, "the muddiest place that I ever was in," according to one visitor—and already smoky. A French general, several years later, pointed out: "This town, when the Indian frontier is thrown back, and the roads are rendered practicable, will certainly become one of the first inland cities of the United States." Standing at the head of "the most beautiful river on earth," as Jefferson called the Ohio, it was the natural junction of the turnpike and river traffic that developed as the country surged westward, the connecting link between old and new America.

Long before the roads were rendered practicable they were thronged with "infatuated emigrants," some on horseback, some afoot, and others nursing wagons over the rude trails; all bent on finding places of settlement in the new country beyond the mountains where each man could be "a prince in his own kingdom."

By 1800 Pittsburgh's population was four time larger than it had been a decade before. Its glassworks, iron foundries, and textile mills, its shipping and outfitting businesses— its surging growth in general, and its throngs of strangers—gave the city the character of a

PITTSBURGH, 1790. Water color by Lewis Brantz.

back-country metropolis—a metropolis turned westward to the extraordinary new world that was being reared in the wilderness beyond.

When the French traveler Michel Chevalier visited Pittsburgh in 1835 he described it as "the first manufacturing town in the Union . . . yet far from what it is destined one day to become." "Nowhere in the world," he reported, "is everybody so regularly and continually busy . . . there is no interruption of business for six days in the week, except during the three meals, the longest of which occupies hardly ten minutes. . . ." Such rapid and unexampled progress, reflected an English visitor who claimed to be proof against American gasconade, presented an amazing political lesson to the world at large, an example of the achievements that were possible in a democracy where power emanated from the people and where the rewards of industry were not withheld from them.

In 1845, within five hours most of Pittsburgh burned flat and most of its rising prosperity turned to ashes. But the city's recuperation from disaster was immediate and something more than complete, in the phenomenal manner of stricken American cities. Almost at once, the smoke of its industrial fires was blacker, and it was more lasting, than the smoke of its accidental holocaust. "Nothing can be more pictur-

The Library of Congress
THE RUINS OF PITTSBURGH, 1845. Lithograph by James Queen after a painting by W. C. Wall. (Detail.)

esque than the site . . ." wrote Anthony Trollope after his visit during the Civil War. "Even the filth and wondrous blackness of the place are picturesque when looked down upon from above. The tops of the churches are visible, and some of the larger buildings may be partially traced through the thick, brown, settled smoke. But the city itself is buried in a dense cloud." To other visitors the spectacle of steamboats lined in profusion along the riverbank was a still more impressive sight.

PITTSBURGH, 1849. Lithograph by Tappan and Bradford after a drawing by B. F. Smith, Jr.
The New York Public Library, Stokes Collection

CHICAGO, ABOUT 1838. Lithograph from Francis de Castelnau, *Vues et Souvenirs de L'Amérique du Nord* (Paris), 1842. Probably the earliest view of the site of Chicago.

Chicago

For almost a half-century after the founding of the nation, Chicago remained a tiny settlement on the Chicago River, at the head of Lake Michigan, almost invisible in the midst of a vast, undeveloped prairie. After being burned down a few times, thought an English traveler in 1846, the village might amount to something. No city on earth was to amount to something more suddenly, burn more thoroughly, and rise again from the flames more lustily. Foreigners commenting on America, classified the extraordinary vitality of Chicago along with Niagara Falls as one of the wonders of the New World.

In 1867–68, when the Reverend Foster Barham Zincke, an Englishman, visited Chicago, "one of the youngest cities in the world," he reported that it well deserved its reputation as a new world wonder. "Its stores, and private houses and churches, are good," he declared, "and would be so considered in any city. Its stores are in buildings, two floors higher than the shops of Oxford or Regent Street, as is generally the case in all the large American cities. . . . In the central parts of the city, where all the buildings are good and massive, and the smoke . . . has put a complexion upon them something like that of London, you could never guess that many of its inhabitants, still young themselves, remember the erection of the first brick house in the place; you would more likely suppose that you were surrounded by the evidence and appliances of the commercial prosperity of many generations."

In October, 1871, the booming city already boasting a population of about 300,000 people, burned level in one of the most horrible catastrophes of the century. "Billows of fire were rolling over the business palaces of the city and swallowing up their contents. Walls were falling so fast that the quaking of the ground under our feet was scarcely noticed, so continuous was the reverberation. Sober men and women were hurrying through the streets from the burn-

THE SHERMAN HOUSE, CHICAGO, 1866. Lithograph by Jevne and Almini.

THE CHICAGO FIRE, 1871. Lithograph by Gibson and Company.

ing quarter, some with bundles of clothes on their shoulders, others dragging trunks along the sidewalks by means of strings and ropes fastened to the handles, children trudging by their sides or borne in their arms. Now and then a sick man or woman would be observed half concealed in a mattress doubled up and borne by two men. Droves of horses were in the streets, moving by some sort of guidance to a place of safety. Vehicles of all descriptions were hurrying to and fro, some laden with trunks and bundles, others seeking similar loads and immediately finding them, the drivers making more money in one hour than they were used to see in a week or month. Everybody in this quarter was hurrying toward the lake shore." Seventeen thousand, four hundred and fifty buildings were destroyed and a large portion of the population left homeless. The city had practically disappeared in ashes even more quickly than it had originally sprouted from the prairie such a short time before.

But Chicago was the inevitable metropolis of the vigorous prairie world in the Northwest. "And it fills one with simple amazement," wrote Edward A. Freeman in 1881, "to see the way . . . Chicago has risen from its ashes. In that great city I could see or hear of nothing older than the fire, save a church-tower . . . and a single detached wooden house of an antiquated type." By a web of railroads, and along all the waterways, the Lake City took tribute from almost the entire West. The vigor of the place was almost frightening. Overnight it had been reborn, as Carl Sandburg would describe it, the "City of the Big Shoulders":

> Hog Butcher for the World,
> Tool Maker, Stacker of Wheat,
> Player with Railroads and the Nation's
>   Freight Handler; . . .
> Laughing the stormy, husky, brawling
>   laughter of Youth. . . .

CHICAGO, 1879. Lithograph by Currier and Ives.

The Chicago Historical Society

SAN FRANCISCO, ABOUT 1851. Lithograph by M. & N. Hanhart after a sketch by F. S. Marryat.

San Francisco

Richard Dana, visiting San Francisco Bay in 1835, found there only a fort, a presidio, and a mission with its surrounding village of Indians. But, he wrote, "if California ever becomes a prosperous country, this bay will be the center of its prosperity. The abundance of wood and water; the extreme fertility of its shores; the excellence of its climate, which is as near to being perfect as any in the world; and its facilities for navigation, affording the best anchoring-grounds in the whole western coast of America—all fit it for a place of great importance."

News of the discovery of gold, when it was heard around the world, made San Francisco an almost instantaneously contrived "metropolis." Except for the lasting wonder of its hills and the glorious bay that spread out beneath them, nothing that could be told of the early city was true six months after it was reported. Week by week the man-built city changed its appearance. People who returned after several months at the mines hardly recognized the San Francisco that had

grown up in the meantime. In 1849 Montgomery Street ran along the water's edge; a year later it was almost in the center of town. The flimsily built city was burned nearly to the ground half a dozen times during the first few years of its growth, but it shot up again after each disaster to harbor a growing population drawn from every corner of the earth. On Christmas Eve in 1849 one block of the inchoate city burned level but it was rebuilt in a month. Five months later three other blocks were consumed by flames and while they were rebuilding another fire destroyed three hundred houses and five million dollars worth of property. Within four months another section of the city burned up and eight months after that twenty-two blocks were laid in ashes. Hardly more than a month passed before a sixth fire ravaged the city. By the end of the Civil War it had over one hundred thousand persons and a history like Aladdin's palace. It was accurately reported to be "far more cosmopolitan than any other American city except New York."

The New-York Historical Society
THE HOUSES OF D. D. COLTON AND CHARLES CROCKER.
SAN FRANCISCO, about 1879. One section of a pano-
ramic photograph.

The simple truth about San Francisco
made a fantastic saga. The city was born for
an extravagant destiny; it was a tall tale
come true. After the gold fever of mid-century abated, the fabulous Comstock and
Mother Lodes, and then the Central Pacific
Railroad, showered wealth on its picturesque hills. Most of the state yielded the
bounty of its soil to the magnificent port, and
directly to it came the products of China,
Japan, and the Sandwich Islands. Marble
palaces rose up beside wooden shanties as the
excitement of speculation electrified life at
every level. "Wall Street can teach Montgomery Street nothing in the way of 'bulling'
and 'bearing,'" wrote Samuel Bowles in
1865, "and the 'corners' made here require
both quick and long breath to turn without
faltering."

NOB HILL AND THE FAIRMOUNT HOTEL, CHINATOWN IN THE FOREGROUND, SAN FRANCISCO, 1906. Photograph by
H. C. White Co.

The Library of Congress

THE PANAMA-PACIFIC EXPOSITION, SAN FRANCISCO, 1915.

"The novelties of the city never cease," reported an eastern newspaperman the same year. "One is constantly reminded that twenty years ago there were only sandhills, with the crumbling cathedral and rude adobe dwellings of a little Spanish post. . . . Our generation has seen no second miracle like the origin and growth of San Francisco. . . . Burned to the ground six times within eighteen months, her growth was not stopped, nor her prosperity impaired; and if a new earthquake were to shake down every building, not leaving one stone upon another, the town would soon be as large and as vigorous as ever."

One of the great disasters of modern times hit San Francisco in 1906, an earthquake and fire that wiped out its entire business district and a large part of the residential section of the city. "The gayest, lightest hearted, most pleasure loving city of the western conti-

nent," wrote Will Irwin, "and in many ways the most interesting and romantic, is a horde of refugees living among ruins. It may rebuild; it probably will; but those who have known that peculiar city by the Golden Gate, have caught its flavor of the Arabian Nights, feel that it can never be the same."

As Richardson had foretold forty years earlier, San Francisco rebuilt with phenomenal speed. Other cities the world over have recovered from disaster, but none so quickly and so buoyantly. That magic of rebirth and all the enchantment of the city's past, Irwin notwithstanding, seemed to materialize in the Exposition City that housed the Panama-Pacific Exposition of 1915. Many Easterners made their first transcontinental trip to wonder at the "dream city of cobweb palaces" which called attention to the vigor and enterprise of the new civilization along the Pacific coast.

Collection of Mrs. J. Insley Blair
BROADWAY AND CITY HALL, NEW YORK, 1819. Water color by Baron Axel Klinckowström.

THE GROWTH OF CITIES

In 1800 the combined populations of the five major cities along the Atlantic seaboard—Boston, New York, Philadelphia, Baltimore, and Charleston—totaled barely 200,000 people. Sixty years later New York alone had four times as many inhabitants and was already the third largest city in the world. Philadelphia was by then more populous than Berlin. Chicago was growing more frighteningly than either of them, and elsewhere in the country, east and west, cities were doubling their populations by the decade. The nineteenth century was, as one embittered country man remarked, "the century of cities." Cities were giving "the twist of progress to the age," and nowhere with more dramatic thoroughness and suddenness than in America.

To a country that grew up on farms and in the woods such rapid urbanization was a violent transition. People who ganged together in cities could not afford the individual freedom of action enjoyed by their country cousins or by those along the frontier. As urban communities grew larger and more complex many of the problems of the individual became matters of common interest, problems whose solution was beyond the reach of individual resourcefulness. The need of protection from fire, crime, and disorder, of an adequate supply of pure water and food, of passable public highways and other transportation routes for the dependable movement of people and supplies, and of a municipal government to supervise the rest—all became matters of daily concern that called for a sense of collective responsibility.

New York's third City Hall, started in 1803 and first occupied in 1811, was a hand-

REAPING ON BOSTON COMMON, 1835—40. Painting by George Harvey.

some symbol of the growing importance that the management of city problems was assuming. Baron Alex Klinckowström, the Swedish artist of the water color reproduced on the opposite page, wrote that it was "built in a light and pretty style." In the sketch, he wrote, "you will get a good idea of this part of New York, which really is attractive . . . you will see the costumes in use here, and also all the vehicles, from the elegant coach down to the modest pushcart, on which the licensed porter is busily transferring the traveller's belongings to the harbour." He might also have remarked, among other things, the scavenger pig rooting along the street, upon whose casual progress the disposal of the city's refuse depended.

At the time Klinckowström drew his picture one could have walked beyond New York's City Hall and been almost immediately in the country. For a time still, a village philosophy allied all American cities with the rural nation just outside their borders. A large percentage of city people were only recently removed from farms or small villages and continued to behave and think very much like their rural countrymen. Even today a heavy rural "lag" differentiates the populations of Detroit, Los Angeles, and other swiftly grown American metropolises from the ancient industrial populations of European cities.

While they were still small and few, cities exercised an influence far out of proportion to the numbers of their people—an influence that was often bitterly resented in the hinterland. As early as 1770 "A Connecticut Farmer," railing against New York, wrote the *New London Gazette* that he hoped "the plumes of that domineering city may yet feather the nests of those whom they have long plucked." However, the cultural and economic forces generated within cities were going to provide, for better or for worse, the dynamics of the new age. Cities were growing at a pace and to a size unknown in earlier history and only an unprecedented co-operative effort could prevent them perishing from the bulk and complexity of their problems.

Collection of Edward W. C. Arnold

CITIZENS SUPPLYING A FIRE ENGINE WITH WATER FROM A PUMP, NEW YORK, 1809 (?). Water color by William P. Chappel. Photograph courtesy of the Museum of the City of New York.

Where buildings huddled together a fire was everyone's affair. The law in many early cities required each householder to keep leather buckets in the hall of his house and, if he himself for good reason could not take them to and use them at a blaze, to throw them into the street when an alarm was heard in his neighborhood. They were picked up by the volunteers who formed a bucket line between the fire and the nearest pump or cistern. Each bucket was marked with the name and address of the owner and was later reclaimed.

Fires were the particular scourge of early American cities, built as they were so largely of wood. Visitors remarked on the nightly—the twice- and thrice-nightly—alarms that often disturbed their sleep. After one such alarm, wrote Basil Hall in 1827, "I was scarcely well asleep again, before a second and far more furious alarm, brought all the world to the windows. The church bells were clanging violently on all hands, and the ear could readily catch, every now and then, a fresh sound chiming in with the uproar with much musical discord. . . . I succeeded by quick running in getting abreast of a fire-engine; but although it was a ponderous affair, it was dragged along so smartly by its crew of some six-and-twenty men, aided by a whole legion of boys, all bawling as loud as they could, that I found it difficult to keep up with them. On reaching the focus of attraction, the crowd of curious persons like myself began to thicken, while the engines came dashing in amongst us from every avenue, in the most gallant and business-like style." Service in early fire departments was voluntary and without monetary compensation. Membership was an enviable distinction and most companies had a waiting list of hopeful applicants. The company rosters included the names of successful and prominent men in every walk of life.

The Maryland Historical Society

FIRE OF THE WAREHOUSE OF HENRY WEBB AND COMPANY, BALTIMORE, 1827. Painting by an unidentified artist.

THE FIRE MASTERS AND OFFICERS OF VOLUNTEER FIRE COMPANIES OF CHARLESTON, 1840. Painting by Christian Meyr. Photograph courtesy of the Carolina Art Association.

The City of Charleston, South Carolina

THE WHITE TURTLE AND THE RED CRAB OF PHILADELPHIA RACING TO A FIRE, ABOUT 1845. Lithograph by Jonas.

"We had as much love for [fire fighting] as we possibly could have for anything else," recalled one volunteer. "We would leave our business, our dinner, our anything, and rush for the engine. The night I was getting married there was a fire. I could see it, and I wanted to go immediately. But the next morning early, before breakfast, there was another fire, and I went to that. So you may judge how we liked it." At the great New York fire of 1835, engines came from neighboring cities, including the Northern Liberty Hose Company of Philadelphia, which dragged its engine over six miles of sandhills en route, where the railroad was not completed.

"The competition to be first [at a fire]," wrote an English traveler in the 1850's, "is so ardent, that ambitious young men sleep as if a part of the brain were left awake to watch for the word 'fire.' . . . They will sometimes put on their boots and great-coats, carry their clothes in their hands, and dress at the fire. In rushing along the streets, sometimes blowing horns, and ringing the large bells attached to the engines . . . they often run down and severely injure passengers who are in their way; or if one of themselves fall, the rest drag on the engine, regardless of his fate, and occasionally break his legs or arms with the wheels. . . . When two engines arrive at a fire at the same time, the companies frequently fight for the first place, and then a desperate and bloody battle will rage for a considerable time, while the flames are making an unchecked progress." Many of the boys and young men who "ran with the machine," as volunteer aides to the volunteers, were irresponsible roughnecks for whom the fighting was a large part of the sport.

Mightiest and most terrifying of all was Mose, the Paul Bunyan of the Bowery, whose proper place at a hydrant was rarely disputed. His strength was as the strength of ten, not because his heart was pure, but because he was built that way. In the heat of competition Mose's natural bludgeon was an iron lamppost or an uprooted oak tree, his favorite brickbat, a paving block.

Cincinnati in 1853 was the first city to install a salaried steam fire department, but other cities soon followed. With the introduction of steam apparatus, fewer men were needed and as cities grew in size, they were needed all the time rather than as a volunteer service. Also, too many buildings burned down during the confusion and rowdyism that attended fire fighting on a voluntary basis. As the Chief Engineer of Cincinnati's new professional department reported in 1854, "Under the present control, the engine-houses are no longer nurseries where the youths of the city are trained up in vice, vulgarity and debauchery; where licentiousness holds her nightly revel. The Sabbathday is no longer desecrated by the yells and fierce conflicts of rival companies, who sought the occasion for the purpose of making assaults upon one another."

But the day of professionalization was a day of mourning for many adventuresome spirits, for, as the London *Times* remarked in 1857, the volunteer firemen had become "a *great* institution."

The Museum of the City of New York
SCENE AT A FIRE ("TAKE OUT DE BUTT"), 1848. Lithograph by E. and J. Brown after a drawing by James Brown. An illustration of *Mose, The Bowery B'hoy,* a play by Chanfrau that immortalized New York's most heroic fire laddy.

FIRE ENGINE, ELIZABETH, NEW JERSEY, ABOUT 1880. Painting by E. Opper.
The Museum of Art, Rhode Island School of Design

The Historical Society of York County
"HYDRANT WATER CONVEYED THROUGH WOODEN
PIPES," YORK, PENNSYLVANIA, 1816. Water color by
Lewis Miller.

For fire fighting, street cleaning, cooking, and drinking, no eighteenth-century American city had better than a primitive system of water supply. The little Moravian town of Bethlehem, Pennsylvania, it is true, had an "excellently contrived water-works" that was piping water to its homes when Schoepf visited there in 1783. But at the time Philadelphia, the country's foremost city, still relied on public hand pumps set at intervals

Collection of Edward W. C. Arnold
THE OLD TEA WATER PUMP AND CART, NEW YORK,
1807. Water color by William P. Chappel. Courtesy
of the Museum of the City of New York. (Detail.)

along the principal streets. New York's modest aqueduct system, inaugurated shortly after, was supplemented by its Tea Water Pump, celebrated for the purity of its outflow which tank carts peddled about the streets at "one ninety-sixth of a dollar per bucket." But the city was clamoring for a more abundant supply. "It seems generally allowed," reported the press in 1799, "that a greater supply of water is wanted in the city of New York, than we have hitherto enjoyed, for the common wants of life, and for the purposes of extinguishing fires, and cleansing the streets." The need was elementary and urgent for every city that hoped to grow and survive.

Philadelphia was the first major city to provide its inhabitants with an adequate public system. The white marble pumping station at Center Square was built by Benjamin Henry Latrobe to house the steam pumps which distributed water from the Schuylkill River through hollowed pine logs. Latrobe's plan was fiercely criticized as being hopelessly visionary when it was projected, but sentiments were reversed immediately when on a January morning in 1801 the city awoke to find clear water abundantly flowing from the new hydrants. Forty years later, Dickens was surprised at the "fresh water, which is showered and jerked about and turned on, and poured off, everywhere" in Philadelphia.

By 1850 eighty-three American cities had public water supplies. New York was the first to reach far out into the country for an adequate supply, tapping the Croton River and carrying its waters over some forty miles of hill and valley to two reservoirs on the outskirts of the city. The elegant Philip Hone visited the reservoirs in 1842 when the system was practically completed. "The clear, sweet, soft water . . . for to be in fashion I drank a tumbler of it . . . is flowing copiously," he reported, "and has already formed two pretty limpid Mediterranean seas, of wholesome temperance beverage, well calculated to cool the palates and quench the thirst of New Yorkers, and to

THE FOURTH OF JULY IN CENTER SQUARE, PHILADELPHIA, ABOUT 1810. Painting by John Lewis Krimmel.

HIGH BRIDGE ACROSS THE HARLEM RIVER; PART OF THE CROTON AQUEDUCT SYSTEM. Painting by an unidentified artist, about 1840. The central arches of the bridge were later converted into a single long span to facilitate river traffic.

diminish the losses of the fire insurance companies."

The successful completion of the Croton System was a good indication that American engineers were learning to cope with the complex and large-scale problems that grew apace with our cities. High Bridge, which carried New York's water across the Harlem River, was comparable to the finest of Roman aqueducts in grace and strength.

New York celebrated the accomplishments with extravagant fanfare. "Nothing is talked of or thought of in New York but Croton Water," wrote Hone in his diary; "fountains, aqueducts, hydrants, and hose attract attention and impede our progress through the streets. Political spouting has given place to water-spouts, and the free current of water has diverted the attention of the people from the vexed question of the confused state of the national currency. It is astonishing how popular the introduction of water is among all classes of our citizens, and how cheerfully they acquiesce in the enormous expense which will burden them and their posterity with taxes to the last generation. Water! Water! is the universal note which is sounded in every part of the city. . . . The moral as well as the physical influence of water pervades everything."

In the 1840's no city dweller took such benefits for granted. After twenty years of continuous agitation, Boston opened its public supply of pure water in 1848 with ceremonies as elaborate as had been New York's. With the mayor and other dignitaries on a stage over the Frog Pond in the Common, with a ringing of bells and a firing of cannon and skyrockets, with the singing of Lowell's Ode beginning, "My Name is Water," water from Lake Cochituate was spouted through a fountain to inaugurate the city-wide system.

That "glory of the plumber's art," the frequent and well-appointed American bathroom, came closer to realization when water ran out of faucets from city mains—and when adequate sewer drainage was achieved. Indoor toilets and baths with running water remained the privilege of well-to-do urbanites for years before they became standard equipment for the average home. Americans were, however, becoming a more cleanly and sanitary people, and for those who kept up such a schedule, new conveniences were making the weekly bath a fairly simple maneuver.

THE WATER CELEBRATION ON BOSTON COMMON, 1848. Lithograph by F. Rowse, after a drawing by B. F. Smith, Jr., published by Tappan and Bradford's Lithography. Daniel Webster, Longfellow, and other well-known personages may be recognized in the foreground.

The Library of Congress

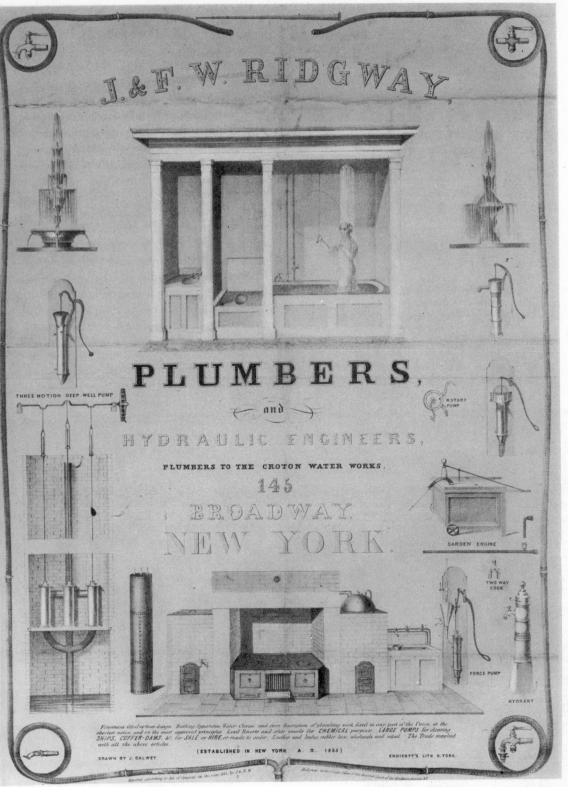

ADVERTISEMENT, 1844. Lithograph by Endicott, after a drawing by J. Galwey.

The Harry Shaw Newman Gallery
THE FARMER AT MARKET, 1840–1850. Lithograph by
August Köllner. Köllner was a German who came to
this country about 1840. In addition to his lithographs, he left many drawings and water colors of
great historical interest to students of the nineteenth
century American scene.

So long as the farmer had easy and quick
access to markets, provisioning the city
remained a relatively simple matter. Even so,
in the hot American summers, perishable
food often spoiled either on the short haul
from neighboring farms or from marketing
time to meal time. "They have their seasons
for the articles of life," reported Janson,
"which, in London, we hardly perceive. . . .
In the beginning and middle of summer it is
difficult to procure fresh provisions of any
kind." "Fresh meat," he wrote, "will . . . keep
no longer than the dinner hour of the morning it is killed; and the morning's milk turns
to curd in the evening." At a dinner given
in New York by President George Washington in 1789, retailed one delighted gossip,
the First Lady "ate a whole heap" of rancid
trifle as though it were an ordinary experience, although her more fastidious or frank

INTERIOR OF A BUTCHER SHOP, ABOUT 1840. Painting by an unidentified artist.

The Newark Museum

THE FULTON STREET MARKET, NEW YORK, ABOUT 1834. Aquatint by William J. Bennett.

husband "changed his plate immediately."

Americans, rich and poor alike, were notorious meat eaters. Scavenger pigs which until well along in the nineteenth century fed on refuse in the city streets, sometimes provided the laborer with pork for his table. But market meat was apparently not always so fresh. During the summer of 1795, recorded one doctor, "meats spoiled uncommonly quick, and those which were brought home, apparently fresh and good in the morning, were often found unfit to be eaten when cooked and brought upon table."

As congestion in city streets increased, the delay and difficulty in getting produce to market discouraged the farmer and further imperiled the city consumer. To relieve the crowds at the older markets and to tempt the farmer into the city, New York opened the Fulton Market in 1821 at a convenient location for the incoming marketman. On opening day, reported the *Gazette*, "it was ornamented with the handsomest exhibition of beef, mutton, pork, &c., ever presented to the public . . . several gentlemen from Europe . . . were unanimous that they had never

seen anything of the kind to equal it, in all respects."

But until there was rapid, dependable transportation and adequate refrigeration, city dwellers took what they could get as soon as they could get it. Those who could afford it sent special messengers into the country to fetch milk and cream when a really fresh supply was wanted.

THE MILK MAN, ABOUT 1840. Water color by Nicolino V. Calyo. Photograph courtesy of the Museum of the City of New York.

137

WILLIAM H. LADD'S EATING HOUSE ("MEALS AT ALL HOURS OF THE DAY"), BOSTON, ABOUT 1840. Lithograph by J. C. Sharp after a drawing by Fitz Hugh Lane.

With the growth of cities people obliged to work at increasing distances from their homes needed eating places where meals could be had at modest prices and, usually, in a hurry. The common American habit of bolting quick-cooked victuals in grim silence was noticed by almost every critical foreigner. According to one European visitor the national motto seemed to be "gobble, gulp, and go."

The tavern of earlier days, with its atmosphere of tippling and its encouragement of protracted conversation, was no place for a businessman's luncheon. In 1827 Basil Hall ate at one of the short-order restaurants that were springing up to take its place, "a curious place called the Plate House, in the very centre of the business part of the busy town of New York.

"We entered a long, narrow, and rather dark room," he wrote, "or gallery, fitted up like a coffeehouse, with a row of boxes on each side made just large enough to hold four persons. . . . Along the passage, or avenue, between the rows of boxes, which was not above four feet wide, were stationed sundry little boys, and two waiters, with their jackets off—and a good need, too, as will be seen. At the time we entered, all the compartments were filled except one, of which we took possession. There was an amazing clatter of knives and forks; but not a word audible to us was spoken by any of the guests. The silence, however, on the part of the company, was amply made up for by the rapid vociferations of the attendants, especially of the boys, who were gliding up and down, and across the passage, inclining their heads first

138

to one box, then to another, and receiving the whispered wishes of the company, which they straightway bawled out in a loud voice, to give notice of what fare was wanted. It quite baffled my comprehension to imagine how the people at the upper end of the room, by whom a communication was kept up in some magical way with the kitchen, could contrive to distinguish between one order and another. It was still more marvelous that within a few seconds . . . the things we asked for were placed piping hot before us. It was really quite an Arabian Nights' Entertainment, not a sober dinner at a chophouse."

For a while yet few people worried much about the purity of the city's food supply. Until mid-century most New Yorkers drank swill milk from cows that lived indoors and fed on mash from the city distilleries. Before the development of the refrigerator car, cattle for the meat market were driven through the city streets to slaughterhouses. The latter, often indiscriminately scattered through the residential districts, were stinking pestholes surrounding by putrefying waste and pools of blood. Only after the Civil War did Chicago, New York, New Orleans, and Boston set up central abattoirs in the interest of public health.

The evolution of great packing centers with plants equipped to slaughter cattle in a hygienic and efficient manner was potentially a great boon to public health. By elimi-

YOUTH. "You needn't be afraid, Ma'am. Stand behind me!"

The Library of Congress
CATTLE EN ROUTE TO THE SLAUGHTER HOUSE. From *Harper's Weekly*, 1859.

nating the long, exhausting trek of the livestock to local markets by cattle car and street way, it also promised the city dwellers better meat. But the city dweller, butcher and consumer alike, also lost sight of the source of his food and its processing.

When Upton Sinclair in his book *The Jungle* (1906) described the filthy conditions in some of the worst packing houses, where everything was saved but "the squeal of the pig and the health of the laborer" who consumed the output, public alarm and indignation forced the passage of Federal laws to protect the distant consumer from unscrupulous practices.

The Library of Congress
PORK PACKING IN THE UNITED STATES, 1872. Detail of a lithograph after a charcoal sketch by H. F. Farney.

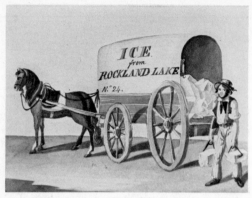

AN ICE CART, ABOUT 1840. Water color by Nicolino V. Calyo. Photograph courtesy of the Museum of the City of New York.

Almost the first novelty of the New World to impress Basil Hall upon his arrival were the numerous covered ice wagons he saw on city streets. The abundance of ice for all purposes in America never has ceased to astonish foreigners. The author of Baedeker's *Handbook to the United States* thought the "musical tinkling" of the ice water was the most characteristic sound of American hotels. A half-century earlier, Mrs. Maury, an Englishwoman, wrote that of all the luxuries in America, she most enjoyed the ice, then a rare and expensive treat in England. "I found it a most refreshing practice," she explained, "to place several jugs of iced water in my bedroom during the great heats; the atmosphere became perceptibly cooled."

The invention of a labor-saving ice-cutting machine in the late 1820's almost immediately cheapened the cost of ice in the city to a point where the refrigerator became "an article of necessity" in the home. In northern cities large companies were formed to cut and distribute the product not only to the inhabitants of local and neighboring communities but to the South, the West Indies, and even to distant India.

Among the prominent by-products of cheaper ice was ice cream for the masses. It had been a delicacy favored by the gentry from early in the eighteenth century—and the staple refreshment at Washington's republican levees while the first President was in residence in New York. By the 1850's *Godey's Lady's Book* conceded that ice cream had become "one of the necessary luxuries of life" and the ice-cream parlor was already a celebrated metropolitan institution. In 1841 William Lee, owner of a well-known estab-

CUTTING ICE AT ROCKLAND LAKE, ABOUT 1845. Lithograph by G. and W. Endicott after a drawing by John W. Hill.

WILLIAM LEE'S ICE CREAM SALOON, BOSTON, 1841. Lithograph by Thayer and Company after a drawing by David Claypoole Johnston. Cover design for a music sheet, "The William Lee Quick Step."

lishment on Washington Street, Boston, was made the subject of a popular quickstep, his quick-stepping attendance on the patrons of his crowded ice-cream saloon having suggested the motive for the music.

According to Chauncey Depew, the first marble soda-water apparatus was invented and patented in 1854 by an English druggist operating in Boston. By the 1870's soda-water fountains, often impressively composed of polished stones and glittering metals and costing as much as ten thousand dollars, were an auxiliary line of many city drugstores. "Few courtships lacked the odorous adjuncts of the soda fountain," writes Professor Schlesinger. "The young lady and her escort, having made their choice of syrups, waited in palpitant ecstasy while the attendant pulled the faucet first this way for the broad, silvery, foaming stream of soda and then that for the sharp hissing spurt which crowned the glass with iridescent bubbles."

A CITY DRUG STORE, YORK, PENNSYLVANIA, ABOUT 1880. Lithograph by an unknown artist. Part of an advertisement.

141

FRESH OYSTERS!

BY WESTOVERS'

AMBOY LINE.

Through by Express on the

NEW YORK & ERIE RAIL ROAD.

For Sale Here,

And by the Proprietors, in all the Principal Towns on the New York & Erie Railroad, and also on the *Chenango Valley*, from *Binghamton* to *Utica*.

Customers dealing with this Line shall be supplied regularly, according to order, through the season, with the best of AMBOY OYSTERS, at the lowest possible prices.

Sept. 10, 1853.   **C. & R. WESTOVER.**

[From Fairmans' Job Printing Office, Elmira.]

The New-York Historical Society, Bella C. Landauer Collection

A REFRIGERATOR CAR, 1853.

In 1842 an announcement of refrigerator-car service on the Western Railroad of Massachusetts was hailed with great enthusiasm. The first cars were small, crude ice-boxes on wheels which were placed between the tender and the passenger cars to give "additional security to the passengers in case of accident." But when the first carload of refrigerated butter was shipped to the Boston market one hot June, news of the event spread like wildfire. For the city it promised a revolution in diet. In the Ogdensburg-Rouse's Point area, within easy reach of the railroad route to the city, the value of dairy farms increased one hundred per cent with the new promise of year-round markets.

But all the railroads and steamboats could do in hastening food to the city was not enough to provide the urban dweller with a year-round supply of varied produce. The annual loss of meat, fruit, and vegetables by decay "transcends all estimate, all conception," reported the New York *Tribune* in 1864. The need for better methods of storage and preservation was brought sharply to focus during the Civil War when huge armies on the move had to be adequately fed and it was during, and immediately after

The New-York Historical Society
ADVERTISEMENT, 1874. From the New York *Daily Graphic.*

that conflict, that canning produce became a large-scale enterprise. By 1870 thirty million cans of food were being put up each year, and soon the urbanite could revel in a choice throughout the year of canned salmon from Oregon, canned tomatoes from Maryland, and canned milk, oysters, beef, and fruit from other widely separated areas. "Even the cook book may yet be obsolete," exulted one housewife, "for every can of prepared food has a label with directions how to cook." The can opener became the indispensable tool of the city kitchen.

FANEUIL HALL, BOSTON, 1867, LINED WITH CANNED GOODS. Photograph by Dodge, Collier & Perkins.
The American Antiquarian Society

THE BANK OF PENNSYLVANIA, 1798. Wash drawing by the architect, Benjamin Henry Latrobe.

THE PHILADELPHIA EXCHANGE, ABOUT 1835. Wash drawing by the architect, William Strickland.

Capital to float the growing commerce of the country inevitably centered in the cities. When James Fenimore Cooper visited Philadelphia early in the nineteenth century he was particularly impressed by the superb buildings that housed "the monied institutions." So much fine architecture, he observed, was "a tribute to gold . . . to be expected here." For several decades following the Revolution Philadelphia was the nation's center of business finance and its banks and merchants' exchange were among the finest American buildings of their time.

By the mid-1820's, however, the New York stock exchange had outdistanced all others in the country. Its "stockjobbers" were already a special breed of city man. The devotion to "le make-money," as one French visitor described it, seemed to most foreigners the most vulgar side of the American character. But others recognized that the feverish speculation of the counting house and the 'change was a normal result of the prevailing optimism of a rich new nation. The present condition of Americans, explained Tocqueville, "is that of an almost exclusively manufacturing and commercial association, placed in the midst of a new and boundless country, which their principal object is to explore for purposes of profit."

Having witnessed the vigorous comeback of New York merchants after a great fire had swept the business district in the mid-1830's, Harriet Martineau thought that the commercial credit of the city could stand practically any shock. Ironically, the Panic of 1837 followed her words before she could get them in print. It was the most severe up to that date of the periodic panics and industrial depressions that were becoming one phase of the nation's economic system. The effect on the hordes of people now gathered in cities, divorced from the food-giving soil, was disastrous. Urban poverty on such a scale and so glaringly obvious was a novel and disconcerting problem in this "new and boundless country," and it posed municipal problems that have not yet been solved. Just twenty years later, another panic spread through the country, again causing widespread want and discontent.

The Museum of the City of New York
"WALL STREET, HALF PAST 2 O'CLOCK, OCT. 13, 1857," A DAY OF PANIC. Painting by James H. Cafferty and Charles J. Rosenberg.

"THE TIMES," 1837. Lithograph by H. R. Robinson after a drawing by Edward W. Clay.
The Museum of the City of New York, J. Clarence Davies Collection

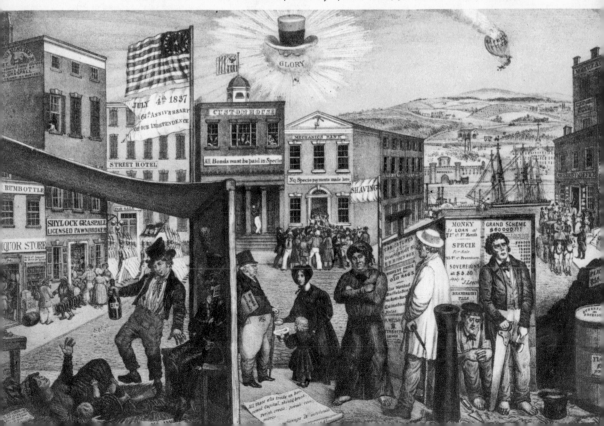

Even colonial cities had had districts favored by the rich and others relegated to the poor; but such contrasts were becoming more blatant as time passed. Broadway, neighboring Bowling Green, was still New York's stylish residential quarter in the 1820's, although the city was starting to move uptown at a formidable rate. "Commerce is gradually taking possession of the whole of the lower extremity of the island," wrote Cooper in 1828, "though the bay, the battery, and the charming Broadway, still cause many of the affluent to depart with reluctance . . . Broadway . . . is the fashionable mall of the city, and certainly, for gaiety, the beauty and grace of the beings who throng it, and, above all, the glorious sun that seems to reign here three days out of four, it may safely challenge competition with most if not any of the promenades of the world."

Not very far uptown, in contrast, New York's Five Points became during the 1820's a notorious slum and a spawning ground for crime and degradation. "This is the place," wrote Dickens in 1842; "these the narrow ways diverging to the right and left, and reeking everywhere with dirt and filth. Such lives are led here, bear the same fruit here, as elsewhere. The coarse and bloated faces at the doors have counterparts at home and all the world over. Debauchery has made the very houses old. . . . Open the door of one of these cramped hutches full of sleeping Negroes. Bah! They have a charcoal fire within, there is a smell of singeing clothes on flesh, so close they gather round the brazier; and vapours issue forth that blind and suffocate. From every corner, as you glance about in these dark streets, some figure crawls half-awakened, as if the judgment hour were near at hand, and every obscure grave were giving up its dead. Where dogs would howl to lie, men and women and boys slink off to sleep, forcing the dislodged rats to move away in

BROADWAY FROM BOWLING GREEN, ABOUT 1826. Water color by William J. Bennett.

Collection of Mrs. J. Insley Blair

quest of better lodgings. Here, too, are lanes and alleys paved with mud knee-deep; underground chambers where they dance and game; the walls bedecked with rough designs of ships, of forts, and flags, and American Eagles out of number; ruined houses, open to the street, whence through wide gaps in the walls other ruins loom upon the eyes, as though the world of vice and misery had nothing else to show ... all that is loathsome, drooping and decayed is here." The grocery stores of the district (see illustration) were meeting places for the worst of New York's early gangs, the Plug Uglies, Dead Rabbits, Shirt Tails, and other groups who devoted their best efforts to mayhem.

The Hot Corn girls were celebrated figures of the Five Points. They peddled more than corn, and for the favors of the prettier and wittier ones, young bloods of the district fought in desperate, sometimes murderous, earnest.

Collection of Mrs. Luke Vincent Lockwood
THE HOT CORN GIRL. Water color by Nicolino V. Calyo, about 1840. Photograph courtesy of the Museum of the City of New York.

FIVE POINTS, ABOUT 1829. Painting by an anonymous artist who depicts himself (?) in the center foreground with a handkerchief held to his nostrils.

Collection of Mrs. J. Insley Blair

The New-York Historical Society
THE ILLINOIS CENTRAL RAILROAD, 1866. Detail of a lithograph by Jevne and Almini.

Historically the city was richer, smarter, and more enterprising than the country, bigger cities more so than smaller ones. In America the big cities were growing faster than the small, and becoming more assertive. The prospect of a gargantuan metropolis feeding with a ravenous appetite on the labors of the countryside and growing fatter and more demanding, seemed, from beyond city limits, to reveal the swollen parasite Jefferson had warned against—an ugly growth on the national body.

Such urban imperialism was enormously increased with the introduction of the railroad. Indeed, the big city of modern times was in large part the creation of railroads. Until they could throw out such life lines into the food-producing hinterlands, and until they had speedy lanes of distribution

The American Antiquarian Society
"THE INSATIATE MONSTER BOSTON. A NIGHTMARE DREAM OF A PATRIOTIC POLITICIAN OF THE INTERIOR." Lithograph by David Claypoole Johnston, about 1840.

NEW YORK-HOBOKEN FERRY, ABOUT 1838. Gouache painting probably by Nicolino V. Calyo. Photograph courtesy of the Museum of the City of New York.

for the products of their industry, vast, modern cities could not develop. Wherever rails were laid, old cities flourished with new vigor, others sprang into being out of little or nothing. In 1856 a Scotch visitor to Chicago found railroad lines then in course of speedy formation that would open 6738 miles of trackage out of the city. "As 5075 miles of these lines pour western and northern and south-western produce into Chicago," he said, "and 1663 miles communicate with the east and south-east, partially bringing produce, but chiefly carrying it away, it is fairly evident that the business centring at Chicago must increase still more rapidly than it has hitherto done."

Manhattan Island, one of the fastest growing population areas in the country, depended vitally upon ferry, as well as railroad, communications with the surrounding world.

Before the first steam ferryboat was put in permanent service on the Hudson River in 1811, the relatively short passage across that river might have taken anywhere from fif-

teen minutes to over three hours, depending on the tide, the winds, and, in the winter, the blocks of ice that swept back and forth with the current. Even on a trip from Brooklyn to New York, across a river barely half as wide as the Hudson, delays and dangers could completely frustrate the traveler. On one crossing of the East River in 1784 seven passengers (the eighth person was drowned) had to abandon a boat that was crushed by the ice and clamber aboard the ice itself which carried them back to the Hudson and into the Narrows before a rescue party could reach them. A cautious traveler might have to wait several days for conditions that would promise a fairly safe and quick passage across either river. However, by 1821 when Timothy Dwight visited New York, steam ferries were in daily operation and that eminent and observant passenger thought they made the passage across to New Jersey and Long Island easier, more pleasant, and safer than if there had been bridges across both rivers.

CASTLE GARDEN, 1866. Wash drawing by Thomas Worth. Castle Garden at the tip of Manhattan Island was made a reception center for immigrants in 1855.

The commencement of railroad service coincided with the first really great wave of immigration to America from Europe. Between 1830 and 1850 nearly two and a half million newcomers arrived in this country from other lands. Many, born to the plow, pushed on to farming lands in the West. Others, without funds to travel farther or with which to buy land and equipment, stopped at the port of entry. New York, like other coastal cities, owed much of its tremendous growth to those foreigners who, once landed, stayed in the city. "All Europe is coming across the ocean," it seemed to the dapper New Yorker Philip Hone in 1836, "all that part at least who cannot make a living at home; and what shall we do with them? They increase our taxes, eat our bread, and encumber our streets, and not one in twenty is competent to keep himself."

Hone was a bad statistician. Not a few of those who were shipped off to the New World by their home parishes were the lame, the halt, the blind, and paupers. Of twenty-two hundred paupers in the New York alms-house in 1832 almost half were recent im-

migrants; in Baltimore the story was much the same. But among the brawny gangs who dug ditches for the gas and water mains, laid the tracks for the railroad, and worked on building construction jobs—among those "competent to keep themselves" by providing the hard, menial labor that the city needed to grow on—the proportion of immigrants was far above Hone's figure.

Tocqueville took a dim view of the mixed peoples who thronged American city streets. The lower ranks of the population, he wrote, "contain a multitude of Europeans who have been driven to the shores of the New World by their misfortunes or their misconduct; and they bring to the United States all our greatest vices, without any of those interests which counteract their baneful influence. As inhabitants of a country where they have no civil rights, they are ready to turn all the passions which agitate the community to their own advantage; thus, within the last few months, serious riots have broken out in Philadelphia and New York. Disturbances of this kind are unknown in the rest of the country, which is not alarmed by them, because the population of the cities has hitherto exercised neither power nor influence over the rural districts. Nevertheless, I look upon the size of certain American cities, and especially on the nature of their population, as a real danger which threatens the future security of the democratic republics of the New World. . . ."

The crimes of violence that were reported so often in the press—and the American press made the most of them—were also attributed by many Americans to the mixture of peoples that were filling the seaboard cities; people with different religious and political principles, people without principles, people of different languages, and people without the attachments to place, government, and one another that might be expected of native stock. Others noted a tendency towards lawlessness in all Americans, an impatience of authority that seemed a natural accompaniment of democratic principles. "Every man his own policeman" was the American motto, according to one visiting Englishman. Whatever the cause, the fact remained that riots and violent disturbances became serious problems in most of the

Collection of Mrs. Luke Vincent Lockwood
THE SOAP-LOCKS OR BOWERY BOYS, NEW YORK, ABOUT 1840. Water color by Nicolino V. Calyo. Photograph courtesy of the Museum of the City of New York.

major cities, and control of the situation was beyond the primitive official police system of the time. New York's Plug Uglies, Dead Rabbits, and Soap-Locks or Bowery Boys, the Crawfish Boys of Cincinnati, and the Rough Skins, Bloody Eights, and Rip Raps of Philadelphia, were terrorist gangs that often had things very much their own way.

"THE SOAP-LOCKS' DISGRACEFUL ATTACK UPON THE GERMANS," NEW YORK, 1840. Lithograph by H. R. Robinson. The Germans apparently had come to the scene to serenade the celebrated dancer Fanny Ellsler whom they claimed as their own. Hoodlums from the Five Points broke up the ceremony, and with it the heads and instruments of the musicians, in a protest against such "un-American" demonstrations.

The Library of Congress

Collection of Edward W. C. Arnold

A CITY WATCHMAN AND HIS WATCH BOX, NEW YORK, 1809. Water color by William P. Chappel. Photograph courtesy of the Museum of the City of New York. (Detail.)

isolated dispirited creature, half ashamed of himself and his office, and utterly inefficient for any public good. . . . In the States the policemen wear no uniform. In New York they wear a badge [a copper, or 'cop'] dangling from a button-hole. Their principal occupation in that metropolis, as far as I could see, was handing ladies over the crossings on Broadway."

It was during the 1850's in New York, and then in Philadelphia and Boston, that a uniformed police force made its first appearance in America. Policemen and public alike at first made strenuous objections to citizens wearing a special dress like a liveried lackey. At an indignation meeting in New York in 1854 a speaker complained that "no man bearing the proud title of an American citizen, desired to appear in any dress that should make him conspicuous among his fellows." But the distinct advantage of being able to identify an officer at a time of trouble weighed heavier than such scruples.

From the earliest days of the Republic the increasing complexity of urban life was clearly reflected by the steady growth of police forces. New York's increased about five times in the twenty years following the Revolution. But nothing like a full-time professional force existed for some time to come. With constables, or marshals on call during the day if necessary, the only street patrol was performed at night by the City Watch. Identified only by his stick and leather hat, the city watchman, or "leatherhead," usually assumed his nightly duties already wearied by a day's labor at his regular job.

While Timothy Dwight reported in 1823 that "New York's finest" were then in full control of the city's polyglot population later witnesses found that the situation had deteriorated there and elsewhere. "In no city of the Union have I seen any appearance of an efficient, well-organized body of police," wrote James Stirling in the 1850's. "Any stray policeman you may encounter seems a poor,

The American Antiquarian Society

A BOSTON POLICEMAN, 1840. Lithograph by Thayer after a painting by W. Lydston.

Commemorating the Bravery of the New York Police during the Draft Riots of 1863 and the Orange Riots of 1871. Lithograph by H. A. Thomas.

THE DISTRIBUTION OF AMERICAN ART UNION PRIZES AT THE BROADWAY TABERNACLE, NEW YORK, DECEMBER 25, 1847. Lithograph by Sarony and Major after a drawing by T. H. Matteson.

The Metropolitan Museum of Art
INTERIOR OF THE METROPOLITAN MUSEUM OF ART, 1881. Painting by Frank Waller.

Side by side with discord and disorder the city provided opportunities for concerted and constructive human effort far beyond the reach of the small town and the countryside. In crowded centers the constant friction of minds warmed the imagination and generated fresh currents of intellectual excitement. Here, too, wealth was concentrated, with which to float the projects of dreamers. Cities might degrade men by magnifying trifles, as Emerson observed, but, as he also observed, the country could ill spare "the commanding social benefits of cities . . . the high social possibilities of a million of men." With their newspapers and periodicals, their lecture halls and music auditoriums, and their libraries, galleries, and museums, cities provided man with the equipment for testing the social purposes of life in every detail.

The American Art Union, organized in New York City in 1839 on a subscription basis, built up a sound relationship between the artist and a nation-wide public that has never been quite recaptured. Each year the best and most representative paintings were exhibited, engraved copies of the judges' choice were distributed, and, on Christmas night, paintings bought out of surplus funds were raffled off to the subscribers. The scheme was early brought to an unhappy end by the state lottery laws, but not before it had sponsored innumerable worthy artists and spread appreciation among many people who had previously considered art as an indulgence for the rich and the effeminate. Within a generation both Boston and New York had well-established and growing art museums.

THE PUBLIC LIBRARY OF CINCINNATI, 1869. Architect's drawing by George W. Rapp. The library building, opened in 1868, had originally been intended to serve as the Handy Opera House. It was bought in at auction before it was completed and adapted for its new purpose.

The Public Library of Cincinnati

BALTIMORE AND CALVERT STREETS, BALTIMORE, MD., ABOUT 1853. Lithograph by E. Sachse and Company.

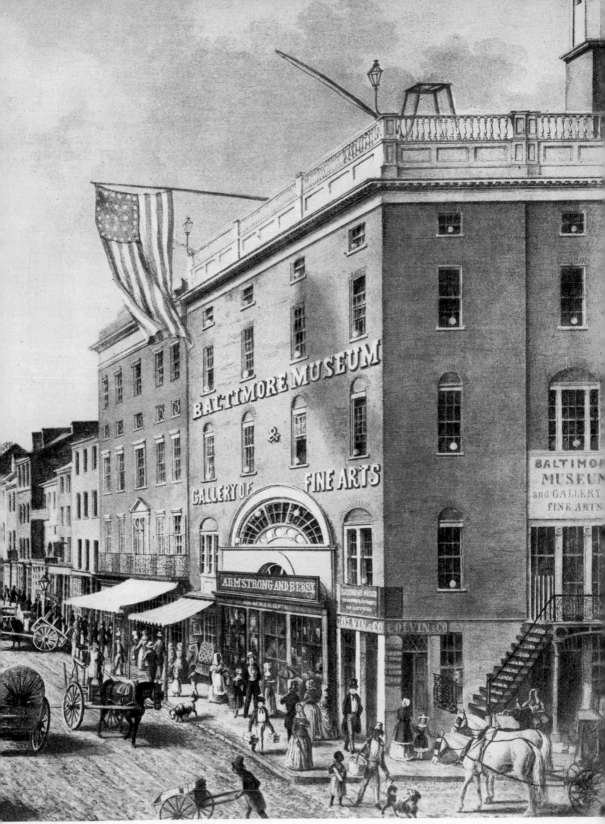

The Maryland Historical Society

St. Paul's Church and the Broadway Stages, about 1835. Lithograph by Pendleton after a drawing by H. Reinagle.

The Harry Shaw Newman Gallery
An Omnibus, about 1840. Lithograph by August Köllner.

By the 1830's, the limits of several cities had already stretched beyond any reasonable walking range, and omnibuses had made their appearance on the streets. The rapid lateral extension of New York, due to its cramped position between two rivers, made the need for some public conveyance there especially acute. It became known at an early date as "The City of Omnibuses." "The whole length of Broadway," wrote a visiting Englishwoman in 1848, "is filled with Omnibus carriages at all hours . . . you might almost say the street was paved with them; the fare is two or three cents, and all ranks make constant use of these conveyances. This indeed is almost a necessity, for the intense heat of the summer precludes the possibility of gentlemen walking in the business hours."

Street traffic was already a trial and a menace to the pedestrian and was fast becoming one of the most vexing and persistent of municipal problems. "There is something confused in this Broadway," wrote Fredrika Bremer when she visited New York in the 1850's, "which makes one feel a little bewildered in the beginning. When crossing it I think merely of getting to the other side alive." Even in the larger cities such streets as were paved at all were usually covered with cobblestones that contributed heavily to the noise and discomfort of urban life.

The "cop," so much maligned in earlier days, had become an indispensable friend to confused pedestrians. It was in the nature of city growth that crowds thickened at the business center during the working hours of the day, mobilizing and dispersing, morning and night, in constantly increasing numbers.

The New-York Historical Society

SCENE IN BROADWAY. From the *People's Journal*, 1853.

"THE TRAFFIC HALT," 1878. Painting by H. Schuldt.

The Rhode Island School of Design

THE PROPOSED ELEVATED RAIL-WAY, BROADWAY, NEW YORK, 1848. Lithograph by R. J. Rayner. (See plan at foot of page.)

In 1867 the *Evening Post* complained that "New York is the most inconveniently arranged commercial city in the world." Among other things, the paper noted, "its streets are badly paved, dirty, and necessarily overcrowded ... the means of going from one part of the city to another are so badly contrived that a considerable part of the working population ... spend a sixth part of their working days on the street cars or omnibuses." At least half a dozen other American cities might have made a similar complaint.

An elevated railway to relieve Manhattan's crowded streets had been suggested as early as 1825. The more elaborate plan illustrated on this page was proposed in 1848, twenty years before the first "el" was actually constructed. Passenger cars were to be propelled by endless ropes operated by stationary steam engines, the passengers being delivered and discharged at the stations by tenders. The system was to be equipped with telegraph and gas lights. "Sofa elevators" were to ascend to a landing where ladies could meet their friends and rest in the Ladies' Pavilions. Beneath improved street pavements, as

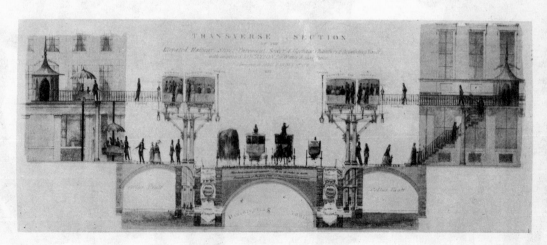

part of the grand plan for city betterment, were to be sewer, water, and gas pipes, "garbage chambers for the reception of offal from each building," and vaults for disinfecting sewage for agricultural uses.

Ingenious as it was, the scheme was discarded. In the opinion of a committee of New York's Common Council such a project would "no doubt destroy the appearance of the street, as well as drive the citizens entirely from it."

Had the city fathers known, nothing could have driven the citizens from the city streets, as later expedients clearly proved. The filthy conditions of the streets in most of our major cities in the middle of the nineteenth century would have frightened anyone conditioned to modern standards of hygiene off to the country in a minute. Even in New York's Broadway, mother of Main Streets, the scavenger hogs were both too "weak in numbers and deficient in organization" to remove the garbage in good time. Civic conscience had not yet developed to a point where such matters were accepted by city dwellers as a pressing social responsibility.

Aside from the garbage, wrote James Silk Buckingham when he visited New York in 1837–40, some of the side streets "are almost impassable in times of rain or snow; and, when not incommoded by a profusion of mud and water, they are prolific in their supply of dust." Broadway itself, he reported, was "wretchedly paved" and either pitted with deep holes or cluttered with loose stones—but it still attracted growing crowds.

The noise of the "tumultuous" New York streets sounded to Walt Whitman in 1870 like a "heavy, low, musical roar, hardly ever intermitted, even at night." But it took a poet to find music in the clatter of lurching carts and omnibuses and the shouting of pedestrians against the din.

Most American cities neglected the need for better-paved streets long after Paris and London had shown the way to improvement with asphalt surfacing. Urban growth was too rapid for all its novel problems to be met as they arose. However, in the 1870's, twenty-five years after the plan illustrated below was conceived, Washington spent over five million dollars on its thoroughfares and became the country's best-paved city. But it was not until the end of the century that any American community could rank in this respect with the older European cities.

PROPOSED PLAN FOR PAVING PENNSYLVANIA AVE., WASHINGTON, D.C., DESIGNED BY HORACE P. ROSS, 1853. Lithograph by Endicott and Co.

The Yale University Art Gallery, Mabel Brady Garvan Collection

Collection of Edward W. C. Arnold
LAMP LIGHTER, NEW YORK, 1806. Water color by William P. Chappel. Photograph courtesy of the Museum of the City of New York. (Detail.)

Overhead, as underfoot, better facilities were wanted to speed the quickening pace of urban life. From the beginning of history the need of adequate light, outdoors and indoors, had been secondary to the cost and inconvenience of providing it. For city man and country man alike, Poor Richard's "early to bed, early to rise" was ancient common sense. The best solution to the problem of artificial illumination, concluded Benjamin Franklin, was to do without it. Daylight saving time, he urged, offered the only answer for sensible people who must live by the clock.

But cities that were supplied by railroads and supported by factories depended on timed operations that went all around the clock. Also, people beyond reach of the cock's crow were more inclined to burn night oil than were their country cousins. The maintenance of whale-oil lamps, set on posts at intervals along the main streets, for the safety and convenience of their inhabitants, had been a large item in the budget of colonial cities. But at best, complained those whose business or pleasure took them abroad after dark, such illuminants barely made the darkness visible. They merely exhibited, wrote one irate early New Yorker, "the somnified gloom of sepulchral tapers."

As early as 1796, novel experiments with gas lighting were performed in Philadelphia; during the War of 1812 gas was used to light the cotton mills at Watertown and

ST. THOMAS'S CHURCH, BROADWAY, NEW YORK, BY GAS LIGHT, ABOUT 1835. Water color by George Harvey.
Collection of Mrs. J. Insley Blair

The Museum of the City of New York

"New-York by Gas-Light. Hooking a Victim." Lithograph by Serrell and Perkins, about 1850.

Providence; and in 1816 Baltimore became the first American city to organize a company for distribution of lighting gas. But there were no foundries in the country that could cast the necessary long iron conduits and it was three years before the company began business. Boston and New York adopted gas for street lighting immediately afterwards. In 1824 the New York *Post* reported that "it appeared perfectly obvious that this mode of lighting our streets, public buildings . . . and dwelling houses, surpasses everything of the kind that has hitherto been attempted by oil or candles." The general public, however, was wary of the newfangled lighting "with smoke." Gas was liable "at all times to give the company the slip," it was reported, as it had done at Mrs. Charles Russell's New York cotillion, and it was still "illy calculated for the ordinary use of a family." But soon city dwellers successfully adapted their lives to such brighter lights.

Neither lighting them with gas nor patrolling them with a uniformed police force made straight and narrow paths of city streets. Every urban center had a lively traffic in vice and sin, casual and organized, that flourished side by side with the prudish decorum recommended by nineteenth-century etiquette books. In the byways of big cities men and women could find a retreat from the ordinary restraints and conventions of life—an escape, at least, from the prying eyes and clucking tongues of neighborhood gossips.

Following the Civil War a spate of books by moralists, reformers, and missionaries gave detailed warnings of the pitfalls and temptations that awaited the innocent in the metropolis. No statistics reveal how many outsiders were lured into the cities by such earnest tracts. But the percentage of the urban to the total population rose from fifteen to forty between 1850 and 1900.

OLD-LAW TENEMENTS, BUILT 1867–1906. Photograph by Berenice Abbott, 1937, after the fronting buildings were torn down.

TITLE PAGE OF THE BOOK BY JAMES WM. BUEL, 1883.

The worst iniquities of city life were rooted in the squalid misery of slums. Dickens had told only the beginnings of the story in his description of the tenements in New York's Five Points. Such rookeries of degradation and pestilence became during the next generation the landmarks of almost all the chaotically growing cities and mill towns of the country—scars deeply cut across the face of America. In those congested corners the bright promise of life in a democracy had turned into festering despair.

In the slum there was freedom, to be sure —freedom with a vengeance; freedom to starve and degenerate, if need be; freedom, certainly, to find life's compensations at the lowest possible level. But the more rewarding freedom of the frontier lands was already beyond the reach of the most lowly city dwellers. To them the railroad tracks were not the high road to the open West but a social barrier that hemmed them in "on the wrong side."

New York with its vast aggregations of

immigrants displayed the problem of urban poverty most conspicuously at the very threshold of the nation. Into the sunless, airless honeycombs of its neglected districts the biggest city was cramming more people into less living space than had ever been accomplished by any community in the history of the world. That extreme of human compression was made more conspicuous by contrast with the palatial residences being piled high in other districts by those who came out on top of the frantic scramble of the metropolis.

Alexander T. Stewart, the "lucky immigrant," in 1869 set a modest precedent for the more pretentious mansions that soon lined Fifth Avenue. Here was *Progress and Poverty* and *Sunshine and Shadow*, as two contemporary books of protest were entitled, in sharpest outline. Other cities showed the same pattern in reduced scale. The slum-mansion combination seemed almost an inevitable sign of urban "development."

The New-York Historical Society
TITLE PAGE OF THE BOOK BY MATTHEW H. SMITH, 1869

ALEXANDER T. STEWART MANSION, NEW YORK CITY, BUILT IN 1869. Photograph about 1883.
The New-York Historical Society

Boston had reserved its famous Common as early as 1640; William Penn, foreseeing the rapid growth of Philadelphia, had set aside five squares for the permanent use of the town's people; and in 1733 New York had leased property to be "inclosed to make a Bowling Green . . . with Walks therein, for the Beauty & Ornament of the Said Street as well as for the Recreation and delight of the Inhabitants." But those were tiny lungs for cities whose civic bodies were rapidly becoming gigantic, whose pulse beat faster every year. No early city father dreamed ahead to the day when the neighboring countryside would be pushed back beyond reach of a large segment of the city population. Yet,

for those condemned to dwell in the shadows, the world of nature was being reduced practically to the few defiant weeds and blades of grass that pushed up through cracks in the pavements and the stubborn trees that made headway in the litter of cramped back yards.

A large "central park" was first suggested for New York City in 1850 as an "essential aid to public health." It was to be a great breathing place for the toiling masses in times of heat, pestilence, and despair—the equivalent of a brief visit to the countryside. The need was urgent enough; New York's death rate was twice that of London's. Among the troglodytes the rate was appall-

CENTRAL PARK, NEW YORK, ABOUT 1864. Lithograph by Charles Magnus (?).
The Museum of the City of New York, J. Clarence Davies Collection

A GERMAN BEER GARDEN IN NEW YORK, 1825. Chromolithograph by H. Breul.

ingly high. Almost every sizable city was prey to epidemics that easily left their frequent breeding place in the slums to invade even the most exclusive districts.

Central Park was completed in 1876 according to the inspired design of Frederick Law Olmsted. He envisioned the park, not as an afterthought—a mere ornament to the growing city—but as an organic element in its development. The inauguration of such parks amounted to an official admission that the ordinary city public must have space and means for recreation as well as for work. A century later the idea seems elementary. At the time it marked a significant break in the traditional pattern of recreational life in America—a pattern that had been shaped by rural conditions and a Calvinistic disapproval of anything that encouraged idleness or amusement for its own sake.

The Puritan tradition of hard-working week days and earnest Sabbaths died hard. Native Americans of the old school were dismayed, for example, by the lager beer gardens that appeared in numerous cities and catered to capacity crowds of German immigrants on Sundays. "The long bar, immense in extent, tells the story," wrote one aroused moralist. "The quantity [of lager] sold in a day is enormôus. A four-horse team from the brewery . . . finds it difficult to keep up the supply." And there were song, games, and dancing and, in some gardens, buxom waitressess.

By the time of the Civil War New York had the third largest German population of all the cities in the world, including those in Germany—and Cincinnati, St. Louis, Louisville, Chicago, and Milwaukee held a great many more. Faster and faster the United States was becoming "not merely a nation, but a teeming nation of nations." Added to the growing native population the alien swarm sent the census figures soaring. The growth and the mixture were perceptible everywhere, on farms, in frontier and manufacturing towns, and in the larger cities, but particularly in the latter which were, faster and faster, draining people from the country, the village, and foreign lands alike.

BROADWAY, 1870. From *La Ilustración de España y América*.

In New York, where the concentration of people, people of all hues and tongues, was greatest, some streets could no longer adequately carry the load of humanity. "Several hundred thousand persons—rich and poor, male and female, wise and simple—earn their living by personal effort in that narrow corner of this island which lies south of Grand Street," wrote one dismayed inhabitant to the press in 1866. "We cannot live here . . . and it is inconvenient to live across the arms of the sea on either hand. We want to live up-town, or in the adjacent county of Westchester; and we want facilities for getting quickly, cheaply, comfortably from our homes to our work and back again. . . . Gentlemen of the Legislature! Give us both the Underground and the Aërial Railway!"

Two years later, in New York City, a trial trip was made on the first elevated railroad in the world, over a quarter-mile of track. Within a decade, after several experiments, the elevated system proved successful, old lines were extended, and new ones opened. Still the crush in the streets increased.

The Brooklyn Bridge, across New York's East River, engineered by the German immigrant, John A. Roebling, gave Manhattan's million and more of people an easy, graceful aerial exit from their cramped island. It also provided an entrance for more and more transients. The day after the bridge opened it was remarked that the city needed more bridges. "It is with the bridge as with railways, "commented *Harper's Weekly*. "When they are first laid along routes upon which the scant travel seemed to make such a road ridiculous, it develops crowds of travellers. . . . The one thing which is indisputable is that the continuous throng across the bridge was wholly unanticipated, and that the practical ability of the trustees to deal immediately with an unexpected and vitally important situation is put to the severest test."

An experimental section of a pneumatic subway under Broadway had been opened in 1870. But the idea was not yet ripe and the project was soon abandoned.

Conditions on the streets and transit lines were made worse by the perpendicular

168

EXPERIMENTAL TRAIN ON THE GILBERT ELEVATED RAILROAD, NEW YORK. From *Leslie's Weekly*, 1878.

BROOKLYN BRIDGE, 1883, THE YEAR IT OPENED. Photolithograph by Shugg Brothers.

The Library of Congress
THE ELEVATOR AT LORD AND TAYLOR'S STORE, NEW
YORK. From *Leslie's Weekly*, 1873.

sity in the many-storied buildings that were rising in the downtown districts of New York and Chicago. In the tall buildings of the latter city, wrote a visitor, "are the most modern and rapid elevators that fly up through the towers like glass balls from a trap at a shooting contest. The slow-going stranger, who is conscious of having been 'kneaded' along the streets, like a lump of dough among a million bakers, feels himself loaded into one of those . . . baskets . . . and the next instant . . . up goes the whole load as a feather is caught up by a gale. The descent is more simple. Something lets go, and you fall from ten to twenty stories as it happens. . . . These elevators are too slow for Chicago, and the managers of certain tall buildings now arrange them so that some can run 'express.'"

growth of the city. Passenger elevators, envisioned in the New York plan of 1848 (p. 160) and put to practical use in the London Crystal Palace Exhibition a few years later, had, by the 1870's, become an established metropolitan convenience, a human neces-

The ever-rising value of city real estate, the perfection of structural steel, the telephone, the elevator, and the growing centralization of business, all went hand-in-hand with architectural daring to produce the skyscraper, America's most distinctive contribution to the art of building. "The Chicago method in putting up these steepling hives," one

THE NEW YORK SKYLINE, 1898. Section of a wash drawing by August Will.

New Yorker explained when the idea was new, ". . . is to construct the actual edifice of steel framework, to which are added thin outer walls of brick or stone masonry, and the necessary partitions of fire-brick, and plaster laid on iron lathing. The buildings are therefore like enclosed birdcages, and it is said that, like bird-cages, they cannot shake or tumble down. The exterior walls are mere envelopes. They are so treated that the buildings look like heaps of mansonry, but that is homage paid to custom. . . . One of these buildings—and not the largest—has a population of 4000 persons. It was visited and its elevators were used on three days . . . by 19,000, 18,000, and 20,000 persons. . . . The reader now understands why in the heart of Chicago every work-day evening the crowds convey the idea that our Broadway is a deserted thoroughfare as compared with, say, the corner of Clark and Jackson Streets." But, as one prophetic Jeremiah complained in 1891, when entire streets were lined with skyscrapers "what disadvantages there would be!" "What disadvantages," the most pessimistic prophet of the 1890's could scarcely foresee!

The Library of Congress
ERECTING THE MUTUAL SAVINGS BANK BUILDING, 1902. Wm. L. Jenney's Home Insurance Co. Building (1883–85) in Chicago was the first true skyscraper to be erected. His Leiter Building (1889), also in Chicago, was one of the first buildings to use a steel skeleton without self-supporting walls, thus opening a new era not only in construction but in urban life.

The Museum of the City of New York, J. Clarence Davies Collection

Kennedy and Company
THE TELEPHONE HABIT. Painting by George Baum-
garden, about 1910 (?).

Without the telephone the huge concentrations of people in office buildings and the
acceleration of business activity would have
been impossible. To have delivered by hand
all the messages that were given to the telephone and telegraph wires would have blackened the city streets and clogged every
elevator, corridor, and stairway of the business world with breathless, colliding carriers.

To most people, at first, there seemed "a
kind of absurdity in addressing a piece of
iron" instead of a flesh and blood listener.
The London *Times* in 1877 referred to the
new contraption as the "latest American
humbug." The native public had been made
more receptive to the new instrument by the
widely publicized experience of the Emperor
of Brazil at the Philadelphia Centennial
Exposition the year before. Casually putting
an experimental receiver to his ear Dom
Pedro exclaimed: "My God! It talks!" and
his surprise was immediately and exultantly
reported throughout the country. Even so,

CENTRAL TELEPHONE OFFICE, NEW YORK CITY, 1888. Photograph by Rosenfeld.
The American Telephone and Telegraph Company

BROADWAY, NEW YORK, ABOUT 1880. Lithograph by J. J. Fogerty.

for some years the instrument was considered "an extravagance for home users; and, for social matters, an intrusion on privacy"—all of which it was.

In the business world, however, the telephone rapidly evolved from a curious electric toy to a practical convenience and then to an insistent necessity. Telephone wires—with those for the telegraph and electric lights—were spreading into a solid copper canopy over the main streets of big cities. If service was to expand it was a simple matter of computation to foresee the necessity of mile-high poles to carry the traffic in words. As early as 1884 New York found it necessary to order all wires put underground.

As the instrument improved and as the invention of the multiple switchboard and the extension of long distance wires provided broader, quicker service, America was well on its way to acquiring the telephone habit. As Thorstein Veblen has pointed out, invention is the mother of necessity; with the telephone conveniently available, people found it necessary to say more than had ever before entered their heads to say. America was becoming the world's most talkative nation. "What startles and frightens the backward European in the United States," said Arnold Bennett when he visited this country early in the present century, "is the efficiency and fearful universality of the telephone." The telephone was, he added, America's proudest and most practical achievement.

GRAND STREET, NEW YORK, AT NIGHT, 1889. From *Harper's Weekly.*

With Brush's invention of the outdoor arc lamp and Edison's invention of the incandescent lamp in 1880 the night life of cities took on a new brightness; and with visibility thus improved, the tempo of city life after dark went up another few notches, both in and out of doors. To keep pace with the new possibilities something swifter than horsecars was needed to quicken street traffic at all hours. In the years immediately following, the development of an efficient dynamo and cheap current revolutionized urban and suburban transportation.

Electric traction had earlier been used in Germany but, in characteristic fashion, America took over the European precedent and applied it on a colossal scale. By the close of the century this country had nine times more trackage for electric cars than Germany. A passenger could soon ride in electric trolleys all the way from Portland, Maine, via New York to Sheboygan, Wisconsin, if any such idea had entered his head.

What was more feasible, the city dweller could get out of the city and back in again, quicker and cheaper on a trolley car than in any other way yet made possible, and cities immediately started to build up their outskirts. Where the railroads had encouraged people to concentrate their lives in compact, massed communities, the electric cars started them sprawling in widening circles of suburban developments.

Within the city, however, streetcars did little to speed up traffic. They merely increased the daily throng of transients struggling for headway in downtown streets. As the author of the American *Baedeker* wrote of Boston in 1898, a typical instance, "men of business after being whisked by the electric car from their suburban residences to the city at twelve miles an hour, sit stoically while the congested traffic makes the car take twenty minutes to pass the most crowded section of Washington Street—a walk of barely five minutes."

"GOING TO CONEY ISLAND," 1896 (?). Photograph from the Byron Collection.

THE CHICAGO LOOP, ABOUT 1909.

TREMONT STREET, BOSTON, AFTER THE INSTALLATION OF A SUBWAY, 1899.

The Museum of the City of New York
"NOT EXPERTS—JUST SARDINES." Original drawing by Rollin Kirby. (Reproduced in the New York *World*. October 8, 1927.)

Boston, following the examples of Budapest and London, was the first American city to seek relief from surface traffic problems by going underground. In 1898 a mile and a half of subway track was opened under Tremont Street to be quickly followed by more extensive routes. A few years later New York built its first subway. But the relief provided in either case was brief. Every effort to relieve urban traffic congestion succeeded only well enough to invite bigger crowds to the scene. The speedy new underground routes encouraged more people than ever to make a daily or frequent trip downtown. Out of the kiosks onto the same old city streets swarmed increasing crowds of transients who, for the privilege of quickly reaching their destination, tolerated travel conditions that would have made cattle complain; conditions that

The Public Roads Administration

EASTER MORNING ON FIFTH AVENUE, 1900. A single automobile can be seen almost in the dead center of the photograph.

got progressively worse. "A Connecticut commuter lost his temper during the downtown morning rush and punched a platform guard," reported the *New York Times* in 1940. "After four years of a sardine existence, he said, something snapped in his brain that morning when the guard tried to jam him into a car that had no room to receive him. The door started to close and hit him on the shoulder, whereupon he suddenly saw red and struck the platform operative. Every honest subway passenger on reading the story will say to himself, 'There, but for the grace of God, go I.'" There were few compensations above ground either. In 1946 Boston, in the name of virtually every other city in the nation, large and small, reported that traffic snarls and congestion were "worse than ever."

Emerson had once hailed the cow as the "engineer" who had laid out Boston's downtown streets. There were, he pointed out, worse engineers. At best, in Boston as elsewhere, streets had been planned to accommodate the pedestrian and horse-drawn traffic that might be expected from four- or five-story buildings. With taller buildings rising everywhere to shelter more people who could hope to enter and leave downtown by improved traction systems, real congestion awaited only the advent of the automobile. So far as can be observed, the single car shown in the photograph above attracted little attention in competition with the fashion display of Fifth Avenue's Easter day parade, but it was a signal no one could recognize at the time, that all existing city streets would soon be obsolete.

THE STEERAGE, 1907. Photograph by Alfred Stieglitz.

THE MODERN CITY

The modern city as it evolved during the later nineteenth century and the first half of the twentieth, in all its complexity and diversity, with its mechanical operations and its mobile power and population, was a new type of community, without precedent in history. It required new techniques of living and a new social philosophy. These, thought John Storer, a farsighted English critic, in 1870, had hardly been investigated, no less perfected. "To mould the vast congeries of life massed around a given center say ten miles around Charing Cross, for instance, into a systematic organism," he wrote, "so as to give the most good possible to every one of the vast human family therein contained, is a matter difficult of achievement, and one admitting a vast improvement over all former precedents."

In America urban growth was even more rapid and disturbing than it was in Europe. Here, historical developments were compressed into a shorter span of time and the pattern of change was revealed more sharply. Indeed, development was so rapid and change so constant, that the typical American city seemed more a process of becoming something than being anything—anything, at least, that could be confidently planned for very far in advance. Here, too, the continual admixture of new, mixed strains to the population heightened every urban problem.

During the early years of the present century, a tidal wave of immigration beat on the American shores. In the first decade there were almost nine million newcomers. Earlier waves had brought the Irish, the Germans, the Scandinavians, and others from Northern Europe, many of whom had sought the country beyond ports of entry, most of whom represented a relatively small problem of assimilation into the American whole.

Now came central and eastern Europeans —Slavs of every stripe, Magyars, Jews from everywhere, Italians, Greeks, peoples from the Danube, the Moldau, the Vistula, the Volga, the Arno—from the steppes of Russia and the shores of the Mediterranean, from mysterious lands whose very names stretched the imaginations of most older Americans. People whom Henry James, himself an expatriate, revisiting Boston, noticed with snobbish annoyance as "gross little foreigners." People who came with many of the same mixed motives that had brought the earliest settlers. People whom nobody could prove had a whit less biological efficiency than the first comers whatever their different appearance and traditions. People who for many

The A. F. Sherman Collection, Ellis Island
IMMIGRANTS, ABOUT 1900. Photograph by A. F. Sherman. Print by Alexander Alland.

reasons settled largely in cities, in separate defensive clusters of their own nationalities.

Most of the native trees, wildflowers, birds, and animals (as Lewis Gannett writes) gave way, in such congested spots as New York, to immigrants from Europe and Asia—to Oriental plane trees and the ailanthus (the tree that grows in Brooklyn), to the "English" sparrows, pigeons, and starlings, to alley cats, rats, and mice of Eurasian origin. The native human stock was more resilient but it, too, was customarily replaced in the worst spots by long and hard-tried foreign strains.

At the turn of the century the more sensitive witnesses broke out in a wave of literary protest at what was happening. The "shame of our cities," the miserable way the "other half" was forced to live, and the "bitter cry of the children" all gave titles to books that described the truth in all its hideous detail.

The torrential flow of new stock was characteristically shunted into the tenement districts, the slums, of the larger and industrial cities. In 1905, New York outdid Bombay by crowding over one thousand persons onto each acre of a thirty-acre area, to live there as they might. In *How the Other Half Lives* Jacob Riis, himself an immigrant, described the full horror of windowless, bathless, airless mass living:

"The hall is dark, and you might stumble over the children pitching pennies back there. Not that it would hurt them; kicks and cuffs are their daily diet. . . . All the fresh air that ever enters those stairs comes from the hall door that is forever slamming and from the windows of dark bedrooms that in turn receive from the stairs their sole supply

"BANDIT'S ROOST," NEW YORK, 1887–88. Photograph by Jacob A. Riis.

The Museum of the City of New York

of the elements God meant to be free. . . . The sinks are in the hallways, that all the tenants may have access—and all be poisoned alike by their summer stenches. . . . When the summer heats come with their suffering, they have meaning more terrible than words can tell. . . . Step carefully over this baby—it is a baby, spite of its rags and dirt. . . . This gap between dingy brick walls is the yard. That strip of smoke-colored sky up there is the heaven of these people. Do you wonder the name does not attract them to the churches? . . . The tenement is much like the one in front we just left, only fouler, closer, darker—we will not say more cheerless. The word is a mockery. . . . What sort of an answer, think you, would come from these tenements to the question 'Is life worth living?'"

The worst districts, settled by successive waves of immigrants, were often hard-by the business center, in the shadow of the cities' proudest monuments. A stone's throw often separated the palatial penthouses and the squalid slums, although the social distance was greater than that which separated the medieval lord from his serf.

Many cities enacted housing laws to diminish the worst of such spectacular contrasts. In Henry Street, New York, some of America's first social settlement houses were established. In Chicago Jane Addams founded the famous Hull House. But half a century later, in 1940, it was estimated that almost one quarter of New York's hordes still lived in antiquated tenements and "substandard" dwellings unfit for human habitation. The drab wooden billets in other cities were only slightly less picturesque.

HENRY STREET, NEW YORK, 1935. Photograph by Berenice Abbott.

The Museum of the City of New York

The Museum of the City of New York.
J. Clarence Davies Collection
NEW YORK'S FIRST TAXIS OUTSIDE THE METROPOLITAN
OPERA HOUSE.

The first motorized taxi service in New York, in 1898, was a huge success at the start. At first there was difficulty finding drivers. Young college men who knew something about electricity and storage batteries were tried, but they did not know the city. Finally old hackies were weaned from their horse carriages to serve as drivers.

By 1907, reported the *Independent Magazine*, there were throngs of cars on New York's Fifth Avenue: "Theatre 'buses at night, the endless procession of automobiles faring out into the country of a week-end, the industrious little electrics, all are eloquent of the hold the sport has taken upon the popular fancy. Sport? It is more than that, this automobilism; it is as necessary as the telephone and the typewriter."

Even before the wide use of automobiles, city streets in downtown central districts were, as we have seen, burdened with an intolerable congestion of humanity and vehicles. Almost every effort to provide relief seemed to add to confusion. To all that went before, the automobile added a new and boundless energy that must be forced, somehow, through already obsolete channels.

As automobiles took over streets already too cramped for horses and wagons and pedestrians the raging traffic in American cities had to be seen to be believed. "For nothing had I seen the traffic in Piccadilly Circus and on Boulevard Montmartre," wrote an English visitor to Chicago in 1920. "I had still to realize the impact upon the

FIFTH AVENUE AND 42ND STREET, NEW YORK, ABOUT 1909.
The Museum of the City of New York, J. Clarence Davies Collection

Ewing Galloway

FIFTH AVENUE AT 51ST STREET, NEW YORK CITY, 1921.

human ear of two lines of trolley cars running over cobbles, on wheels that are never oiled; this, combined with several hundreds of motor vehicles with their throttles open; this combined with a double line of elevated railways whose couplings are never oiled; and this combined with a policeman who acts as a master of the revels by means of a whistle! . . . It was magnificent. I had a sense that here was something animal and untamed. . . . Here is no hint of leisure, nor of mercy, for mercy is a draft on time and life— in Chicago there is no time for life."

By 1924, motorized traffic on New York's Fifth Avenue had been slowed to five miles an hour along the busy stretches. Later, as the dials on the dashboards of improved cars showed potential speeds up to and beyond one hundred miles an hour, traffic in the same spot would often be reduced to two or three miles per hour. At times it was even slower than that. Speed was a futile conquest under the circumstances.

The Boston Herald

WASHINGTON STREET, BOSTON, 1949.

183

SUBURBIA. HOUSING IN FLUSHING, LONG ISLAND.

In the mid-1920's some two million people entered a limited area of Manhattan Island in one day, most of them during brief rush hours of the morning and evening. Fifteen years later on a typical business day the number was well over three million. Dwelling along the choked and clamorous routes of such enormous crowds had few compensations.

The same automobiles, which had done so much to make urban living difficult, did even more to encourage an outward movement of the permanent population. Undeterred by hours of necessary commuting, breadwinners filled their purses in the city and fled to the more or less remote outskirts for domestic comfort, in gigantic daily pulsations of the population. The suburbs which sprang up along the quickest and easiest transportation routes often developed as chaotically as had the cities themselves, a fact hardly disguised by the excessive regularity of their appearance.

Swift and easy means of communication, transportation, and power transmission made it no longer necessary, as it once had been, for people to mass in huge clots in order to organize social forces or to enjoy most of the facilities and conveniences of daily living. New communities could be planned that provided both the pleasures of country life and the main advantages usually associated with life in the city. Such integrated dwelling systems could also avoid the bleak, haphazard character that the speculator's suburb usually presents.

In 1929 Radburn, New Jersey, was laid out as a present-day garden city, with the functions of domestic living divorced from the noise and traffic of streets, with a continuous belt of park space built about residential superblocks, with schools, playgrounds, swimming pool, and safe footpaths all planned as organic features of a vital community life. It was the first town built anywhere to incorporate many of these designs for balanced living.

In 1936, to demonstrate the full possiblities of the idea, the U.S. Government sponsored a trio of "greenbelt towns." In the necessities of living and in many of its luxuries, reads one recent appraisal of the experiment, "the people who live in Greenbelt are richer than those who live on Park Avenue. The Greenbelt kids, at least . . . are richer than the families who live in our 'best' suburbs, for they share a kind of socially balanced, democratic living that hardly exists any longer except perhaps in the town-meeting country. And they are richer than the inhabitants of the slums and the to-be-slums that increasingly fringe our cities, because they live in a physical and social equilibrium that has not been matched in ten years of housing and planning effort."

National Housing Administration
GREENBELT CHILDREN RUNNING THROUGH AN UNDERPASS ON THEIR WAY HOME FROM SCHOOL. Photograph by Gretchen Van Tassel.

GREENHILLS, OHIO, 1938. One of the Greenbelt towns planned by the U.S. Resettlement Administration.
The Library of Congress

By the very nature of their purpose and construction city streets and buildings assume more or less lasting patterns. On the other hand, thanks to the advances of modern technology and sociology, the habits, needs, and ideals of city life change with increasing rapidity. At just what point it becomes economically and humanly unfeasible *not* to abandon the city, to raze it and start fresh, suggests an interesting speculation.

The dilemma is largely hypothetical. Cities have grown on their historic sites for good geographic and economic reasons that are permanent elements of their importance. In the semi-rigid framework of their streets and structures enormous sums have been invested over long periods of time. Inevitably, razing and rebuilding proceeds as patchwork, sometimes instigated by private initiative and opportunism, sometimes by an officially administered city plan. Thanks in good part to government encouragement during the Great Depression, eleven hundred American communities had by 1940 created planning commissions to secure some sort of co-ordination in urban and regional development.

The national government itself played the leading rôle in the mounting war against inadequate housing and recreational facilities. In 1939, for the first time in a century, the slums of America were on the decrease, according to the U.S.H.A. Administrator. Large-scale, comprehensively planned rehousing operations were undertaken in cities all over the country. But inordinately high land values in more desirable spots within a city often made it an "economic necessity" to plant the new projects, cheerful enough in themselves, in the noisiest and dirtiest sections. And still, it was pointed out in 1942, at the current rate of construction it would take New York alone two hundred years to rehouse all the population then living under substandard conditions.

New York, November, 1946. Photograph by Todd Webb.

QUEENSBRIDGE HOUSES, THE LARGEST PUBLIC HOUSING DEVELOPMENT IN THE UNITED STATES WHEN OPENED IN 1939.

FINANCIAL DISTRICT, SUNDAY. Photograph by Todd Webb.

"Week-ends and holidays in summer reveal the city in its starkest reality," reported the International Congress for Modern Architecture in 1942. "As a place for working, it has ceased to function; as a place for living, it has been abandoned. Men have fled its hot pavements to seek the freedom of nature —space for play in the open air and sunlight . . . the holiday is sandwiched between a yesterday of crowds departing and a morrow of crowds returning — stations mobbed by thousands, roads choked with traffic, transportation lines in a general paralysis. The evacuation of the city is living evidence of its failure to provide space for recreation for the enjoyment of the many." The contrast between New York's Wall Street and Coney Island of a Sunday morning in summer offers an emphatic illustration.

CONEY ISLAND, SUNDAY.

International News Photo

Fairchild Aerial Surveys, Inc.

THE CHICAGO LAKESHORE.

In numerous American cities have appeared the beginnings of new highway systems scaled to the speed of the automobile
and the eagerness of a host of people to quit
the urban center as often and as quickly as
possible. Instead of leaping spasmodically
from stop light to stop light along horse-
and-buggy street patterns, the motorist takes
to long stretches of speedway free from pedestrian intrusion, curving and looping to
avoid unnecessary, dangerous, and delaying
intersections.

In Chicago, New York, and some other
cities major highway improvements have incorporated park, playground, and landscape
features to provide some of the essential
open space, beauty, and recreational opportunity that had been lost in earlier urban
development. Neglected shore lines have
been restored to remind city dwellers of the
natural setting of their communities, long
lost to view as river fronts and lake fronts
developed into industrial wasteland.

The Museum of the City of New York
TRIBOROUGH BRIDGE, 1937. From a negative by Berenice Abbott.

Unlike the urban communities of Europe that gradually developed from ancient villages, the American city shot up with uncontrollable speed, sometimes out of a blank wilderness. In neither case were these modern communities simply villages grown large. They were entirely new forms of social and economic organizations demanding a new way of life of those who lived in them and, in good measure, also of those who came within their orbit.

"We can ill spare the commanding social benefits of cities," Emerson wrote in an essay a century or so ago. Today we can hardly avoid them wherever we live. Neither can we escape the demeaning influence of urban conceits which Emerson complained about in the same essay. Modern cities have generated explosive forces that are breaking down many of the old differences, grown so acute during the nineteenth century, between city and country. And, good or bad, urban standards tend to call the tune everywhere in matters of fashion, habits of thought, forms of entertainment, and social attitudes.

With every advance in communication and transportation the influence of certain major urban centers has spread in a series of widening circles, some of them covering tremendous areas. New York, as a prime example, has become the economic, cultural, and social nerve center for a "metropolitan region" that includes parts of four states, two-hundred and seventy-two other incorporated communities, and all the rural districts that lie between. By 1940 Chicago, San Francisco, Los Angeles, Detroit, Boston, and well over one hundred other such key cities had brought within the range of their central influence almost half the people of the nation. Here was a new type of population grouping, typical of America and largely made possible — or inevitable — by the commonplace character of automobiles, telephones, electrical transmission of power, and other such facilities in our national life.

Within each of these super-communities people read the same newspapers, frequent

METROPOLIS, 1946. Photograph by Todd Webb.

The U.S. Coast and Geodetic Survey

MIDTOWN NEW YORK, VIEWED THROUGH A NINE-LENS CAMERA.

or are dependent upon the same principal trading or distributing center, face overlapping problems of public concern—sewage disposal, health, crime, transportation, and other matters, although they maintain various separate local governments for approaching their common difficulties.

In many ways the power exercised by these regions of interdependent interests is, in fact, greater than that exercised by any existing political state. The nuclear energy, so to speak, developed within those irregularly-shaped super-communities has put new strains on our federal system which the Founding Fathers could never have anticipated. Some students have suggested that such areas be organized into radically new administrative units that would bring city and country into more realistic governmental patterns.

VIII
ROADS
TO UNION

ROADS TO UNION

INTRODUCTION

ONLY the heat of war had brought the colonies to a point of fusion. As the flames of the Revolution subsided, it was confidently predicted by many observers, the union of states would separate again into its components. "They can never be united into one compact empire..." said the Dean of Gloucester; "a disunited people till the end of time, suspicious and distrustful of one another, they will be divided and subdivided into little commonwealths or principalities, according to natural boundaries, by great bays of the sea, and by vast rivers, lakes and ridges of mountains." The possibility was real enough. Washington noted with dread a tendency of sections of the country to fall apart under the strain of poor communications. His vision had been sharpened by his grim experience at Valley Forge when desperately needed food went unsold a short distance away because of transport difficulties. "Open *all* the communication which nature has afforded between the Atlantic States and the Western territory, and encourage the use of them to the utmost," he urged, "...sure I am there is no other tie by which they will long form a link in the chain of Federal Union."

The American people at the time numbered less than four millions, scattered over almost eight hundred thousand square miles. Beyond the east coast areas served by the more heavily traveled thoroughfares, the population lived in small clusters almost entirely out of touch with one another. Even by way of the best roads, between Boston and New York, communication was vexingly slow. In 1788 James Madison waited nine impatient days at New York for an important letter from Boston. From Richmond to New York the mail might be hurried through in a week, but two weeks was common. Inland, off the principal highways, travelers found only crude and hazardous paths leading through forests on a scale Europe had not known for millennia. In bad seasons any road was virtually impassable. Sizeable towns might be isolated for days after a heavy rain.

With travel so tedious, individualism was an almost necessary virtue, localism an unavoidable weakness. Even James Madison, as he wrote to Jefferson in 1786, knew as little "of the affairs of Georgia as of those of Kamskatska." The ordinary citizen, with no timely knowledge of his countryman's activities in another section, could find little interest in them and could recognize no sense of mutual obligation or common purpose. To the majority of people, schooled by tradition in local attachments and aware only of local conditions, the national government seemed a distant and sometimes alien force.

While the main body of Americans was confined to the eastern seaboard the problem of national integration was serious enough. But, as Washington foresaw, almost immediately after the revolutionary war years the population started streaming west at an incomparable pace. "We are greatly and rapidly,—I was about to say fearfully, growing," Calhoun told Congress in 1817. "This is our pride and our danger, our weakness and our strength." Like Washington, he urged every effort to bind the Union together by road and canal. The nation was then more than twice as large as it had been when Washington made his plea thirty years before and the population was scattering to its farthest limits. To hold the social and political fabric intact while the Republic expanded with such explosive force challenged individuals and government alike.

Reviewing his western travels in 1839 Frederick Marryat concluded that to speak of the United States as a nation would be absurd. "The inhabitants of the cities . . ." he wrote, "know as little of what is passing in Arkansas and Alabama as a cockney does of the manners and customs of . . . the Isle of Man." Society, ranging from "a state of refinement down to one of positive barbarism," had spread too rapidly and too distantly to settle into fixed, recognizable patterns or to give any semblance of unified purpose. Yet, at the time Marryat wrote, the more settled parts of the country were already feeling the cohesive force of the network of turnpikes that had been thrown over the East, of the Erie and other canals (as well as the National Road) that linked the vast Mississippi Basin with the Atlantic seaboard, and of the steamboats that trafficked far beyond reach of road or canal.

America was an ideal trying-ground for the steamboat. The lack of enough good roads flanking the rivers, particularly in the West, spared the new invention serious competition from stagecoaches along those primary routes. The almost endless inland waterways of the West provided the sheltered conditions required by the frail early vessels. Wood, which served as fuel in the young days of steamboating, grew abundantly along the riverbanks. And a migratory people welcomed every "lift" that would speed them on their way to someplace else.

One light-spirited observer characterized the typical western steamboat as a thing of "wood, tin, shingles, canvas, and twine" that looked like "a bride of Babylon." A playful slap from an ocean wave, he remarked, would reduce the entire contraption to kindling. However, these indigenously contrived paddle-wheelers were admirably designed for their place and purpose and won respectful notice around the world. Their role in winning the West and cementing the Union can hardly be exaggerated. By their agency, wrote an American in 1841, national colonization and national production had been advanced by at least a century. Elsewhere it was noted that steamboats by stepping up the means of communication over wide reaches of the continent promoted the cause of democracy as effectively as could be done by electoral laws. "There isn't anyone," observed Tocqueville, "who does not recognize that the discovery of steam has added unbelievably to the strength and prosperity of the Union, and has done so by facilitating rapid communications between diverse parts of this vast body."

Remarkable as their exploits were, and in the yarns of Mark Twain and others steamboats were all but amphibious, they could not navigate the arid Plains or the lofty Rockies. Where they left off emigrants contrived other means to reach farther goals. In 1843, as those who had trudged off from the headwaters of the rivers were already pressing into Oregon, congressional spokesmen ridiculed the notion that such a remote territory could ever be incorporated into the Union. Since it would take ten months for representatives from the coast to travel to the District of Columbia and back again, representative government was implausible.

But the most extravagant boosters of the western borderlands were closer to reality than the sober-sided congressmen. ". . . The time is not far off," rhapsodized one exuberant prophet who passed for a comedian at the time, "when the locomotive will be steaming its way to the Rocky Mountains, with a mighty big train of cars running after it. Yes, the whistle of the engine will echo through the South-west Pass, and sharply hint to the free people of that great territory the approach of hundreds and thousands tew, who are to be their neighbors." Within less than a generation not only was Oregon a state of the Union but representatives were speeding from the Pacific coast to the Capital by a timetable instead of a calendar —almost as quickly as Madison's letter had come to New York from Boston barely eighty years before. Or they were flashing their messages instantaneously by wire.

The transcontinental railroad, one of the proudest achievements of the age, was only the main strand of a growing web of iron connective tissue that was spreading over the land. With frequent, fast, and regular service, with large-scale organization, and with endless capital the railroads swiftly and inexorably cut into the steamboats' impor-

tance in the years after the Civil War. ". . . eight years ago," wrote Mark Twain in 1883, "a boat used to go up the river with every stateroom full, and people piled five or six deep on the cabin floor; and a solid deck-load of immigrants and harvesters down below, into the bargain. To get a first-class stateroom, you'd got to prove sixteen quarterings of nobility and four hundred years of descent. . . . But it's all changed now; plenty staterooms above, no harvesters below—there's a patent self-binder now, and they don't have harvesters any more; they've gone where the woodbine twineth— and they didn't go by steamboat either; they went by the train."

The railroad proved itself the most powerful consolidating force civilization had yet known. With it and the telegraph the Union, full-grown and richly peopled, endured and flourished. In less than a century after the Dean of Gloucester's gloomy prediction it was all done, from buffalo trace to iron horse, from straggling, haggling newborn states to an iron-bound union of imperial domain. Space and time had been all but annihilated; complete annihilation awaited the advent of the automobile and the airplane.

"VIEW FROM BUSHONGO TAVERN 5 MILES FROM YORK TOWN ON THE BALTIMORE ROAD." Engraving from the *Columbian Magazine*, 1788.

ROADWAYS AND TURNPIKES

Washington was not the only statesman who pleaded for better communications in the interest of a firm federal union. "To make the crooked ways straight and the rough ways smooth," Gallatin told Congress, would unite the people in interest, "which is the most effectual means of uniting the human race." But with one main exception, the famous National Road, private initiative, not government authority, promoted the public welfare by better roads. As the eighteenth century gave way to the nineteenth, turnpike companies were lacing the countryside with improved highways and collecting a tidy income in toll charges. By 1811 the state of New York alone had chartered one hundred and thirty-seven road corporations whose combined capital was over seven and a half million dollars voluntarily invested by people confident of a quick and high return on their money.

As opposed to natural roads, turnpikes were constructed on a firm bed with drainage facilities. When possible they followed a level route with tollgates about every ten miles where country roads turned into the 'pike. The new roads attracted an immense trade. Stagecoach and wayside tavern flourished as never before. But, like almost all later developments in American transportation, turnpikes ultimately set in motion more traffic than they could adequately handle. As public enthusiasm switched to canals, steamboats, and railroads, interest in highways lapsed until, long later, bicyclists and automobilists pointed out that practically nothing had been done to improve them for sixty years.

For two decades after the Declaration of Independence, until the beginnings of the turnpike excitement, the new Republic had not a single well-paved road to help bind its straggling parts together. The thin network of post and stage roads, largely concentrated near the coast, offered more discouragement than inducement to wheeled traffic. Even the well-traveled "roads from Philadelphia to Baltimore," it was reported, "exhibit, for the greater part of the way, an aspect of savage desolation. Chasms to the depth of six, eight, or ten feet occur at numerous intervals. A stage-coach which left Philadelphia on the 5th of February, 1796, took five days to go to Baltimore." Horses floundering up to their bellies in thick mud were a frequent spectacle. At times the road eluded the traveler altogether and left him, bewildered, in what seemed a trackless wilderness.

On what was probably the best road, that between Boston and New York, two stages and a dozen horses were means enough to accommodate all the passengers and freight during the first years under the Constitution. The trip took four to six days on the average and was usually an adventure long remembered. The cost of inland transportation over such rudimentary highways was enormous.

Under the circumstances, traveling for pleasure was a diversion reserved for later generations. It is easy to understand Jefferson's concern for Washington's safety when the President made a necessary southern tour in 1791. "I shall be happy to hear that no accident has happened to you in the bad roads," he wrote the President, ". . . that you are better prepared for those to come by lowering the hang [body] of your carriage and exchanging the coachman for two postillions . . . which [are] . . . essential to your safety."

Travelers who might well expect to help the horses drag their vehicle through the rutted mire, or to abandon the vehicle altogether and foot it through the mud, as Washington had to do when on his way to meet Congress, understandably preferred horseback, if travel they must. Even horsemen often had to mount and dismount to make any progress, according to the Marquis de Chastellux. In Virginia, observed Hugh Grigsby, "coaches were rarely seen. There were thousands of respectable men in the Commonwealth who had never seen any other four-wheeled vehicle than a wagon and there were thousands who had never seen a wagon."

The Metropolitan Museum of Art

A VIEW NEAR PHILADELPHIA. Engraving from John Scoles after a drawing by Jacob Hoffman. From the *New-York Magazine*, 1795.

So long as many citizens and their federal representatives would be living more than three hundred miles from the national capitol, claimed Richard Henry Lee in 1788, government as proposed under the Constitution would be impossible. Time and distance were too great obstacles to such a federal union. (Lee did not mention it but the expense of a long journey would in itself have been prohibitive for poor people, should any be elected to office.) Much the same objection was raised to the proposed admission of Oregon into the Union seventy years later, although the "impossible" distance by then had increased to three thousand miles, and even at that, was shrugged off by forward-looking representatives. Nevertheless, in a land so thinly peopled, so widely scattered, and so poorly articulated as America in 1790 the hope of any lasting union lay in quickening communications.

The conquest of distance was, and remained, instinct with America's destiny.

Traveling in the relative luxury of his own coach, Josiah Quincy recalled that it once had taken him a month to reach Washington from Boston. By public conveyance the trip might easily have been slower. An average of three or four miles an hour was fair speed for a stagecoach during the 1790's. Some of the difficulties of keeping even that pace are suggested by the plaintive scribble on the waybill shown below: "Gentleman proprietors unless you order your Drivers to drive faster on the meadall [?] of the road we had better quit the Bisniss   the Stage neaver of late Comes to Bristoll untill Six and Seaven oclock   then my horsis has to travel after Dark and very often Dont Get in to phila untill 9. & 10. oclock   itt will kill my horsis if Some alteration is not made on the Rote   they vary often have to Return

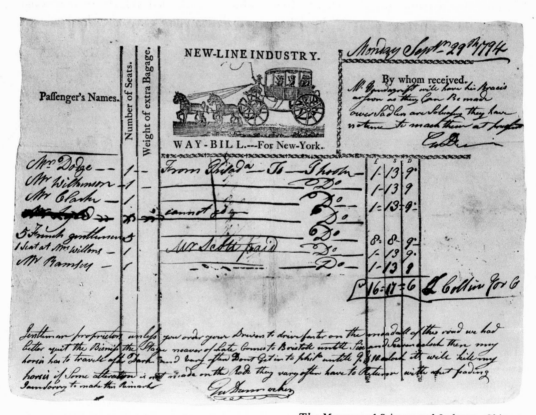

A WAYBILL, 1794.

The Museum of Science and Industry, Chicago

The Metropolitan Museum of Art

THE CHARLES RIVER BRIDGE. Engraving by John Scoles. From the *New-York Magazine*, 1795.

without feading I am sorry to make this Rimark."

In and about the major cities the roads showed some slight improvement, enough, at least, to permit the heavier flow of traffic through those more crowded areas. Enough, too, to encourage the use of the private vehicles—"carriages, phaetons, and chairs"—of which the German traveler Johann Schoepf noted so many in 1783–84. At the end of the eighteenth century Bostonians alone owned one hundred and forty-five of one sort or another. For years such luxury was practically unknown in the hinterland. When Governor Turnbull visited Norwich, Connecticut, in a chaise during the Revolution all work in the village stopped as the inhabitants gathered to stare at the curiosity.

It was in and near the cities, too, that the worst difficulties were first met by public improvements. To overcome the awkwardness of being at times isolated from the mainland by high tides, Boston spanned the Charles River by a permanent bridge in 1786. Built by Lemuel Cox, the construction was hailed as an engineering triumph. It

was over one thousand five hundred feet long and forty-two feet wide, with a railed passage for pedestrians on either side, a draw that could be raised by two men, and "forty elegant . . . lamps to illuminate it when necessary."

Like many other public improvements of the day it was a privately financed speculation, undertaken through voluntary subscription in the cause of good business as well as social progress.

The Worcester Art Museum, Goodspeed Collection
TRADE CARD, 1795. Engraving by Samuel Hill.

THE CORNER OF GREENWICH AND WARREN STREETS, NEW YORK, JANUARY, 1809. Water color by Baroness Hyde de Neuville.

In city and country alike northern travelers welcomed the winter snows that smoothed the way for sleighs. "Carriages fitted up this way," wrote Robert Sutcliff of his American experiences in 1804–6, "glide along with such silent celerity, that the laws require the horses should have small bells fixed to their harness, that passengers in the streets may have notice of their approach; otherwise they would be liable to many accidents. . . . The noise of carriage wheels, which is, in general, very considerable, especially in the principal streets; is now supplanted by the tinkling of bells on every hand."

As cities became more specialized in their commercial interests and more dependent upon the surrounding countryside for food and fuel, the need for better roads in all directions became critical both for the townsman and the farmer. Snow enough to make the way easy was seasonal and regional. In most seasons and in wide areas getting farm produce and other needed supplies to the markets of growing cities was an increasingly vexing problem. "In December last," complained a writer of the early Republic, "the roads were so intollerably bad that the country people could not bring their forage to market, though *actually offered the cash on delivery.*"

"They are making a Capital Turnpike Road from Philadelphia [to] Lancaster, wch was very much wanted as the Old one is very bad, indeed," came another, more hopeful report in 1795, "the Work people Employed on the Road (many of whom are

The Maryland Historical Society
COUNTRY ROAD WITH OXCART, EARLY 19TH CENTURY. Water color attributed to Benjamin Henry Latrobe.

Moravians with Long Beards like Jews) say it will be finished by the End of November." It was. The Philadelphia and Lancaster Turnpike Road Company, chartered in 1792, had sold two thousand two hundred and twenty-six shares at thirteen dollars each within a few hours after its subscription books were opened. Over protesting cries of "monopoly" the company went on to construct a sixty-two-mile highway which contemporaries agreed was a "masterpiece of its kind . . . paved with stone the whole way and overlaid with gravel, so that it is never obstructed during the most severe season." This first macadamized road in this country, built at a cost of almost a half million dollars, opened a new era in American communication.

The pike opened a new era in American capitalism, as well, and posed a new problem in corporation control. A promise of handsome returns attracted private capital to the better-roads movement in a fever of speculation. The new Lancaster road gave Philadelphia a fresh hold on the inland trade. Baltimore immediately countered with a turnpike to Reisterstown. And so the competition flourished up and down the country. Before 1801 at least sixty-six turnpike companies had been incorporated, most of them in New England.

Tollgates were placed at convenient intervals along the way to collect different rates from carriages, horsemen, drovers, and commercial vehicles. The controlling companies had the right to penalize those who took "shun pikes" around the gates to avoid charges. "Turnpikes are aristocratic," complained the critics who felt that roads were a matter for public management, not private speculation, ". . . the common roads are good enough for all." But they were not good enough and the aristocrats of roads attracted heavy traffic. On the Dauphin turnpike in Pennsylvania the keeper of one gate recorded sixteen thousand people passing his post from March through December, 1817.

The Metropolitan Museum of Art
A Toll Gate on the Baltimore-Reisterstown Road. Engraving after a drawing by Francis Blackwell Mayer.

The Metropolitan Museum of Art
THE DILIGENCE STAGE NEAR TRENTON, 1811-1813.
Water color by Paul Svinin.

Overland travel in the new Republic, even over the better roads, had few rewards beyond the simple satisfaction of reaching a destination in one piece. "My nerves have not yet quite recovered from the shock of the *wagon*," wrote one native traveler after a trip from Baltimore to New York in 1790. Foreign visitors were usually louder in their complaints. Moreau de Saint-Méry reflected that no European could understand why Americans, who were so eager to "go places," put up with such conditions. The ordinary stages, he wrote in 1794, "are usually drawn by four horses and have nine or twelve places, on benches without backs, three people to each bench. The space is hardly ever sufficient for three. From the elbow height of a seated person to the top, the carriages have leather curtains on three sides, fastened to studs by buttonholes in leather straps. The front is open, because the driver always sits on the first bench. It is through the front that one gets into the back of the carriage, by stepping over the benches. . . . The carriages are very high, long and narrow, and the drivers, who are almost always slightly drunk, drive so fast that accidents are excessively common."

Saint-Méry's countryman, Brissot de Warville, after a drive through a rainy Connecticut night thought that heaven alone had preserved him from accident, at which he was "much astonished." "I knew not which to admire most in the driver," he reflected, "his intrepidity or dexterity. I cannot con-

The American Antiquarian Society
ADVERTISEMENT FOR A COMMERCIAL MAIL STAGE, "THIRTY-NINE HOURS FROM BOSTON TO NEW YORK," 1815.
Engraving by Brunton.

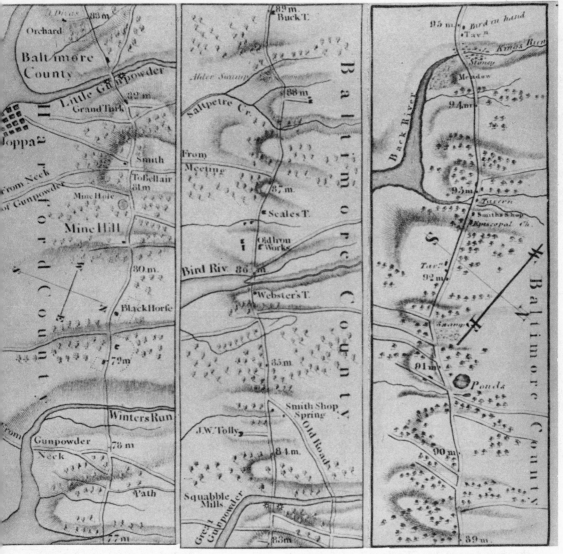

PORTION OF A ROAD MAP. From S. S. Moore and L. W. Jones, *The Traveller's Directory*, 1804 (2d edition).

ceive how he avoided twenty times dashing the carriage to pieces." Drunk or sober, East or West, the American stage driver developed over the years a reputation for extraordinary skill.

Whatever the conditions Americans, during the last years of the eighteenth and the early years of the nineteenth century, were taking to the road in constantly increasing numbers. "To give an idea of the internal movements of this vast hive," wrote an English visitor in 1817, "about twelve thousand wagons passed between Baltimore and Philadelphia in the last year, with from four to six horses, carrying from thirty-five to forty hundredweight. . . . Add to these . . . the innumerable travelers on horseback, on foot, and in light wagons, and you have before you a scene of bustle and business, extending over a space of three hundred miles, which is truly wonderful." Road maps had long since become a practical necessity.

The Library of Congress

The "Colossus" Bridge over the Schuylkill at Philadelphia, built in 1811. Engraving from Klinckow-ström's *Atlas*, Stockholm, 1824.

Where roads were broken by large streams, rivers, and tidal waters early travelers faced not only discomfort and delay, but, often, real danger. A ferry crossing in winter, in a small, flat-bottomed scow carrying excitable beasts along with humans and their vehicle, could test the courage of a veteran. Even the redoubtable General Horatio Gates was once discouraged from making the passage from New Jersey to New York when he saw how shaken the incoming passengers were from the perils of their trip.

As travel increased, however, bridges were thrown up at key points, usually by a privately financed company such as had built the one across the Charles. Paul Svinin, a Russian traveler who visited the United States in 1811–13, marveled at the way private initiative was answering the wants of the country. "Bridges in this country," he wrote, "merit the particular attention of a European. Many of them are truly beautiful, notably those of Philadelphia, Trenton, Washington and Boston. But the most wonderful one, and the most remarkable in point of construction, is the bridge which was built across the Schuylkill River near Philadelphia in 1811. It is a single arch, with a span of 340 feet and an exceedingly gentle rise. It is built entirely of wood and

seems to be suspended in the air. It is so delicate in appearance as to make you doubt its strength, but reassurance comes as you step upon it, even though you have not examined its construction. Daily it is traversed by several heavy drays drawn by ten huge horses."

Beyond the terminals of the turnpikes, roads to the West degenerated into thin, rutted clearings in the forest, not yet cleared of tree stumps. Off the main routes the difficulties of overland freighting made almost any point on the western riverbanks seem nearer to world markets than a place twenty miles distant by bad roads from the Atlantic coast ports. Before the end of the eighteenth century seagoing vessels, built on the Monongahela and Ohio Rivers, were sailing from Pittsburgh, Marietta, and other western cities to European and West Indian ports (see pp. 208, 209). In all, some sixty-seven known ships, exclusive of gunboats, were launched on western waters before the Ohio and Mississippi demonstrated how formidable they could be to unwieldy, ocean-going craft. The very thought of a square rigger sailing from Pittsburgh to Italy, via the Ohio, the Mississippi, the Gulf of Mexico, and the ocean, completely baffled the customs inspectors of Europe.

FERRY SCENE, 1811-1813. Water color by Svinin.

THE ROAD TO THE WEST. Water color by George Tattersall.

The American Antiquarian Society
A KEELBOAT DESCENDING THE OHIO RIVER. Drawing by Charles Lesueur.

MAP OF PITTSBURGH, 1805, SHOWING THE SCHOONERS *Allegany, Amity,* AND *Conquest;* THE BRIGS *Ann, Jane, Bison, Fayette,* AND *Nanina;* AND THE SHIPS *Western Trader, General Butler,* AND *Pittsburgh.* Wash drawing by William Mason.

The Maryland Historical Society

A SCENE ON THE NATIONAL ROAD. A reconstructed drawing by T. C. R., 1869.

As already told, flatboats and keelboats did a huge trade along the western rivers, mostly downstream. When the steamboat solved the worst difficulties of upstream transportation a large part of the growing trade of the interior of the continent threatened to by-pass the East altogether. For a while, at least, freight charges by steamboat to the upper Ohio were considerably less than the cost of wagon transport from Philadelphia and Baltimore. Farmers who lived along the Mississippi system could exchange their wares for merchandise from the West Indies and Europe via New Orleans more easily than they could trade by land with eastern centers.

To bring East and West together by a direct overland route had been talked about and legislated in Congress a number of years before construction actually started on a National Road in 1811. The new route was to be built as straight as might be through the mountains from Cumberland, Maryland, where it connected with a state road, to Wheeling, West Virginia, and the western waterways. As it slowly progressed, the "National Pike" became a coursing thoroughfare for emigrant, travelers, and

Public Roads Administration

THE ROUTE OF THE NATIONAL PIKE.

freight to the West. "It looked more like a leading avenue of a great city than a road through rural districts," wrote one historian of the road.

In some areas, particularly on the roads to the West out of Philadelphia and Baltimore, Conestoga wagons handled much of the heavy trucking. In 1815 the number of them arriving in Pittsburgh from the East was estimated at close to six thousand. Gaily colored, even to the reins, and often with belled horses, these were the most picturesque outfits on the road. A four- to six-horse team of carefully matched, well-cared-for animals hauling a load of several tons stretched sixty feet along the road. With the teamster always on the left, the wagons inaugurated a "keep to the right" traffic. Other vehicles, attracted to the ruts left by the Conestoga's broad wheels, followed the precedent.

In the East, too, overland traffic was starting to crowd the roads. During the War of 1812, when much of the intercoastal traffic was driven from the seas, swarms of freight wagons were called into service. Half hu-

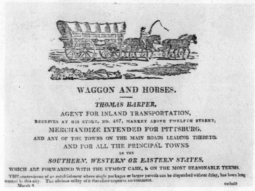

WAGGON AND HORSES.

THOMAS HARPER,
AGENT FOR INLAND TRANSPORTATION,
RECEIVES AT HIS STORE, NO. 467, MARKET ABOVE TWELFTH STREET,
MERCHANDIZE INTENDED FOR PITTSBURG,
AND ANY OF THE TOWNS ON THE MAIN ROADS LEADING THERETO,
AND FOR ALL THE PRINCIPAL TOWNS
IN THE
SOUTHERN, WESTERN OR EASTERN STATES,
WHICH ARE FORWARDED WITH THE UTMOST CARE, & ON THE MOST REASONABLE TERMS.

The Free Library of Philadelphia
ADVERTISEMENT. From the *Aurora*, March 8, 1814.

morously, half earnestly, they were often given such pseudo-maritime names as *Neptune Metamorphosed, Mud-Clipper,* and *Sailor's Misery* and it was suggested for the benefit of anxious shippers at both ends of the route that they be logged by their "skippers" in and out of the "ports" they passed through. One "fleet of fast-sailing wagons" was reported by the press to have been sighted "scudding under bare poles" through the mud of a stormy day.

NORTH EAST CORNER OF SECOND AND RACE STREETS, PHILADELPHIA, 1825-1830. Engraving by Robert Tiller, Jr., after a drawing by G. Strickland. A westward-bound freight wagon is loading in the foreground.

The Worcester Art Museum, Goodspeed Collection

MERRY-MAKING AT A WAYSIDE INN, 1811-1813. Water color by Svinin.

H. ROSE.

A bird in the hand is worth two in the bush.

Collection of H. Morgan Brainard

AN INN SIGN FROM COVENTRY, CONNECTICUT, EARLY 19TH CENTURY.

By the end of the 1820's the American stagecoach had become a much improved vehicle and roads were spreading in an ever wider net. In 1826 the *American Traveller* reported: "Now we have more than 70 different lines of 4 and 6 horse stages which regularly depart, from this city [Boston] in every direction. . . . If this species of improvement continues to advance with the same gigantic strides (and we see nothing to prevent), the time cannot be far distant when a complete consolidation of the interests and feelings of the people of the United States will be brought about."

During the turnpike era the roadside inn was a social institution as important to local residents, if any, as to teamsters and travelers—a clearing house for mail, gossip, news, business, and argument, and a place of general entertainment. The American innkeeper, as James Fenimore Cooper patiently explained to his English correspondents, was something more than an ordinary publican. "He is often a magistrate, the chief of a battallion of militia, or even a member of a state legislature," wrote Cooper. "He is almost always a man of character . . . frequently [with] a peculiar pride in his profession." He was, in other words, quite as important within his orbit as he pretended to be, and altogether as independent. According to a frequently told anecdote Louis Philippe, the future king of France, was once booted out of a Cincinnati tavern into the gutter by a landlord to whom he had tried to show condescension. Prince and commoner slept in any bed they found empty "or occupied by but one person," as the Duke of La Rochefoucauld-Liancourt reported, "without inquiring . . . who that person may be."

As travel quickened — in 1826 Josiah Quincy, this time in a public stage, traveled from Boston to Washington in eight days— more specialized institutions took over the various functions of the tavern at key points on the road. Some served as tippling houses,

The Museum of Science and Industry, Chicago
AN EARLY FLAT-TOP COACH BETWEEN PHILADELPHIA AND BALTIMORE, 1832-1835. Engraving by Tudor Horton after a drawing by Henry Smith (?).

some as boardinghouses, and others as hotels. In the larger cities where the concentration of travelers was greatest the city hotel burgeoned into a peculiarly American establishment where every need and convenience of the guest was anticipated, including many he was slow to recognize. Englishmen were astonished to learn that in some of these public palaces they could have their shirts washed and ironed while they bathed. The tinkling of ice was heard everywhere in every season of the year.

SANDERSON'S FRANKLIN HOUSE, CHESTNUT ST., PHILADELPHIA, ABOUT 1835. Engraving by John Rubens Smith.
The Yale University Art Gallery, Mabel Brady Garvan Collection

A CANAL DROVER. From a bank note engraving.

THE CANAL ERA

The waterways were the natural, the easiest, and the most popular highways of early America. To a very large extent colonial culture and economy developed along the rivers and about the bays of the land. Roads —and even some early railroads—were considered more as necessary links between water routes than as independent traffic lanes. To improve on nature and supplement the existing rivers with artificial watercourses was an old dream. As Benjamin Franklin pointed out before the Revolution, "rivers are ungovernable things." Canals, he suggested, being "quiet and always manageable" should be encouraged to speed the country on its way and in new directions.

A rage for canal and lock navigation swept through the Union during the 1790's. Philadelphia alone planned to build three, work was actually started on a canal through the Mohawk Valley, and every state had its separate projects, some of them actually completed. While roads were as few and as bad as they were, the need for easier communications was obvious enough. It was pointed out early in the 1800's that for the cost of moving a ton of merchandise from England to America one could have moved the same load barely thirty miles overland in America; coal from Liverpool at that time sold for less in Philadelphia than coal from Richmond,

Virginia, so tedious was transport by land.

Every enterprising seaport on the Atlantic coast wanted to tap the bulging larders of the western territory, to dissuade the western farmer from sending his harvest downstream to New Orleans. But so long as it cost a dollar to send a bushel of wheat to New York that could be raised in Illinois for fifty cents most of the grain, pork, whiskey and other produce from the West drifted down the Ohio and the Mississippi. With the revived craze for canals that grew with the development of the West, the Erie Canal, after twenty-five years of planning and hoping, finally came to fruition.

Clinton's "Big Ditch" that extended New York's commercial empire far into the back country was only one of the artificial rivers to fortune that was built in the fever of competition. But it was typical of the enterprise as a whole and was, in many ways, the most imposing achievement of all. Along its muddy waters developed a whole library of folklore that recalls its large place in the history of American life. For many emigrants the Erie was the way to the West, the road to destiny. It is small wonder they sang of it in Michigan:

> Then there's the state of New York,
>   where some are very rich,
> Themselves and a few others have dug

BUILDING THE ERIE CANAL. Lithograph by Anthony Imbert. From Cadwallader Colden, *Memoir . . . of the Completion of the New York Canals,* 1825.

a mighty ditch,
To render it more easy for us to find
   a way,
And sail upon the waters of Michigania,
   Yea, yea, yea, to Michigania.

The Erie Canal was actually started in 1817 with all the discouragements that faint and perverse hearts could present to the sponsors. Even Jefferson had said that the "talk of making a canal *three hundred and fifty miles long through a wilderness*" was "little short of madness." It did take magnificent vision and determination just short of madness. At the start of the project "wild Irish bog trotters from West Ireland, cutting out the trees the width of the canal track, were set to work knee deep in the wet muck; they could wear nothing but a flannel shirt and a slouch cap, and there were no tools that could be used. Shovels and spades were out of the question and a rectangular side-board wheelbarrow equally useless. . . ."

That primitive scene was soon replaced by a prospect of strange new machinery developed out of the unprecedented demands of the giant cut. Great hoists for removing infinite stumps and full-grown trees, scrapes and plows with special blades to cut deep-lying roots, cleared the ditch; a new variety of hydraulic cement solved the problem of stonework. In eight years the way was clear from Lake Erie to New York Bay.

The completion of the canal was jubilantly celebrated along its entire length. On October 26, 1825, Governor DeWitt Clinton and a distinguished group of companions on board the *Seneca Chief* started the unprecedented trip from Buffalo to New York by water. At every town by which the party passed there were artillery salutes, banquets, and speeches. New York was reached in nine days and here the celebrations climaxed. A

CELEBRATING THE OPENING OF THE ERIE CANAL, NEW YORK HARBOR, NOVEMBER 4, 1825. Painting by Anthony Imbert.

keg of water from Lake Erie was emptied into the Atlantic in a symbolic rite and twenty-two gaily decorated steamboats, a flotilla of extraordinary size for that day, were on hand for the ceremonies. It was probably the most important occasion New York harbor has ever known. For the first time the road to and from the West was wide open,

and New York was its main terminal.

It was the culmination of a broader interest. "The western settlers," Washington had written in 1784, "stand as it were on a pivot. The touch of a feather would turn them any way . . . smooth the road, and make easy the way for them, and then see what an influx of articles will be poured upon us; how amaz-

ingly our exports will be increased by them, and how amply we shall be compensated for any trouble and expense we may encounter to effect it." The next year Washington promoted a canal company to facilitate transportation along the Potomac Valley.

But it was principally by means of the Erie that the way was finally made easy. The "in-flux" was pouring in and West and East were bound together by a new tie. With the progress of the National Road and the rapid development of steam-powered transportation during the same years, America seemed for the first time in a fair way to bind the whole wide continent together in a secure Union.

A Scene on the Erie Canal, 1831. Water color by John W. Hill.

Even before the canal was completed the tolls began to exceed the interest charges on the state's debt. The year after the canal was opened to its full length, the income was over three quarters of a million dollars. No longer called a ditch, the Erie was now known the country over as The Grand Canal. Fifty gaily painted boats leaving Albany for the West in a single day was a common occurrence. At some locks that were in use night and day, sixty or seventy boats might be seen awaiting their turn. From the West they came laden with wheat, grain, timber, whiskey, and pelts. A single cargo of furs in 1826 was valued at one hundred thousand dollars. In that same year 19,000 boats floated past one town along the route. From the East went salt, furniture, and merchandise of every description.

To the consternation of Philadelphia merchants, hungry as any for western trade, it was pointed out in an Ohio newspaper that while it took thirty days and cost five dollars a hundred pounds to transport goods from Philadelphia to Columbus, the same articles could be brought from New York in twenty days by the Hudson and the Erie Canal for half the cost. The governor of Georgia observed that wheat from central New York was cheaper at Savannah than wheat from central Georgia. By 1847 the canal business concentrating at Albany was greater than that derived by New Orleans from the trade of the whole Mississippi River system.

No single agency up to this time had given such an impetus to westward migration. The new canal, "the most stupendous chain of artificial navigation in this or any other country," as one guidebook described it, immediately became the principal gateway to the basins of the western lakes and the Mississippi River. Travelers of every stripe, from

A Scene on the Erie Canal, about 1830. Aquatint by Hill.

griping English authors laden with note-books for recording their criticisms, to yodeling Swiss farmers still in native dress and burdened with their wagons and farming tools, took to the Erie in a continuous surging procession.

Horace Greeley recalled his journey on one of the "cent and a half a mile, mile and a half an hour" Erie packets with no great pleasure. Like Dickens and other fastidious travelers he found the facilities for washing, sleeping, and eating on board far short of perfection. But for poor emigrants the cheap travel rates more than compensated for the snail's pace and the relative discomforts. A great part of the population of the western states remembered that it was the Erie that had set their destiny.

The floating population of "Canawlers" who lived and worked on the muddy ditch have left countless legends of the rough and riotous heyday of the Erie. Walter Edmonds, Harold W. Thompson, and others have summarized some of them in their books, including one memorable chant:

We were forty miles from Albany,
Forget it I never shall,
What a terrible storm we had one night
On the E-ri-e Canal.

Oh the E-ri-e was a-rising,
The gin was getting low;
And I scarcely think we'll get a drink
Till we get to Buffalo.

We were loaded down with barley,
We were chuck up full of rye;
And the Captain he looked down at me
With his goddam wicked eye.

Oh the girls are in the Police Gazette,
The crew are all in jail;
I'm the only living sea-cook's son
That's left to tell the tale.

LOCKPORT, NEW YORK, 1836. Lithograph by J. Bufford after a drawing by W. Wilson.

Everywhere along the route booming towns sprang up to tap the passing commerce. In 1821, according to a tourists' guide, Lockport had consisted of two houses. A few years later its five ascending and five descending locks, "the most stupendous work on the whole route," made it a key point on the

FORT ERIE FROM BUFFALO CREEK, SITE OF THE CITY OF BUFFALO, ABOUT 1810. Water-color drawing probably by Edward Walsh.

canal and a flourishing community. At the western terminal of the waterway Buffalo grew in the most phenomenal manner.

"Buffalo is one of the wonders of America," exclaimed Captain Marryat in 1839. "It is hardly to be credited that such a beautiful city could have risen up in the wilderness in so short a period. In the year 1814 it was burnt down, being then only a village; only one house was left standing, and now it is a city with twenty-five thousand inhabitants. . . . The city of Buffalo is remarkably well built; all the houses in the principal streets are lofty and substantial, and are either of brick or granite. The main street is wider and the stores handsomer than the majority of those in New York. It has five or six very fine churches, a handsome theatre, a town-hall, and market, and three or four hotels, one of which is superior to most others in America; and to those we must add a fine stone pier, with a light-house, a harbour full of shipping and magnificent steam-boats. It is almost incomprehensible, that all this should have been accomplished since the year 1814. And what has occasioned this springing up of a city in so short a time as to remind you of Alladin's magic palace? —the Erie Canal, which here joins the Hudson river with the lake, passing through the centre of the most populous and fertile states."

Commerce on Lake Erie, from Buffalo to and from the West, took on enormous importance. The incredulous Indians who lived along the shores of the lake had seen their first steamboat, the *Walk-in-the-Water*, in 1818. With the opening of the Erie, as Marryat observed, the lake swarmed with up-to-date steam vessels along with increasing clouds of sail. The Great Lakes formed a gigantic natural extension of New York's canal. When they were joined with the Mississippi River system the nation had a continuous network of waterways from New York to New Orleans and the Northwest.

The success of the Erie released a frenzy of canal building throughout the country. At one point America threatened to become a

The William L. Clements Library, University of Michigan

THE *Walk-in-the-Water*, DETROIT IN THE BACKGROUND, 1820. Gouache drawing by George W. Wistler.

Venice of interlocking waterways. Obstacles only tempted the audacity of inspired promoters. Pennsylvania did everything but make water run uphill. To complete its system of inland waterways canal boats were carried in sections for thirty-six and a half miles over mountains twenty-three hundred feet high by inclined planes between Hollidaysburg and Johnstown.

BUFFALO FROM LAKE ERIE, 1836. Aquatint by W. J. Bennett after a drawing by Hill.

The New-York Historical Society

CINCINNATI, 1835. Water color by J. C. Wild.

DETROIT, 1794. Water color by E. H.

Most of the new cuts opened fresh avenues to a population westward bent and to the eastbound products of the rich inland country. Ohio started to link the Great Lakes with the Mississippi by canals almost immediately after the completion of the Erie. Already flourishing, Cincinnati felt the canal's magic touch and boomed as never before. With an outlet in both directions it became a crossroads of an active traffic and a funnel for the farm produce of a wide area. "In March and April last," reported *Niles's Register* in 1831, "about 58,000 barrels of flour, 7,000 do. whiskey, 12,000 do. pork, 18,000 kegs of lard, 750 hhds. of hams and 1,800,000 lbs. bacon passed down the Miami Canal."

When the Erie Canal was opened Detroit was little more than a frontier fortress. The American flag had not been raised over the settlement until 1796 and, until it burned to the ground in 1805, it was only a small cluster of wooden buildings covering a few acres of ground and surrounded by a stockade. But it, too, was on the main route to the West and once the great migration started the little village, almost as old as Philadelphia, suddenly awoke from its long sleep.

A few years later Marryat noted that there still wasn't a paved street in Detroit. In winter the mud was knee-deep; in summer the dust obscured everything. As a consequence the inhabitants made their morning and evening calls in one-horse carts which backed up to the door of a house to receive its passengers and carried them to their destination where the cart was again backed up to the door to land the callers dry and clean. Nevertheless, concluded Marryat, Detroit would soon become one of the most up-to-date and flourishing cities of America. At Detroit in 1836, Harriet Martineau remarked that "thousands of settlers are pouring in every year; and of these, many are Irish, German, or Dutch, working their way into the back country, and glad to be employed for a while at Detroit, to earn money to carry them further." Cleveland, founded in 1796, was also an outpost one day, a great port the next.

DETROIT, 1836. Aquatint after a painting by W. J. Bennett.

The New-York Historical Society

PLAN OF JOHN FITCH'S STEAMBOAT. Engraving from the
Columbian Magazine, January, 1787.

STEAM IS UNION

Robert Fulton's journey up the Hudson River in 1807 in the *North River Steamboat of Clermont,* popularly known in later years as the *Clermont,* was by no means the first successful demonstration of a steamboat. His compatriots James Rumsey, Oliver Evans, John Stevens, and John Fitch, not to mention a list of European pioneers, had shown the way with earlier experiments. Fulton himself had demonstrated a steamboat on the Seine in France four years before his *Clermont* chugged its way from New York to Albany. Some earlier steamboats had "sailed" farther and faster. But Fulton's Hudson River trials were a practical success; they paid dividends. From that moment the evolution of steamboats proceeded in an unbroken curve of accomplishment. It was a turning point in history.

". . . steam," reported the New York *Mirror* during the early history of the invention, "—the tiny thread that sings from the spout of a tea-kettle, that rises from our cup of shaving-water, suddenly steps forth . . . and annihilates time and space. . . ."

Fulton's frail craft, laboring and fuming up the Hudson at the rate of five miles an hour "like the devil in a sawmill," hardly annihilated time and space. News of the craft's progress upriver traveled faster than the *Clermont.* But as time dragged on over the thirty-two hours it took to reach Albany, more and more jubilant witnesses came to the riverbanks to hail the successful voyage.

"What is this steam going to lead to?" asked the editor of the *Mirror.* "Till now, man has been bound to a single spot like an oyster, or a tree. . . . [Steam] is going to alter, in a degree far more remarkable than any previous change, the condition of mankind. . . . *Steam is union.* It connects minds. . . . It will diminish the size of the globe. . . . Human beings will become one single people, one nation, one mind, one heart. Mankind will see, feel, act together. *The vulgar,* the million, the cheated and oppressed people, will be as united on great questions of general interest as were the Spartans at Thermopylae, or the Americans at Bunker Hill." Steamboats did not quite reach those advanced goals. But they did, within a relatively few years, reach almost every point in the nation where a few feet of water would take them.

From the start Fulton provided extravagant arrangements for his fares. The *Paragon,* his third Hudson River boat, was a spectacle of wonder to the Russian visitor, Paul Svinin. Its large and elegant sections, one for men, another for women, its dining saloon that daily accommodated one hundred and fifty persons, its kitchen where the cooking was done by steam, and its quarters for the crew, were all astonishing. "Gleaming silver and bronze, shining mirrors and mahogany are everywhere, and the most fasti-

ROBERT FULTON'S STEAMBOAT . . . KNOWN AS THE *Clermont*, PASSING WEST POINT, NEW YORK, ABOUT 1810. Lithograph by de F. Berthaux, Dijon, France, after a sketch by Charles Balthasar Julien Fevret de Saint-Mémin.

FULTON'S *Paragon*, 1811-1813. Water color by Svinin.

The New-York Historical Society
STEAMBOAT LANDING, NEW YORK CITY, 1830. Sepia drawing by Charles Burton.

dious person of the most refined taste can find here everything to his liking," wrote Svinin. "... the best wines, all manner of dainties, and even ice-cream in the hot season ... everywhere there are comfortable seats which lure the passengers thither. . . . It is a perfect masquerade where everybody is at home, where everybody is master for his money. . . . It is . . . a whole floating town!" For a public unfamiliar with such luxury Fulton posted regulations admonishing the passengers to remove their boots before lying down in the berths, not to sit on the tables, and otherwise to show due regard for propriety and the fittings under pain of a fine.

With such attractions steamboating caught the public fancy almost at once. "The amount of travel from one important commercial place to another in our country," noted a New York editor in 1827, "has lately increased to an astonishing degree. . . . The bringing of such a number of steamboats on that [the Hudson] river seems to have multiplied rather than diminished the number of passengers in each. Every new boat is immediately filled, and yet the decks of the old ones seem only to swarm with additional numbers." At least one hundred steamboats were on the river by 1840. It was a profitable traffic for the lines that could survive the competition.

Rate wars between competing companies were at times so fierce that the fare from New York to Albany once dropped to ten cents; at another point nothing at all was charged for passage, although meals were extra. Agents for the different lines so earnestly pressed their business at the steamboat landings that sometimes a traveler went by one line and his luggage, grabbed by a runner for a competing line, went by another.

Within a very few years of the *Clermont's* first run, steamboats had ventured out from the protected river courses into the relatively open water of Long Island Sound, Chesapeake Bay, and the Great Lakes. As early as 1809 the *Phoenix,* built by John Stevens of Hoboken, took to the ocean on a short but dangerous trip around Sandy Hook and down the New Jersey coast to the Delaware. By the year 1900, it was early prophesied, steam vessels *might* be crossing the Atlantic under their own power.

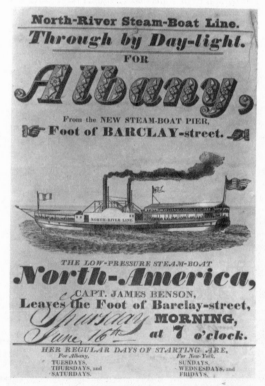

The Harry Shaw Newman Gallery
STEAMBOAT ADVERTISEMENT.

PORTLAND PIER, LAKE ERIE. Painting by George Harvey, about 1840.

THE LADIES' SALOON IN THE LONG ISLAND SOUND S.S. *Atlantic*, ABOUT 1846. Lithograph by G. & W. Endicott.

Iron Witch, BUILT 1844. Painting by J. V. Cornell.

Unlike the steamboats on western rivers those on the Hudson and Sound carried little freight beyond baggage and express goods. Speed and comfort were their primary attractions and it was in facilitating travel that they served their major purpose. As an alternative to the stagecoach, whose service was fairly regular but definitely uncomfortable, and to the river and sound sloops, which were comfortable enough but at the mercy of tide and wind, the steamboat offered the advantages of both its rivals with none of the disadvantages.

The Hudson River, lordly, picturesque, and strategic, rich with history and legend, provided a magnificent natural highway leading far into the interior of the country. Captain Marryat thought it was "incomparably more beautiful" than the Rhine; it was as he imagined the Rhine to have been in Caesar's day. To the distinguished Swedish spinster, Fredrika Bremer, the Hudson recalled the Dala and Angerman rivers of her native land, "excepting it was broader and on a larger scale." Its very size, however, was an obstacle to cross-traffic that had to cope with wind and currents. The shorter the distance to be covered the more vital, proportionately, was dependable, scheduled service. Steam ferries removed a serious uncertainty from travel and transportation between New England and the South.

Within less than a generation after Fulton's pioneer voyage the Hudson had become a thoroughfare teeming with steam traffic. "Now come the steamboats," wrote Miss Bremer in 1849, as she watched the panorama from Newburgh, "thundering like tempests among the hills. Two or three chase each other like brilliant meteors; two others plow along, working heavily, laboring and puffing, and pulling a whole fleet of larger and smaller craft. The little town of Newburgh alone maintains, by its trade from the country back of it, two or three steamboats. When one sees the number and magnificence of the Hudson steamers, one can scarcely believe the facts. . . ."

THE HUDSON RIVER *S.S. St. John*, 1864. Lithograph by Currier and Ives after F. F. Palmer.

WEST POINT FROM THE FERRY LANDING AT PHILLIPSTOWN, NEW YORK. ABOUT 1858. Lithograph by an unidentified artist.

THE DAY BOAT ON THE HUDSON RIVER. From *Harper's Weekly.*

The Metropolitan Museum of Art

SALOON OF THE *S.S. Drew.* Lithograph by J. N. Allan.

The New-York Historical Society

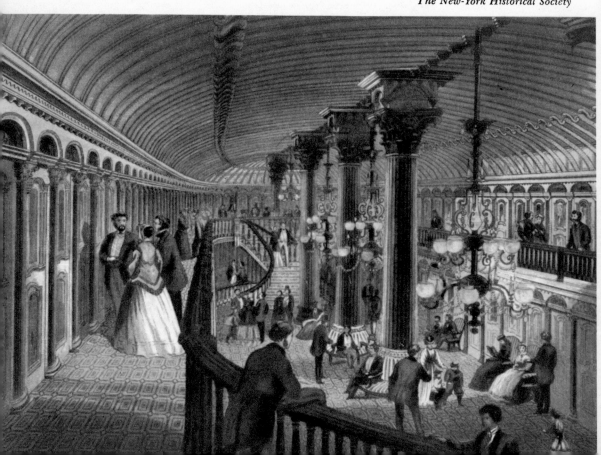

The Hudson River steamboats held an irresistible lure for all manner of travelers, from the earnest young Horace Greeley who strained his ten dollars-a-week budget to take a Sunday excursion, to the abandoned women who, moralists warned, "literally overran the night liners to Albany." Long after the railroads had opened a faster route along the shore the steamboats plied up and down the magnificent valley with heavy pay loads of enthusiastic passengers. In the year 1851 nearly a million people patronized the river steamers. Six years later the *New World*, "a gigantic specimen of steamboat architecture," carried one thousand persons up the river on a single trip.

Even to a generation inured to almost daily triumphs of its material civilization, "the grandest palace drawing room steamers in the world" that appeared on the river during the forties and fifties held fresh wonders. Their slim, sharp, glistening white hulls, topped by high superstructures with generous deck space for sight-seers, were two and three time the length of Fulton's pioneering *Clermont*.

The *New World* was three hundred and seventy-one feet long with a thirty-five-foot beam, and rival vessels were often not a great deal smaller. Newspapers referred to "our mile-long steamers" that were cutting up and down the river at amazing speeds, hitting well over twenty miles an hour when the race was on against time or a rival claimant for the record. The *South America* made one trip in 1843 from Albany to New York in seven hours and twenty-one minutes. The press called such vessels the "fastest boats in the world" and more than one handsome craft blew up or burned down in the process of trying to prove it.

The elegance of the interiors of those fleet leviathans taxed description. The ornate woodwork of the *Drew*, finished in white and gold, its rich upholstery and carpeting, elaborate gas chandeliers, and spacious "grand stairway," with its band "pervading the atmosphere with the strains of musical renditions of culture, harmony, and pleasurable rhythm"—its all but indescribable splendor —spread the vessel's fame to far lands. Here, truly, democracy had its palace.

THE STEAMBOATS *Drew* AND *St. John* OF THE PEOPLE'S EVENING LINE, BUILT IN 1860 AND 1863 RESPECTIVELY. Lithograph by Currier and Ives, 1878, after C. R. Parsons.

The New-York Historical Society

THE STEAMBOAT
ON WESTERN WATERS

With his magnificent plans for steamboating, Robert Fulton, like "Poor John" Fitch before him, had his eye on the vast waterways of the Mississippi River system. Nowhere in the world was there such a field of promise for the new invention. As Mark Twain appraised it, the Mississippi carried to the Gulf of Mexico the water of fifty-four subordinate rivers, draining a basin larger than the combined areas of Spain, Portugal, Germany, Austria, Italy, and Turkey. To that interior empire the Mississippi was, in James Madison's words, "everything ... the Hudson, the Delaware, the Potomac, and all the navigable rivers of the Atlantic States, formed into one stream."

In the estimation of Mark Twain, however, that one stream was by all odds the longest, the crookedest, and the most inconstant of all rivers. Fulton's deep-hulled boats were impractical in its turbulent currents and unpredictable channels. In 1816 when Henry Shreve, an experienced bargeman, developed a vessel with a flat hull, a high-pressure engine installed on the main deck, and another deck above for additional carrying space, a distinctive Mississippi steamboat had appeared. Those essential characteristics have never been changed. In 1827 Mrs. Trollope, arriving at the mouth of the Mississippi, saw innumerable such "fly waggons" of the rivers, totally unlike any she had seen in Europe, "and greatly superior to them," she added with rare charity. They most resembled, she thought, the floating baths at Paris. Their appearance was far less important than the fact that at the very beginning they could travel from New Orleans to Louisville and beyond, against the current and over all but the shallowest spots, in far less than half the time of a keelboat.

A WESTERN STEAMBOAT, 1832. Lithograph by Bénard, Paris, France, after a painting by A. St. Aulaire.
Kennedy & Co.

MAP SHOWING THE BASIN OF THE MISSISSIPPI. From William C. Woodbridge, *School Atlas*, 1843.

Collection of Joseph Verner Reed

CAIRO, ILLINOIS, 1838, ALLEGEDLY THE "EDEN" THAT LURED DICKENS'S MARTIN CHUZZLEWIT INTO THE WILDERNESS. Painting by Antonio Mendelli. The only objection to the site of Cairo, according to one contemporary of Dickens, arose from the fact that "it was subject to inundation at times."

Two years after Shreve's *Enterprise* made its pioneering journey up the Mississippi in 1815 it was exultantly claimed in Kentucky that "the Steam Boats have brought N. Orleans to our doors." Goods that had been sweated by road over the Alleghenies at the cost of five to eight dollars were soon being shipped from Philadelphia via New Orleans by steamboat for one dollar. Steamboat building quickly developed into a major business in the West. "The invention of the steamboat was intended for us," declared the Cincinnati *Gazette* in 1815. "The puny rivers of the East are only as creeks, or convenient waters on which experiments may be made for our advantage."

Those who plodded their weary way across the mountains to the West increasingly took to the new craft once they reached the western rivers. With their passion for clearing the wilderness and turning up fresh soil Americans were flocking into the Mississippi Valley at a formidable rate. Out there, the legend ran, the squash vines grew so fast they were known to chase droves of squealing hogs more than half a mile through the fields while the earth thundered under their weight. Watching the hordes of purposeful emigrants pouring through Pittsburgh towards that promised land, Henry Schoolcraft concluded that "they meant, in their generation, to plough the Mississippi Valley from its head to its foot. There was not an idea short of it. What a world of golden dreams was there!" According to the *Western Messenger* in 1836 the human multitudes that crowded every conveyance down the Ohio from Cincinnati were as thickly wedged as the wild pigeons that blackened the skies overhead—"their forest resting-places, stripped of foliage and beechnuts, and broken down by their innumerable company, afford a happy analogy to the hotels and inns, whose dining tables are swept clean, and whose dormitories are crammed full with the ever-swelling torrent from the traveling caravans."

The steam packets that carried their share of the migrant hosts wherever the water would float a shallow hull created their own legends. Rather than build up steam for enough speed to keep ahead, one captain of an Ohio River packet, for example, turned his helm to let a streak of lightning pass his boat—a little shamefacedly, to be sure. As always there was more than a hint of real meaning in the tall tale. The heaviest-muscled keelboatmen rarely pushed the one thousand three hundred and fifty miles from New Orleans to Louisville in less than three months' time. In 1853 the steamboat *Eclipse* made the upstream trip in four days, nine hours, and thirty minutes.

There was still room on the great river for all kinds of craft. Almost three thousand flatboats drifted into New Orleans in 1846—

The Mariners' Museum, Newport News, Virginia
FERRY FROM ILLINOIS TOWN TO ST. LOUIS, 1832. Detail from a lithograph by Becker after a painting by Leon Pomarede.

an all-time record. But by then Mississippi steamboats were already carrying ten million tons of freight—nearly double the foreign commerce of the United States—up and down the river. They went on, for another decade or two, to greater activity and glory. The man-powered craft retreated to the remote, shallow upstream reaches and slowly disappeared.

THE EXPRESS LINE PACKET *Prairie State*. Lithograph by O. Becker.
The Mariners' Museum, Newport News, Virginia

The New-York Historical Society
FRONT STREET, ST. LOUIS, 1840. Lithograph by J. C.
Wild. (Detail.)

At the crossroads of the Mississippi system St. Louis was able to levy a toll on the river trade in all directions. After the *Yellowstone's* pioneering trip up the Missouri in 1823, steamboats poked ever farther into the back country until in 1859 one vessel came within fifteen miles of Fort Benton, three thousand five hundred and sixty miles from the sea. Furs from the Northwest, annuities to the Indians, Mormon exiles, military personnel and supplies, emigrants, gold seekers —first California bound, then for Montana— all found space on the Missouri River boats; and St. Louis was the terminal of the traffic. Manufactures, hogs, grain, and other produce arrived from Ohio and Illinois river ports for transshipment. "All these advantages combine to make [St. Louis] a place of

great trade," wrote F. B. Mayer in 1851. "It's inhabitants . . . all wear the anxious & care worn looks of 'men of business.' " Almost always, Mayer added, nearly one hundred steamboats could be counted on the levee, "taking in and discharging freight, letting off steam, & pushing out or arriving. . . . There is probably no busier scene in America in the same space. For two miles a forest of smoke stacks is seen towering above the 'arks' from which they seem to grow. All between this and the line of warehouses is filled with a dense mass of apparently inextricable confusion & bustle, noise & animation. More steamboats are probably seen here than at any port in the world . . . ."

In the rivalry between the Atlantic ports and New Orleans for the western trade, Cincinnati occupied a strategic place with convenient outlet in either direction, down the Ohio or by way of the Erie Canal. The downriver route was long favored for bulkier products destined for the east coast. At one time eighty per cent of the pork and grain from Cincinnati went down the Ohio. The long line of steamboats and the masses of merchandise piled on the levee were a sign of the "Queen City's" flourishing prosperity. Dickens remarked that it had risen out of the forests like an Arabian Nights city. Even Mrs. Trollope was impressed by the activity along its waterfront. "Its landing is a notable place," she wrote, "extending for more than

A SECTION OF THE CINCINNATI WATERFRONT, 1848. Daguerreotype by Fontayne and Porter.

The Historical and Philosophical Society of Ohio

THE STEAMBOAT *Charles Carroll*, BUILT IN 1846 (?). Engraving.

a quarter of a mile. . . . I have seen fifteen steamboats lying there at once and still half the wharf was unoccupied." In 1848 more than four thousand steamboats arrived at Cincinnati during the twelve months.

Boats, large and small, were fitted up with comforts and conveniences to attract the excursion trade. Parties were often formed for a festive journey down the Beautiful River and past the varied sights along the lower Mississippi which were so pleasantly strange to northern eyes. "Our river boats," explained Charles Wessen, "are quite as comfortable as . . . a first rate hotel. You will have a large bar for refreshment—also a hair dressers and shaving store (first rate and no mistake)." The *Charles Carroll,* he wrote of the vessel shown in the accompanying illustration, "trades to New Orleans from this port [Cincinnati?], a distance of 1400 miles . . . [she] can accomodate 600 passengers. . . . The engines . . . burn nothing but wood, you can see one of the firemen taking some wood from a large pile marked *X*. . . . The windows between the two decks are bed rooms. The door marked *O* leads from the saloon, for those who wish may walk under the veranda."

The Cincinnati Public Library

RED RIVER CARTS FROM FORT GARRY, 1845-50. Painting by Paul Kane.

The Minneapolis Institute of Arts
THE GORGE OF THE ST. CROIX RIVER, 2100 MILES FROM NEW ORLEANS, 1847. Detail from a painting by Henry Lewis.

Steamboats were also feeling their way far out into the back-country fringe of the river system, searching for cargo and transporting a fabulous assortment of humanity. Before the Civil War more than forty tributaries of the Mississippi River had been navigated by steamboats.

When the *Virginia* puffed up to Fort Snelling in 1823 a new era had opened for the far North. Each spring in the years that followed, a caravan of ox-drawn carts, loaded with the spoils of the hunt, lumbered from the Red River colonies near the Canadian border down to the head of navigation. The Red River carts were made entirely of wood and rawhide, with no metal. On still days the creaking of their wheels sounded a cacophony that could be heard for miles. A single file of one hundred and twenty carts pulled into St. Paul, which replaced Fort Snelling as an entrepôt, on July 10, 1847, and by 1858 about six hundred were arriving at that city each year. Until well after the Civil War steamboats offered the quickest and cheapest outlet for those isolated, northern posts, carrying away their furs, lead, and grain and bringing, in exchange, tobacco, alcohol, manufactured and other goods.

More than two thousand miles down the river and a world apart from the northern headwaters, the New Orleans levees were handling a huge share of the river traffic. Before the railroads were built alarmed Easterners feared that the southern city might drain off not only the sugar and cotton from its own back yard, but, as well, all the precious trade of the whole western continent. In 1832 steamboats were "arriving and departing every hour," wrote one observer at the levees, and for about a decade to come the gay, exotic, and rapidly growing city was the first port of the nation in the value of its exports. At one point the steam tonnage on western waters exceeded that of the entire British merchant marine and New Orleans was the financial and commercial emporium of the trade.

The Bland Gallery, Inc.

A SCENE ALONG THE LOWER MISSISSIPPI, 1883. Detail from a painting by William Aiken Walker.

SUGAR LEVEE, NEW ORLEANS, 1853. Painting by Hippolyte Victor Valentin Sebron.

Tulane University

"WOODING UP" ON THE MISSISSIPPI, 1861. Lithograph by Currier and Ives after F. F. Palmer.

For long, sometimes picturesque, sometimes weary miles thick forests grew right down to the banks of western rivers. Only a small part of the cargo capacity of the vessel had to be reserved for fuel since most steamboats took on wood twice daily. During a long journey "wooding up" provided an interesting pause for the passengers. On the wild reaches of the upper Missouri, Indian

The Metropolitan Museum of Art
ON BOARD A RIVER STEAMER, PLAYING AT "SEVEN UP," 1870. Engraving after a drawing by A. B. Houghton.

hostilities made wood hawking a perilous trade. The log of one steamboat in 1868 recorded: "Found seven woodchoppers and their dog murdered at a woodyard at Round Butte." Later, Indians found it more rewarding to go into the business themselves. To the south, along the Mississippi the hazards from Indian violence were few. But, reported Mrs. Trollope, woodcutters there still had the assurance of early death. "Only a miserable cow and a few pigs, standing knee-deep in the water," she wrote, distinguish the huts of the more prosperous of the ague-ridden, dropsical tribe. Cordwood actually became an important cash crop of farmers living along the rivers.

Every vessel carried a cross section of humanity, people of many tongues and several colors traveling with a great variety of purposes. The unhappy custom of separating the gentlemen's and ladies' saloons on some vessels, wrote one European, reduced the men "to their own devices for amusement . . . playing cards, drinking, chewing tobacco, smoking, talking politics, or . . . the

240

THE STEAMBOAT ON WESTERN WATERS

idle employment of whittling." (Whittling the furniture or the woodwork of the ship was in most cases, however, specifically forbidden.)

From moment to moment of its endless life the river was making prodigious jumps across necks of land, radically changing the relative positions of towns and landmarks. It moved sidewise, bodily, so shifting its course that, as Mark Twain put it, the whole thirteen hundred miles which La Salle floated down was, two hundred years later, solid dry land. It built up islands that moved upstream as the current of the muddy water added here, subtracted there, to and from a deposit of earth. The land seemed to flow in a ceaseless counterpoint to the river. Whole trees, islands of trees, and parts of trees—trees that lurked just beneath the surface and others that floated as tall obstructions—vagrant currents, enormous whirlpools, shallow rapids, widespread floods, everything that nature could contrive to tax the skill

The Metropolitan Museum of Art
THE PILOT-HOUSE OF A MISSISSIPPI STEAMBOAT. Illustration from Edward W. King, *The Great South*, 1875.

and nerve of the navigator gave the Mississippi its character as a "wicked river." In order to be a Mississippi steamboat pilot, concluded Mark Twain, "a man had got to learn more than any one man ought to be allowed to know; and . . . he must learn it all over again in a different way every twenty four hours."

SNAGS ON THE MISSOURI RIVER, 1833. Aquatint after Bodmer. From Maximilian, Prince of Wied, *Atlas*. For other examples of Bodmer's work see Chapter II.

The New York Public Library

Western steamboats varied from "the very filthiest of all filthy old rat-traps" to those floating worlds in miniature whose elegance "bordered on magnificence." When he stepped on board one of the latter, wrote Mark Twain, the traveler "entered a new and marvelous world . . . inside, a far-receding snow-white 'cabin'; porcelain knob and oil-picture on every stateroom door; curving patterns of filigree-work touched up with gilding, stretching overhead all down the converging vista; big chandeliers every little way, each an April shower of glittering glass-drops; lovely rainbow light falling everywhere from the colored glazing of the skylight; the whole a long-drawn, resplendent tunnel, a bewildering and soul-satisfying spectacle!"

When trips may have lasted for many days or even several weeks, a good table was an important consideration. On the better boats the richness and variety of food served to the cabin passengers in a multiplicity of badly balanced courses was the ruination of tender digestions. In general, travelers' guides warned against overeating from the abundant fare that customarily faced the passenger at mealtimes. On the squalid lower deck and at any level in the lesser boats, no such caution was necessary.

During the years that eastern ports watched the record runs of their clippers with breathless expectancy the Mississippi Valley waged its separate war against time. A race between two celebrated rivals, announced weeks in advance, brought the whole valley to "a state of consuming excitement." People lined the riverbanks by firelight to cheer their champions through the night—and waited anxiously, sometimes for long days after, to learn the result of a race. Mark Twain pictured the spectacle in all its brilliance—the "fairy palaces" with their chimney tops, cut to counterfeit a spraying crown of plumes, pouring out a sable roof of smoke from "furnaces crammed rosin and pine," starting off into the great river under a tremendous pent-up head of steam that shrieked through safety valves; stately ships, stripped of every possible encumbrance and "trimmed" down to the hair of the steamboatman, which was parted in the middle with a spirit level, whistling by the shore like the wind. The nation still remembers the great race of 1870 when the *R. E. Lee* beat the *Natchez* from New Orleans to St. Louis in 3 days, 18 hours, 30 minutes.

Steamboating had already had its heyday when the *R. E. Lee* raced to glory. Railroads were converging upon the Mississippi and Missouri Rivers from numerous parts of the East, leaping the water over remarkable bridges to continue across the rest of the continent, and reducing "the leviathan artery of the North American continent" to a feeder of the railways. Before the bridges were built it was the steamboat's sacrificial gesture to carry the life line for its rival across the river.

The Missouri Historical Society
INTERIOR OF THE STEAMBOAT *Grand Republic*, 1867.
Photograph by E. Boehl.

"Champions of the Mississippi," 1866. Lithograph by Currier and Ives after F. F. Palmer.

The Steamboats *Denver* and *Colorado* Unloading Material for the Union Pacific Railroad at Omaha, 1869.

THE RAILROAD

On one of his river trips it seemed to Mark Twain that the boat might as well have gone by land, the way it clambered over reefs and snags along the river bed. There were steamboats on western waters, others boasted, that needed only a heavy dew to float them on their way. Lacking dew the suds of a keg of beer tapped over the side would moisten the keel enough for a long voyage. But steamboats still stayed within the river beds.

The railroads knew no such weakness. As early as 1813 Oliver Evans of Philadelphia was forecasting steam-driven carriages traveling over their own selected routes, "almost as fast as birds fly, fifteen or twenty miles an hour"; traveling on double tracks so that the "carriages . . . may pass each other in different directions, and travel by night as well as by day; and the passengers will sleep in the stages as comfortably as they now do in steam boats." Evans's own early invention, the amazing *Orukter Amphibolos*, or amphibious digger as he called it, steamed along over land and water alike.

Not many shared Evans's vision. Neither national nor state governments thus early considered the possible developments im-

portant enough to justify their encouragement or attention. That the public interest might be deeply involved was beyond consideration. Yet within a lifetime the railroads were affecting American life at countless points. They were underwriting the development of the country and the private organizations which controlled them exercised more power than had any other group in the history of the nation. We had, as Thoreau remarked, constructed a fate that would spin the thread of our destiny. It peopled the country where the oxcart and steamboat left off. It played a large part in the development of the iron and steel industry. It helped determine the growth of agriculture. It heavily influenced the outcome of the Civil War. It "greased the way for big business and high finance," and played an important rôle in national politics. It was, indeed, the typical achievement of the age.

Even more important, perhaps, it shaped a way of thinking. To follow a train of thought was no mere figure of speech. To do things "railroad fashion" became the byword. Thoreau was surprised that even his more dilatory neighbors caught the train to

The Worcester Art Museum, Goodspeed Collection

AN EARLY RAILROAD. Lithograph by Pendleton after a drawing by David Claypoole Johnston, 1826. Granite blocks for building the Bunker Hill monument were hauled from the quarry to tidewater over one of the first roads in this country to use iron rails.

Boston. Railroads were as punctual and as inexorable as the fates. When the bell rang the people learned to be at the station. "Getting left," that colloquialism of a timetable era, was a privation few would endure. "Thus," wrote Henry David Thoreau, "one well conducted institution regulates a whole country."

Following a much earlier English precedent, the first American railroads were intended for horse-drawn cars. They were designed simply as mechanically improved turnpikes. As contemporary encyclopedias pointed out, they were "a species of road or carriage way, in which the tracks of the carriage wheel being laid with bars or rails of wood, stone, or metal, the carriage runs with so much greater facility that one horse will perform the work of many."

Before the practicability of steam locomotion had been thoroughly demonstrated in America the Baltimore and Ohio Company had built twenty-five miles of roadbed over which cars had been successfully propelled by horses, a manually turned winch, a sail, a steam locomotive, and in one experiment, by two dogs. Horses, either between shafts or operating a treadmill, remained for a while the favorite source of power. They cost little, carried their own fuel, and gave off no sparks.

Several such roads were laid during the early years of the nineteenth century. But the subject of steam railroads won public interest slowly. "When we reflect upon the obstinate opposition that has been made by a great majority to every step toward improvement," wrote Evans in 1812, ". . . it is too much to expect the monstrous leap from bad roads to railways for steam carriages, at once."

The Harry Shaw Newman Gallery
BUZZARD'S ROCK ON THE ROUTE OF THE B. & O. R. R. Lithograph by Endicott and Swett, 1831.

The Harry Shaw Newman Gallery
A LOCOMOTIVE ON THE BALTIMORE AND OHIO R. R.
Lithograph by Endicott and Swett, 1831.

The York engine designed and built by Phineas Davis, probably the one illustrated in the left column, won a contest staged by the B. & O. in 1831 for the best steam locomotive. It successfully hauled four cars weighing fifteen tons up hills and around curves and, by itself, ran at twenty miles an hour. It was not the first or only conclusive demonstration but for some years to follow, horses continued on the tracks of most railroads.

The Pioneer Fast Line advertised it would carry passengers by rail and canal from Philadelphia to Pittsburgh in four days, and often nearly kept its word. Two daily lines of horse-drawn cars left from the door of Third Street Hall, which was erected in 1834 for the accommodation of travelers and others at the Philadelphia end of the line. This "elegant and commodious establishment," with its "105 rooms, numerous private parlours and bath rooms, where travellers can be accommodated with hot or cold

RAILWAY CAR OF THE "PIONEER FAST LINE" TO PITTSBURGH. From *Atkinson's Casket*, 1834.
The New-York Historical Society

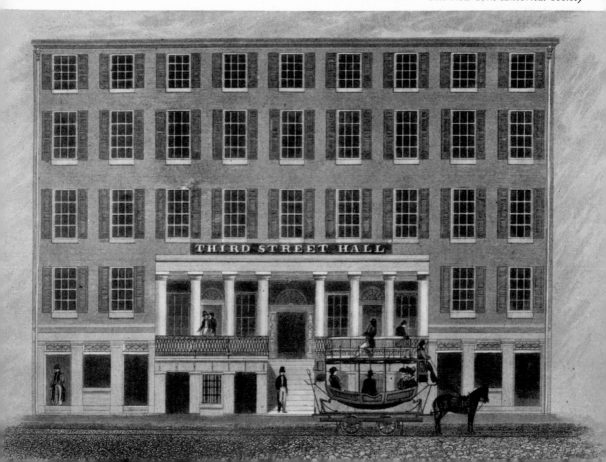

The Museum of Science and Industry, Chicago

AN EARLY LOCOMOTIVE, POSSIBLY INTENDED TO REPRESENT THE "TOM THUMB," DRAWING A "BRIGADE" OF CARS, ABOUT 1830. Engraving by Alexander Robb.

baths at all hours," was a hotel of the new order. Such an increase in facilities, both for transportation and comfort, reported *Atkinson's Casket*, "staggered belief."

"A number of persons visited Monument Square yesterday," reported a Baltimore newspaper in 1830, "for the purpose of examining a very elegant railroad passenger carriage just finished by Mr. Imlay, and intended to be placed immediately upon the road. . . . The body of the carriage will contain about twelve passengers and the outside seats at each end will receive six, including the driver. On the top of the carriage is placed a double sofa, running lengthwise,

which will accomodate twelve more. . . . The whole is surmounted by an iron framework with an awning to protect from the sun or rain. The carriage which is named the 'Ohio' is very handsomely finished and will, we have no doubt, be a great favorite with visitors to the railroad."

Early experiments exposed travelers to the hazards of showering sparks, boiler explosions, collisions, and violently jolting progress. The barrier car of cotton bales, to act as a cushion in case of accident, and the brass band for diversion, which the *West Point* pulled in its "brigade," were planned to protect and reassure the passengers.

The Smithsonian Institution

THE "WEST POINT," THE SECOND LOCOMOTIVE BUILT IN AMERICA, ON THE CHARLESTON AND HAMBURG ROAD, 1830-1831. From William H. Brown, *The History of the First Locomotive in America*, 1871.

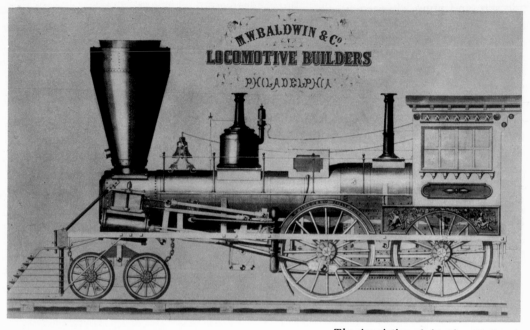

BALDWIN PASSENGER LOCOMOTIVE; TYPE USED IN 1853.

The Association of American Railroads

The Harry Shaw Newman Gallery
ANNOUNCEMENT, 1849.

Demonstrations, each one improving on the last, quickly disclosed the practicability of the locomotive although resistance was stern in some quarters. Turnpike and canal operators, tavern keepers and freight handlers, farmers and the timid of heart, all felt their interests threatened by a shift to steam locomotion. To travel at a speed of fifteen or twenty miles an hour, protested some, was in itself a sinful deviation from the Lord's plan for mankind. The extent to which public enthusiasm was excited might be measured by the "alarmed complaint," part prophecy, part humor, that appeared in one newspaper in 1830: "It will set the whole world a-gadding. . . . Grave plodding citizens will be flying about like comets. All local attachments will be at an end. It will encourage flightiness of intellect. Veracious people will turn into the most immeasurable liars. All conceptions will be exaggerated by the magnificent notions of distance. . . . It will upset all the gravity of the nation. . . . Upon the whole, sir, it is a pestilential, topsy-turvy, harum-scarum whirligig. . . . None of your hop skip and jump whimsies for me." But more stood to gain than to lose by the success of the railroad.

Railroads were not an American invention, but their development in this country was special and independent. Distances were vast, mountain grades and sharp curves were unavoidable, wood for fuel was abundant and cheap, and Americans were in an inordinate hurry to "get there." The massive, rigidly constructed English engines, admirable though they were but suited to relatively straight and level roads, could not operate satisfactorily under American conditions. Swivel trucks, or track feelers, in the front to ease the locomotive around bends in the road, balloon stacks accommodated to wood-burning furnaces, and paired driving wheels on either side of the engine evolved as distinctive features of the American locomotive.

Improvement was constant and rapid and the engines grew steadily larger. "When in the thirties a locomotive collided with a cow, the locomotive had to be sent to the repair shop; in the forties, the company had to pay for the cow." The losses in both cases caused the development of the elaborate "cow catchers."

Once committed to the idea of steam locomotion America turned to railroad building with uninhibited zeal. Over thirty thousand miles of track were laid before the Civil War. Capital resources in the early days were limited and construction had to be speedy to satisfy the temper of the people as well as their rapidly growing needs; there was never time to lose and much ground had to be covered. To one European, at least, the American locomotive seemed a "crazy affair, as loose-jointed as a basket"; to another it seemed "the incarnate spirit of opportunism." So with the wooden bridges that often seemed hastily and cheaply contrived. Time would not wait for costly, permanent structures at the start. No European crossed over the ingenious, inflammable, and swaying wooden trestles that so casually spanned rivers and gorges without a muttered prayer. Speed, not safety, was the goal; "Go ahead," not "All right," was the slogan, of American railroads.

TRESTLE BRIDGE ON THE BALTIMORE AND OHIO RAILROAD NEAR CUMBERLAND, MD. Built by Wendel Bollman, 1857. The locomotive is No. 56 built by William Mason and put in service in 1856. Photograph courtesy of the Association of American Railroads.

The Baltimore and Ohio Railroad

TRAVEL ON A PLANK ROAD, ABOUT 1850. Engraving from a bank note.

For a few years of the mid-century the waning interest in turnpikes was given a brief boost by the introduction, via Russia and Canada, of sawed lumber surfaces—the so-called plank roads. The sensation when riding upon a plank road was described as "similar to that of riding in a sleigh when the sleighing is good. But 'the going' on a plank road is always good . . . without regard to weather." "The railroad," reported one magazine, "is the thoroughfare for the citizen away from home—for travel; but the plank road is for home use." They were, without doubt, the smoothest highways built in America until the advent of the asphalt and concrete roads of recent years. But experience proved that depreciation was prohibitively rapid and by 1857, after a period of intense promotion, the idea was discarded.

The railroad's great influence as a binding force was not felt immediately. Like most of the first improved highways the early railroads were planned to attract trade from the surrounding countryside into the individual cities, rather than to connect separate regions. Independent operators used different-gauge tracks to discourage rivals from connecting with their lines. The average length of the first ninety-five roads was barely forty-one miles.

The early railroads offered few of the creature comforts so lavishly provided by contemporary steamboats. Even native

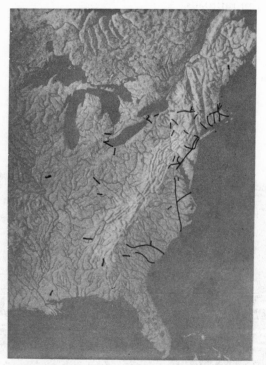
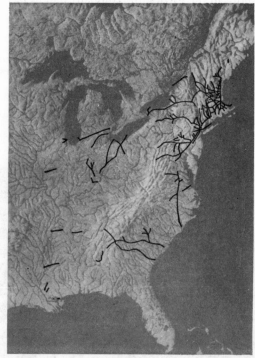

RAILROADS IN OPERATION, 1840 and 1850. From Clifford and Elizabeth H. Lord, *Historical Atlas of the United States.*

The Harry Shaw Newman Gallery

"THE EXPRESS TRAIN," REPRESENTING A SCENE ON THE BOSTON AND ALBANY RAILROAD IN 1842. Lithograph by Currier and Ives.

Americans toughened to the rigors of overland travel in the new country objected to being treated as "live lumber" in dirty, overcrowded, ill-equipped cars. As usual, visiting foreigners were more critical. "There is a great deal of jolting, a great deal of noise, a great deal of wall, not much window, a locomotive engine, a shriek, and a bell," wrote Dickens, describing an American railroad in 1842. "The cars are like shabby omnibusses, but larger: holding thirty, forty, fifty people. The seats, instead of stretching from end to end, are placed crosswise."

The fixed principle of one-class travel, that obliged visiting gentlemen to travel in close quarters with any of the democratic rabble that had the fare, added indignity to discomfort and to what most of them felt was downright danger. In 1836 Harriet Martineau had thirteen holes burned in her gown by cinders during a brief trip.

By 1850 over nine thousand miles of track had been laid, the roads were becoming systematized, and through trains were piercing the East in all directions. The revolution in the life of the country which the railroads were to accomplish was implicit in what had already been done. The West was as yet untouched by the iron rails, but there was already talk of uniting the world, by a system of railroads, under the leadership of the United States.

Whatever its immediate shortcomings the railroad lastingly captured the imagination of America during the 1830's and '40's. It held the key to the future in which Americans preferred to live and dream. It was, as Whitman pronounced it, the "type of the modern! emblem of motion and power! pulse of the continent!" It symbolized the march of progress and promised to conquer the distances that lay between impatient man and his goal. Its "fierce-throated beauty" was a challenge to time. The principal memory one French traveler had of his trip across the Atlantic in an American packet, during which he was continuously and miserably seasick, was of having heard the word railroad mentioned at least once every ten minutes. When he landed he discovered that there was "a perfect mania" on the subject in the New World.

A COACH ON THE BALTIMORE AND OHIO, 1861. From the *London Illustrated News.*

The American railroad coach quickly evolved from a carriage-like vehicle into the basic type which persists today. By the time the change was completed, Americans traveled everywhere, whether by canal boat, steamer, or train, in long, narrow saloons, often literally rubbing shoulders with their fellow travelers. "In the centre of the carriage," wrote Dickens of the railroad coach in which he traveled, "there is usually a stove, fed with charcoal or anthracite coal, which is for the most part red-hot. It is insufferably close; and you see the hot air fluttering between yourself and any other object you happen to look at, like the ghost of smoke. . . . The conductor, or check-taker, or guard, or whatever he may be, wears no uniform. He walks up and down the car, and in and out of it, as his fancy dictates; leans against the door with his hands in his pockets and stares at you . . . or enters into conversation with the passengers about him."

As trains equipped with headlights covered ever greater distances by night as well as by day, the problem of passenger comfort got the close attention of rival railroad companies eager for the travel trade. The democratic notion that every traveler was entitled to a fair measure of comfort played hand in glove with an enthusiasm for patent furniture that developed in the 1850's. The standard of comfortable coach travel, with fully adjustable seats, that was set at an early date persists today at a level no other country has rivaled.

"Distances are long in America," wrote Trollope, "and he who declines to travel by night will lose very much time." Everything in the country, he added, "is done by a new and wonderful contrivance; and of all their wonderful contrivances that of their railroad beds is by no means the least. For every four seats the negro builds up four beds. . . . Two are supposed to be on the level of the ordinary four seats, and two up above on shelves which are let down from the roof. Mattresses slip out from one nook and pillows from another. Blankets are added and the bed is ready."

Imperfections in the first arrangements, however, were quickly pointed out. "Is it not, then, a little strange that in our sleeping-cars no provision is made for extending to women the delicate consideration which they need?" wrote a female correspondent to the press. "No woman of delicate instincts would care to sleep in the same room with twenty or thirty men. Yet this is what she is required to do in a sleeping-car. She cannot undress in public of course, and therefore has to rid herself of her outer garments after she has climbed into her berth and drawn the curtains. Of the difficulty of this operation any woman who has tried it can speak in pathetic terms; but it is easy in comparison with the difficulty of getting into one's clothes in the morning. . . .

"I say nothing of the unpleasant necessity

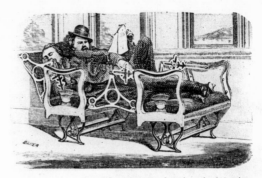

The New-York Historical Society
TRAVELING IN COMFORT. From the *Pacific Rural Press*, 1871.

of having to contemplate a car full of half-dressed men, who are engaged, with the charming indifference of their sex, in putting on boots and collars, or in watching with anxiety for a glimpse at some lady similarly occupied. It is rather hard, however, that young girls should have to be thus familiarized with that unattractive object, a sleepy and unwashed man. That trial should at least be postponed until marriage has rendered it inevitable."

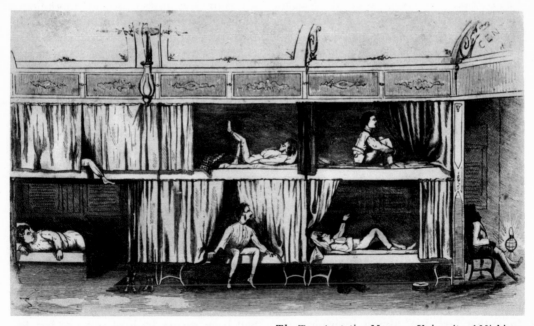

The Transportation Museum, University of Michigan

A SLEEPING CAR OF THE 1850's.

THE RAIL ROAD SUSPENSION BRIDGE NEAR NIAGARA FALLS, 1856. Lithograph by N. Currier after C. Parsons.

Some American railroad bridges were attracting wide attention by the 1850's. Roebling's suspension bridge over the Niagara River was almost as great a spectacle as the famous falls. "For more than ten years," wrote J. G. Kohl, "men have been spinning like spiders the iron web that connects Canada with the Union; have tried with great labour various experiments, and when their work has been destroyed by the powers of Nature, have begun again; and at length triumphed over all obstacles. As the river here is almost as deep as it is broad, the erection of piers was out of the question, and since the river runs at the Narrows with fearful velocity, there could be no bridge of boats. . . . Nothing remained, therefore, but to adopt the plan of the spider, when he flings his fine thread from tree to tree through the air. Paper kites were prepared, and, when the wind was fair for the attempt, sent across, loaded with the first thin wires . . . and now from that first thin, almost invisible wire, we have arrived at a grand and beautiful sus-

pension bridge, that is, perhaps, unequalled in the world. The chains on which it hangs are as thick as ship's masts, and more than a thousand feet long, and the towers that support them are masterpieces of modern architecture. They are about 250 feet high, and divided into two stories; through the upper one runs a railroad, and through the lower a broad and spacious roadway for passengers, horsemen, and carriages."

In its airiness Roebling's span, the first large railroad suspension bridge in the world, recalled the wooden trestles of earlier days. Here, at least, was displayed the same economy of means, materials, and time that had shaped the earlier structures and that was becoming a hallmark of American construction in general. In Europe where costs, manpower, and speed of construction were relatively minor considerations, iron bridges perpetuated the proportions familiar in the massive, laboriously contrived spans that had been earlier built of stone to last forever. A bridge across the celebrated gorge in the European manner, reported Roebling to the directors of his company, would have cost ten times as much "without securing a better purpose, or insuring greater safety."

Wherever the railroads found their way through the countryside shopping habits were altered. At every main stop along the route such facilities for buying and selling a variety of commodities developed as had previously been known only in larger cities along the main waterways. Every important railway depot was becoming an economic center for its surrounding area. "The railways are the true roads of America," wrote a witness of the process; "they have made the towns, and the towns turn to them in grateful acknowledgment, not banishing them to the back regions, but receiving them in their very midst."

"It is now considered as an axiom in modern political economy," concluded a somewhat fatuous philosopher of the 1860's, "that the construction of railways from large cities through rural districts not only must increase the population and industry of such districts, but must act as a most effective agent of social reform. The natural overflow of the city into the country necessarily carries with it an element of refinement and culture, so that we find society, in every vil-

WHOLESALE STORE
AT
LYON'S FALLS!
THE RAILROAD TERMINUS!

A. H. TYLER & Co. would respectfully announce to the Merchants and Citizens of LEWIS and adjoining Counties, that they have on hand and are daily receiving A LARGE STOCK of

GROCERIES!
DRY GOODS!
BOOTS and SHOES, Nails, &c.
Which they will sell at a small Advance of Cost.

Call & Examine our Teas!
Look at our
SUGARS, COFFEES, PRINTS and
Ready Made Clothing!

The Collecton of Regional Art, Cornell University BROADSIDE, 1866.

lage which is touched by the railroad, slowly and surely improving...." Those who felt differently about the city observed that many families were using the railroads to escape its "murky and unhealthy haunts" and to make the acquaintance of that nature they had known only in books.

THE 9:45 A.M. ACCOMMODATION, STRATFORD, CONNECTICUT, 1867. Painting by Edward Lamson Henry.
The Metropolitan Museum of Art

Americans, visitors unfailingly remarked, were always on the move. Their mobility was an ingrained inheritance that got every encouragement to develop in the open reaches of the New World. "Our forefathers wandered here," explained James K. Paulding in 1843, "and their posterity has been wandering ever since." To that instinctive urge "to go places" the steamboat and the railroad gave a sharp spur.

"Travelling seems to increase in even a greater ratio than the facilities," wrote one editor in the early days of the railroad. "Great as these are, by railroads and steamboats, the locomotive propensities of our countrymen seem to keep pace or to exceed them. For every traveller ten years ago, there are a hundred now, and we are sometimes fearful the comforts and conveniences with their cheapness, will make us a nation of travellers, always in motion, and that the art will be brought to such perfection, that it will be cheaper to travel than to stay at home and pay rent—indeed we are not sure but

that it is so already." The remark was prophetic of the auto-trailer migrations of the Great Depression a century later.

Even more than the steamboat the railroad fundamentally changed concepts of time and distance. For those who depended on the trains, God's time was replaced by the timetable, a schedule "as inexorable as fate." We were fast developing into a nation of people, as one sociologist described it, endlessly and anxiously catching its trains.

It had been constantly pointed out that each advance in easy, rapid communication would strengthen the Union. With the railroad, and with the telegraph, America would become "more and more one people, thinking more alike, acting more alike, and having one impulse." Beyond that, prophesied one writer, the railroad would unite the entire world. "Everything will be built on a grand scale. Everything will be built for *mankind!* There will be called meetings, not of a town or towns, not of countries or states, not national conventions, or even

"TEN MINUTES FOR REFRESHMENTS." Eating en route before dining car service was common. Lithograph published by the Great Atlantic and Pacific Tea Co., 1886.

The Harry Shaw Newman Gallery

Collection of Mrs. T. K. Boardman, Jr.

SCENE ON THE BRATTLEBORO AND WHITEHALL RAILROAD, NEAR BRATTLEBORO, VT., 1860-70. Photograph by Lucius H. Tatham. Courtesy of the New-York Historical Society.

delegates of nations—but meetings of *the world!"*

Others wondered if it were not the railroad companies instead of the government or the people that was gaining the most strength. Great thoroughfares had, from the dawn of history, been public highways. With the railroad the most perfect and important roads yet known to mankind were controlled by gigantic and growing private organizations. Their motives were challenged and their methods questioned, but in terms of travel and transport the nationalization of the country advanced with every new mile of track. At mid-century, with swarms of Americans finding their way into California and Oregon, national unity became quite suddenly a coast-to-coast problem; and in October, 1849, more than eight hundred delegates met at a convention in St. Louis to declare that a transcontinental railroad was a vital national need.

The destiny of the nation and the lives of its people became so inalienably associated with the progress of the railroad, as it thrust its rails and sounded its whistle deeper into the countryside, that the iron horse seemed to Thoreau the vehicle of America's own restless spirit. It was more than a laboring engine of democracy. It became, to remain for later generations, a fire-steed for the imagination.

"When I meet the engine with its train of cars moving off with planetary motion," wrote Thoreau at Walden, "—or, rather, like a comet, for the beholder knows not if with that velocity and with that direction it will ever revisit this system, since its orbit does not look like a returning curve,—with its steam cloud like a banner streaming behind in golden and silver wreaths . . . as if this travelling demigod, this cloud-compeller, would ere long take the sunset sky for the livery of his train; when I hear the iron horse make the hills echo with his snort like thunder, shaking the earth with his feet, and breathing fire and smoke from his nostrils (what kind of winged horse or fiery dragon they will put into the new Mythology I don't know), it seems as if the earth had got a race now worthy to inhabit it."

257

PAINTING BY JOHN GAST, 1872.

BEYOND THE MISSISSIPPI

The great trains of oxcarts that trundled across the plains and the prairies, picking up where the railroads left off, set no dizzy pace. But the stagecoach that flashed by them seemed a miracle of celerity. "In 1864," wrote A. D. Richardson, "Ben Holladay rode by a special coach from Folsom, California, to Atchison, Kansas, (almost two thousand miles) in twelve days and two hours. . . . That was a trip worth the taking! —a history of the last generation—a prophesy of the coming Pacific railroad, the grandest material enterprise of all time. . . . Whirling over the Sierra Nevadas, along the perilous edge of many a dizzy precipice—spinning through the all enveloping dust of the Great Basin, with its endless alkaline wastes—rattling along frowning canyons of the Rocky Mountains—shooting across the sands of the measureless desert, and then rolling merrily over the gentle swells of the flower-spangled prairie! Night and day, through storm and sunshine, shivering in bitter frost, panting in tropical heat, shrinking under pelting hail, cowering in the lightning's fiery track— across the continent, from the serene ocean

to the turbid river!" Small wonder that a western youth, being told that Moses led the Children of Israel out of captivity across the hundred miles of fearful desert in forty years, retorted: "Humph! Ben Holladay would have fetched them through in thirty-six hours!"

Then it was the brief-lived Pony Express that streaked by the Overland Stage in the night, as Mark Twain told it, "so we heard only a whiz and a hail, and the swift phantom of the desert was gone before we could get our heads out of the windows . . . like a flash of unreal fancy." Easterners like Horace Greeley who traveled overland by stagecoach to see the land beyond the Mississippi could contrast the constant driving motion of the West with the scene along more familiar waterways and railways. It was just those decades that saw the steamboat reach the peak of its majesty. As far as the rivers and bays would reach they teemed with vessels not content just to "get there" but to break the record in the bargain. Not all of them, of course, but it was the ideal. The time on the New York–Albany run had already been cut to less than eight hours. It had become an all daylight trip. In 1853 the *Eclipse* churned 1024 miles up the Mississippi from New Orleans to Cairo in just over three days —an upstream speed of more than fourteen miles an hour for the full trip.

But the iron rails were flanking the steamboat routes and stealing the trade. By 1860 lines from the East had reached the Mississippi at a number of points and were already nosing into wagon-train and stagecoach territory. Hardly a decade more and transcontinental train travelers, thundering past the covered wagons that continued for some time to trek across the prairies, mistook them for traveling circuses. The nuisance of distance in a large land had become as obsolete as the ox train. "The railway," pronounced *Leslie's Weekly* in 1870, "has so abridged time and space, that the continent is rapidly losing its romance and becoming prosaic. . . . We have almost ceased to speak of the frontier."

As emigrants, miners, and adventurers streamed across the prairies and mountains to the far West, the clamor for better communications between the remote western outpost and the settled East became more and more insistent at both ends of the country. In the uncertain days before the Civil War, political expediency as well as social and business needs demanded a more effective liaison between the far-separated regions of the sprawling nation.

Under Jefferson Davis, as Secretary of War, five lines of survey were run to the Pacific in 1853 and 1854 to determine "the most practicable and economical route for a Railroad from the Mississippi River to the Pacific." Each survey concluded by vigorously recommending the particular route it had explored. Davis quite naturally supported the southernmost, along the thirty-second parallel. But Congress, acutely conscious of sectional rivalry, delayed action for almost a decade.

THE UNITED STATES PACIFIC RAILROAD EXPLORING AND SURVEYING PARTY IN THE GILA AND SIERRA DE LAS ESTRELLAS, 1853-56. Lithograph after Albert H. Campbell from the official report of the expedition.

The Library of Congress

Congress did appropriate funds to bring camels from the Near East to use as experimental transports across the arid lands of the Southwest. They were "the most docile, patient and easily managed creatures in the world and infinitely more easily worked than mules," remarked their commander. "General Beale and about fourteen camels stalked into town last Friday week," reported the Los Angeles press in January, 1858, "and gave our streets quite an Oriental aspect. . . . These animals are admirably adapted to the travel across our continent and their introduction was a brilliant idea the result of which is beginning most happily." For a number of years "these outlandish brutes" saw service in various parts of the West. In a plowing contest in Alabama a camel easily won over a mule. But prejudice was everywhere too strong against such exotic beasts, the herd was scattered, and the serious experiment survived only in the legend of a huge white camel occasionally "seen" by incredulous Westerners on the empty deserts.

Long before the railroad could make the great leap from the Mississippi to the Pacific men were dreaming ahead to that day. Meanwhile, a growing inland empire, dotted with isolated communities, clamored for goods and news from the outside world. To supply such settlements not only with the necessities of a halfway civilized life, but with any odd convenience, that might plausibly be transported, including such disparate commodities as oysters and mouser cats, was a profitable business. In the late 1850's almost every person in the western region who could commandeer a vehicle entered the freighting business. For years after the railroad had spanned the continent caravans of ox-drawn vehicles continued to serve the regions beyond the immediate reach of the iron rails.

The largest of many organizations that evolved to handle this traffic enterprise was Russell, Majors, and Waddell's. In 1858 the firm practically monopolized the great freighting business of the Plains, operating some 6250 wagons and 75,000 oxen in that service. At Leavenworth, Kansas, in 1859, Horace Greeley noticed "Such acres of wagons! Such pyramids of extra axletrees! such herds of oxen! such regiments of drivers and

A Camel Train Encampment near Carson Valley, 1856. Photograph of a sketch, from *Visscher's Pictorial of California*, 1870.
The New-York Historical Society

other employees!"—all belonging to this one firm—that it took an eye witness to believe it.

Another visitor to a western freighting town observed "huge freight wagons on every street, at every corner. . . . There is heard the lumbering of these 'prairie schooners,' the bellowing of oxen, braying of mules, cracking of long lariats (whips) . . . the hollowing—yelling—of teamsters, mingled with more oaths than I ever heard before in all my life together."

With three to five tons of freight per wagon, carefully packed against the exigencies of rough travel and manned by a motley crew of bullwhackers, mule skinners, and sundry assistants, trains of from twenty-five to one hundred wagons were often launched from their terminal towns with moral exhortations (Waddell was a pious temperance man) that must have sounded wonderfully incongruous in the wild atmosphere of those brawling communities. Sometimes, as the trains filed over the immense wilderness to their destination, their canvas tops stretched out beyond reach of the eye. In 1860, a traveler reported passing almost two thousand westbound freight wagons on the 350-mile

The Union Pacific Railroad
A WAGON TRAIN IN ECHO CANYON, UTAH, 1869 (?).

stretch between Denver and Fort Kearney.

From four to six weeks were required for ordinary freighting between the Missouri River and Denver in the right season. Even the "quick freighting," done with horses and mules throughout the year, was much too slow for the mails or impatient human cargoes. From every part of the West came a clamor for roads and mail, for speedy communications.

A WAGON TRAIN CORRALLING IN A DENVER STREET, 1886.

The Denver Public Library Western Collection

The Denver Public Library Western Collection
BEN HOLLADAY'S OVERLAND EXPRESS, AT KIMBALL'S,
1867.

After a decade of experimentation, a daily stagecoach service was started from the Missouri to the Pacific coast. The Overland Route, as it was popularly known, was never more than a temporary expedient until a railroad could be built. But for two decades it added a new legend to the story of the Great West. Ben Holladay was for several years the most prominent of the traffic organizers of the plains. His reputation did not suffer in Mark Twain's accounts of his journey in a Holladay stage.

The journey took about twenty-five days. "Twenty-four mortal days and nights—twenty-five being schedule time—must be spent in that ambulance," wrote one seasoned traveler on whom the romance of the adventure was lost; "passengers becoming crazy with whisky, mixed with want of sleep, are often obliged to be strapped to their seats; their meals, dispatched during their ten-minute halts, are simply abominable, the heats are excessive, the climate malarious; lamps may not be used at night for fear of non-existent Indians; briefly there is no end to this Via Mala's miseries."

Stage stations were posted about every twelve and a half miles along the route. "The buildings," according to Mark Twain, "consisted of barns, stable room for twelve or fifteen horses, and a hut for an eating room for passengers. ... In a corner [of the latter] stood an open sack of flour, and nestling against its base were a couple of black and venerable tin coffee-pots, a tin teapot, a

THE CALIFORNIA-NEVADA STAGE LEAVING THE INTERNATIONAL HOTEL AT VIRGINIA CITY FOR CALIFORNIA VIA DONNER LAKE. From Lawrence & Houseworth, *Gems of California Scenery*, 1866 (2d edition).
The Library of Congress

little bag of salt and a side of bacon. By the door of the station keeper's den, outside, was a tin wash-basin on the ground. Near it was a pail of water and a piece of yellow bar soap, and from the eaves hung a hoary blue woolen shirt, significantly—but this latter was the station keeper's private towel."

Stage keepers were tough individuals of necessity. "Robber's Roost" was for a while the home of Slade, a notorious character of the time, and a rendezvous for all the desperadoes of the county.

Popular representations rarely pictured the stages slowly plodding through shifting sands or feeling their way over rocky sections of the route. Yet there was some truth in the dashing illustrations that advertised their service. "The whips crack, and the two cars of the desert go rolling forward. . . ." recounted one responsible journalist of his own trip in 1865. "Along plains, over hills, and down steep winding canyons our horses leaped at their utmost speed. One route of eight miles we traveled in thirty minutes! . . . We spent only seventy-two hours upon

The New-York Historical Society
BEN HOLLADAY'S CALIFORNIA EXPRESS, ABOUT 1867.
Lithograph by Vincent Brooks, Day & Son.

the five hundred and seventy-five miles of desert road between Salt Lake, and Virginia, Nevada. . . . Reaching Austin our vehicle whirled around the last street-corner, ran for several yards poised upon two wheels, while the others were more than a foot from the ground, but righted again; and with this neat finishing stroke ended our ride of four hundred miles, accomplished in fifty-one hours."

ROBBER'S ROOST AT VIRGINIA DALE, LARIMER COUNTY, COLORADO, 1868-78. A stage station on the Overland Route. Photograph by William H. Jackson.

The Denver Public Library Western Collection

THE PONY EXPRESS CROSSING THE SIERRAS IN A SNOWSTORM, "SWIMMING THE STORM," AND ON THE PLAINS. From *Hutchings' California Magazine*, 1860.

The promise of both a telegraph and a railroad across the continent raised to an almost unendurable pitch the general impatience for more speedy communications. In January, 1860, plans to establish "an independent horse express across the Plains to California" were announced in the papers. Within two weeks an appeal was made for "two hundred gray mares, from four to seven years old, not to exceed fifteen hands high, well broke to the saddle, and warranted sound, with black hoofs, and suitable for running the 'Overland Poney Express.'" On April 3 the St. Joseph *Weekly West* reported that the first "horse and rider started off from St. Joseph amid the loud and continual cheers of the assembled multitude. . . . The rider is a Mr. Richardson, formerly a sailor, and a man accustomed to every description of hardship, having sailed for years amid the snows and ice bergs of the Northern ocean . . . before this paragraph meets the eyes of our readers, the various dispatches contained in the saddle bags will have reached the town of Marysville on the Big Blue, one hundred and twelve miles distant—an enterprise never before accomplished even in this proverbially fast portion of a fast country."

Each horseman covered the forty to a hundred and twenty-five miles of his route at a steady gallop where possible, changing horses in a matter of seconds at intermediate stations and carrying a maximum of twenty pounds of mail. "No matter what time of the day or night his watch came on," wrote Mark Twain, "and no matter whether it was winter or summer, raining, snowing, hailing, sleeting, or whether his 'beat' was a level straight road or a crazy trail over mountain crags and precipices, or whether it led through peaceful regions or regions that swarmed with hostile Indians, he must always be ready to leap into the saddle and be off with the wind!" In spite of all difficulties and hazards, the Pony Express covered a total of 650,000 miles in its brief history and, it is said, lost only one mail.

Actually the project was a desperate adver-

FROM THE LEAVENWORTH *Weekly Herald,* FEBRUARY 4, 1860.

tising bid for government contracts to carry the mail across the Plains. It was well conceived but enormously expensive. Special light saddles were designed; the distance between stations was ten to twenty miles depending upon circumstances, the riders changing mounts some seven to twelve times in their runs; five hundred horses were bought for the service (the freighting bill for feed was itself a huge item); eighty experienced riders and hundreds of station keepers were hired at the start, all sworn not to drink, curse, or quarrel; and a fee of five dollars per half-ounce was established as a carrying charge. Every trip was a heavy expense to the operators.

THE PONY EXPRESS MEETS THE TELEGRAPH. From *Harper's Weekly*, 1861.

Nothing could have dramatized the need and the eagerness for speedy communications between East and West more than the almost superhuman regularity and punctuality of the pony expressmen. Every rare delay or disruption of their scheduled service—caused by swollen mountain streams, blizzards, Indian attacks, stumbles in the dark—was noted in the papers as a matter of serious public concern, particularly in the West. These were fateful days; the dissolution of the Union hung in the balance. To speed the delivery of Lincoln's inaugural address from Washington to California the distance to be raced by each horse was reduced to a ten-mile stretch. As a result the 1950-mile transit was completed in seven days and seven hours.

The bankrupt firm of Russell, Majors, and Waddell, which was operating the Pony Express, gave up its project when the first telegraph wire spanned the continent. In October, 1861, just a few months after Lincoln had pronounced the idea a "wild scheme" and "next to impossible," over three and a half thousand miles of wire between New York and San Francisco were opened for public service, at both ends of the circuit.

"It was thought last year and truly too," remarked a Kansas paper, "that the Pony had accomplished wonders. . . . But now the Pony had become a thing of the past—his last race is run. Without sound of trumpets, celebrations, or other noise demonstrations, the slender wire has been stretched from ocean to ocean, and the messages already received from our brethern on the Pacific coast, most conclusively show that the popular heart beats in unison with our own, on the absorbing question of the preservation of the Union."

Wells, Fargo and Company had bought out Ben Holladay for two and a half million dollars and proceeded to spruce up the equipment and extend the service on the Overland Route. "A novel sight was presented in the Concord Railroad Yard, at noon Wednesday," reported the Concord (New Hampshire) *Daily Monitor*, April 15, 1868, "in the shape of a special train of fifteen long platform cars, containing thirty elegant coaches . . . and four long box cars, containing 60 four horse set harnesses . . . all consigned to Wells, Fargo & Co., Omaha and Salt Lake City, the whole valued at $45,000 perhaps." "The coaches are finished in a superior manner," continued the newspa-

The American Antiquarian Society

A CONSIGNMENT OF CONCORD COACHES MADE BY ABBOTT DOWNING CO., CONCORD, NEW HAMPSHIRE, 1868.

per, "the bodies red, and the running part yellow. Each door has a handsome picture, mostly landscapes, and no two of the sixty are alike. They are gems of beauty and would afford study for hours. . . . They are designed for nine persons inside, and eight or ten outside."

Among the most famous Concord coaches, which were sold to far parts of the earth, was the Deadwood Stage, which ran the perilous route from Cheyenne to Deadwood via Laramie. It ran through Buffalo Gap, Lame Johnny Creek, Red Canyon, and Squaw Gap, all notorious haunts of road agents— Peg-legged Bradley, Dunk Blackburn, Curley Grimes, and others—not to mention Sioux Indians. The old coach survived more than one running gun fight, and during its career carried a varied human freight, including Calamity Jane and Buffalo Bill.

THE DEADWOOD COACH, BILL MCCUNE, DRIVER, JOHN NELSON "RIDING SHOT GUN" ON TOP. 187?.

The National Archives

UNION PACIFIC RAILROAD SURVEYORS AT WORK. Lithograph by Vincent Brooks, Day & Son, from William A. Bell, *New Tracks in North America*, 1869.

"To feel the importance of the Pacific Railroad, to measure the urgency of its early completion, to become impatient with government and contractor at every delay in the work," wrote Samuel Bowles in 1865, "you must come across the Plains and Mountains to the Pacific Coast. Then you will see half a Continent waiting for its vivifying influences. You will witness a boundless agriculture, fickle and hesitating for lack of the regular markets this would give. You will find mineral wealth, immeasurable, locked up, wastefully worked, or gambled away, until this shall open it to abundant labor, cheap capital, wood, water, science, ready oversight, steadiness of production. . . . You will find the world's commerce with India and China eagerly awaiting its opportunities. . . . It is touching to remember that between Plains and Pacific, in country and on coast, on the Columbia, on the Colorado, through all our long journey, the first question asked of us by every man and woman we have met,—whether rich or poor, high or humble,—has been, 'When do you think the Pacific Railroad will be done?' "

With the passage of the Pacific Railway Act of 1862, surveys had finally been started for the long-envisioned transcontinental project. "Each of our surveying parties," wrote General Dodge, Chief Engineer of the Union Pacific, "consisted of a chief who was an experienced engineer, two assistants, also civil engineers, rodmen, flagmen, and chainmen, generally graduated civil engineers but without personal experience in the field, besides ax men, teamsters, and herders. When the party was expected to live upon the game of the country, a hunter was added. Each party would thus consist of from eighteen to twenty-two men, all armed. When operating in a hostile Indian country they were regularly drilled, though after the Civil War this was unnecessary, as most of them had been in the army. Each party entering a country occupied by hostile Indians was generally furnished with a military escort. . . . Notwithstanding this protection the parties were often attacked, their chief or some of their men killed or wounded, and the stock run off. . . ."

Under such circumstances twenty-five

thousand miles of exploratory reconnaissances and fifteen thousand miles of instrumental lines were run before the actual grading and construction work could follow.

When the transcontinental railroad was started no line yet crossed Iowa to Council Bluffs, opposite Omaha which had been chosen as the starting point for the westward leap. Materials and supplies of every variety were either hauled across Iowa by oxen and ferried across the Missouri or shipped up the river. Omaha was a striking example of what railroads were doing to the face of the land. "There is nothing in Europe in any way like to these western railway settlements," wrote Anthony Trollope. "With us in England, it is difficult to realize the importance which is attached to a railway in the States, and the results which a railway creates. We have roads everywhere, and our country had been cultivated throughout . . .

before our system of railroads had been commenced, but in America . . . the railways have been the precursors of cultivation. They have been carried hither and thither, through primeval forests and over prairies, with small hope of other traffic than that which they themselves would make by their own influence."

In a few short years of railroad activity Omaha sprang from a small frontier settlement to what one early visitor described as "the liveliest city in the United States. Streets were being graded, sidewalks thronged with returned gold seekers, discharged soldiers, farmers selling produce, speculators, Indians, and other strange characters of border life. . . . The railroad disbursed a quarter of a million dollars per month." Wherever the railroads ended or started they gave rise to such colorful and prospering communities.

OMAHA, FOURTEENTH AND DOUGLAS STREETS, 1868.

The Union Pacific Railroad

BUILDING THE UNION PACIFIC RAILROAD: CUTTING "TUNNEL NO. 2" AT THE HEAD OF ECHO CANYON, UTAH.

PLACING A STONE ABUTMENT FOR A BRIDGE IN WYOMING, 1868.

The surveys completed, instructions were to go ahead no matter what the cost. So it happened: "Thirty seconds to each pair of rails . . . three blows to each spike, ten spikes to a rail, 400 rails and 4000 spikes and 12,000 blows to a mile. To every mile some 2500 ties . . . at $2.50 each, delivered. The roadbed is ever calling for more and more; the six- and eight-horse or mule teams toil on from end o' track with spoils from the immense tie-piles; in the mountains, the tie camps are heaping others by the thousands."

Forty miles of track for the Union Pacific were laid in 1865, two hundred and sixty-five in 1866, two hundred and forty-five in 1867, four hundred and twenty-five in 1868, and the remaining one hundred and five miles in the first few months of 1869. "We found the workmen, with the regularity of machinery, dropping each rail in its place, spiking it down, and then seizing another," reported A. D. Richardson. "Behind them, the locomotive; before, the tie-layers; beyond these the graders; and still further, in mountain recesses, the engineers. It was Civilization pressing westward—the Conquest of Nature moving toward the Pacific."

In the heat of intense competition during the last days of construction the Union Pacific crews laid a record eight miles of track in twenty-four hours, to be topped by the Chinese laborers of the Central Pacific who countered with ten miles in one day.

For long stretches above and below Omaha the banks of the Missouri River were stripped of timber to provide the millions of crossties that were needed. Until the tracks reached the summit of the first range of the Rockies, where there was good timber, wood and all other supplies had to be hauled the ever-increasing distance from the East.

A STRETCH OF OLD TRACK ON THE UNION PACIFIC ROAD. Photograph by Captain A. J. Russell.
The Union Pacific Railroad

As the railroads advanced from two directions into the unoccupied waste that separated their spearheads, the terminal camps that supplied the "front" of operations with building materials, provisions, and all the necessaries of community life hopped from point to point in the immediate rear. They were, someone remarked, the terminals for the stage, for the railroad, and for many a life. In these "Hells on Wheels," as Samuel Bowles appropriately called them, concentrated all the reckless excitement generated by the dangers, the difficulties, and the tension of the undertaking. "Hell would appear to have been raked to furnish them," wrote Bowles, "and to it they must have naturally returned after graduating there." In such brawling spots was re-created the riotous drama of the mining towns—the almost instantaneous growth, the unbridled passion of men of action temporarily thrown together far from conventional scenes, the gradual assertion of law and order, and, more frequently than not, the sudden removal of all human life out of the flimsy shell of the community.

"We are now . . . *in the West,*" wrote one eyewitness in 1868 of Ellsworth. "Here is *life.* The fine spun theories, the moon-eyed inventions, the old time manners, and obsolete customs of the East are unknown. The houses here are alternately Beer Houses, Whiskey Shops, Gambling houses, Dance houses and Restaurants. There is little difference however as the Beer houses sell whiskey, and the whiskey houses retail beer, while the Club rooms and Restaurants all dispense the lightning (here sweetly called 'Tarantula juice'). The dance houses combine the worship of Bacchus with terpsichorean amusements of a very high order. They used to 'have a man for breakfast here every morning' as they pleasantly spoke when chronicling the nightly murders in the

A "HELL ON WHEELS" TOWN AT THE END OF THE RAILROAD TRACK IN WYOMING, 1868.

The Union Pacific Railroad

town, but, as they pensively admit, 'business is very dull now.' "

Some "hells" sprang out of the prairie, blossomed briefly with corruption, disorder, and death, and, once deserted by the railroad crews, gave up their streets and false-fronted, rickety buildings to wolves and coyotes that wandered in from the surrounding wilderness. Elsewhere, as in the case of Cheyenne, the terminal town for the winter of 1867–68, when the concentrated turmoil was relieved and the railroad moved ahead, communities settled down to a relatively quiet and enduring existence.

As the railroads pushed on every mile of progress was contested by the wilderness, by mountain gorges and wastelands, often by cruel weather, and sometimes by the savage natives for whom the onrushing "bad medicine wagon" was the latest in the long series of threats to their freedom which had aroused the Indians since colonial days.

The United States Geological Survey
CORINNE, UTAH, 1869. A "hell town" that boomed and busted. Photograph by William H. Jackson.

THE DALE CREEK BRIDGE, NEAR SHERMAN, WYOMING. The wooden framework structure was six hundred and fifty feet long and one hundred and twenty-seven feet high, the largest of its kind on the road.

The Union Pacific Railroad

The Union Pacific Railroad

THE COMPLETION OF THE TRANSCONTINENTAL RAILROAD AT PROMONTORY POINT, UTAH, MAY 10, 1869.

On May 10, 1869, just twenty-one years after the New York *Herald* with wild inaccuracy had protested that "this whole project [of a transcontinental railroad] is ridiculous and absurd. . . . Centuries hence it will be time enough to talk of such a railroad . . ." the tracks were joined at Promontory Point, Utah.

"The two trains pulled up facing each other," wrote General Dodge, "each crowded with workmen who sought advantageous positions to witness the ceremonies and literally covered the cars. The officers and invited guests formed on each side of the track, leaving it open to the south. . . . Prayer was offered; a number of spikes were driven in the two adjoining rails, each of the prominent persons present taking a hand, but very few hitting the spikes, to the great amusement of the crowd. . . . The engineers ran up their locomotives until they touched, the engineer upon each engine breaking a bottle of champagne upon the other one, and thus the two roads were wedded into one great trunk line from the Atlantic to the Pacific."

Bret Harte wrote the poem of the day:

What was it the Engines said,
Pilots touching, head to head
Facing on a single track,
Half a world behind each back?

And, after allowing the locomotive from the East to describe the wonders of civilization it was bringing to the empty wilderness of the West, he quoted from the western locomotive:

You brag of the East! You do?
Why, I bring the East to you!
All the Orient, all Cathay,
Find through me the shortest way;
And the sun you follow here
Rises in my hemisphere!

The country rejoiced with processions, thanksgiving services, and ringing of the Liberty Bell, as the golden spike was driven into the last tie. The completion of the gigantic job, said *The Nation*, "gives us a road to the Indies, a means of making the United States a half-way house between the East and West, and last, but not least, a new guarantee of the perpetuity of the Union as it is!"

The exultant cry that the wealth of the Indies now lay close at hand, reiterated constantly in the literature of the day, sounded curiously like the triumphant boasts of navigators three centuries earlier.

"Never again," wrote Paxson, historian of the frontier, "could the wild Indians range the plains from the Rio Grande to the Assiniboin. The Pacific Railroad split the northern and the southern plains forever. . . . The year after the celebration at Promontory Point, the section of the Union Pacific that crossed the plains was paralleled from Denver to the Missouri . . . by the Kansas Pacific . . . which was connected with the main line at Cheyenne."

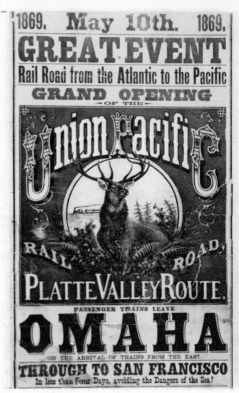

The Union Pacific Railroad
ADVERTISEMENT, 1869.

THE FIRST TRANSCONTINENTAL TRAIN FROM SACRAMENTO, MAY, 1869. Painting by Joseph Becker.
Collection of Mrs. Harry MacNeill Bland

THE EADS BRIDGE ACROSS THE MISSISSIPPI AT ST. LOUIS, COMPLETED IN 1874. Lithograph by the Democratic Lithograph Printing Co.

As different railroads converged on the Mississippi and Missouri Rivers to take off across the rest of the continent, bridges sprang up to expedite the East-West traffic flow. The bridge at St. Louis, built by James B. Eads between 1867 and 1874, was the most costly and important of the early ones. Carriages and railroads traveled on separate levels sixty feet above the water. Revisiting St. Louis after the bridge had been built

DINING SALOON OF A HOTEL EXPRESS TRAIN, 1870. From *Leslie's Weekly*.

Mark Twain reviewed the melancholy and woeful sight of a half-dozen "sound-asleep steamboats" where once there had been a mile of wide-awake ones. "Remains of former steamboatmen told me," he wrote, ". . . that the bridge doesn't pay. Still, it can be no sufficient compensation to a corpse to know that the dynamite that laid him out was not of as good quality as it had been supposed to be." Steamboating as Mark Twain remembered it was all but dead.

Accommodations on the best transcontinental trains, as developed by the inventive genius of George M. Pullman, Webster Wagner, and others, offered conveniences and luxuries that a great many people did not command in their own homes. Travelers reported through the *New York Times* of speeding *"twenty-seven miles in twenty-seven minutes"* while their champagne glasses, filled to the brim in the new dining cars, spilled not a drop. After dinner the passengers gathered in the drawing-room car to sing hymns with an organ accompaniment while the train "with its great, glaring Polyphemous eye, lighting up long vistas of prairie, rushed into the night and the Wild. Then to bed in luxurious couches, where we slept the sleep of the just and only awoke the next morning . . . at eight o'clock, to find ourselves at the crossing of the North Platte, three hundred miles from Omaha—*fifteen hours and forty minutes out.*" Mark Twain, recalling his own recent trip across the Plains in Ben Holladay's coach, found the new state of things hardly credible.

In 1900, with tracks crisscrossing the country in a gigantic web, the United States had a greater mileage of railroads than all Europe. It was not done without corruption and waste and disorder. But the very scale of the achievement left the nation with an affection for railroads that remains part of the American character.

"And when I think how the railroad has been pushed through this unwatered wilderness and haunt of savage tribes," wrote Robert Louis Stevenson, ". . . how at each stage of the construction, roaring impromptu cities, full of gold and lust and death, sprang up and then died away again, and are now but wayside stations in the desert; how in these uncouth places pigtailed Chinese pirates worked side by side with border ruffians and broken men from Europe, talking together in a mixed dialect, mostly oaths, gambling, drinking, quarrelling and murdering like wolves; how the plumed hereditary lord of all America heard, in this last fastness, the scream of the 'bad medicine wagon' charioting his foes; and then when I go on to remember that all this epical turmoil was conducted by gentlemen in frock coats, with a view to nothing more extraordinary than a fortune and a subsequent visit to Paris, it seems to me, I own, as if this railway were the one typical achievement of the age in which we live, as if it brought together into one plot all the ends of the world and all the degrees of social rank. . . . If it be romance, if it be contrast, if it be heroism that we require, what was Troy town to this?"

A BUFFET, SMOKING, AND LIBRARY CAR, 1900. Photograph by Detroit Photographic Company.
The Library of Congress

The Public Roads Administration

SHIPS OF THE PLAINS NEAR BIG SPRINGS, NEBRASKA, 1912.

A NATION ON WHEELS

The growth of railroads during the last two thirds of the nineteenth century had gradually chilled the enthusiasm for every other kind of travel and transportation within the country. Less than a generation after its first serious outbreak the canal fever had subsided. The inland waterways were no longer the primary routes they long had been, although both canal boat and steamboat continued to carry an enormous bulk of slow freight. But as the iron horse monopolized long-distance overland hauling the early zeal for turnpikes had dwindled to nothing. By about 1900 there were more miles of railroad per person in America than ever before or since and, conversely, fewer good highways than might have been found in any other civilized country.

Gallatin's century-old dream of uniting "by intimate community of interest the most remote quarters of the United States" was hardly realized by such a transportation system. The railroads had built into the body of the nation a gigantic steel skeleton on which the country's main traffic depended.

But, impressive as that was, it provided only a rigid, sparse frame. It remained for the automobile to cover the whole structure with a supple web of thoroughfares through which people, supplies, and ideas could circulate with almost boundless freedom.

At the time of the automobile's first popularity the existing roads were, largely, feeders to the railways, relatively short stretches with only local importance. Those that developed in following years took on an independent life, following, joining, or leaving the rails and leading to or avoiding the depots as convenience dictated. Slow to win official attention, the need for better and longer highways took on a breathless urgency as millions of far-ranging cars streamed off the assembly lines. No other country in the world was so ready, so eager, and so able to put the automobile into general service as America. "It is probable," reported President Hoover's Committee on Social Trends, "that no invention of such far-reaching importance was ever diffused with such rapidity, or so quickly exerted influences that ramified through the national culture, transforming even habits of thought and language."

A car in his garage, like a full dinner pail, was the valid expectation of virtually every American citizen. With well over forty-four million registered motor vehicles traveling more than four hundred billion vehicle miles (in 1949) there was still no clear indication that a saturation point was reached. How safe enough roads could be built quickly enough to serve the growing torrent of vehicles was not clear either. But it was clear that the open highways of the continent had become the latest "frontier" of American development. When it was settled the nation might become, for the first time, something like the "single neighborhood" of Gallatin's vision.

In a sense it was the bicycle that cleared the path for the automobile. "The bicycle is not a toy," one clergyman boldly prophesied in 1882. "Class it with the flying-machine if you will; but only by way of contrast; that was a failure, this, a success . . . as my farmer parishioners say of the potato-bug, 'It has come to stay.' " In 1896 when a mere handful of automobiles were registered in the United States, four million bike riders were enjoying their sport. Through the League of American Wheelmen, organized in 1880–81 to promote cycling and its interests, began a vigorous "good roads movement." It was the first time the matter had been effectively pressed since the end of the turnpike era sixty years before. In 1893 Congress was persuaded to vote $10,000 to the Secretary of Agriculture to promote an inquiry into the subject. There was as yet no existing government mechanism to handle a really big job.

A MEETING OF THE LEAGUE OF AMERICAN WHEELMEN, ABOUT 1881.

The Smithsonian Institution

AN UNIMPROVED ROAD NEAR BROOKINGS, SOUTH DA-
KOTA, ABOUT 1904.

As late as 1908 there were only six hundred and fifty miles of macadamized road in all the United States and not yet a single mile of concrete. From the wide areas in between the rail lines people found their way to the nearest depots as best they might along dirt roads, roads that ran into each town from the surrounding countryside rather than from one town to the next, and that were deep in mud or dust according to the season. Such primitive routes were the charge of localities whose property owners often worked out their road taxes with pick and shovel.

Meanwhile the automobile was winning a secure place in Europe. In 1901 *Vogue* reported that "certain circles" in Paris were avoiding the hurly-burly of railway travel

SCENE IN FRONT OF THE VANDERBILT HOUSE, 58TH STREET AND FIFTH AVE., NEW YORK CITY, ABOUT 1902.

altogether by taking to their motor cars, as the King of the Belgians did on his frequent trips between Brussels and Paris. "Is it not truly a royal way of getting about . . . ?" asked *Vogue*.

America's "royalty" also made the news by puttering about in charmed circles. Two years before the fashion report from Paris the *New York Times* regaled its readers with social notes of the Newport colony extravagantly racing around the Ocean Drive in horseless carriages. Society had taken up automobiling as a fad, importing its cars when the baby industry in this country could not match the demand for smart turnouts.

For the first few years of the new century there were probably more motorcars in England than in America, largely because road conditions there were so much more favorable. However, the early clubs of pioneer automobilists in this country added their protest to that of the cyclists. For them, hazarding out of town onto the existing rural roads was pioneering in a serious sense of the word, fraught with hardship and discouragement, if not often with mortal peril. But the "fashion" of automobiling did not last long in America. Almost immediately the common man wanted a car he could afford and the keen rivalry of the early manufacturers soon brought prices down to an unfashionable level. By 1907, according to one magazine, the auto had become a "necessity," and the auto salesman a permanent, increasingly important feature of the American economy.

SMITH AND MABLEY'S AUTOMOBILE SALESROOM, NEW YORK CITY, 1905. Photograph by Byron.
The Museum of the City of New York

The Public Roads Administration
AN ATTEMPT TO ACCUSTOM HORSES TO AUTOMOBILES, BRETTON WOODS, NEW HAMPSHIRE, 1904.

Early drivers were up against a big prejudice. Their spluttering devil cars were endangering unconditioned pedestrians and disturbing the ancient peace of the countryside. "Perhaps the time will come," remarked a senator from Texas in 1909, "when horses will be educated to the point where they will not be afraid of automobiles; but I doubt that for I have not seen the time yet that I was not afraid of them." To overcome such apprehension, advised *The Happy Motorist* in 1906, motorists must be subtle and artful. "An elaborate drawing up before the horse which the country farmer is doing his best to scare into panic; a ceremonious reduction of speed to a crawl while passing the old lady in her barouche, so that she shall not be dusted; a generous treatment of the country parson and squire when encountered—these belong to the subtleties, the guile, the worldly wisdom of a threatened pastime."

Quite aside from the simple annoyance caused by the obtrusive and noisy machines the farmer detected in the clamor for better roads a threat of additional taxes. But the promise of some relief from rural isolation and all its traditional inconveniences won the National Grange to the good-roads movement in 1907.

The Museum of the City of New York,
J. Clarence Davies Collection
TOURING, 1904-5.

Even stronger prejudices favored the new machines. Americans were mobile by temperament and habit; the country was large, the distances great, and the scenery full of interest; Americans liked speed, they loved to tinker, and they wanted to keep up with the Joneses; the per capita wealth of the country was increasingly high and the cost of a good car was being reduced; automobile manufacturers, road builders, tire makers, oil industrialists, and a host of others stood to profit by getting America out of the mud and motoring along adequate highways. From every angle the public eagerness for cars and the complementary promise of a good market for a variety of industries, once conditions were favorable, stimulated a widespread pressure for improved roads.

When a hard-surfaced, all-weather highway to span the continent—the Lincoln Highway—was projected in 1912–13 there were no maps by which any succession of local roads could be charted as a connected route. In picking a connected trail from the Missouri River to the Pacific, explained the officers of the Lincoln Highway Association, they used the maps and mileages of railroad timetables in endeavoring to link up the various sections of disconnected county and township improvement. However, the notion of a national highway excited the public imagination and a new westward movement of pioneers gradually got under way. By 1915 official road guides were promoting transcontinental auto trips to the Panama Pacific Exposition in San Francisco. If trouble was experienced near Fish Springs, Utah, counseled one guidebook, "build a sage brush fire. Mr. Thomas will come with a team. He can see you twenty miles off." The latest frontier was far from settled; it was advancing in all directions.

THE PRESIDENT AND VICE-PRESIDENT OF THE LINCOLN HIGHWAY ASSOCIATION MAROONED IN A MUD-HOLE EN ROUTE TO THE PANAMA PACIFIC EXPOSITION, LINCOLN HIGHWAY, NEBRASKA, 1915. Photograph courtesy of the Public Roads Administration.

The Nebraska State Highway Department

ONE DAY'S OUTPUT (1000 CARS) AT THE FORD FACTORY, HIGHLAND PARK, MICHIGAN, 1913.

"The commodities that conduce to civilized living," wrote Henry Ford in a philosophic mood, "are thus far enjoyed by only a small fraction of the world's inhabitants. The experience of the Ford Motor Co. has been that mass production precedes mass consumption and makes it possible, by reducing costs. . . . If the production is increased 500%, costs may be cut 50%, and this decrease in cost, with its accompanying decrease in selling price, will probably multiply by 10 the number of people who can conveniently buy the product. This is a conservative illustration of production serving as the cause of demand instead of the effect."

Ford had made his first famous Model T in 1909 and by 1914 his factory was turning out almost as many cars as all others combined. Between 1909 and 1927 fifteen million of the unpretentious little cars rolled off the Ford assembly lines in a constantly larger volume that startled the entire world and put wheels under a good part of the nation's people. The joke that a Ford could go anywhere except in society was well put. The man who could not afford a "tin Lizzie" was poor indeed. The man who owned one enjoyed no distinction on that score over millions of his countrymen.

Farmers, particularly took the flivver to their hearts. The price of a Ford had dropped from $780 in 1910–11 to $360 in

1916–17 and second-hand models could always be had from $25 up if the monthly instalments on a new car were too steep. By 1920 the rural roads of America swarmed with the beloved, temperamental, efficient little cars that were "built for the multitude."

Such widespread car ownership increased the clamor for better roads. Better roads invited the production of improved cars. Improved cars attracted more buyers who

THE SAME ROAD BEFORE AND AFTER IMPROVEMENT, 1914–1915 (?). The liberated vehicle on the right

increased the clamor for better roads. The process became a self-perpetuating crescendo that has not yet abated. With several million cars of various makes already on the roads before World War I, inadequate highways had become an intolerable nuisance, menace, and extravagance. While the Ford could travel over all but an open field (in 1909 Ford himself won a transcontinental race in a Model T, covering the all but

appears to be the same Model T Ford as that shown on the left, none the worse for its earlier difficulties.

unexplored route from New York to Seattle in twenty-two days and fifty-five minutes), autos in general not only needed better roads but they emphasized the need by rapidly destroying the old roads, especially when heavy trucks began pounding over the light-surfaced routes originally planned for horse-and-buggy traffic. Like floods, droughts, and insect pests, motorists constantly overran state bounds and the problems they excited had to be thought out on an interstate, regional, and national scale.

A Federal-Aid Road Act of 1916 was the first important move of the national government to share responsibility with the states in providing durable highways to supplement the existing railroad network. The act was designed to develop an interstate system of highways and to centralize road construction in the hands of state highway departments staffed by experienced engineers. The need for such a broad approach was dramatized during the war that immediately followed when the Army Motor Transport Corps, in a "daring adventure," sent a fleet of motor trucks, en route to France, on a "nearly impossible" trek from Detroit over the Alleghenies to Baltimore in winter. Two years later a military convoy of motor transports managed to cross the continent, 3242 miles from Washington to San Francisco, in sixty-two days.

The facts and figures of automobile ownership and operation in America make giddy statistics. By 1913 registration had risen to one and a quarter million; in 1919 the figure was almost six times greater; in 1925 nearly twenty million cars were registered; and after World War II more than forty-four million motor vehicles were in service. All in all, between 1900 and 1942 sixty-nine million cars had been manufactured, three and three-quarter million passenger cars alone in the single year before Pearl Harbor. After the halt called by the war the figures again started to leap upwards. In such a favored state as California, claimed its governor, there were two automobiles for every five people, compared with one for every four as a national average.

With such a mounting flow of cars heading each year for the roads the Highway Act of 1916 had quickly proved obsolete. A new act in 1921 concentrated federal aid upon "such projects as will expedite the completion of an adequate and connected system of highways, interstate in character." The old act was designed to improve rural roads, often of limited reach and objective; the new one was continental in scope, planned to accommodate the cross-country habits of the new cars and their touring passengers. Every new model could carry more people farther and faster than earlier ones had done, and frequently did over all obstacles, including an increasing number of unfortunate pedestrians and fellow motorists. The mortality rate from automobile accidents rapidly developed into a large item in actuary tables. The loss of time and money from congestion on the roads was a less poignant matter but it helped to underline the fact that auto travel needed to be humanized, that wide, safe, and efficient roads were not being engineered as fast as the traffic required.

SCENE ON THE BOSTON POST ROAD IN CONNECTICUT, 1923.

The Public Roads Administration

The Public Roads Administration

HOLIDAY PEAK TRAFFIC OVER THE ARROYO SECO NEAR PASADENA, CALIFORNIA, 1941.

DROUGHT REFUGEES STALLED ON THE HIGHWAY, NEAR LORDSBURG, NEW MEXICO, 1937. Photograph by Dorothea Lange for the Farm Security Administration.

To a people whose forefathers had hacked their way through solid forests, plodded across immeasurable plains, and scaled towering mountains, overcoming every obstacle to their ceaseless movement, any sort of road was an open highway to the future. Theirs was a land of magnificent distances and enchanting scenic variety, three and a half million square miles of beckoning country without tariff barriers or passport difficulties and, by the 1930's, interlaced with several million miles of passable roads. With a cheap and flexible means of transportation within almost everyone's reach and with billions of dollars available for the purpose (in 1937 five billion dollars were spent on motor travel), the nation took to wheels as a matter of course.

At what point the country would have all the cars that might conceivably be put to use was anyone's guess. To own an automobile was by the 1930's not an expectation but the realization of most American families. Yet, to President Hoover, two cars in every garage seemed a plausible standard of sufficiency.

The family's car was generally held to be its most precious possession. "I'll go without food before I'll see us give up the car," reported one woman to the Lynds in their survey of a typical American community. A mother of nine children stated that she would "rather do without clothes than give up the car." During the depression of the 1930's many desperate people made just that choice, clinging to their jalopies with grim faith in mobility as an ultimate resort.

More people were making longer trips in their cars than had ever traveled by any means before. But, according to a report

Life Magazine

Main Street on a Saturday Night in a Midwestern Town (Franklin, Indiana), 1941. Photograph by Bernard Hoffman.

made in 1930 to President Hoover, most automobiles observed on the road were engaged in trips of less than fifty miles, and a great many in trips of less than half that distance. Obviously, people were also moving about more quickly and more frequently in their own localities than had ever been possible before. For rural folk, going to town—anywhere from five to two hundred miles—developed from a weekly, monthly, or seasonal expedition to a swift, easy passage. From an infrequent opportunity it became a routine social necessity.

In the dark days of the depression five times as many American farms had automobiles as had piped-in water. One housewife when asked why the family kept a car when it owned no bathtub replied, with real surprise, "Why, you can't go to town in a bathtub." The very phrase "going to town"

became a general slogan for making the most of things.

Actually it was the town that was going to the country, by automobile, as by movie and radio. Urban values derived from the industrial city and the metropolis were spreading a standard of culture all over the land. As a sort of symbol, New York's Broadway was projected in an endless series of replicas from one boundary of the continent to the other. The dazzle of white lights, the movie palace, the facilities for spending time and money, all are available on a variable scale to motorized rural populations, as any Main Street scene on Saturday night clearly shows. The automobile had spanned the historic gulf between town and country that had seemed so impassable a few generations earlier. Wherever the need and whatever it was, you could go by car.

The Museum of the City of New York

BUS TERMINAL, NEW YORK CITY, 1936. Photograph by Berenice Abbott.

Ewing Galloway
TRANSCONTINENTAL TRUCKING ACROSS THE ROCKIES
ON "VICTORY HIGHWAY."

The automobile had been conceived, or accepted at least in its earliest days, as a pleasure vehicle, limited in all practicality to city streets and best suited to the amiable diversions of the well-to-do. But by 1907 it was already spoken of as being as indispensable as the telephone and the typewriter in the ordinary affairs of life, and it was already assuming its rôle of a common carrier in the larger communities. By the mid-1920's motor buses were offering transcontinental service in competition with the railroads. Before World War II the number of passengers, including children in school buses, had risen to almost five billion fares in a single year. In the years following the war buses were carrying more than one third of the nation's intercity passenger traffic.

Trucks, too, had long since followed the tourist out onto the long roads while they continued to clog city streets on their innumerable short hauls. The four and a half million drivers required for the six million trucks that found their way to the streets of the city and to every corner of the country constituted the largest occupational class in the nation, excepting farmers. The farmers themselves were, of course, generally motorized with truck, tractor, and sedan. In 1949 it was estimated that about half the communities in the United States were served exclusively by motor transport.

No nation had ever undergone such a quick, radical, and complete revolution in its habits as America with its automobilism. It was proving to be a far bloodier revolution than the War of Independence. The incessant, roaring passage of motors, from huge road liners carrying twenty tons of freight to tiny pleasure cars that traveled a mile on a teaspoonful of gasoline, was accounting for forty thousand deaths and a million and a quarter injuries each year.

Even for people enchanted with their machines and dependent on them for the necessities as well as the joys of life, that was a fearful toll. It was made worse by the fact that in many areas the very number of cars on the road slowed their progress down to something less than a horse-and-buggy pace.

Out of the desperate need to relieve traffic paralysis "and sudden death" new types of highways were wanted faster than they could be engineered—broad-laned thoroughfares that separated opposing streams of cars, that provided grade separations to eliminate the conflict of cross traffic, that controlled entry and exit points, that skirted population centers and removed the car from pedestrian traffic, and that were insulated from abutting property by landscaped rights-of-way, free from obstructive and disfiguring billboards.

A SECTION OF THE MERRITT PARKWAY, CONNECTICUT.

The Portland Cement Association

CAHUENGA PASS, LOS ANGELES, CALIFORNIA. Photograph by Andreas Feininger.

In the 1940's, with thirty million miles of road—the most extensive system in the world—the United States still did not have enough adequate major highways. Traffic had continued to increase until, on main-traveled routes, the passage of cars through night and day was incessant. Year by year the definition of an adequate highway that would carry such a burden and speed the vehicles safely along their way had to be revised. Broader roadbeds, heavier grading, and more durable surfaces were built into routes that often ignored the accidents of terrain by cuts and fills and that called for new degrees of engineering skill.

The old bottlenecks to continuous fast travel, in areas about large centers of population and where rivers and bays presented obstacles, were transformed into "magic motorways" that in their sheer functional beauty are monuments to the automobile era. Within six years, 1931–37, two long-cherished dreams were realized when the lower Hudson River and San Francisco Bay were bridged with soaring highways that gave New York and San Francisco direct, unbroken motor communication with the main bulk of the continent.

The dream of the moment, to extend such facilities throughout the nation by a country-wide system of integrated super-highways, is already taking concrete form. "Even before the project is complete," reported the *New York Times* in 1947, "its effects on the life of the nation will be profound. All are not now foreseeable, but such a system of interstate highways is bound to develop new population centers, open new factory locations, establish new freight routes, stimulate business and lessen regional friction. Most of all it will bind the people of this country into one vast neighborhood where the wants of all can be freely supplied and the ideas of all can freely circulate. It will mark the final peaceful conquest of an empire by the internal combustion engine."

"MAGIC MOTORWAYS," NEW YORK.

The Port of New York Authority

The Port of New York Authority

THE GEORGE WASHINGTON BRIDGE, NEW YORK, COMPLETED 1931.

A TRAFFIC "SWITCHBOARD" ON THE GRAND CENTRAL PARKWAY, NEW YORK CITY, 1939.

The Public Roads Administration

WINGED VICTORIES

In their passion for speed Americans had long talked—in tall tales—of supersonic travel. Paul Bunyan once had to reverse a speeding train on the B. & O. back up a few hills so that the locomotive whistle could catch up with the train in time to signal the crew to apply the brakes and avoid a crash. At that pace not only Bunyan's station stop at Washington, but international barriers, are hard to see. At supersonic speed it is easier to see that human beings must become "one single people, one nation, one mind, one head," as the New York *Mirror* forecasted a century ago of the coming age of faster communications. With the airplane that age has dawned and most of the habitable world has been mechanically reduced to a single travel area. With the likely prospect of soon being abe to leave New York at high noon and, by traveling through the air faster than the earth turns on its axis, arrive at San Francisco in the forenoon of the same day, Paul Bunyan's exploits seem modest enough.

To whatever degree world fellowship may be served by the newly opened skyways, America is in a fair position to play an important rôle. The country has provided a splendid training ground for international air service. Populous centers were far enough apart to promote the most rapid transportation. Every sort of flying condition from arctic blizzard to tropical storm,

THE DEPARTURE OF DR. JOHN JEFFRIES AND PIERRE BLANCHARD FROM ENGLAND (OPPOSITE) AND THEIR ARRIVAL (BELOW) IN FRANCE, JANUARY 7, 1785. French engravings.

The Institute of Aeronautical Sciences

the two daring adventurers took off from Dover Castle and several hours later, after a perilous trip, landed in the Forest of Guines. In France they received a royal welcome at Versailles and numerous other "honors and attentions" which Jeffries thought were "much above our merit."

After forty-four successful ascensions in Europe Blanchard arrived in America for an exhibition tour in 1793. Armed with a passport signed by Washington, who witnessed the take-off, Blanchard ascended from the courtyard of a Philadelphia prison to a deafening volley of artillery fire and the playing of music. Three quarters of an hour later he landed in New Jersey where his passport saved him from embarrassment at the hands of suspicious rustics. It was the first actual aerial voyage in this country.

conceivably to be met with in a single flight within the country, encouraged experimentation and the development of equipment suitable for any airway on earth. By and large the aviation industry in America had to win its wings through such general public service as it could provide, without serious intervention or subsidy by the government during its growing period. Air transport, less bothered by military expediency in America than in many other countries, here could concentrate on economy, comfort, safety, and speed as important factors in a serviceable commercial aviation.

The first American to make an aerial voyage shared one of the outstanding flights in aeronautical history. Dr. John Jeffries, a Boston physician, bought permission from the French aeronaut, Pierre Blanchard, to accompany him on a balloon flight across the English Channel. On January 7, 1785,

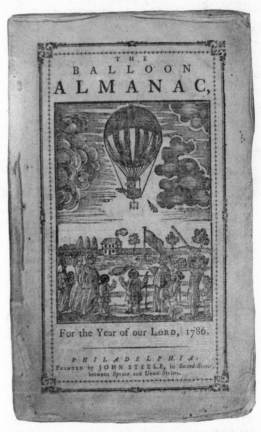

The Institute of Aeronautical Sciences
ALMANAC TITLE PAGE, PHILADELPHIA, 1786.

THE BALLOON ASCENSION OF 1834 AT BALTIMORE. Painting by Nicolino V. Calyo. Photograph courtesy of the Frick Art Reference Library.

"What is the use of the new invention?" someone asked Benjamin Franklin who had witnessed the earliest ascensions in France. "What is the use of a new-born child?" retorted Franklin. He pointed out elsewhere that the invention might well mark a turning point in human affairs. Franklin suggested that even the most potent sovereign could not protect his dominions from enemy troops dropped out of the sky—a considera- tion which, he added, might convince rulers of the folly of war.

For a while after Blanchard's early flights interest in ballooning subsided in America. A quarter-century later, however, visiting French demonstrators revived a dormant enthusiasm and by 1834 ballooning had become such an active pursuit in Baltimore that the press complained of it as a public nuisance. Again some thought they recog-

nized a borning revolution in travel and transportation in those numerous flights. That same year another portion of the press echoed Franklin's forecast. "Conveyance by air," reported the Silliman's *Journal,* "can easily be rendered as safe as by water or land, and more cheap and speedy, while the universal and uniform diffusion of the air over every portion of the earth, will render aerial navigation preferable to any other.

To carry it into effect there needs only an immediate appeal, on a sufficiently large scale. . . ." But little that developed during the nineteenth century did much to justify their faith in "aerostation." Others observed that it was little more than a circus of ups and downs. As one contemporary newspaper remarked: "They all 'gracefully ascend' and 'gracefully descend,' and there is an end of the matter."

INFLATING THE TRANSATLANTIC BALLOON, *Great Western*, SEPTEMBER, 1860.

PROFESSOR L. S. C. LOWE IN THE GONDOLA OF HIS BALLOON, ON AERIAL RECONNAISSANCE OF CONFEDERATE LINES DURING THE CIVIL WAR.

INFLATING A RECONNAISSANCE BALLOON DURING THE CIVIL WAR.

Until the successful development of dirigibles in the present century the problems of control and motive power kept lighter-than-air flight close to the entertainment level. But serious efforts were constantly made to achieve some practical results with the balloon. According to one estimate as many as eight thousand people had taken part in about three thousand ascensions in America during the fifty years before 1859. Many of the flights were made by earnest aeronauts at the peril of their lives. Thaddeus Sobieski Constantine Lowe, a New Hampshire-born zealot, was one of two experienced balloonists who planned to use the prevailing easterly winds for flights to Europe in 1859. Scientific minds thought it a feasible stunt and public interest in the adventures ran high. Lowe's *Great Western* was destroyed by the wind before it left the ground. On a second trial flight in another balloon, taking off from Cincinnati, Lowe landed in South Carolina just before hostilities broke out between the North and the South. He was imprisoned briefly as a Yankee spy but was released.

Lowe achieved tangible results during the war years immediately following by developing the first air corps in United States Army history. Both sides in the conflict recognized the importance of his reconnaissance work aloft. The Confederate forces paid Lowe the high tribute of trying constantly to destroy his balloons by artillery fire and sabotage. "Even if the observer never saw anything," remarked General Alexander of the Confederate Army, "his balloons would have been worth all they cost, trying to keep our movements out of sight." But Lowe saw, interpreted, and reported.

"It may safely be claimed," wrote the Chief of the Union Army Signal Corps, "that the Union Army was saved from destruction at the battle of Fair Oaks . . . by the frequent and accurate reports of Professor Lowe."

Another, and probably the most brilliant, American aeronaut of the nineteenth century was John Wise whose numerous successful flights were so commonplace that they filtered down into an elementary textbook of the period. "If Mr. Wise can ascend in his balloon 4 times in 1 week," read *A Pictorial Primary Arithmetic* of 1867, "how many times can he ascend in 3 weeks? Why?" Wise was the first man to carry mail by air in this country which he did on a brief hop in 1859. The same year, on the first leg of a projected trans-Atlantic voyage, Wise traveled over 800 miles in less than twenty hours, a record for air travel not surpassed until 1910.

Fourteen years later Wise persuaded the owners of the New York *Daily Illustrated Graphic* to finance the construction of a gigantic balloon for the overseas trip which he insisted could be successfully made. After public excitement was fired to white heat the enormous, elaborate craft, equipped for every contingency, took off for Europe on

The Institute of Aeronautical Sciences
INTERIOR OF THE CAR OF THE *Daily Graphic* BALLOON, 1873. From the New York *Daily Illustrated Graphic*.

October 6, 1873 (without Wise who had disagreed with his sponsors) and landed a few hours later in the Catskills.

However few were the sustained, solid accomplishments of Lowe, Wise, and other pioneers, their innumerable ascents, stunts, and claims had made a commonplace of man, after long centuries, actually free of the earth. From the Mother Goose Melodies of the 1830's to the dime novels of the 1880's and 1890's, including Tom Sawyer's aerial adventures over the Sahara Desert, American literature contributed generously to the air-mindedness of the country. People impatient with the delay of practical aerial navigation were buoyed by the occasional optimist who promised the coming day when "floating palaces of the people, far more numerous and splendid than excursion steamboats," would sail the skies. There was much serious writing as well as fantasy, which probed the questions yet to be settled before men could direct their own course through the air. And there persisted the happy vision, reshaped by a Wall Street broker in 1879, that air travel would wipe out all international boundaries and result, at long last, in a congress of United Nations.

To a nation that was leaping over the continent in enormous strides by railroad and steamboat, practical conquest of the air could not remain an utterly implausible vision. "Steam eagles" that would take Washingtonians to Boston for a dinner party and home again of an evening, stream-lined propeller-driven "Aeroports," "aerial locomotives" eight hundred feet from bow to stern, that would journey to the California gold fields and back in seven days, heavier than air "steam-kites" of unrecorded pretentions, all were attempted or dreamed by earnest enthusiasts, and lampooned by scoffers. Some incorporated ideas prophetic of future successes. None amounted to anything practical.

At the turn of the present century there was a growing conviction in some circles that "God never intended man to fly," at least until he won his angel's wings; to fly,

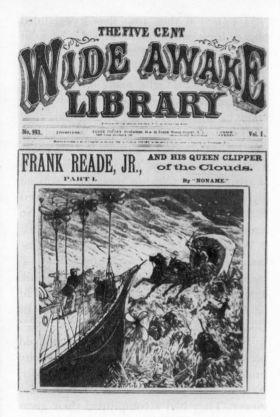

THE COVER OF A DIME NOVEL, 1890.

SONG

By an Exquisite, in 1934, at breakfast.

"Tell John to set the kettle on
I mean to take a drive;
I only want to go to Rome,
And shall be back by five.

Tell cook to dress those humming birds,
I shot in Mexico;
They've now been killed at least two days
They'll be un peu trop haut.

I'll try that wine, too, a la rose,
Just brought from Ispahan;
How could those Goths of other times,
Endure that vile Champaign?

The trip I took the other day,
To breakfast in the moon,
Thanks to that awkward Lord Bellaire,
Has spoiled my new balloon.

For steering through the Milky Way,
He ran against a star,
And turning round again too soon,
Came jolt against my car.

Such fellows ought to keep below,
And never venture there;
If he's so clumsy he should go
By no way but the Bear.

My steam is surely up by now—
Put the high pressure on;
Give me the "breath bag" for the way—
All right—hey—whizz—I'm gone."

that is, with the freedom and purpose that birds flew. Even as late as the autumn of 1903 Simon Newcomb, a world-famous astronomer, admonished the public that such freedom in the air was not a likely development. "May not our mechanicians . . . be ultimately forced to admit," he asked, "that aerial flight is one of that great class of problems with which man can never cope, and give up all attempts to grapple with it?" But an increasing number of Americans were tackling the fundamentals of heavier-than-air flight. Following European precedents gliding trials by the Montgomery brothers in California during the 1880's, by Octave Chanute in the '90's, and by the Wright brothers and others, had brought new understanding to the vital matter of using the pressure of air to control soaring bodies.

A PROPHETIC CARTOON OF 1834. From *Peabody's Parlour Journal.*

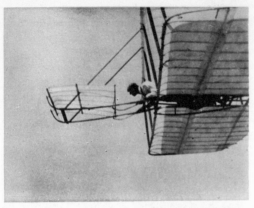

The National Archives
A SOARING FLIGHT AT KITTY HAWK, NORTH CAROLINA, 1901.

By 1902 the Wright brothers had, through patient study and laborious experimentation, evolved a very satisfactory glider. In two months' time they made between seven hundred and one thousand flights on the windy slopes of Kill Devil Hill at Kitty Hawk, North Carolina. Those long hours in the air gave them invaluable experience none of their predecessors or immediate contemporaries had enjoyed in their quest of powered flight.

"Damned if they ain't flew!" exclaimed one witness when man, in the shape of Orville Wright, raised himself in full flight under controlled power and sailed forward into space. The flight, made on December 17, 1903, lasted just twelve seconds, long enough to capture one of the oldest of human dreams. The press was still ridiculing the near-success of Samuel P. Langley in a similar attempt just nine days before, and it spared little space to report the winged victory at Kitty Hawk. In all its implications that first flight was too nearly incredible to make good reportage. Man had flown!

What was even more important the same man—or men—proved by continued successes in days following, flying with the wind, against the wind, in a straight course, and in circles that their flight was no freak of circumstance.

Ten years later Orville Wright looked back with amazement at his own audacity under the circumstances of the first flight. Neither he nor his brother was a trained engineer. They had accomplished their great feat by practical mechanics, perseverance, and ingenuity. During those ten years their continued progress in the air attracted more

ORVILLE WRIGHT FLYING, WILBUR WRIGHT AT THE WING TIP, KITTY HAWK, DECEMBER 17, 1903.
The Institute of Aeronautical Sciences

WRIGHT AIRPLANE AT FORT MYER, VIRGINIA, 1909.

attention in Europe than in America.

The slow progress of aviation in America was in part caused by the difficulty of inventors and experimenters in securing financial aid in their work.

With very serious doubt that its specifications could be met, the United States Army agreed to accept from the Wrights a plane that could carry for one hour a pilot and passenger, not less than three hundred and fifty pounds in all, at a top speed of forty miles per hour and with fuel for one hundred and twenty-five miles. Orville Wright sealed the $25,000 contract with a successful trial at Fort Myer, Virginia, in September, 1909.

WILBUR WRIGHT IN ENGLAND, 1909.

OFFICIAL PROGRAM OF THE FIRST AMERICAN AVIATION MEET, LOS ANGELES, 1910.

With a trail through the air clearly blazed America held its first aviation meet in 1910 before a daily audience of from twenty to fifty thousand spectators. When the meet closed, all aviation records save one had been broken. Louis Paulhan of France and Glenn H. Curtiss of the United States set most of the new marks. "Their majestic, even, steady flight filled the thousands at Dominguey Field with a delirium of delight," reported the press. "Men cheered on and on as though there would be no end. And right then and there every man, woman and child of the multitude wanted to fly— fly up in the blue, cut away from the earth— fly—fly—oh, the ravishing delight of it!" Within five minutes, the report concluded, every member of the audience wanted a flying machine of his own. However, in spite of all that enthusiasm, until 1913 just five airplanes were sold to private individuals.

Writing to a French acquaintance in 1784 at the height of the first ballooning craze, George Washington not altogether jokingly remarked that if newspaper reports could be trusted one might "suspect that our friends at Paris, in a little time, will come flying thro' the air, instead of ploughing the ocean to get to America." In 1844 the idea seemed plausible enough to enable Edgar Allan Poe to perpetrate an enormous hoax. His fictitious account of an East-West aerial crossing was printed in the New York *Sun* as a news fact that covered a full page of an extra edition.

Until such a flight was actually achieved, crossing the Atlantic by air stood as a supreme challenge to those who would be "at home with the wind." Melville Vaniman's attempt to realize the dream in 1912 in the semi-rigid airship *Akron* met disaster before the final take-off. But the dare was almost immediately accepted by others. Seven years later the British fliers Alcock and Brown opened a new road above the clouds by a non-stop crossing from Newfoundland to Ireland in their Vickers-Vimy biplane.

THE SEMI-RIGID *Akron* AT ATLANTIC CITY BEFORE A PROJECTED TRANS-ATLANTIC FLIGHT, 1912.

The National Archives

LOADING THE *Spirit of St. Louis* AT CURTIS FIELD, LONG ISLAND, MAY 20, 1927.

In May, 1927, an unheralded young aviator, Charles A. Lindbergh, flew from San Diego, California, to New York making record time in the *Spirit of St. Louis,* a plane he had reconstructed according to his own ideas. A few days later he took off for the field of Le Bourget in France—unceremoniously, alone, with five sandwiches and a canteen of water for provisions, and to the shaking of many heads. Thirty-three and a half hours later he arrived precisely at his goal.

The enthusiasm with which he was greeted, he remarked, created more hazards than all the rest of his adventure. The whole civilized world applauded. That the Atlantic flight had been made was not in itself news; others had flown the ocean before. But the quiet assurance of the young aviator, the apparent simplicity of the operation, and, most of all, the precision with which his flight was accomplished won universal and ungrudging admiration.

The measure of Lindbergh's success can be read in the record of the thirty-one trans-Atlantic flights that were attempted in the following two years. Not one achieved an announced destination, although many spanned the ocean itself, and a score of lives were lost in the efforts that were made. But that one perfect flight had secured public confidence in aviation's future. In the months that followed his return to America Lindbergh flew the *Spirit of St. Louis* on a tour of the forty-eight states, visiting eighty-two cities and covering 22,350 miles in two hundred and sixty air-hours, always on schedule or ahead of the specified time. With all eyes fixed on his progress the time-table orderliness of the young hero's tour advertised the dependability of the airplane to every corner of the land.

Air transport in America on an established commercial basis had its beginnings before Lindbergh's flights, although for some years Europe's network of airlines for passengers, mail, and express outmatched any developments in this country. Under the Civil Aviation Act of 1926, Congress recognizing the growing commerce in the air laid out a federal airways system to expedite and help organize the traffic. With the evolution of fast, highly dependable, and versatile planes in the 1930's, most importantly the DC-3 which quickly became standard equipment on most major airlines in the United States (and elsewhere), commercial aviation advanced towards unlimited horizons. By the mid-1930's service in America was setting the standard of efficiency and safety. In the Civil Aeronautics Act of 1938 the government prepared, among other things, long-range programs in anticipation of future developments in both civil aeronautics and air commerce. Flying the Atlantic Ocean was still in an exploratory stage in 1939. But as a foretaste of tomorrow's travel one American, Howard Hughes, had already flown around the world in less than four days' time.

The Douglas Aircraft Co., Inc.

LOADING A DC-3 TRANSPORT PLANE.

A DC-3 ON TOP OF THE WORLD.

The Douglas Aircraft Co., Inc.

At the outbreak of World War II the total output of American airplane factories was less than 6000 units a year. In May, 1940, President Roosevelt asked the industry to gear-up to an annual production of at least fifty thousand planes, a staggering increase at a time when designs were undergoing constant changes. Yet, once plans were stabi-lized, production figures mounted in a spec-tacular curve. In 1944 the planes of all types manufactured in the nation totaled almost one hundred thousand for the year.

Airplanes had become commonplace vehi-cles, production could apparently be geared to almost any demand, and the airways of the globe offered endless room for flight. Fly-

TAIL SECTIONS OF B-17F BOMBERS ON THE ASSEMBLY LINE AT THE BOEING PLANT, SEATTLE, 1942. Photograph by Andreas Feininger for the Farm Security Administration.

The Library of Congress

American Airlines System

CONTROLLING AIR TRAFFIC, LA GUARDIA FIELD, NEW YORK, 1946. Photograph by Merle J. Oelke.

ing the Atlantic had been reduced from a challenging stunt to the routine schedule of hundreds of planes each week. The thousand days of Magellan's epic trip about the globe had been reduced to a flight of ninety-six hours by a plane that never put wheels to the ground en route (Magellan's was surely the more interesting trip!). But those are simply statistics and records that are superseded as they are written of. With the sky full of fast, comfortable, and safe planes the familiar problem of traffic became one of the frontier problems of aviation. The heavens are immeasurably spacious—there is room for all who would fly—but in poor weather they become for all practical purposes no larger than a radio beam and its thin path to a safe return to earth. At such times a few planes are enough to jam the airways.

As elsewhere remarked, the success of American democracy can be properly measured only in terms of the scale of its development. To have created a free, working government over a continental area is a unique achievement in world history. Without the agencies of the steamboat and the railroad it would have been all but impossible. With the automobile it was accelerated and enhanced.

With men able to roam the heavens that stretch in unbroken highways over all the earth America's historic need to knit together her sprawling parts became inseparable from the larger need to help knit the nations of the world into a neighborhood of free people. There was no turning back from the responsibilities man acquired with the realization of his dream of owning wings.

IX
THE DEMOCRATIC MOLD

THE DEMOCRATIC MOLD

MOLD

INTRODUCTION

To WIDE PORTIONS of the world the emergence of America as a new nation was a matter of small moment. In 1797 when young John Quincy Adams, son of the President, arrived in Prussia to represent his country as American Minister, he was confronted by one dashing officer of the guards who admitted without a blush that he had never so much as heard of the United States of America. Countless other Europeans no doubt knew as little and cared less about the events that were taking place across the Atlantic. But to some they seemed to be matters of supreme importance. Benjamin Franklin's English friend, the Reverend Dr. Richard Price, wrote that next to the introduction of Christianity the American Revolution might prove to be "the most important step in the progressive course of human improvement." Writing to Price, Turgot, minister of finance under Louis XVI, remarked that the new nation was "the hope of the human race. It may become the model," he wrote. "It ought to show the world by facts, that men can be free and yet peaceful, and may dispense with the chains in which tyrants and knaves of every colour have presumed to bind them, under pretext of the public good. The Americans should be an example of political, religious, commercial and industrial liberty. The asylum

they offer to the oppressed of every nation, the avenue of escape they open, will compel governments to be just and enlightened; and the rest of the world in due time will see through the empty illusions in which policy is conceived. But to obtain these ends for us, America must secure them to herself; and must not become, as so many of your ministerial writers have predicted, a mass of divided powers, contending for territory and trade, cementing the slavery of peoples by their own blood."

As Turgot indicated, there were others, Frenchmen and Prussians as well as English clergymen, who had no such faith in or hope for America's future as an independent, unified nation. "In the present state of affairs," wrote the French chargé d'affaires in New York, also in 1787, "it is impossible to unite under a single head all the members of the Confederation. Their political interests, their commercial views, their customs and their laws are so varied that there is not a resolution of Congress which can be equally useful and popular in the South and in the North of the Continent...." Frederick the Great argued that the mere size of the country made disunion or a monarchy inevitable.

The basis for any prediction was slim. There were, at least, no valid historical precedents by which to forecast the future when in 1788 America adopted a written constitution as a chart for its destiny. This trial in government was undertaken in a manner, on a scale, and under circumstances which made it seem, as H. G. Wells has written, "like something coming out of an egg." In the Declaration of Independence the signers had, so far as they were able—and they were exceptionally able men—stripped the matter of political relationships down to its fundamentals. They had re-examined the "inalienable rights" of men who must live together in a governed society.

In writing the Constitution the founding fathers, although in many ways not of a mind with Jefferson's Declaration, hoped to provide a system of government strong enough to secure those rights to all the people, but limited to the point where it could never encroach on the liberties it existed to protect. They aspired to guarantee a lasting unity to the nation while safeguarding the local freedom of each part.

There was nothing new in the problem. How to reconcile maximum individual freedom with adequate social authority, how to preserve liberty within empire, was one of the most ancient of political dilemmas and to the men of the Constitutional Convention the most immediate and important. The Constitution, although soundly based on the experience of the past, was enlightened with new and courageous thinking. With it America made an outstanding contribution to political history.

Gladstone once wrote that the American Constitution was "the most wonderful work ever struck off at a given time by the brain and purpose of man." But those who helped to strike it off, and a majority of their countrymen, held no such conviction. The document was written in the heat of violent controversy.

To a revolutionary generation that could "snuff the approach of tyranny in every tainted breeze," to a generation trained in local loyalties, the assumption of broad powers by a remote, central authority had the stale smell of the imperial control that had

just been cast off. Patrick Henry warned that "that paper," referring to the proposed Constitution, was "the most fatal plan that could possibly be conceived to enslave a free people." Others of different counsel prevailed, but by the slenderest of margins. With his customary sagacity Benjamin Franklin pointed out that in the long run, regardless of the forms the Convention adopted, the fate of the government would be determined by the temper of the people themselves.

The final document was a result of serious compromises. It was incomplete. And it was bitterly opposed by a large number of the people. But it was, as Washington and others averred, the best that could be done at the time—and it could be changed if it were once accepted by enough of the states.

Two years before Washington's inauguration Benjamin Rush, signer of the Declaration of Independence, had warned his countrymen against the common fallacy of confounding the War of Independence with the American revolution. "The American war is over," he wrote, "but that is far from being the case with the American revolution. On the contrary, nothing but the first act of the great drama is closed."

America had cast away the customary props of state—royalty, aristocracy, and an established national church—and framed its federal structure in the name of all the people. Few among the leaders of the new Republic held that confidence in popular sovereignty which the Declaration had implied, however. Democracy, indeed, was a tainted word. But, as George Mason remarked, the genius of the people was for democracy and the rapid growth of democratic purposes beyond any intention of the founding fathers was a continuous peaceful revolution that caught the world's attention.

If America, born of rebellion, could achieve stability; if a society made of mixed peoples with no ancient roots in the land and few, if any, common, time-hallowed traditions could find some binding faith; if a people committed to the dangerous principle that freedom of religion, speech, assembly, and the press was not only permissible but desirable; if that nation could survive conflicting ideas and unlimited criticism from within, and if America could demonstrate all this on a continental scale, then by its example alone, by the unanswerable power of contrast, it would be a threat to every other existing form of government.

Actually the questions were never finally answered. Each succeeding generation of voters had to meet the issues over and over again. The problems had to be thought out afresh with each changing season of opinion and each new development of circumstances.

An Allegorical Salute to the States under the
Constitution. Frontispiece of the *Columbian
Magazine*, 1788. Engraving by Trenchard.

AMERICA,
"THE HOPE OF THE WORLD"

Act Two of the "great drama," as Benjamin
Rush termed the continuing nature of the
American revolution, opened with the rati-
fication of the Constitution in 1788. Patrick
Henry warned his countrymen that the very
first line of the script, starting "We, the people," threatened a new phase of the revolution "as radical," he claimed, "as that which
separated us from Great Britain." With
others Henry felt—and felt with blazing conviction—that if local liberties were to be
protected the phrase must instead read "we,
the *states*." This novel experiment in federalism that called for the sacrifice of state
sovereignty must be forestalled.

Without the support of Washington the
Constitution would never have been accepted. Washington understood as clearly as
any that the nation was taking a revolutionary step, that the men who framed the Constitution had done so without authority
from their states, and that proposing to
maintain order and equity by dividing sovereignty between federal and state governments was running in the face of logic and
experience. He knew, too, that his countrymen were incurring heavy responsibilities
in their plan to form a more perfect union
and to secure to themselves the blessings of
liberty. The world would be watching them
with hope and interest. "The preservation
of the sacred fire of liberty and the destiny
of the republican model of government," he
counseled in his first inaugural address, "are

A DISPLAY OF THE STATES UNITED. Engraving by Amos Doolittle, 1788.

justly considered, as *deeply*, perhaps as *finally* staked, on the experiment intrusted to the hands of the American people."

The people themselves had no part in framing the document which starts, "We the people" — "that poor little thing," as Henry scornfully called the phrase. The Constitution was drafted by men who firmly believed that affairs of government could not safely be referred to popular opinion. "The proposition that the people are the best keepers of their own liberties," warned John Adams, "is not true." To that point of view Washington, Jay, Marshall, Madison, and most other leading Americans of the time solemnly, if sometimes reluctantly, subscribed. The "popular tumults" that had occurred during the days of the Articles of Confederation had given them all cause to

fear that a broad electorate would only lead to anarchy and that anarchy would end in despotism.

Shays' Rebellion in 1786–87, a protest of debt-burdened farmers without political power to obtain relief, had been reported to Washington as an unfortunate indication of the "levelling principle" and the "desire for change" that were prevalent among many of the people — two characteristics which, forty years later, Tocqueville thought were outstanding aspects of a flourishing American democracy.

Jefferson, who heard about the Shays' outburst in France, wrote to Abigail Adams: "I like a little rebellion now and then. It is like a storm in the atmosphere."

Here spoke America's foremost democrat, that *Man of the People,* as Mrs. Adams apos-

The John Carter Brown Library

A PEEP INTO THE ANTIFEDERAL CLUB. Thomas Jefferson (standing on the table), the Devil (lower left), and their Subversive Associates, Including the Eminent Astronomer David Rittenhouse, President of the Democratic Society of Philadelphia (envying the government on Saturn, spied through his telescope), a Cutthroat, a French Revolutionary, an aspiring Negro, and Others Voicing the Democratic creed. A satire published in New York, August 16, 1793. Engraving by an unidentified artist.

WASHINGTON AND HIS STAFF AT FORT CUMBERLAND, MARYLAND. Review of the Troops Summoned to Quell the Whisky Rebellion, October, 1794. Painting by an unidentified artist. Photograph courtesy of Victor Spark.

trophized him, with utter distaste for his views. Upon his return to America Jefferson became the earnest champion of democratic principles and an easy target for those who did not share his views—for most of those, that is, then in positions of political authority.

Distrust of government was the heritage of Americans, a natural consequence of their colonial troubles and of that freedom of individual action which conditions in the New World made possible. The right of the people to resist when they felt that their interests were neglected or their liberties invaded was, after all, hallowed by the Declaration of Independence.

The threat of rebellion within the union and secession from it recurred on several occasions, from different areas, during more than seventy-five years after Washington's inauguration. The subject was frequently discussed in all sections of the country during this time. In 1792 Abigail Adams wrote her sister from the capital in Philadelphia,

"I firmly believe if I live Ten Years longer, I shall see a devision of the Southern & Northern States, unless more candour & less intrigue, of which I have no hopes, should prevail."

Two years later the whisky distillers of western Pennsylvania revolted against the injustice of Hamilton's excise tax which, from beyond the mountains, seemed as unfair as the stamp tax had seemed to eastern colonists a quarter of a century earlier.

Exercising his constitutional power, the President called out the militia to put a stop to such "anarchy and confusion." To the surprise of some, the organizations of four states, fifteen thousand strong, answered the summons to police their fellow citizens, and the revolt collapsed. The vigor of federal authority over individual insurgency was demonstrated in an almost operatic manner by "Hamilton's army," as that oversize punitive force was called. But the question of insurgency of a section, of secession and of States' rights, remained wide open.

In his last words of advice to his countrymen, Washington warned them to discountenance "even a suspicion" that the sacred ties of union might be loosened. Yet within a very few years separation from the Union, for different reasons, was openly discussed in various sections of the country. Radical Republican opinion in Virginia in 1798–99 was prepared for physical resistance to the National government even, some claimed, to the point of erecting an armory and drilling the militia—rather than submit to the "palpable violations" of justice imposed by the Alien and Sedition Acts. "Perhaps the Potomac, the Delaware, or the Hudson, like the Rhine," reported the *Connecticut Courant*, "may part rival, hostile nations, and the shores of one of them be perpetually crimsoned with the blood of the inhabitants."

Farther west, settlers had long been seriously disaffected by the national government's apparent neglect of their need of a secure life line down the Mississippi River and had threatened more than once to set up their own government. Jefferson, philosophically, was inclined to let them do it. ". . . if they see their interest in separation," he wrote in 1803, "why should we take side with our Atlantic rather than our Mississippi descendants? It is the elder and the younger son differing. God bless them both, and keep them in union, if it be for their good, but separate them, if it be better."

Through the early 1800's Yankees continually grumbled over the "corrupt and corrupting influence and oppression of the aristocratic democrats of the South," not to mention the political antics of the "wild men" from the West who were just beginning to take their places in the nation's

The Hartford Convention or *LEAP NO LEAP.*

MASSACHUSETTS, CONNECTICUT, AND RHODE ISLAND CONTEMPLATE ABANDONING THE UNION. A Commentary on the Hartford Convention, 1814. Engraving by William Charles.

THE STAR SPANGLED BANNER IN THE ROCKET'S RED GLARE OVER FORT MCHENRY, 1814. Painting by an unidentified artist.

councils. It was the Westerners who descended upon Washington in 1811, organized the Twelfth Congress with Henry Clay as Speaker, and called for war against England. A battle cry was raised against British arrogance on the high seas and for "free trade and sailors' rights." Actually, the land-hungry War Hawks wanted more room and greater freedom along the western frontier. New England wanted only peace and the freedom to take its own chances on the ocean, but over its protests war was declared and thus in its turn New England questioned the inseparability of the states. When, in 1812, Timothy Pickering, once Washington's Secretary of War, said, "Let the Union be severed," he was but echoing sentiments earlier expressed by Josiah Quincy, "Such a severance holds no terrors for me." One year later the *Columbian Centinel* of Boston reported that *"the States are separated in fact when one section . . . perseveres in measures fatal to the interests and repugnant to the opinions of another section."*

Yankee resentment grew as the unfortunate war continued. In 1814 delegates sent by the legislatures of Massachusetts, Connecticut, and Rhode Island and by counties in New Hampshire and Vermont met at Hartford to discuss "means of defense against dangers . . . proceeding from acts of their own government." As earlier in the South and in the West, the final step of secession was not taken in the North, the war soon ended, and before very long New England, by and large, enjoying peace and prosperity, was hotly denying the constitutional right of other states to consider secession as a solution of sectional issues.

A half century passed before the constitutionality of that question was finally tested on the battlefield. But for the moment America was weary of sectional discord. In spite of defections suffered from within and humiliations imposed from without, America emerged from the War of 1812 with a new sense of unity and national dignity—feelings strong enough to justify calling that otherwise futile conflict our "second war of independence.

One of the happiest by-products of that war was "The Star Spangled Banner," written by Francis Scott Key after the British bombardment of Fort McHenry. For a country of such brief traditions and with so few official ceremonies or trappings to dramatize its purposes, the flag provided a symbol of peculiar importance. Key's verses became immediately and lastingly popular. The star spangled banner was accepted by all sections as the emblem of that lusty nationalism that grew out of the war. (One hundred and seventeen years later the song was officially proclaimed the national anthem.)

A MILITIA DRILL IN 1832. Lithograph by David Claypoole Johnston. The artist depicts himself with a cap, fifth man from the left.

For almost a century and a half America had been involved in the major wars of Europe because she was both intimately concerned and also too weak to stand apart and alone. With the Treaty of Ghent in 1815 the country turned its back to the Atlantic, self-confident in its independence. The size of America and its distance from first-rate military powers provided an immunity from aggression that lasted down to the present generation. Few nations in modern history have enjoyed such prolonged and undisturbed security. Not until 1898 did we again become seriously involved in international affairs, and then it was because we were strong.

Until a very recent day the idea of a standing army of any size has always been unpopular in America. Even during the Revolution civilians looked askance at a regular army. The Boston Massacre was still fresh in people's minds as an example of the dangers inherent in a professional soldiery. At the Constitutional Convention the power of Congress to maintain a permanent military force excited great alarm. The common militia, it was maintained, would serve the interests of the new nation sufficiently well.

Actually the militia system was a weak prop but, since no serious threats to security developed, the system lingered on. The periodic local muster, its participants often overdressed in gaudy outfits to compensate for their lack of militaristic temper, sometimes with no equipment at all, was in its latter days primarily a social occasion. Few nations have felt so free to play at the arts of soldiering and to work at the arts of peace.

When Tocqueville visited America he observed virtually no one in uniform and a complete lack of military spirit among the people. He prophesied accurately that Americans would always be reluctant to interrupt their profitable peacetime pursuits to engage in war, that they would always be unprepared for military emergencies, but that

THE UNITED STATES MILITARY ACADEMY, WEST POINT, N. Y. Aquatint by J. Hill after George Catlin, about 1830–35.

once the threat of war destroyed their chances of peaceful speculation, the same passions that made them attach so much importance to peace would be turned to arms. "Hence it is," he wrote, "that the self-same democratic nations that are so reluctant to engage in hostilities sometimes perform prodigious achievements when once they have taken the field."

Washington, who in a period of supreme trial again and again lacked enough soldiers for his purpose, was thoroughly aware of the inadequacies of the militia system in times of crisis. "The subject . . . is not a fit one to be publicly known or discussed," he wrote to his nephew with extreme bitterness. "I am wearied to death all day . . . at the conduct of the militia, whose behavior and want of discipline has done great injury to the other troops, who never had officers, except in a few instances, worth the bread they eat."

"However pacific the general policy of a nation may be," he wrote several years later, "it ought never to be without an adequate stock of military knowledge for emergencies. . . . The art of war is at once comprehensive and complicated; it demands much previous study." He urged the creation of a school to develop a core of military learning that could serve the nation at times of crisis.

The United States Military Academy long advocated by Washington and Knox was finally established by Act of Congress in 1802. It was primarily an engineering school, the only one in the country for its first twenty-three years. At the start of the War of 1812 it existed largely on paper. Real development began in 1817, under Brevet Major Sylvanus Thayer, "the Father of the Military Academy." The custom of choosing entrants from each congressional district has always given our small standing army, at least among its officers, a representative, broadly national character. The great bulk of the army itself has in every war been civilian by training and preference.

AN ELECTION SCENE IN FRONT OF THE STATE HOUSE, IN PHILADELPHIA (INDEPENDENCE HALL), ABOUT 1818. Painting by John Lewis Krimmell.

THE FRANCHISE TO LIBERTY

In the period following the War of 1812, for the first time in its history, the nation felt free and able to consolidate its latent powers without distraction from abroad or defection within. It was time for self-determination and self-development. It was an era as contemporaries said of good feelings. The anxieties and antagonisms that had flared up following the acceptance of the Constitution twenty-five years before seemed to be contained, if not quenched. America could, for the moment, get on with its business of peaceful revolution.

To Tocqueville, who visited the country in 1828, the frequent and spirited public elections to determine the will of the people —a people, as he observed, with a taste for change and self-assertion regardless of conse-

quences—seemed like a series of minor revolutions in themselves. The intention of those who framed the Constitution to safeguard the new government against the "excesses" of democracy was already being defeated, as witness the general commotion attending election days.

Most of the new states admitted into the Union reduced suffrage qualifications to a minimum and opened legislative and administrative offices to adult males in general. Religious considerations in either case were fast disappearing. In the East the voting privilege and the right to hold office were more slowly, but inevitably, extended to the great mass of white male citizens and even in some states to free Negro males. Even Massachusetts and Virginia, two principal seats of the tie-wig and knee-breeches political con-servatives, called constitutional conventions to consider, among other things, the ques-tion of broader suffrage rights. In 1821 Massachusetts after heated argument cast aside property qualifications for the fran-chise, as most others among the original thir-teen states had already done. In the Virginia Convention of 1829–30 arguments just as hot were offered on either side in a brilliant contest of opinions. "I fear the excessive democratic spirit coincident to victory after a hard-fought battle continued to the last extremity," wrote John Marshall during the debates, "may lead to universal suffrage or something very near it. . . . I wish we were well through the difficulty." Although the Virginia franchise was somewhat extended, the commanding persuasion of Marshall on the side of conservatism, supported by such able elder statesmen as Madison and Mon-

roe, limited the political gains of the com-mon man. In other respects the Constitution was liberalized in accordance with the wide-spread tendency of the times.

Every extension of the right to vote, how-ever slight, automatically increased the need of extending that right farther. At the time of his visit Tocqueville concluded: "In America the principle of the sovereignty of the people is . . . recognized by the customs and proclaimed by the laws; it spreads freely, and arrives without impediment at its most remote consequences. If there is a country in the world where the doctrine of the sover-eignty of the people can be fairly appreci-ated, where it can be studied in its applica-tion to the affairs of society, and where its dangers and its advantages may be judged, that country is assuredly America." That the doctrine was not without serious dangers, Tocqueville readily admitted.

The New-York Historical Society

THE VIRGINIA CONSTITUTIONAL CONVENTION OF 1829–30 AT RICHMOND. Painting by George Catlin. James Monroe occupies the chair and James Madison the floor; John Marshall sits behind Madison in the front row and in a direct line from the chairman and speaker. There are 101 identified portraits in the scene.

THE OLD HOUSE OF REPRESENTATIVES, 1821–22. Painting by Samuel F. B. Morse. The painting includes portraits of 86 people, among them those of the Justices of the Supreme Court standing against the back wall on a raised dais with Chief Justice John Marshall and Justice Story at the right of the group, Jedediah Morse, Benjamin Silliman, and a Pawnee chief in the gallery, and pages and attendants. The scene was depicted at candle-lighting time while members of the House were assembled for an evening session.

Among "the shoals of democracy" Tocqueville considered as most dangerous the diminishing talents of the directly chosen representatives of the people. His visit coincided with the advent of the Jackson democrats and he felt that the statesmen of that era were "very inferior" to those who guided the nation fifty years earlier. "On entering the House of Representatives at Washington," he wrote, "one is struck by the vulgar demeanor of that great assembly. Often there is not a distinguished man in the whole number. Its members are almost all obscure individuals, whose names bring no associations to mind. They are mostly village lawyers, men in trade, or even persons be-

longing to the lower classes of society. In a country in which education is very general, it is said that the representatives of the people do not always know how to write correctly."

James Fenimore Cooper, who visited the House of Representatives that same year, was, on the other hand, "struck by the sim-

ple but imposing aspect of this assembly," by the unembellished grandeur of the setting, without "swords, chains, collars, stars, bayonets, nor maces," but with a quiet architectural dignity that reflected "the sacred uses of the place" and the sovereignty of law.

One could view the scene either way without distorting the truth. Democracy, working at the common level, staged a mediocre show. With conspicuous exceptions, men of real ability were ceasing to seek the modest and dubious rewards of the political arena; men of special distinction had only a limited chance of winning popular support. On the other hand this was a government "of laws, and not of men" and faith in its mission to the world was, in these decades of the nineteenth century, rapidly taking on the fervor of a state religion.

With Jackson's elevation to the Presidency the "horrible ravages of universal suffrage" were apparent all over the nation, nowhere more glaringly than in the West. Nine years before, Josiah Quincy, speaking for the *ancien régime* of the East, had complained to Congress: "You have no authority to throw the rights and property of this people into the 'hotch-potch' with the wild men on the Missouri, nor with the mixed, though more responsible race of Anglo-Hispan-Gallo-Americans who bask on the sands in the mouth of the Mississippi. . . .

Do you suppose the people of the Northern and Atlantic States will, or ought to, look with patience and see Representatives and Senators from the Red River and Missouri pouring themselves upon this and the other floor, managing the concerns of a seaboard fifteen hundred miles, at least, from their residence?"

So it happened, however, and by way of celebrating the triumph of the masses over the classes not only in the new democratic West and South but also in the developing industrial areas of the East, Jackson's supporters made a "people's day" of his inauguration. "The White House was invaded by a mob of men, women, and boys, who stood on chairs in their muddy boots, fought for the refreshments, and trod glass and porcelain underfoot. 'It would have done Mr. Wilberforce's heart good,' wrote an onlooker, 'to have seen a stout black wench eating in this free country a jelly with a gold spoon at the President's house.' Jackson was glad to escape by a window; and the mob was

The American Antiquarian Society

DAVY CROCKETT ADDRESSING CONGRESS. From the *Davy Crockett Almanac*, 1844. Crockett, coonskin philosopher, Indian fighter, and "ring-tailed roarer," made himself as much at home on the floor of Congress as he did on the frontier.

A CANDIDATE FOR OFFICE ADDRESSING AN AUDIENCE.
Drawing by George Caleb Bingham.

Edwards. Nevertheless I think I can govern you pretty well. I do not think it will take an extraordinary smart man to govern you; for to tell the truth, Fellow citizens, I do not think you will be very hard to govern no how."

In rough and rude paraphrase that last clause was very close to Jefferson's democratic creed. If man was a rational animal, endowed with an innate sense of justice along with his natural rights, then he could, as Jefferson claimed, "be restrained from wrong and protected in right, by moderate powers, confided to persons of his own choice and held to their duties by dependence on his own will." Surely the world could offer few better places to test the merits of such a creed than America of the mid-nineteenth

"A MEMBER OF CONGRESS" AS DESCRIBED BY MRS. TROLLOPE. Lithograph by Hervieu from Mrs. Trollope's *Domestic Manners of the Americans*, London, 1832.

finally drawn off like flies to honey, by tubs of punch being placed on the lawn. Washington society thought of the Tuileries on the 10th of August, and shuddered."

The gloomy predictions of the chaos that would follow Jackson's election, like similar ones made when Jefferson had become President, did not, for all the antics of henchmen and followers, quite materialize. The success of this relatively untutored son of the people in the supreme office of the land, indeed, re-enforced a growing feeling that almost any honest man was a fit candidate for government office. "Fellow citizens," argued one aspirant from Illinois in very much that spirit, "I offer myself as a candidate before you, for the office of governor. I do not pretend to be a man of extraordinary talents, nor do I claim to be equal to Julius Caesar or Napoleon Bonaparte, nor yet to be as great a man as my opponent, Governor

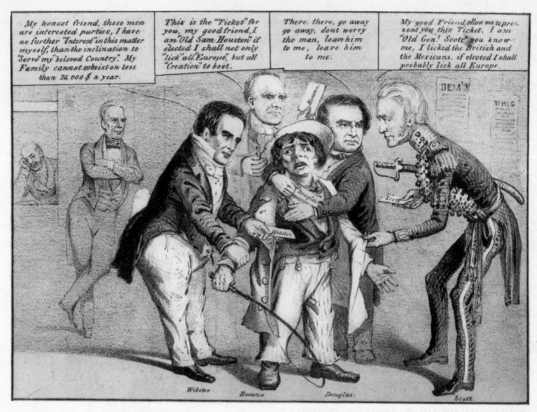

SOLICITING A VOTE, 1852. Lithograph from *The Old Soldier by His Son John.*

century. The main business of the country was the conquest and exploitation of a large, rich, and undeveloped continent. And that job could best be done with a minimum of governmental restriction and a maximum of individual liberty. Even without the reasoned leadership of such democratic statesmen as Jefferson, however, this credo would have been improvised to match the conditions of the time. Political freedom and social equality were, as the late Carl Becker pointed out, the casual and lavish gift of nature quite as much as the results of any reasoned theory of politics and society.

Fifty years after the Constitution had been adopted, the ideal of popular sovereignty had been worked into a hard political fact. Contrary to every intention of the signers of that document, and with hardly a change in its written form, America was developing into a more thorough democracy than the world

had yet seen. Every election season witnessed the results of broadening suffrage. Although throughout the country there was much sound political thinking in this period, it was often drowned out by the clamor of "popular" campaigning. Gigantic parades, torchlight processions, campaign songs, and barbecues were planned to arouse the unthoughtful and tempt them to the polls on the side of the right candidate.

The presidential campaign of 1840 was one of the noisiest and jolliest of all, and set a pattern for others to follow. "Men's minds," wrote Philip Hone to his diary, "are wrought up to a pitch of frenzy, and like tinder a spark of opposition sets them on fire." At Indianapolis, delegates to the Whig convention marched in a mile-long procession. Twenty thousand men converged on Columbus from all parts of Ohio through the rain, snow, and mud of a trying winter to march

AN ELECTION SCENE DURING THE HARRISON-VAN BUREN CAMPAIGN, 1840. Water color by Francis H. Schell.

THE VERDICT OF THE PEOPLE. Painting by Bingham, about 1854.

eight abreast in columns two miles long in honor of their candidate. At a Cleveland rally no building could hold the crowd of partisans, so "the temple of nature was used." The din of political drums reached practically every citizen of the land.

In many respects it was the apotheosis of the American political campaign. Men of inconspicuous talents, or military heroes—in any case men with a minimum of enemies—were offered as candidates on the merits of their built-up campaign personalities. General Harrison, well-born but mediocre member of a wealthy Virginia planter family, was pictured as a simple man content to live in a log cabin. Van Buren, a truly self-made man of humble origins, was pictured by the opposition as a fop who perfumed his whiskers and laced himself with corsets. Vital issues were soft-pedaled by both parties in the fear of alienating one or another segment of the

population. And political machinery ground out as much noise as possible with what little could be found safe for discussion.

It is another curious and ironic development that the fathers of the Constitution had believed that they were safeguarding their government from the menace of political parties—in his farewell address Washington had specifically warned his countrymen against the "baneful effects" of party spirit—and that within a few brief years it was the party system that provided the working machinery of the Constitution. As they evolved during the first fifty years American political parties drew their support from all classes, sections, and interests within the country. Each party appealed to very much the same broad cross-section of opinion, progressive and conservative, poor and rich, and, for a while yet, northern and southern. Neither could afford to differ too radically from the other without sacrificing an important element of support. Both took both sides of every vital question. As Herbert Agar has pointed out, "Instead of seeking 'principles,' or 'distinctive tenets,' which can only divide a federal union, the party is intended to seek bargains between the regions, the classes, and the other interest groups. It is intended to bring men and women of all beliefs, occupations, sections, racial backgrounds, into a combination for the pursuit of power."

Whatever their banners and slogans, all parties tended to emphasize the fundamental unity of the electorate rather than its diversity—a precarious unity that must be achieved by almost any compromise if a whole wide continent of conflicting interests and principles were to be kept in step and advancing to some common goal. That such a system of government, crude and wasteful as it often seemed, could survive the basic test of a civil war provided a measure of its vitality.

To Jefferson and his contemporaries the spectacle of a candidate for high office addressing himself directly to the people, pleading for votes and often making himself ridiculous in the process, would have seemed like demagoguery of the most debased sort. The carnival spirit in which the electorate responded to the drums of the 1840 campaign would have seemed like the reverse of that counterfeit coin. But it worked out all right. Few people even pretended to believe that the majority was always and necessarily right. That, as Thoreau put it, would be "the most palpable of all impostures." But majority rule did provide the only practical working principle of government.

So long as the majority decision was undetermined, argument flourished at white heat, or at any level of heat which might be generated by the usual campaign methods. But once the verdict of the people was announced political tempers cooled, defeated candidates sent messages of congratulations to victorious rivals whom they had vilified the day before and whom they had charged with the most subversive motives, and both

friends and opponents of a disputed issue accepted the electoral decision with reasonable grace. As William James said, Americans had developed "the habit of trained and disciplined good temper toward the opposite party when it fairly wins its innings."

With the exception of the Civil War the nation faced few serious crises until quite recently. The country was living out a lush period of its history and in normal times could afford to be casual, even careless, about the public business. However inefficient and extravagant political machinations might seem, they adequately served a purpose and there was freedom, security, and wealth enough left over for almost everyone. Up until the Civil War and then after it, few minority groups felt so hopelessly dispossessed that they lost faith in the polls. However capricious the majority will might seem, a coming election always promised the possibility of redressing the balance. In those halcyon days democracy could afford to make mistakes and take the time to correct them

The American Antiquarian Society
MAJOR BEN. PERLEY MOORE OF NEWBURY, MASS., PAYING OFF AN ELECTION BET HE LOST TO COL. ROBERT I. BURBANK OF BOSTON. Lithograph by J. H. Bufford after a photograph by Turner and Cutting. Moore wheeled a barrel of apples from his to Burbank's house, a distance of 36 miles. On the third day he arrived with his load and was greeted by "at least 30,000 enthusiastic spectators."

GOING TO CHURCH. Painting by George H. Durrie, 1853. The original of a well-known Currier and Ives lithograph.

CREEDS, COLORS, AND RACES

In Europe by the end of the eighteenth century national societies had long ago become stabilized around old mixtures of people, had developed into nations of more or less homogeneous populations with dominant patterns of religious behavior. In America, for more than a century and a half, every shipload of immigrants had increased the diversity of the population. The Americans who declared themselves independent in 1776, although, of course, predominantly of British origin, were nevertheless a conglomerate breed of people, drawn from numerous lands representing a variety of racial strains, and professing a wide assortment of creeds.

But compared to the stream of immigrants that peopled the colonies before the Revolution and the torrent that flowed over the country in the century after the Treaty of Ghent, the influx of newcomers from 1775–1815 was barely a trickle. For more than a generation, thanks to wars and turmoil,

America enjoyed a unique shake-down period. The nation had time to become home-born and home-bred, time for its motley population to develop a national spirit broad enough to accommodate all remaining differences.

Less mixed to start with, New England enjoyed that respite longer than some of the other sections and developed a vigorous, homogeneous sectional culture that, as Crèvecoeur remarked as early as 1782, exhibited "a most conspicuous figure in this great and variegated picture." The ideas and ideals that shaped the Yankee character became a fixed and singular attitude towards life. Everywhere they went, and they went everywhere, the sons of New England left the stamp of their convictions and opinions. The meetinghouse spire that rose from the dead center of early New England community life became an elementary, lasting American symbol, even for those who came

ROGER SHERMAN, CONNECTICUT YANKEE. Painting by Ralph Earle. John Adams called Sherman "an old Puritan, as honest as an angel and as firm in the cause of American Independence as Mount Atlas."

AMERICAN FRIENDS GOING TO MEETING IN SUMMER. Engraving from Robert Sutcliff, *Travels in Some Parts of North America,* 1815.

to America much later and from distant lands and who settled in remote parts of the country. High above each village it stood as a witness to the stability and order of the society below, a witness that the people within its shadow lived and governed themselves not alone by patriotism, but also by reverence and self-control.

Lord Bryce felt that the influence of the church was, and had been since the days of the Pilgrims, deeper and greater here than in any European country except Scotland. Even in the worst times, he observed, religion and conscience, however they were manifested, were a constantly active force in American life and had helped to allay and conquer the moral and political evils which threatened the country. A century earlier Crèvecoeur had pointed out that in America any and every religious opinion was entertained and freely took its chances with others, which, he thought, exerted a unifying rather than a disruptive force in society. "This is a problem," wrote Crèvecoeur, "which a great many people in Europe could

not comprehend, prejudiced as they are by the ancient manners and customs of the society in which they live."

The first amendment to the Constitution, assuring all Americans that the federal government would not interfere with their freedom to worship as they chose, in fact merely confirmed a long-standing state of affairs. Since the early days of the Massachusetts Bay Colony few people in this country had suffered serious inconvenience because of their faith, and few have since. "There is not a country in the world," wrote Bryce half a century ago, "where Frederick the Great's principle, that every one should be allowed to go to heaven his own way, is so fully applied. This sense of religious peace as well as religious freedom all around is soothing to the weary European, and contributes not a little to sweeten the lives of ordinary people."

The Quakers, once whipped and dragged through the streets of Puritan New England as "Notoriouse Heratiques," had built a haven in Pennsylvania long before the Revo-

338

"A VIEW OF THE INSIGHT (*sic*) OF THE OLD LUTHERAN CHURCH IN YORK, PA. 1807." Drawing by Lewis Miller. Hung about the gallery are paintings of the twelve apostles, the three kings—Saul, David, and Solomon—Adam and Eve, Abraham, Isaac, and others (the latter paintings are at the right, in front of the choir and organ).

lution and had opened the gates to people of every persuasion. The example they set, and which Voltaire found so admirable, involved more than religious tolerance. The equality these people felt before God implied equality among men and women in the affairs of the world. That implication was not carried out in their governmental practice; indeed, there were those in Pennsylvania who spoke bitterly of Quaker overlords and tyrants. But other sects accepted the idea, applied it in a broad political sense, and in the process overthrew the Quaker oligarchy in the colony they had founded.

Among those who were attracted in great numbers to Penn's colony were German Lutherans and Calvinists, members of the two Protestant state churches of the Fatherland. In the New World they took their place side by side with those of other denominations without preference and, for the most part, without prejudice. The pietist elements among the Germans—the Mennonites, Dunkers, Amish, Moravians, and others —were a deeply religious people who, like

the Quakers, renounced the rule of priests, secure in the faith that each individual was an equally endowed and responsible citizen of God's commonwealth. Also like the Quakers, they practised a benevolent humanitarianism that helped earn their state above all others a reputation for social progress.

AMISH MEN ATTENDING AN AUCTION, LANCASTER, PA., 1942. Photograph by John Collier for the Farm Security Administration.

*The Library Company of Philadelphia,
Ridgway Library*
THE GENIUS OF AMERICA ENCOURAGING THE EMANCI-
PATION OF THE BLACKS, 1792. Painting by Samuel
Jennings, presented to the Free Library Company of
Philadelphia by the artist. Liberty is placing the
catalogue of the library on a pedestal; "as an emblem
of aversion to slavery, a broken chain is placed under
her feet"; some Negroes pay homage to Liberty while
others are "in attitudes expressive of Ease and Joy."

Both the Quakers and the German sectarians opposed slavery on religious and moral
grounds. It was the distinguished Mennonite
leader, Francis Daniel Pastorius, who voiced
the first formal protest at the Friends Meeting, Dublin Township, in 1688. This was at
the start of Penn's Holy Experiment, when
he was advertising for settlers. "And those
who steel and robb men, and those who buy
or purchase them, are they not all alike?"
Pastorius asked. He looked for assurance
that he and his followers might "satisfie like-

Kurze Nachricht von der Abscheulichkeit des Neger-Handels.

The Historical Society of Pennsylvania
A PENNSYLVANIA-GERMAN TRACT AGAINST THE SLAVE
TRADE. From the *Neue Reading Kalendar*, 1819.

wise our good friends and acquaintances in
our natif Country, to whom it is a terrour or
fearful thing that man should be handled so
in Pensilvania." During the century that
followed, the Quakers themselves kept alive
the argument against human slavery.

The word slavery was not mentioned in
the Constitution although the problem was
actually dealt with in several compromise
measures. In almost every state there was a
growing party in favor of abolition. Slavery
was already all but extinct in the North and
had been banned from the Northwest Territory. Even in the South, except in Georgia
and South Carolina, it was looked on as an
evil—a necessary evil, perhaps, but one
openly deplored by many of the South's
most eminent citizens (and slaveholders). "I
tremble for my country," wrote Jefferson,
"when I reflect that God is just; that his justice cannot sleep forever." Anyone could
hope, in 1790, that the necessary evil might
become less necessary and ultimately disappear. No one could foresee the effects of the
cotton gin and the textile machinery soon to
be developed.

Without an established national church
America was free of a conservative authority
which broadly influenced the destinies of
most other nations. The Church of England
had played an important part in colonial life
and it carried a social prestige which
attracted many prosperous dissenters from
their former faith. It was, usually, the church
of the royal governors; and even the Penns
soon rejoined that denomination. But generally speaking Americans were nonconformists and, often, nonconformists to
nonconformism. Among most of the Protestant sects that were transplanted to America
new variants constantly stemmed from the
parent tree in a bewildering variety of native
growths.

The Baptists, vigorous advocates of religious equality and disestablishmentarian-
ism, won a wide following among the "plain
people." Although here, too, the main sect
subdivided into divergent groups, all believed in adult baptism and total immersion.

"They are christened in rivers after they have reached the age of thirty," wrote Svinin to whom those rites were strange. "These christenings take place on the first Monday of each month, regardless of the weather . . . during the winter, holes are cut in ice for the purpose. In spite of the temperature of ten below zero, and in spite of the fact that those who are to be baptized must stand waist deep in water for an hour, there is no record of any of them falling ill: such is the virtue of a warm faith and enthusiasm. . . . Barefoot and bare-headed, with flowing hair, they step solemnly into the river, while a choir sings."

Svinin was only one visiting European who was surprised and bewildered by the multitude of different sects that seemed to flourish in America. "I sincerely believe," wrote the irrepressible Mrs. Trollope, "that if a fire-worshipper, or an Indian Brahmin, were to come to the United States, prepared to preach and pray in English, he would not be long without a 'very respectable congregation.'" It was true that conditions encour-

Photograph from the American Antiquarian Society
NONCONFORMISM TO NONCONFORMISM. Half of a New Bedford meetinghouse being removed to a new site as the result of a church quarrel, 1816. Drawing by Charles Lesueur. The dissenting half of the congregation sawed the building in two and removed their part elsewhere by an ox train.

aged wide experimentation in religious performances, some of which seemed eccentric to travelers from countries where religious habits were more settled and were prescribed by immutable traditions. Often those new variations were the true witness of a new, developing civilization.

A BAPTIST CEREMONY, 1811–13. Water color by Paul Svinin.

The Metropolitan Museum of Art

A METHODIST CAMP MEETING, 1836. Lithograph by E. W. Clay.

The evangelical Protestantism that swept in successive waves throughout the colonies and the states, in the camp meeting and its revival ceremonies brought a unique American contribution to Christianity (see Chapter Six). To some the emotional excitement fired by these "awakenings" seemed miraculous; to others it seemed fantastic. In any case it represented a rebellion against all religious doctrine that had settled into formal patterns. It carried the Gospel in an enthusiastic manner to places beyond the reach of ordinary church practices. It caused still newer groupings within the older sects. And wherever it carried, by preaching the doctrine of the liberated individual, it furthered the cause of democracy.

In spite of such a wide variety of religious expression America remained an overwhelmingly Protestant Christian country during the first decades of the new Republic. Barely one per cent of the country's population was Catholic in 1810 and there were even fewer Jews. Another century passed before the United States became the greatest world center of Jewry, but by the 1840's, against many discouragements, the Catholics had increased their numbers, almost entirely by immigration, to a million in a total population of some seventeen million.

The Roman Catholic church had been quick to realize its opportunities and its responsibilities following the Revolution. John Carroll, cousin of Charles the Signer, who had been born in Maryland but educated in France, returned to America and became this country's first Roman Catholic bishop (of Baltimore) in 1790. The year before, he had founded Georgetown College which opened its doors in the District of Columbia in 1791. Near-by in Baltimore, after a faltering start, St. Mary's Seminary developed into the largest and most influential institution of its kind in the country.

Beyond the Appalachians the early labors of the Jesuit missionaries of New France had set a heroic example for those who followed, although their missions among the Indians lay neglected for almost a generation after the French and Indian Wars. Within ten years from 1791–1800, under Bishop Carroll's direction, twenty-seven priests were sent beyond the mountains to resume the work. As has so often happened, the tragedy of Europe was a blessing to America, for many of the missionaries were French priests driven from their own country by the revolution there.

Father Badin, the first Roman Catholic priest ordained in the original states, was despatched over the mountains to the "dark and bloody ground" of Kentucky. There in 1812 was founded the Sisters of Loretto, an order devoted to the Christian training of girls, which grew, colonized, and set a standard for other convent schools in the West. With Father Nerinckx, a Belgian who joined him, Father Badin built an episcopal palace of logs at Bardstown, the center of a parish embracing the entire northwest territory of the United States and containing at the start a mere thousand followers.

A half century later Thomas Low Nichols wrote: ". . . everywhere in America, in the best society, the most . . . influential ladies have been educated in convents, and though they may never go to Rome they love and respect their teachers, and defend them from the attacks commonly made against them."

The Maryland Historical Society
THE CHAPEL OF ST. MARY'S SEMINARY, BALTIMORE, 1807. Drawing by the architect, Maximilian Godefroy. One of the earliest American buildings in the Gothic Revival style, it still stands. The critical Mrs. Trollope called it "a little *bijou* of a thing."

LITTLE LORETTO, A CATHOLIC EDUCATIONAL ENTERPRISE IN KENTUCKY, ABOUT 1812. Engraving by Courtois, a Belgian artist who had obviously never seen the original.

The Museum of Fine Arts, Boston

Although in total figures immigration to America from Europe was slight during the years immediately following the Revolution, a relatively large number of Frenchmen, driven by uncertainty and turbulence in their own land and in French colonies, sought a haven in the New World. While it was the national capital, Philadelphia attracted a particularly distinguished group of *émigrés* who treated Penn's "green county town" to the novel spectacle of French counts teaching Quaker lads to fence and Quaker lasses to dance, of the Duke of Orleans—the future "citizen king" Louis Philippe—holding court in his residence on Fifth Street, of Talleyrand rehearsing international intrigue on the shores of the Schuylkill, and of the gastronomist Brillat-Savarin, after several months' fare in a local boardinghouse, dedicating his life to the improvement of cookery. A settlement named Asylum on the bank of the Susquehanna was even prepared for Louis XVI, should he need a safe retreat. But the monarch lost his head and his distant faithful subjects never quite succeeded in mastering the wilderness.

More humble exiles made up the bulk of the French immigration. As told in Chapter Two, some lost their fondest hopes and all but their shirts in the Scioto land fraud. Twenty-five years later another group of hopefuls, hastily and indiscriminately organized as the Society for the Olive and the Vine, moved into Alabama on the strength of a grant from Congress to establish the town of Aigleville on the Tombigbee River. Once again the land title was not clear and some of the colony supported by a contingent of anti-Bonapartists from France, equipped more like a plundering expedition than an agricultural one, pushed on to establish a new soldier colony, the Champ d'Asile, on the plains of Texas.

It was a short-lived experiment in New World colonization but its failure was significant. Along with the military discipline

THE FRENCH MILITARY COLONY, CHAMP D'ASILE, IN TEXAS, 1817, AS ENVISIONED BY A EUROPEAN ARTIST. Aquatint after Yerenrag.

The Chicago Historical Society

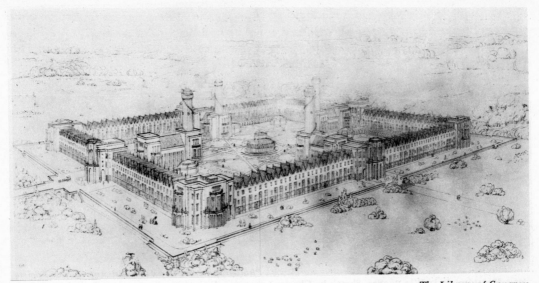

ROBERT OWEN'S COLONY AT NEW HARMONY, INDIANA, AS CONCEIVED BY AN ENGLISH ARCHITECT. Lithograph by Ingrey and Madeley. Public buildings are situated at the centers and extremities of the sides, each 1000 feet long, of the square enclosure with members' dwellings in between. Botanical and other gardens and exercise grounds are in the interior of the square. The plan was intended "to form a new combination of circumstances, capable of producing permanently greater physical, moral, and intellectual advantages to every individual, than have ever yet been realized in any age or country."

the leading colonists felt was necessary, the rigors of frontier life and the hostility of the Indians and Mexicans caused the early abandonment of the project. Once again experience made clear that pioneering in the West was a highly specialized business and might better be left to the native breed who by heritage and training were experts at it.

In spite of land frauds and natural obstacles the hope of finding an Eden somewhere in the open spaces of America grew larger than ever in the middle years of the last century. Both in the name of reason and in the face of it, organized groups of all descriptions and of native and foreign conception—Transcendentalists, Fourierists, Perfectionists, Impressionists, Harmonists, Separatists, Millenarists, Shakers, and a dozen others, each intent on building a perfect community according to their lights—dotted the country with their experiments. "We are all a little wild here with numberless projects of social reform," Emerson wrote to Carlyle in 1840. "Not a reading man but has a draft of

a new community in his waistcoat pocket."

From European shores, too, the New World still seemed the most likely place for men to float their dreams of a better life. The communitarian colony established at New Harmony, Indiana, on the banks of the Wabash in 1825 by the English reformer Robert Owen was one of the bravest efforts of all to reclaim man from social evils. Owen had the good luck and good sense to find and to prefer a site that had already been cleared and built upon by an earlier group of pioneering idealists, the German Rappists, who sold out to return east. His settlement attracted a thousand eager colonists from almost every state of the Union and from most of the countries of northern Europe, including numerous men of marked ability and high purpose.

New Harmony never did build according to its architect's plan. Among other reasons, in America individual opportunity was so great, wages were so high, and the promise of competitive effort was so bright that not

Photograph from the American Antiquarian Society
NEW HARMONY AS IT WAS IN 1831. Sketch by Charles Lesueur, a distinguished naturalist who joined Owen's colony. At the left is a rear view of the community hall where the artist had his studio.

many people could be induced to sacrifice the chance of fortune, or at least prosperity, for the relatively modest security offered by a planned society. The vision of a better world burned brightly enough but that, it still seemed likely, would be realized in America's burgeoning democracy in the natural course of events if everyone were allowed his full measure of freedom in thought and enterprise.

Since Sir Thomas More's day few emigrants have crossed the Atlantic without some vision of Utopia in their luggage. Of what actually lay beyond the ocean they often had but a hazy notion. A half century after the Revolution, Englishmen were still applying to the British Colonial Office for passage to "the Virginia Plantation." The German press carried news from Virginia and Texas in its accounts of South America, a continent which enjoyed great favor among German emigrants. A growing body of literature purported to describe the real America and some volumes were reliable, but for many Europeans this country remained as vaguely known as it had been to the earliest colonists. For poet and peasant alike, however, the New World remained a land of new beginnings. *"Amerika du hast es besser,"* wrote Goethe in 1831, and within a few years of his remark the flow of humanity toward the New World was so great that European ports of departure were congested and surrounded by encampments of emigrants waiting their turn to sail.

Although the Germans and the Irish outnumbered them in the period 1840–1900, the British continued to immigrate in considerable numbers. More than two million Englishmen, Scots, and Welshmen came during these sixty years. Whole villages in Germany sold out and, headed by their clergymen, set out for the nearest port. "It is a lamentable sight," wrote a British observer of that exodus in the 1840's, ". . . to see the long files of carts . . . carrying the whole property of these poor wretches who are about to cross the Atlantic on the faith of a lying prospectus."

That the crowds of departing individuals and families were great and that the prospectuses were often misleading was true enough. But all those who took to the road and the sea were by no means "poor wretches." A better-informed German who crossed the Atlantic in 1849 listed among his traveling fellow countrymen "clerks, artists, musicians, architects, miners, mechanics, men of many professions . . . several families of Jews," as well as peasants—people of different motives and talents who enriched American culture at almost every level. Some came with indefinite enthusiasms about establishing a new and liberal Fatherland in America. Others clustered in ideal communities such as the Amana Society of Iowa. Milwaukee became, for a time, virtually a German town. In a few years New York contained more Germans than any city in the world except Berlin and Vienna. Most immigrants preserved a fond respect for their traditional culture. But in general, the Germans accepted the American way of life more readily than others. Most Germans settled in the North and, like the Irish, joined the Democratic Party as an influential faction which would not blindly follow the party line. Abraham Lincoln was soon studying German as a political expedient. To his cause and his party a decisive number of

EPISODES IN THE ODYSSEY OF A GERMAN IMMIGRANT. Lithographs from the *Fliegende Blätter*, Cincinnati, 1847. Baron Biesele and his *hofmeister*, Dr. Eisele, were cartoon characters whose antics were a popular feature in the German prototype of this short-lived Cincinnati periodical of the same name.

a. BARON BIESELE going through the customs at Le Havre.
b. Ocean passage; *mal de mer*.
c. BARON BIESELE, upon his arrival in America *(in German)*: "Hey, fellow countryman, where can we find a German tavern?"
   COUNTRYMAN *(in German)*: "Damme. Do you think I'm a no-good like you? I am an American."
d. BARON BIESELE, first week after arrival *(in German to another recently arrived German)*: "Well,

Marianel, how do you like it in America?"
   MARIANEL *(in German)*: "Oh, Baron, the language, the language. I'll never learn it in all my life."
e. BARON BIESELE, two weeks after arrival *(in German)*: "Can you tell us—Hey, beautiful Marianel, isn't that you?"
   MARIANEL *(in English)*: "You are mistaken. I don't talk Dutch."

The New-York Historical Society

IMMIGRANTS' ARRIVAL AT NEW YORK, 1847. A section of a panoramic painting by Samuel B. Waugh in 1855. The presence of the Chinese junk has not yet been satisfactorily explained

Germans rallied in the years shortly to come.

The Irish arrived in even greater numbers than the Germans. French, Scandinavians, Poles, Bohemians, and others joined the great migration until the incessant traffic of ships from Europe to America all but bridged the Atlantic. Existing fleets proved too small to carry all the human cargo that clamored for passage. "Since the period when the Gothic tribes, under their hereditary kings, strode down the banks of the Borysthenes, and overwhelmed Greece and Germany and the whole empire of Rome," exclaimed one witness on the American side in 1852, "no migration of men has occurred in the world at all similar to that which is now pouring itself upon the shores of the United States. In extent none, anterior to

the Gothic or since, has equalled it. In a single week we have again and again received into the bosom of our society, numbers as great as a Gothic army.''

For the majority of newcomers the land of promise proved to be the land of performance. There were exceptions, of course, and there were often miserable periods of adjustment. Following the potato famine of 1846, overseas emigration authorities dumped thousands of Irish paupers on American shores; refugees whose way to a decent living was not easy. But most of them found the way by hard and willing labor which the native population considered beneath their attention. By 1850 one out of twenty-three persons in America was Irish-born and, thanks in good measure to Paddy's brawn,

A SUCCESSFUL IRISH IMMIGRANT "HOMEWARD BOUND," 1854. Lithograph by W. & N. Hanhart after a painting by J. Nicol.

managed to blame most of the country's troubles on the immigrants or the Roman Catholic Church. The competition of cheap labor, the Sabbath merrymaking by people of continental backgrounds, the growing influence of the Catholic church, the corruptibility of inexperienced voters, and the subversive notion, suggested by some, that the rampant opportunism of American life might not hold the final answer to human happiness, were all held against these groups.

Because of their disputiveness, their Catholicism, and their genius for politics, the Irish bore a major share of the resentment. However, after a brief, stormy period that rabid nativism burnt itself out, and for years to come the foreign-born hopeful was left relatively unchallenged. Actually, between those who came earlier and those who came in the great mid-century migration, in spite of the fact that the former were called

the railroads were being built at a phenomenal rate. Like those of other origins, the Irish were eager to write home of their success, exciting fresh interest in America wherever their letters were read. Some returned home in person, to enjoy their new prosperity among scenes of their leaner days, each one a living advertisement of American opportunity.

In some sections of this country the enormous influx of aliens provoked a violent resentment among "real Americans"—that is among those who by chance had arrived earlier. Some of this sentiment was based on real grievances, but much was selfish or shortsighted. In the 1850's, under the slogan "Americans Shall Rule America" and under the guise of patriotism, the Know-Nothing organization, so-called because its members were sworn to secrecy about their purposes,

A POLITICAL DEBATE BETWEEN TWO IRISHMEN, ABOUT 1850. Painting by William Hudson.

A COMMENTARY ON THE KNOW NOTHING EXCITEMENT IN BALTIMORE. Sketch by an unknown artist, 1856. The Blood-Tubs, Rip Raps, etc., were gangs of young toughs who sometimes operated under the guise of political clubs.

"settlers" or "colonists" and the latter "immigrants," there was little real difference. All were colonists, all were immigrants, all provided Americans with ancestors. So polyglot was the American population even by 1775, that as Arthur M. Schlesinger has put it, a perfectly legitimate member of those societies which admit only the descendants of Revolutionary and Colonial Americans, "might conceivably have nothing but pure Hebrew blood or French or German blood in her veins."

AN EDUCATED ELECTORATE

If Americans *were* to rule America, if native-born and newcomer were to choose their governors wisely by free access to the ballot box, schooling was needed on a scale never before attempted. Virtually every responsible leader of the new Republic recognized that need and even those who did not favor extending the franchise very far, urged the development of a widespread educational system.

Only people with "a certain degree of instruction," Jefferson remarked, were sure guardians of their own liberties; an ignorant or uninformed electorate would be the dupe of tyrants and demagogues. Adequate schooling, insisted John Adams, must be provided for "every class and rank of people, down to the lowest and poorest." And Washington, with the unique authority his words commanded, added his plea for nothing less than a national system of instruction. The keen

interest of such men in public education held one of the brightest assurances for America's future.

No nation in history so far had accepted and applied the dangerous principle that teaching and learning should be free and available to all. Like the idea of universal suffrage and inseparable from it, it was a revolutionary notion that, although not universally accepted at first, developed with growing force. In the seventeenth century Governor Berkeley had thanked God that there were no free schools or printing in Virginia. For, he wrote to the Lords Commissioners of Trades and Plantations, "learning has brought disobedience and heresy and sects into the world, and printing has divulged them and libels against the best government. God keep us from both!" His fears were justified. A century later the most

The Historical Society of York County, Pennsylvania
LUDWIG MILLER TEACHING A CLASS IN THE OLD LUTHERAN SCHOOLHOUSE AT YORK, PENNSYLVANIA, in 1805. Drawing by Lewis Miller.

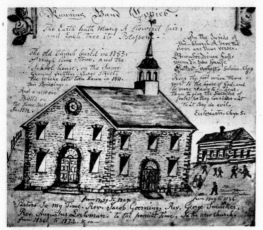

The New-York Historical Society
THE OLD LUTHERAN CHURCH (BUILT IN 1753) AND THE ADJOINING LOG SCHOOLHOUSE AT YORK AS THEY APPEARED BEFORE 1811. Drawing by Miller.

disobedient of the king's subjects were the learned men who drafted the Declaration of Independence; men who had come about their learning with or without the benefit of free schooling and who felt convinced, following the Revolution, that learning must be made general if their new experiment in government was to succeed.

The idea that good education for all and at every level should be tax-supported and otherwise free was by no means universally conceded. To many property owners who never dreamed of sending their children to common schools, state-levied taxes to educate other people's children seemed little short of tyranny. To others the idea of sending their children to free public schools, as the poor were obliged to do, suggested they would be accepting charity. To still others free textbooks in the common schools could only mean the entering wedge of radicalism in American life. Some held a strong feeling against book-learning. Compulsory attendance represented an invasion of parental authority to many dutiful fathers and mothers. Those accustomed to confiding educational matters to the church found something godless in relinquishing them to the state. All along the line the larger idea met such opposition which only gradually,

and then not entirely, disappeared. Between the state and the church the field of education has remained a contested area for generations.

In most sections of early America the church had been the traditional custodian of education and under its auspices had been founded such early institutions of higher learning as Harvard, Yale, and Princeton. Each sect had a strong interest in promoting learning according to its lights. In a country where so many denominations competed side by side for attention every religious group faced a challenge and a danger. Their eagerness to train a competent clergy and their rivalry in properly guiding the minds of the young gave an impetus to education that carried far into the nineteenth century and that reached to the most unlikely places. Because of their firm desire to keep learning close to the people, wherever they scattered, even the early frontier had its sprinkling of little denominational institutions offering schooling at various levels and competing with one another for prestige.

Transylvania Seminary, founded in 1780 by the Presbyterians in what was not yet the state of Kentucky, and ten years later to become a college, was the first pioneering school for "higher education" in the western wilderness. Within a generation or two the West was studded with similar sectarian institutions—beacons for prospective settlers and the joy of local real estate operators.

The Harry Shaw Newman Gallery
THE PRINCIPAL BUILDING OF TRANSYLVANIA UNIVERSITY. Engraving by E. G. Gridley after M. H. Jouett.

The development of a good common school system was slow and uneven, particularly in the South. Even in New England where the principle was firmly established at an early date, the working system fell far short of perfection until Horace Mann, with his new State Board of Education in the 1830's, overcame formidable resistance and lethargy and set an example in Massachusetts that inspired educators not only of other states but of distant countries. Until then, although some areas enjoyed adequate state-provided facilities, others continued to rely largely, beyond the primary grades, on privately supported academies and still others were without adequate schools of any description.

Many distinguished men taught school at some period of their lives, but in the early years of the nineteenth century the typical schoolmaster was a poorly paid incompetent. By tradition and often by necessity he was a strict and harsh disciplinarian. Although McGuffey's *Eclectic Reader* explicitly described the office of teacher as "the noblest on earth," the future rulers of democracy, testing their sovereign rights of independence at an early age, often made it no office for a sensitive spirit.

For all that, Paul Svinin returned to Russia in 1814 with the rosy impression that young America was being splendidly educated. Every *muzhik* in America, who was schooled side by side with the bankers' sons, he reported to his countrymen, could intelligently discuss subjects which would be incomprehensible to a Russian peasant. Svinin was very partial to American institutions, but fifteen years later, Tocqueville, a highly objective critic, also thought that America had better schools and more of them than any other nation.

AN EARLY NEW ENGLAND SCHOOLROOM SCENE. Lithograph by T. Moore after David Claypoole Johnston, 1839.

The American Antiquarian Society

EXTRA-CURRICULAR ACTIVITY UNDER THE APOSTLE OAK, 1841. Painting by George Harvey. "You send your boy to the schoolmaster," wrote Emerson, "but 'tis the schoolboys who educate him. You send him to the Latin class, but much of his tuition comes, on his way to school.... He hates the grammar and the 'Gradus' and loves guns, fishing-rods, horses and boats. Well, the boy is right, and you are not fit to direct his bringing up if your theory leaves out his gymnastic training."

The New York Public Library
"THOSE WHO DO NOT GO TO PUBLIC SCHOOLS." Engraving by Alexander Anderson, 1850.

The final achievement of a universal common school system which provides free learning to all on equal terms has been rightly called one of the landmarks of American democracy. Opposition to the principle, largely in the more conservative eastern states, died hard. There were still those who questioned the wisdom of educating everyone, and even more so of doing it at state expense. To a "plain farmer, or a mechanic," remarked one state legislator in 1829, education was not only useless "but rather a detriment," while a Yale professor about that same time felt that public money spent for such purposes was being thrown away. In their *Growth of the American Republic* Professors Morison and Commager quote a couple in Illinois who "didn't think folks was any better off for reading, an' books cost a heap and took a power of time. 'Twant so bad for men to read, for there was a heap of time when they couldn't work out and could jest set by the fire; and if a man had books and keered to read he mought; but women had no business to hurtle away their time, 'case they could allus find something to do, and there had been a heap of trouble in old Kaintuck with some rich men's gals that had learned to write."

However, the principle that "knowledge and learning generally diffused through a community [are] essential for the preservation of a free government" was enshrined in most of our state constitutions and gradually it was hammered into working form. Not only from the top level of inspired leadership but from the ranks of the people the demand grew more insistent. ". . . until means of equal instruction shall be equally secured to all," resolved one working-man's party in 1830, "liberty is but an unmeaning word, and equality an empty shadow. . . ." Most labor groups felt the same way. By 1850 over three and a third million children were attending over eighty thousand elementary schools and more than a quarter million pupils had stepped up to secondary levels, figures that were doubled in the next twenty years.

Schooling in America has never been a simple means of formal instruction. It has always had the broad social purpose of teaching the common habits necessary to American life to pupils of many different backgrounds—to children of immigrants

The New-York Historical Society
GENTLEMAN *(to crying newsboy)*: "So your father has whipped you; well, don't cry about it."
BOY: "I don't mind the licking, but he's a darned foreigner."
A by-product of Americanization. From *Jonathan's Whittlings*, 1854.

from abroad and from other American regions, to country-born children suddenly transplanted into the confusion of city streets, to children whose family fortunes were widely different and, often, rapidly changing. At the elementary level and in urban communities the work to be done was greatest. *"These children all about your streets, who cannot speak your language,"* warned one educator, *"are your future sovereigns. Is it not important that they be well educated?"* It was, of course, important, and the common school did develop into a profound force for Americanizing the nation's mixed society. Unfortunately, as the accompanying illustration suggests, indoctrinating the young with American ideas and ideals sometimes opened an unhappy breach between generations of immigrant families.

The spread of educational facilities of all sorts was turning America by degrees into "the land of the general reader." The average American, in turn, was developing into a generally well-informed, opinionated, and intensely curious person. "He may be wrong in his views," wrote an Englishman, "but he can always offer you reasons for them. In this, how favourably does he contrast with the unreasoning and ignorant multitudes in other lands! All Americans read and write.

Collection of Edward W. C. Arnold
"Extra, Sir?" Drawing by A. H., about 1850. Photograph courtesy of the Museum of the City of New York.

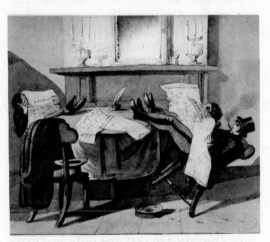

The Museum of the City of New York
"Reading Room," about 1840. Drawing by Nicolino V. Calyo.

Such children and adults as are found incapable of doing either are emigrants from some of the less favoured regions of the older hemisphere, where popular ignorance is but too frequently regarded as the best guarantee for the stability of political systems."

Much of the credit for the very wide distribution of newspapers was due to Benjamin Henry Day whose New York *Sun,* founded in 1833, was the first successful one-cent daily. Day, James Gordon Bennett, and Horace Greeley can be considered the nineteenth-century fathers of the respectable American press.

The American's addiction to his newspaper and the wild energy of the city newsboy caught the attention of visiting foreigners. "You are amazed at the energy of the newsboys," wrote one Englishman, "... as they rush hither and thither with their arms full of wisdom, at a penny an instalment."

A Lyceum Lecture by James Pollard Espy, Meteorologist, at Clinton Hall, New York, about 1841. Drawing by an unknown artist.

At mid-century journalism was already a highly competitive field, and the daily press was already given to sensationalism in the reach for wider audiences, a feature that disgusted people like Dickens. At its best Emerson thought the ubiquitous American newspaper was an important instrument of freedom. Tocqueville had earlier remarked that only a newspaper "can drop the same thought into a thousand minds at the same moment" and that only through the newspaper could the innumerable "little" people who constitute a democracy meet and unite in their feelings and opinions. The discerning Frenchman also observed that the newspapers multiplied not because they were cheap but because more people more urgently felt the need of intercommunication and combination. If that was so the

growing multiplicity of newspapers revealed a passionate search for their common interests among Americans the country over. It was also true, however, that improved presses and shrewd merchandising had brought the newspaper within the reach of everyone at a penny a copy. With "scraps of science, of thought, of poetry . . . in the coarsest sheet," wrote Emerson, the daily paper brought the university to every poor man's door, along with scandal and trash.

The earnestness with which a great many adult Americans carried on their education, or compensated for the lack of formal schooling, amounted to a virtual crusade against ignorance in the middle years of the last century. Organized in 1826 and dedicated to the "general diffusion of knowledge," the Lyceum movement all but covered the

nation with lecturers who spoke on every conceivable subject to large and tireless audiences. In 1841 Philip Hone wrote that the theaters of New York were deserted—"flat on their backs"—while the Tabernacle, "the omnium gatherum and holdall of the city . . . spacious as it is, is filled every night to hear the lyceum lectures, and the course at Clinton Hall is well carried out on the original program." Lecturers trod on one another's heels to satisfy overflowing audiences, far into the West. Emerson, who, for all his intellectual refinements, competed successfully with turbid evangelists on the western circuit, was better known as a Lyceum lecturer than as a man of letters to the great majority of Americans of the 1840's. Thoreau found the only dependable income from his literary efforts came

from reading them on the lecture platform.

That hunger for uplift may have reflected the earnest zeal with which Americans assumed their responsibilities as guardians of their government and society. More generally it meant that to most Americans education was considered the key to success. In a country where everyone had a reasonable expectation of moving up in the world there was an irrepressible incentive to hold that key.

"It is a matter of wonderment," wrote one startled Englishman, ". . . to witness the youthful workman, the over-tired artisan, the worn-out factory girl . . . rushing . . . after the toil of the day is over, into the hot atmosphere of a crowded lecture room." "Going to lectures," he added, "is the next most important duty to going to church."

For long years after the Revolution, as in the colonial period, privileged American girls could cultivate the graces and learn the accomplishments proper to their sex at a variety of private seminaries established for that purpose. Young ladies were, however, generally spared or denied the rigors of real intellectual discipline. "We don't pretend to teach ye female part of ye town anything more than dancing, or a little music perhaps . . ." John Eliot wrote to Jeremy Belknap in 1782, "except ye private schools for writing, which enable them to write a copy, sign their name &c, which they might not be able to do without such a privilege."

In the heated days of the Constitutional Convention Abigail Adams entered a wistful plea that the Founding Fathers ponder that peculiar injustice in their debates. "If you complain of education in sons," she wrote, "what shall I say in regard to daughters, who every day experience the want of it? . . . If we mean to have heroes, statesmen, and philosophers, we should have learned women." But the world of men passed her protest by.

Speaking of American young women in general Tocqueville confessed that he was often surprised and almost frightened by the ease and boldness with which they could think and talk their way through a conversation where a philosopher would have stumbled at every step. He concluded that education was indispensable to protect women from the manners and institutions of democracy. However, for some time to come most American young ladies continued to talk themselves in and out of those dangers without benefit of formal instruction.

There were men and women who would not concede that females were too fragile to

CEREMONIES AT A YOUNG LADIES' SEMINARY, 1810–20. Painting by an unknown artist. The young ladies in the center apparently represent the graduating class.

Collection of Col. and Mrs. Edgar W. Garbisch

THE GEORGE BARRELL EMERSON SCHOOL IN BOSTON, ABOUT 1850. Daguerreotype by Southworth and Hawes.

be seriously educated or that it was absurd to think of sending them on to college. To most others, however, it came as a surprise that the ninety young ladies at Emma Hart Willard's Troy Female Seminary, which opened in 1821, could withstand the strain of mathematics, physics, history, and other subjects. Mrs. Willard and other inspired and inspiring feminists such as Catherine Esther Beecher and Mary Lyon, founder of the Mount Holyoke Female Seminary, bucked a tide of unsympathetic criticism in advancing the cause of female education,

and their efforts were awarded by immediate and lasting success.

The earliest true colleges opened to women were founded in the West. In 1833 Oberlin Collegiate Institute, starting its first semester with twenty-nine men and fifteen women, became the first coeducational college in the world. (Oberlin admitted Negroes, a further radical step that invited persecution from small-minded people.) Throughout the West other colleges followed Oberlin's lead and one after the other opened their doors to women. In the East

THE CAMPUS OF THE UNIVERSITY OF MICHIGAN, ABOUT 1854. Drawing by Adeline B. Mead.

The University of Uppsala
"A STUDENT AT THE UNIVERSITY IN CAMBRIDGE, MASSA-CHUSETTS." A sketch from the manuscript journal of Emanuel Sundelius. Photograph courtesy of the *Harvard Alumni Bulletin*.

where conservative opposition was stronger, the older colleges remained strongholds of the male. However, thanks largely to the liberality of several wealthy philanthropists, separate colleges were opened for women alone, but for the most part not until after the Civil War.

The crowning achievement of the American public school system was the state university, a distinct type of educational institution native to this country. The idea of state-supported schools for higher education is older than the Constitution. It was clearly recognized in the Northwest Ordinance of 1787 which set aside two entire townships in each prospective state "for the purpose of a University." But fifty years passed before it first came to full flower in the University of Michigan.

With his keen interest in public education Jefferson had lighted the way for the broader experiments that followed when he argued for a free and secular university, to be supported and controlled by his native state in which he had led an unremitting struggle against ignorance. When the University of Virginia opened its doors, one of his fondest

THE UNIVERSITY OF VIRGINIA IN 1856. Lithograph by E. Sachse & Co. Jefferson's home, Monticello, can faintly be seen on its mountain top in the background, beyond Charlottesville.

projects materialized. For the new school Jefferson envisioned and proceeded to design and to have built "an academical village" rather than one large building. Separate lodges for the professors were joined by dormitories "opening into a covered way," all surrounding a lawn. In carrying out that plan Jefferson gave the nation one of its outstanding architectural monuments. But beyond that he conceived of a truly modern university dedicated to freedom of learning and teaching free from denominational control or influence, and with a secular curriculum of elective subjects to promote vocational training, scientific studies, and professional learning.

The northeastern states, well equipped with their older, privately endowed colleges of sectarian origin, showed little early interest in true state universities. The earliest embryonic state "universities" (usually little more than secondary schools at their inception) were in the South, but in the West the liberal educational concepts that developed after the Revolution found their broadest expression. In 1816 the constitution of Indiana outlined the ideal. "Knowledge and learning generally diffused throughout a community being essential to the preservation of a free government . . ." the constitution read, "it shall be the duty of the general assembly . . . to provide by law for a system of education, ascending in regular gradation from township schools to a State university, wherein tuition shall be gratis, and equally open to all."

After numerous tentative beginnings in various states, the University of Michigan evolved as the first full-fledged state university—the first to have a well-rounded variety of professional schools, the first of the state institutions to admit women, the first to establish vocational training as part of the curriculum, and in other ways the first to broaden the opportunity for higher education. Other universities followed in quick succession, and older institutions were improved and expanded. Some of the new establishments rose on land that had but a short time before been the battleground of Indian wars. Huxley's great educational ladder, with one end in the gutter and the other in the university, was firmly placed up the side of American society.

THE AMERICAN WAY

With every passing decade of the last century America became increasingly an object of Europe's curiosity. Life in this country, most visitors from abroad agreed, differed perceptibly from life in Europe. The catalogue of differences, both favorable and unfavorable to the American way of life, included everything from the popularity and omnipresence of ice water to the general habit of spitting. Few who found their way into print were qualified to explore the deeper issues that were involved, but all found a ready market for their opinions. "Have a passage ready taken for 'Merrikea," advised Mr. Pickwick's friend Weller, ". . . then let him come back and write a book about the 'Merrikens as'll pay all his expenses, and more. . . ." Dickens later made capital of his own observations of the American scene in his *American Notes* and in *Martin Chuzzlewit*.

With the rest of the passing critics, Dickens agreed that everything and everybody in this country was in a state of everlasting motion. By a natural screening process the New World inherited the more restless people of earth, people who found their natural bent given a fresh twist by the conditions of life in America. Michel Chevalier, who came here from France in 1834 to study our public works, was intrigued by what he saw in passing and stayed on to broaden his observations. "If movement and the quick succession of sensations and ideas constitute life," he wrote, "here one lives a hundred fold more than elsewhere; all is here circulation, motion, and boiling agitation. Experiment follows experiment; enterprise succeeds to enterprise. Riches and poverty follow on each other's traces, and each in turn occupies the place of the other. . . . Fortunes last for a season; reputations, during the twinkling of an eye. An irresistible current sweeps away everything, grinds everything to powder, and deposits it again under new forms. Men change their houses, their climate, their trade, their condition, their party, their sect; the States change their laws, their officers, their constitutions. The soil itself, or at least the houses, partake of the universal instability. The existence of social order, in the bosom of this whirlpool seems a miracle, an inexplicable anomaly. One is tempted to think, that such a society, formed of heterogeneous elements, brought together by chance, and following each its own orbit according to the impulse of its own caprice or interest,—one would think, that after rising for one moment to the heavens, like a water-spout, such a society would inevitably fall flat in ruins the next; such is not, however, its destiny."

Chevalier's mention of houses on the move referred to a point in his travels when, between Albany and Troy, he was stopped by a house of more than forty feet front, rolling along the road. That American practice of raising houses bodily and moving them back, forward, or for a considerable distance across the landscape, never failed to amuse and amaze foreigners. On his trip to the West Dickens met a house, as he wrote, "coming down-hill at a good round trot, drawn by some twenty oxen!"

In the spring the prevailing restlessness reached a yearly peak on moving day. To forewarn immigrants of what they might expect, *The British Mechanic's and Labourer's Hand Book, and True Guide to the United States* in 1840 pointed out: "The year in New York begins on the first of May. . . . There is but little chance of a renewal [of a lease], for such is the nature of property, particularly in this city, that house rent is continually on the advance, all places at a premium for each successive year . . . [on moving day] the whole population appear in confusion as if alarmed by some extensive conflagration."

MOVING A HOUSE IN PHILADELPHIA, 1799. Engraving by W. Birch and Son. The Walnut Street Jail is in the background.

MOVING DAY IN THE CITY, ABOUT 1840. The otherwise unidentified artist of the painting has pictured himself in the left foreground. The locale depicted is also unidentified but it might have been any large northeastern city of the period.

The Library of Congress

An Advertisement of the Moline Plow Co., 1881. Lithograph by Gies and Co.

Changing living quarters each year was not just a city custom. From the hinterland came stories of families whose chickens were so accustomed to moving on every year that each spring they came up to the house of their own accord and crossed their legs, waiting to be trussed for the next step westward. To a people so inveterately mobile any move or change seemed a good thing, something identified or confused with progress.

Europeans were, and still are, puzzled by the American's nostalgic reference to his "home town," a place where he *had* lived at some other time, rarely his residence at the moment. To be born in one place, to remove from there and then to marry in a third place, to settle somewhere else and, finally,

to die still farther on along the road was a common enough experience to make good advertising copy, as the illustration above indicates. "All the enjoyments of heaven," remarked Fredrika Bremer, "would not suffice to keep an American in one place if he were sure of finding another farther west, for then he would have to be there to build and cultivate. . . . He never stops. His work and will is to be always working, building, starting fresh or beginning something new. . . ."

That penchant for keeping on the move and the buoyant optimism that often inspired it provided the real estate agent with a fabulous opportunity in this country. "Be keerful of speckelators" was sound advice to any newcomer, although the words

366

were usually wasted. Martin Chuzzlewit was not the only investor who found a lonely waste instead of Eden at the wrong end of a real estate boom. But the typical migrant was a man of greater faith than Chuzzlewit. He knew in his bones that his chosen site, whatever it seemed at the moment, would be "a great country some day."

Everyone in America, it appeared to Chevalier, was speculating on the future. ". . . the whole country," he wrote, "has become an immense *rue Quincampoix.* . . . The unparalleled growth of some new towns has turned the heads of the nation, and there is a general rush upon all points advantageously situated; as if, before ten years, three or four Londons, as many Parises, and a dozen Liverpools, were about to display their streets and edifices, their quays crowded with

The New York Public Library
AN EARLY HOME IN MISSOURI. Woodcut from Bryan and Rose. *A History of the Pioneer Families of Missouri*, 1876. "Their houses were built of rough logs, with puncheon floors, clapboard roofs, and great, broad, flaring chimneys, composed of sticks and mud. . . . Iron nails were not to be had, and the . . . roofs were . . . weighted with poles and stones."

THE REAL ESTATE AGENT OFFERING "VALUABLE LOTS." Painting by Francis W. Edmonds.
The Harry Shaw Newman Gallery

The American Antiquarian Society
A SCENE IN A FASHIONABLE BOARDING HOUSE. Lithograph by Bufford.

Every American had a natural and reasonable expectation not only of moving on but of moving up in the world. The economic alternatives were so attractive that few men or women chose to work for another for very long. From the earliest colonial days down to the time of Dover egg beaters, corner delicatessens, and other housekeeping aids, Americans have had to cope with a chronic shortage of servants. Two hundred and fifty years ago Cotton Mather, in a pious note to himself, promised he would serve the Lord with greater fidelity if only he would be blessed with a good servant. Even George Washington's advertisement for a cook and a coachman ran in the New York papers for a month and a half before it was withdrawn. But the Father of His Country may have asked too much since he expected only servants "perfect in the business."

warehouses, and their harbours bristling with masts, in the American wilderness. . . . Pestilential marshes and naked precipices of rock have been bought and sold for this purpose. In Louisiana, the quagmires, the bottomless haunts of alligators, the lakes and cypressswamps, with ten feet of water or slime, and in the North the bed of the Hudson with 20, 30, or 50 feet of water, have found numerous purchasers."

The situation was no better toward the middle of the last century when the servant problem, among other causes, induced many urban Americans to try life in a boardinghouse. "For some reason or other, which English people are not very likely to understand," wrote the acid critic, Mrs. Trollope, "a great number of young married persons

FAMILY PORTRAIT, ABOUT 1840(?). Painting by an unidentified artist.
The Museum of Fine Arts, Boston, M. and M. Karolik Collection

Mrs. McCormick's General Store, Catskill, N. Y., 1844. Painting by Alburtis D. O. Browere.

board by the year, instead of 'going to house-keeping,' as they call having an establishment of their own. Of course this statement does not include persons of large fortune, but it does include very many whose rank in society would make such a mode of life quite impossible with us. I can hardly imagine a contrivance more effectual for ensuring the insignificance of a woman, than marrying her at seventeen, and placing her in a boarding-house. Nor can I easily imagine a life of more uniform dulness for the lady herself; but this certainly is a matter of taste."

In spite of the perils of boardinghouses and amid all the change, hurry, and moving about, most critics of our evolving society agreed that American family life was sound. The phrase so often heard in Europe, "a poor man with many children," was anomalous in this country; a man with many children soon ceased to be poor. In large areas of the country until the rise of urban industrialism the family was a production unit and the normal bonds of affection were secured by ties of mutual economic interest.

The same critics were likely to agree that American children enjoyed a unique freedom which could be very annoying. In America each generation of children was expected not only to succeed in life but to outdistance its parents in the race for success. With their resourcefulness, independence, and frequent bad manners they seemed to many witnesses to be bent on eliminating their elders from the race altogether by a campaign of painful extinction.

Many foreign visitors felt that the American's worst trait was his inveterate habit of bragging. Yet the habit had an ancient and honorable history. The first settlers had drawn the long bow out of an urgent desire to "sell" the New World to the Old. Captain John Smith himself was a master of overstatement and even Francis Higginson soberly maintained that "a sup of New England air" was "better than a whole draft of old England's ale."

What developed in necessity survived as a habit. Hyperbole became a national idiom; mixed with a deliberate comic strain as the tale grew taller, it constituted a sort of humor that sometimes confused Europeans. The tales of Davy Crockett riding a streak of lightning or of Paul Bunyan yanking crooked rivers straight or uprooting forests were told deadpan, as though they might,

just possibly, win credence. Anything was possible in America. You could laugh too soon like the English sceptics who scoffed at Audubon's story of a snake that raised its tail and rattled it.

In Leatherstocking, Cooper drew a romantic portrait of an American in the full enjoyment of his freedom and independence who was neither bumptious nor a braggart. To many Europeans who had never seen an American this resourceful hero, probably the most original character in American fiction, was more vital and convincing than any of the living mediocrities who featured the reports of returned travelers. Here was a man who, secure in his self-reliance and his higher moral purpose, lived beyond need and reach of man-made laws—the completely free individual, the perfect democrat of Jefferson's and Emerson's dream.

LEATHERSTOCKING DEFIES THE LAW. Painting by John Quidor.

The New York State Historical Association

PAUL BUNYAN. Lithograph by William Gropper, 1939.

AN AMERICAN IN EUROPE

FRENCH GENTLEMAN: "Permit me, Madame, the honor of introducing to your notice my friend, Mr. John Paul Jefferson Peabody, from the United States of America."

MADAME: *"Ma foi!* An American! He's white!"

From the *Lantern*, August, 1852.

Most Europeans who read Cooper's stories were undoubtedly less interested in Leatherstocking as a symbol of democracy than in his breathless adventures among the savages who with uncanny skill hunted through the forests of the New World. The American Indian had been widely and variously advertised abroad, and even among Europeans otherwise reasonably well informed it was vaguely believed that most if not all inhabitants of North America were redskins.

Faith in the perfectability of human institutions never burned more brightly than in nineteenth-century America. After fifty years of successful self-government, a period of abounding material progress, it seemed only simple logic that the union of states was setting an example for the world to follow. This was a chosen people and by God's will it had a manifest destiny. That self-righteous mantle, so comfortably assumed more than a century ago, has never worn out although it has become threadbare in spots and decidedly less comfortable.

It was never altogether a homespun attitude. In many foreign countries there were men of objective judgment who, like the German philosopher Hegel, saw America as

"the land of the future . . . the land of desire for all those who are weary of the historical lumber-room of Europe." To innumerable others, both abroad and at home, it was still Utopia, or a land where Utopias could be realized. For reformers and humanitarians of every stripe the country offered a wide, richly endowed laboratory for staging experiments that might solve society's problems and correct its evils. Whatever their project, few failed to attract a zealous following.

As a single example the temperance movement had enlisted more than a million Americans by 1825 and within the generation that followed, liquor-control legislation had been passed in thirteen states. Timothy Shay Arthur's *Ten Nights in a Barroom*, written more out of respect for a profitable market than out of reformist zeal, was only one tract among hundreds that kept the issue blazing. Militant as it was and led as it was, in part, by the highest authorities, the campaign tem-

"FATHER, COME HOME!" Illustration from the first edition of Timothy Shay Arthur, *Ten Nights in a Barroom*, 1854.

SIGNING THE PLEDGE, 1846. Lithograph by J. Ropes. Dedicated to the Washingtonians (a temperance society) commemorating their Declaration of Independence from the dominion of King Alcohol.

porarily dwindled away before the larger issues of the 1850's.

During those same decades scores of other crusades of lesser and larger moment kept the country in a ferment of restless aspiration and led to a variety of enthusiasms, some benign, some bigoted. Asylums for the insane were instituted by the tireless efforts and zeal of Dorothy Dix; plans were evolved and realized for the education of the blind by Samuel Gridley Howe; at one point large groups draped in ascension robes prepared for the millennium that had been carefully calculated by William Miller; thanks largely to Dana's *Two Years Before the Mast* flogging was abolished in the Navy; conditions in pri-

sons were humanized in many states; the Fox sisters attracted a numerous following and convinced Horace Greeley that spirit rappings were true indications from the beyond (although Greeley thought they made "dull music at best"); Catholic churches and convents were burned in the name of "good Americanism"; the Shakers, Mormons, and other sectarians won enthusiastic converts; and so on down a much longer list.

"There was an indefinite hope, and there was an assurance that all particular mischiefs were speedily coming to an end ..." wrote Emerson in his *New England Reformers.* "What a fertility of projects for the salvation of the world!"

"THE FOLLIES OF THE AGE, VIVE LE HUMBUG." An unidentified lithograph, about 1850. Represented in caricature are: the craze for trotting, railroad wrecks that resulted from hasty operations, explosions on the Collins
Line of steamships, the temperance movement, real estate speculation, patent medicines, the militia, Jenny

The American Antiquarian Society

Lind's money-making tour under Barnum's direction, free-love societies, Mormonism, the German's fondness for lager beer, political bombast, abolitionism, and other features of life at mid-century.

Nothing in American life presented such a long-standing anachronism as the position accorded to women. In a land where they were shown uncommon deference, a land which according to Tocqueville owed a large share of its progress to their superior qualities, women remained politically and legally almost nonexistent for generations after the Revolution.

The age of chivalry, noted one traveler of the mid-century, was not dead; it had never been born until the day of American democracy. Yet while such observations were being recorded it was still legal in most states for a husband to beat his wife "with a reasonable instrument"—anything from a horsewhip to a stick no thicker than a certain judge's thumb. In all states women were without the vote. And in the civil courts they were considered in a class with minors and incompetents. And when the woman's rights movement really got under way in America, it was largely derived from the earlier work of such women as Mary Wollstonecraft and Fanny Wright in England.

In 1776 when her husband was in Philadelphia helping to draw a charter of freedom for his country, Abigail Adams wrote to him that unless particular care and attention were paid to the political and civil rights of women, "we are determined to foment a rebellion, and will not hold ourselves bound to obey the laws in which we have no voice or representation." Rebellion was slow in coming, although with every passing decade of the next century woman's opinion became a more active agent in the ferment of democracy. Led by militant feminists, women gave ardent support to every growing crusade for human improvement. They fought for temperance, they agitated for peace, they called for higher educational standards, they chal-

The Library of Congress

THE MAY SESSION OF THE WOMAN'S RIGHTS CONVENTION—THE ORATOR OF THE DAY DENOUNCING THE LORDS OF CREATION. FROM *Harper's Weekly*, 1859.

lenged contemporary dress and diet, and they spoke out for the abolition of slavery.

In 1848 at Seneca Falls, New York, was held the first convention in the history of the world to argue the question of woman's rights. A Declaration of Sentiments, modeled on the Declaration of Independence, announced the purposes of the convention. "We hold these truths to be self-evident," the women's protest stated, listing those inalienable rights which thus far were not shared by American women. "... [man] has endeavored, in every way that he could, to destroy ... [woman's] confidence in her own powers, to lessen her self respect, and to make her willing to lead a dependent and abject life."

"Aggrieved, oppressed, and fraudulently deprived of their sacred rights," the ladies present at the convention asked for an equal voice in the home and in the state. Although from 1850 on similar conventions were held annually, and although liberal male opinion supported the movement, the militant

women met with less applause than abuse, even from a large proportion of their own sex. The relatively few who had the temerity to adopt the so-called Bloomer costume which would aid the wearer to attain a "position side by side with man ... his co-worker in life and its duties ... and give a more correct idea of the natural proportions of the human form," were heaped with ridicule.

In the year of the Seneca Falls convention, New York State granted women a few limited rights in the control of their own property. In 1854 the supreme tract of the times, one which was read throughout the world, came from the pen of a woman. In *Uncle Tom's Cabin* Mrs. Harriet Beecher Stowe wrote perhaps the most influential novel in all history. The cause of abolition was the one great reform movement of the era that eclipsed all others, feminism included. Ten years after the publication of Mrs. Stowe's book, when the states were locked in war, President Lincoln said to the author, "So you're the little woman who made the book that made this great war."

The Library of Congress
THE BLOOMER COSTUME. Lithograph after J. Queen.

NORTHERN INDUSTRY. Lithograph by N. Currier.

THE QUESTION OF UNITY

The issue to which Mrs. Stowe's "little book" called attention in such melodramatic style was far from new in American life. From the seventeenth century slavery had been a cause of agitation and disquiet. Throughout the decades before the Revolution an intermittent pamphlet war was waged on the Peculiar Institution by various groups and individuals. Thomas Jefferson mentioned the subject in his first draft of the Declaration of Independence, but others struck out his words. However, the final version of that document, though it did not mention the word slavery, in naming "liberty" as one of the "inalienable rights" of man, implied, for many, an indictment of every form of human bondage. Forty-four years later, during the bitter dispute over Missouri's admission into the Union, John Quincy Adams declared that the seeds of the Declaration of Independence were yet maturing. The harvest, he prophesied, would be a sublime but terrible day in American history.

That harvest was not reaped for forty more years. Between times it occasionally seemed that the dreadful crop might never have to be gathered, that by some ingenious political exercise slavery and the Declaration of Independence might be proved compatible within the frame of democracy, and that the heirs of liberty and union could live out their lives in peaceful fraternity. But by 1850 even a people trained in the practical

wisdom of compromise felt they could concede nothing further on the subject of slavery. Whatever the nature of the political issue—the tariff, currency and banking control, free homesteads or westward expansion —slavery was the irreducible factor.

Between the Missouri Compromise of 1820 and the final Compromise of 1850, America had undergone changes which steadily sharpened the issue. During that single generation heavy and mounting waves of immigration washed over the northern states depositing a large, conglomerate population upon which arguments for state sovereignty and the merits of slavery were alike wasted. As the population pushed westward, state beyond state, all local allegiances were weakened at the expense of a stronger national sentiment—and along the northern routes, in areas unprofitable for slavery, the population had moved on to the extreme limits of the land. The North, thus constantly recruited and extended in its interests, was also being charged by the dynamic magic of a new technology. Every fresh development of the Industrial Revolution seemed to multiply and glorify the promise of free, individual enterprise. Even the humblest immigrant put to the meanest labor felt he had a stake both idealistic and practical in universal freedom. "The great mass of foreigners who come to our shore are laborers, and consequently come into competition with slave labor," remarked a Louisiana editor. "It is to their interest to abolish slavery."

The South underwent no such changes. Warned by their guidebooks, most immigrants shunned the southern states. Without their helpful hands it was difficult for the South to promote manufactures. With increasing fixedness the region settled into a pattern of staple agricultural production manned by slave labor. The world's oldest form of economy struggled for parity with the newest within the same democratic government—and the oldest was supported by a diminishing minority of the nation's population.

Midway in time between the Compromise of 1820 and that of 1850, the French traveler Chevalier noted the serious rift that was developing. "In the North," he wrote, "the removal of all restrictions on the right of suffrage, without the creation of any counterpoise, has destroyed all equilibrium. In the South, the old foundation borrowed from ante-Christian ages on which it has been attempted to raise the superstructure of a new social order in the nineteenth century, shakes and threatens to bury the thoughtless builders under the ruins of their half-finished work. . . . The dissolution of the Union, if it should take place, would be the most complete of all revolutions. . . . But I have a firm faith, that a people with the energy and the intelligence which the Americans possess; a people which has . . . the genius of industry, which combines perseverance with the resources of ingenuity, which is essentially regular in its habits and orderly in its disposition, which is deeply imbued with religious habits, even when a lively faith is wanting, such a people cannot be born of yesterday to vanish on the morrow. . . . For such nations, the most violent storms are wholesome trials which strengthen . . . teach, elevate, and purify them."

The New York Public Library

A SOUTHERN COTTON PLANTATION. Lithograph from Henry Lewis, *Das Illustrierte Mississippithal*, Düsseldorf, 1857.

As the conflict drew nearer more and more was heard of the moral aspects of slavery. The South defended its Peculiar Institution as vehemently as it was attacked in the North. To William Lloyd Garrison's impassioned appeals, as to Mrs. Stowe's little book, the South replied that slavery was vindicated by the Bible, that it provided the best basis for free institutions, and that it compared favorably, in its humane aspects, with the wage system of the industrial North that reduced so many "free" whites to actual slavery. On the last count, at least, some Northerners could agree. "I am more and more convinced of the injustice we do the slaveholders," wrote a Boston clergyman during a trip to Virginia in 1842; "Of their feelings toward their negroes I can form a better notion than formerly, by examining my own toward the slaves who wait on my wife and mind my children. It is a feeling most like that we have to near relations. . . . They are unspeakably superior to our Northern free blacks. . . ."

There were other Northerners—Daniel Webster chief among them—who felt passionately that above all other considerations the Union must be preserved in peace. "I speak today for the preservation of the Union. Hear me for my cause," Webster pleaded in defense of the Compromise of 1850. But the Compromise included a vigorous Fugitive Slave act, and Webster's support of that "filthy enactment," as Emerson called it, won him the opprobrium of anti-slavery people who felt that for political ends he had compromised them beyond the limits of their conscience.

> Of all we loved and honored, naught
>   Save power remains—
> A fallen angel's pride of thought,
>   Still strong in chains.
>
> All else is gone, from those great eyes,
>   The soul is fled;
> When faith is lost, when honor dies,
>   The man is dead!

So wrote Whittier of the aged senator whose moral courage had been strained to the utmost to meet the crisis of the hour.

The Worcester Art Museum, Goodspeed Collection

"CONQUERING PREJUDICE OR FULFILLING A CONSTITUTIONAL DUTY WITH ALACRITY." Lithograph by P. Kramer, about 1850, lampooning Webster's support of the Fugitive Slave Law (he is depicted in the central figure) in the name of the Constitution.

A PRO-SLAVERY BROADSIDE PUBLISHED IN BOSTON, 1850. The lithograph was undoubtedly inspired by the criticisms of slavery made by the English crusader, George Thompson, during his second visit to America in 1850. The fact that it was published in Boston points to the anti-abolition sentiment in the North which did not wish to have the question agitated.

Widespread disobedience in the North greeted the Fugitive Slave provisions of the Compromise. In Emerson's opinion no self-respecting man could obey them or help in their application. However, so long as the South nominated the candidates that northern Democrats elected, as was said at mid-century, pro-slavery interests would always be protected by national policy. Such seemed still to be the case in 1854 when the people's representatives, through the strength of the Democratic Party, repealed the Missouri Compromise of 1820. That time-hallowed compact had banned slavery "forever" from certain large territories. Now the issue of slavery or freedom in those areas was to be decided by popular sovereignty, "squatter sovereignty" as it was called, when the residents appealed for statehood. But the new measure, called the Kansas-Nebraska Act with reference to the territories immediately involved, tended to unite northern sentiment more firmly than ever. "The Fugitive Law did much to unglue the eyes," remarked Emerson, "and now the Nebraska Bill leaves us staring."

Kansas was the first and last testing ground of the rash bill; and in "Bleeding Kansas" civil war soon had a miserable rehearsal. Emigrants from North and South moved into the contested area to save Kansas for their cause. Some came with good will to settle permanently as free or slaveholding residents. Others from both sides came only to vote and leave. In either case emigrant aid societies in North and South urged them on and helped finance their move. Among the newcomers were zealots and ruffians of both persuasions, men prepared to "wade to the knees in blood" to defeat their adversaries. "Border Ruffians" from pro-slavery Missouri sacked the town of Lawrence to eliminate its abolitionist influence. In retaliation John Brown, a stern and God-fearing abolitionist, with his sons, raided the slavery party on Pottawatomie Creek and, one by one and

BORDER RUFFIANS INVADING KANSAS. Drawing by F. O. C. Darley.
The Yale University Art Gallery, Mabel Brady Garvan Collection

in cold blood, five men were slaughtered. Guerrilla warfare raged until federal troops restored order, with the issue still unsettled.

The issue, indeed, could now only burn brighter and hotter. Three years later Brown made his historic raid on Harper's Ferry, was captured by Colonel Robert E. Lee and Lieutenant "Jeb" Stuart of the United States Army, and was tried, convicted, and hanged for murder, for inciting slaves to revolt, and for treason. Before he was put to death Brown told his inquisitors, ". . . I think, my friend, you are guilty of a great wrong against God and humanity—I say it without wishing to be offensive—and it would be perfectly right for any one to interfere with you so far as to free those you wilfully and wickedly hold in bondage. I do not say this insultingly . . . I pity the poor in bondage that have none to help them; that is why I am here; not to gratify any personal animosity, revenge or vindictive spirit. It is my sympathy with the oppressed and the wronged, that are as good as you and as precious in the sight of God. . . . *I wish to say, furthermore, that you had better—all you people at the South—prepare yourselves for a settlement of that question that must come up for settlement sooner than you are prepared for it.* The sooner you are prepared the better. You may dispose of me very easily. I am nearly disposed of now; but this question is still to be settled—this negro question I mean; the end of that is not yet. . . ."

Northern newspapers of both parties condemned Brown's fanaticism; a Christian burial for his body was obtained only with difficulty; and virtually all political incumbents and aspirants denounced the deed. But through the clamor of repudiation and indignation sounded the voices of Emerson, Thoreau, and other northern oracles. "Some eighteen hundred years ago," said Thoreau, "Christ was crucified; this morning, perchance, Captain Brown was hung. These are the two ends of a chain which is not without its links. He is not Old Brown any longer; he is an angel of light."

The Metropolitan Museum of Art
THE LAST MOMENTS OF JOHN BROWN. Painting by Thomas Hovenden, 1881. One of numerous *ex post facto* versions of the subject; apparently inspired by Whittier's rather dull poem on the subject.

The plantation country, remembering the murderous uprisings in Haiti and Santo Domingo, trembled with the thought of what might happen should Brown or anyone like him succeed in arming any considerable number of slaves. When at last the Democrats lost the Presidency in 1860 no words of Lincoln could still the fear that southern welfare was no longer compatible with the majority will of the Union, now dominated by a largely sectional and northern party.

"To those, however who really love the Union," Lincoln said in his first inaugural address, "may I not speak?" And he ended: "In your hands, my dissatisfied fellow countrymen, and not in mine, is the momentous issue of civil war. The government will not assail you. You can have no conflict without being yourselves the aggressors. You have no oath registered in heaven to destroy the government, while I shall have the

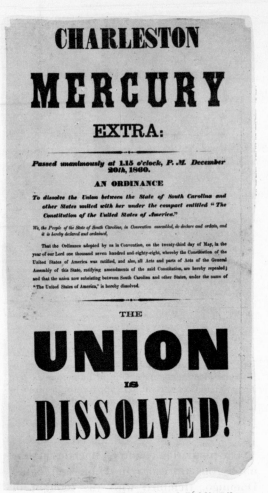

CHARLESTON

MERCURY

EXTRA:

Passed unanimously at 1.15 o'clock, P. M. December 20th, 1860.

AN ORDINANCE

To dissolve the Union between the State of South Carolina and other States united with her under the compact entitled " The Constitution of the United States of America."

We, the People of the State of South Carolina, in Convention assembled, do declare and ordain, and it is hereby declared and ordained,

That the Ordinance adopted by us in Convention, on the twenty-third day of May, in the year of our Lord one thousand seven hundred and eighty-eight, whereby the Constitution of the United States of America was ratified, and also, all Acts and parts of Acts of the General Assembly of this State, ratifying amendments of the said Constitution, are hereby repealed; and that the union now subsisting between South Carolina and other States, under the name of " The United States of America," is hereby dissolved.

THE

UNION

IS

DISSOLVED!

The New York Public Library

HEADLINES FROM THE CHARLESTON *Mercury*, DECEMBER 20, 1860.

most solemn one to 'preserve, protect, and defend' it.

"I am loath to close. We are not enemies, but friends. We must not be enemies. Though passion may have strained, it must not break, our bonds of affection. The mystic cords of memory, stretching from every battlefield and patriot grave to every living heart and hearthstone all over this broad land, will yet swell the chorus of the Union when again touched, as surely they will be, by the better angels of our nature."

By then a large bloc of southern states had already seceded; first South Carolina, which announced her separation from the Union on December 20, 1860; then, before Lincoln's inauguration, Georgia, Florida, Alabama, Mississippi, Louisiana, and Texas. Whether the southern states had a constitutional "right" to secede was, fundamentally, an idle question although much was made of it. In the past all sections of the country had claimed that right and in turn denounced it as treason as national union furthered or impaired their vital interests. Not many years before, during the great ascendancy of the plantation interests, the aged John Quincy Adams had proposed the secession of the northern states, that last desperate move of a frustrated minority.

But the test of union lay beyond the confusions of legal theory. As Lincoln remarked in that same inaugural address, physically speaking the states could not separate. "Can aliens make treaties easier than friends can make laws?" he asked. "Can treaties be more faithfully enforced between aliens than laws can among friends? Suppose you go to war, you cannot fight always; and when, after much loss on both sides, and no gain on either, you cease fighting, the identical old questions as to terms of intercourse are again upon you."

In the last resort the test of sovereignty is power; and Southerners had been repeatedly warned by their own statesmen that there could not be peaceful secession—war must follow, and that would determine the seat of power. At 4.30 A.M., April 12, 1861, the first shot was fired at Fort Sumter. The inhabitants of Charleston swarmed to the waterfront to watch the cannonading and to await the surrender of the fort that followed on the next day. "In the afternoon [of the 15th]," one Charleston lady wrote in her diary, "Mrs. Preston, Mrs. Joe Heyward, and I drove out around the battery. We were in an open carriage. What a changed scene—the very liveliest crowd I think I ever saw, everybody talking at once. All glasses were still turned on the grim old fort."

In New York news of the attack was heard on the night of the fort's surrender. ". . . I

CHARLESTON HARBOR FROM THE BATTERY DURING THE BOMBARDMENT OF FORT SUMTER, APRIL 13, 1861. Painting by W. A. Walker after a sketch made by the artist in 1864 when he was a member of the Confederate States Engineers Corps. At the left is Castle Pinckney, the Confederate gunboat *Juno*, and, in the distance, Fort Moultrie. Fort Sumter is in the center. Fort Johnson is at the extreme right.

heard in the distance the loud cries of the newsboys," recalled Walt Whitman, "who came presently tearing and yelling up the street, rushing from side to side. . . . I bought an extra and cross'd to the Metropolitan hotel (Niblo's) where the great lamps were still brightly blazing, and, with a crowd of others, who gather'd impromptu, read the news, which was evidently authentic. For the benefit of some who had no papers, one of us read the telegram aloud, while all listened silently and attentively. No remark was made by any of the crowd, which had increas'd to thirty or forty, but all stood a minute or two, I remember, before they dispers'd. I can almost see them there now, under the lamps at midnight again."

Was this self-determination or rebellion? Jefferson Davis told his fellow Confederates that they were "the last best hope of liberty." Lincoln, with equal fervor, insisted that the United States—North and South inseparably united—was "the last, best hope of earth." The only answer history can give rests on which side achieved its purpose. As Herbert

Agar points out, the difference between a rebel and the father of his country is solely a matter of success. The roar of cannon over Charleston Harbor drowned out the contending voices of statesmen. For all practical purposes the truth could now only be found on the battlefield.

Neither South nor North was prepared for war. It has been the habit of America until very recent years to prepare for war only when war came. In 1861, as in 1917 and in 1941, new armies had to be created, equipped, trained, and battle-tested. At the outbreak of hostilities the entire United States army consisted of about sixteen thousand men (out of a population of more than thirty million people), most of them scattered in small posts throughout the Indian country. Few of the junior officers had seen more than a handful of soldiers gathered together at one time and, aside from that small professional group, few Americans had ever given serious thought to military matters before the day Sumter was fired on. All this changed in the years that followed.

Cooper Union Museum for the Arts of Decoration
A YANKEE SOLDIER. Sketch by Winslow Homer. Photograph courtesy of the Frick Art Reference Library.

In 1860 the American who would fight the Civil War was a civilian in an overwhelmingly civil society. Five years later, as Denis Brogan remarks, he was—if he lived through that interval—again a civilian in a society as civilian as ever, a society in which it was possible to live for many years without ever seeing a professional soldier. But for the years that intervened he was in the ranks, on one side or the other, of the largest military forces that had yet been brought to battle.

It was the first big war fought by civilian armies. "Probably no future age can know, but I well know," wrote Walt Whitman, "how the gist of this fiercest and most resolute of the world's warlike contentions resided exclusively in the unnamed, unknown rank and file; how the brunt of its labor of death, to all essential purposes was volunteered. The People, of their own choice, fighting, dying for their own idea."

That was written in retrospect. At the time of decision there were more than a few who volunteered their services, or their faith, only after anguished deliberation. Colonel Robert E. Lee, the greatest soldier of the United States army, deplored slavery (he emancipated his own slaves) but scorned the tactics of the abolitionists; he held that secession was not a constitutional right and he held his own pledge of allegiance to his government as a sacred trust; but, as he wrote his son, he could not raise his hand against his native state, his family and relatives, and his home. He was offered the command of the United States army. Reluctantly Lee resigned his commission and took command of the opposing force. One hesitates to imagine the agony that decision cost him.

There were others who faced their souls as bravely and as grimly. As in the Revolution, American families of honest convictions were often divided among themselves. Men from every southern state fought with the North because they felt the Union must be preserved. There were Confederate soldiers from every northern state, men who approved of the South's stand and fought to support it. Many more fought without a question in their minds; still more fought because they were conscripted.

Just how many men there were in the two armies has never been satisfactorily determined, probably no less than two and a half millions. But, as has been truly said, "for the number of men involved, the amount of space traversed, the coast line blockaded, of material consumed and results achieved" the Civil War surpassed all the wars of history up to that time.

It was also a very sanguinary war. More than six hundred thousand men lost their lives during its course, in addition to the hundreds of thousands who were wounded or made permanent invalids. "One of the first things that met my eyes . . ." Walt Whitman wrote his mother from the camp where his brother was stationed in 1862, "was a heap of feet, arms, legs, etc., under a tree in front of a hospital. . . ." In the 1860's the world was not accustomed to such spectacles. "Mother," Whitman wrote a year later, "one's heart grows sick of war, after all, when you see what it really is; every once in a while I feel so horrified and disgusted—it seems to me like a great slaughterhouse and the men mutually butchering each other—then I feel how impossible it appears, again, to retire from this contest, until we have carried our points (it is cruel to be so tossed from pillar to post in one's judgment)."

Probably no other war has been so minutely studied and restudied by historians, amateur and professional, American

The National Archives
A Camp Scene. Photograph by Mathew Brady.

and foreign, as the Civil War. For Americans, as Brogan observes, it is still *the* war; "its heroes on both sides give their names to forts and training camps (Sheridan, Thomas): from its leaders, on both sides, tanks take their names (Grant, Sherman, Stuart). From 1868 (the first post-war election) to 1900 inclusive, every man elected President

The Carver Hospital, near Washington, D. C. Photograph by Brady.

The National Archives

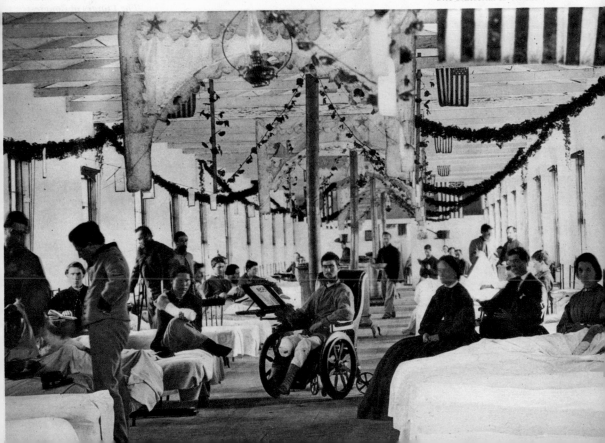

"A CONFEDERATE BULL TRAIN PREVIOUS TO THE BATTLE OF BULLS RUN." Drawing by an unidentified artist.

of the United States had with one exception been an officer in the Union army; all but one were ex-generals. Round it legend of all kinds clustered; it is still a sure-fire subject for fiction and the movies. Its battlefields and war cemeteries are sacred in an especial way. Chancellorsville, Fredericksburg, Vicksburg, Stone River, Chickamauga, Lookout Mountain, Atlanta, Petersburg—these are still fighting names. The tactics, the strategy of the war are fought over again in magazines, in reviews, in books. South of the Potomac it is still a near-fighting word to call this conflict anything but 'The War Between the States.' There are still unreconstructed rebels in Georgia and men who still think treason odious in Vermont — and northern Tennessee." The effect of the war on Ameri-

GALLANT CHARGE OF HUMPHREY'S DIVISION AT THE BATTLE OF FREDERICKSBURG, 1862. Drawing by A. R. Waud.
The Library of Congress

can life was, indeed, immeasurably deep and lasting.

At the time, its outcome was awaited with anxious interest across the Atlantic. On the eve of the war Tocqueville heard the rumblings from abroad and wrote: "I earnestly hope that the great experiment in self government which is carried out in America will not fail. If it did, it would be the end of political liberty in our world." He never knew the result, for he died within six months. But there were others who continued to watch with no less concern. Many could see no reason to hope for—or fear—a northern victory. The South was fighting for its freedom, its homes, and the threatened security of its own society. The North was fighting merely for an imponderable idea of

THE ARMY OF THE POTOMAC ON THE MARCH, JANUARY 21, 1863. Drawing by Waud.

union. Even slavery was a secondary consideration.

"My paramount object in this struggle," Lincoln wrote to Horace Greeley in August, 1862, ". . . is not either to save or destroy slavery. If I could save the Union without freeing any slave, I would do it; and if I could save it by freeing all the slaves, I would do it; and if I could save it by freeing some and leaving others alone, I would also do that. What I do about slavery, and the coloured race, I do because I believe it helps to save the Union; and what I forbear, I forbear because I do not believe it would help to save the Union. I shall do less whenever I shall believe what I am doing hurts the cause, and I shall do more whenever I shall believe doing more will help the cause." That faith, that vision, and that singleness of purpose Lincoln transferred by his own personal magic to the common people of the North. With Lincoln, wrote one of his enemies, the Union, in sentiment, "rose to the sublimity of religious mysticism."

Even before his letter to Greeley was written, Lincoln had decided that slavery must die that the nation might live. In September, 1862, he announced that all "persons held as slaves" within areas "in rebellion against the United States" would be emancipated at the end of the year—a proclamation for which he was damned both in the South and, by conservatives and Democrats, in the North. As a last desperate gesture the South, in March, 1865, authorized the employment of slaves in military service. "The day you make soldiers of them," objected one Southerner, "is the beginning of the end of the revolution. If slaves will make good soldiers our whole theory of slavery is wrong." As Union officers could testify, they did make good soldiers, many of them. But neither that fact nor the

The Metropolitan Museum of Art

LINCOLN SIGNING THE EMANCIPATION, A SOUTHERN VIEW. Etching by Adelbert Volck.

The New-York Historical Society

SLAVES ON A SOUTH CAROLINA PLANTATION, 1862. Photograph by Henry P. Moore from the *Philadelphia Photographer*, 1865.

Proclamation of Emancipation, nor yet the policies of Reconstruction, gave the Negro any solid stake in American society. For that he is often still waiting. The South's use for troops was almost over. In that same March, Lincoln, at his second inauguration, pledged that "if God wills that [the war] continue until all the wealth piled by the bondman's two hundred and fifty years of unrequited toil shall be sunk, and until every drop of blood drawn with the lash be paid with another drawn by the sword, as was said three thousand years ago, so still it must be said, 'The judgments of the Lord are true and righteous altogether.'

"With malice toward none; with charity for all; with firmness in the right, as God gives us to see the right, let us strive on to finish the work we are in; to bind up the nation's wounds; to care for him who shall have borne the battle, and for his widow, and his orphan—to do all which may achieve and cherish a just and lasting peace among ourselves, and with all nations."

A month later to the day the Union forces entered Richmond, pressing hard after Lee's grim, harassed troops. The work was almost finished.

With the infinitely sad scene at Appomattox the long, desperate struggle came to an end. The nation had survived, slavery had been abolished, and a curious, colorful civilization was all but destroyed. But, to paraphrase Ralph Henry Gabriel, the American democratic faith remained not only intact but heightened. Both Blue and Gray believed that theirs was the true witness for democratic liberty. One conquered in battle, the other suffered martyrdom—the faith each claimed as truth had won a double triumph.

NORTHEAST, SOUTH, AND WEST

Although the Union had survived the convulsions of a gigantic war, sectionalism did not disappear from American life with the end of hostilities. Indeed, beside the war-ravaged South and the highly geared industrial North, a new trans-Mississippi West had grown to power during the conflict. All three sections played very distinct parts in the developments of the coming generation. Political and economic rivalry among them was sometimes bitter. But the threat of violent dismemberment of the Union would apparently never again be raised.

In the post-war South reporters saw only desolation. Columbia, once "the gem of South Carolina," was barely discernible among its ashes. "It is now a wilderness of ruins," wrote a northern traveler. "Its heart is but a mass of blackened chimneys and crumbling walls. Two thirds of the buildings in the place were burned, including, without exception, everything in the business portion." But, he added, "the ruin here is neither half so eloquent nor touching as that at Charleston: This is but the work of flame, and might have mostly been brought about in time of peace. Those ghostly and crumbling walls and those long-deserted grass-grown streets show the prostration of a community—such prostration as only war could bring."

Richmond, Atlanta, New Orleans, and other centers in the South bore their deep scars as did the surrounding countryside. Yet, despite the trials and burdens of the Reconstruction period, the South rebuilt with miraculous speed. "As ruin was never before so overwhelming," said Henry Grady,

THE RUINS OF RICHMOND. Photograph by Brady.

a great post-war leader of the South, "never was restoration swifter. The soldier stepped from the trenches into the furrow; horses that had charged Federal guns marched before the plow, and fields that ran red with human blood in April, were green with the harvest in June."

Within fifteen years of Appomattox the cotton crop was larger than ever. In 1873 Edward King, a Connecticut Yankee, found New Orleans doing a bustling business. ". . . when the season is at its height," he wrote, "clerks and patrons work [at the Cotton Exchange] literally night and day. . . . New Orleans is accused of a lack of energy, but her cotton merchants are more energetic than the mass of Northern traders and speculators. . . . One well-known cotton factor . . . gets to his desk, during the season, long before daylight,—and that, in the climate of the Gulf States, comes wonderfully early." However, many aspects of the southern economy did not recover for generations.

The National Archives

THE RUINS OF THE CATHOLIC CATHEDRAL, CHARLESTON. Photograph by Brady.

THE COTTON MARKET IN NEW ORLEANS, 1873. Painting by Edgar Degas. The artist's brothers were successful cotton merchants of New Orleans.

Musée de Pau, France

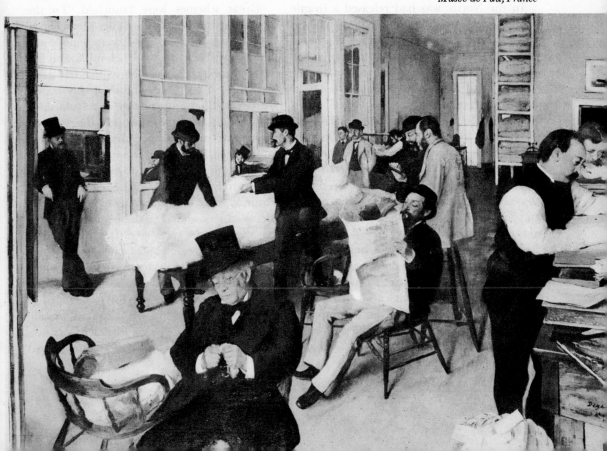

CONSTRUCTION WORK IN NEW YORK, 1868. Painting by Alessandro Mario. The scene is along 46th Street looking west from Third Avenue.

In the North, war had released a titanic charge of vitality and enterprise which was still mounting in 1865 and which the peace diverted into new channels. "Probably, the parallel of this is not to be found in the world's history," wrote an English observer of northern conditions. "All records, of whatsoever period, show, that during fierce and desolating struggles, the populations engaged in them have suffered fearful privations and miseries, and that protracted periods have elapsed before they have been able to recover from their effects. America, which in so many respects has shown herself superior to ordinary rules, has . . . shown that the heaviest and most costly civil conflict can be borne not only without exhaustion, but even with an increase of national prosperity." Self-confident, exuberant, and prosperous almost beyond credence, the triumphant North surged forward with reckless haste to new conquests.

Great schemes were launched. To the saviors of the Union all things seemed possible. Cities rose, grew, and were remade at a giddy rate. Everywhere mines, mills, and factories tapped the seemingly inexhaustible resources of the land, absorbed the brawn, energy, and patient courage of a fresh flood of immigrants, and equipped the country with new material trophies. Forests were obliterated, the earth was plundered, and people found their way or lost it in a mammoth treasure hunt. Waste could not be counted when so much appeared in prospect. Between 1860 and 1870 the per capita wealth of the North grew greatly. Millionaires seemed to increase almost as rapidly as paupers. Tariff walls rose and, in the lee, railroads flung their rails to all points of the compass to carry the products of countless new industries along with myriad passengers, each with a golden gleam in his eye.

The lifeblood of the nation now flowed

The New-York Historical Society

A Scene in the Great Railway Station at Chicago, 1870. Engraving after Thomas Hogan from *Appleton's Journal*.

east and west along the rails instead of through the old circulatory system of waterways that ran north and south. The Middle West had taken a commanding place in the nation's economy. It had all but won the war. It had raised, equipped, and fed a lion's share of the Union armies and it had given the Union cause its leader in "the man from Illinois." It was, as that man said, "the great body of the republic."

One traveler of recent years, crossing the United States for the first time by rail and after several days journey finally reaching Santa Fe, remarked that it was small wonder Columbus had discovered America; it was hard for him to see how anyone could have missed it. America's struggle for "a more perfect union" can only be understood in relation to that enormous scale of operation.

Even while the Civil War was being fought a constant stream of noncombatants flowed westward, spreading out in a loose pattern over a continental area that could barely be envisioned east of the Mississippi. In the first year of peace the flow of westering people increased; one witness found the prairie trails as thick with traffic as the eastern highways. That same year the first tracks were laid to link the farthest West and the East with a railroad. With the completion of that iron bond in 1869, an eastern editor wrote that the Union stood on the threshold "of a destiny higher and better than any nation has yet fulfilled." "And," he added, "the great West is to rule us."

Between 1865 and 1872 the railway mileage in the country doubled. Even before the transcontinental span was finished the arrivals and departures of trains at Chicago alone exceeded two hundred a day. Chicago was the railway hub of the nation, gateway to the receding frontier, and, for an undetermined horde of migrants, the crossroads of destiny—the threshold of the future.

The National Archives
PACK MULE AND PACKERS ON THE WHEELER GEOLOGICAL SURVEY, 1871. Photograph by T. H. O'Sullivan.

It was only after the Civil War that the nation as a whole became truly aware of its continental dimensions. The discovery of America seemed to be taking place all over again as news reports, filed by an army of journalists during the first decade of peace, described the unfamiliar treasure-house of the Great West. Almost to a man the report-ers were awed by what they saw. Almost to a man, too, they returned, "with fuller measure of the American Republic and larger faith in its destiny," and with a message to their readers of "the real breadth and capacity, the necessities and possibilities of the American Nation."

The government sent out a succession of expeditions conducted by Clarence King, Lieutenant George M. Wheeler, Major John Wesley Powell, and others—men keenly alive to the epic character of their assignments to map the facts of this new New World. Even the official reports of these parties bristle with excitement and wonder over what was seen and learned. They found none of the prowling mastodons that Jefferson had warned Lewis and Clark to look for. But they found natural wonders of every conceivable variety that taxed their powers of description. To the man in the street the reports, official and otherwise, brought a sense of adventure that unlocked his imagination. The photographs and paintings that supplemented the survey reports were among the first

SAND DUNES, CARSON DESERT, NEVADA, 1867. Photograph by O'Sullivan, for the King Survey.
The National Archives

adequate graphic accounts of the far western scene to reach the public and they stirred the East to even bigger dreams.

Henry Adams met King, "saturated with the sunshine of the Sierras," and talked long hours with him in the western mountains. "None of his contemporaries had done so much, single-handed," wrote Adams in his *Education,* "or were likely to leave so deep a trail. . . . He had organized, as a civil—not military—measure, a Government Survey. He had paralleled the Continental Railway in Geology; a feat as yet unequalled by other governments which had as a rule no continents to survey. He was creating one of the classic scientific works of the century."

King's various writings on the West he knew so well and loved so ardently appealed to a far wider audience than scientists. He was the first of the western nature writers to win a public. Only John Muir surpassed him in powerful and brilliant descriptions of what the grandeur of the virgin West was really like, though for a hundred years no topic has been more popular.

The Museum of Modern Art
ANCIENT RUINS IN THE CAÑON DE CHELLY, ARIZONA, 1873. Photograph by O'Sullivan for the Wheeler Survey.

LIEUTENANT WHEELER'S SURVEY PARTY IN THE YOSEMITE, IN THE 1870'S.

Collection of Philip Medicus

THE TETON RANGE. Painting by Thomas Moran, 1897.

The Metropolitan Museum of Art

The United States Geological Survey
MAJOR POWELL AND AN INDIAN ACQUAINTANCE, ABOUT
1869. Photograph by John K. Hillers.

John Wesley Powell's account of his run down the Colorado River through more than a thousand miles of the Grand Canyon is one of the great adventure stories in American literature. In 1869 Powell, a maimed veteran of the Civil War, made the first of his trips through the wild rapids and other unexplored perils of that terrible river, sometimes sunk more than a mile deep between its canyon walls. The Indians considered the feat preposterous. The Colorado was a river of mystery and fear and should not be tempted to disclose its awful secrets. "The rocks h-e-a-p, h-e-a-p high," they told Powell; "the water go h-oo-woogh, h-oo-woogh; water pony [the special partly decked rowboats Powell had constructed for his trip] h-e-a-p buck; water catch 'em; no see 'em Injun any more! no see 'em squaw any more! no see 'em pappoose any more!" But Powell, one-armed as he was, completed his adventure from Green River Crossing, Wyoming, to a point just above the present Boulder Dam. White man had never before braved the hazards of that muddy torrent

nor looked up at those giant, brilliantly colored cliffs. But it was no mere stunt; Powell was after topographical and geological data and he repeated the trip two years later to complete his information. Generally speaking, the first proper maps of the United States were made of the far western territories—in most cases better than any that existed of the East.

In his lifetime Powell contributed enormously to a true knowledge of the West. It was he, above all other contemporary spokesmen, who defined the distinctive character of the semi-arid country beyond the 100th meridian—the conditions rooted in geography which, when properly understood, would demand new land laws, new governmental policies, and new types of institutions. As director of the United States Geological Survey, he led a pioneer effort to use the scientific resources of the national government in ameliorating the lot of the public. It might be said he was, in a sense, one of the earliest proponents of the welfare state. Powell believed that the disclosures of science would usher in the golden day and that nowhere would its revelations be brighter than in America.

The United States Geological Survey
POWELL'S BOATS, 1869. Photograph by Hillers.

THE GRAND CANYON, 1872. Photograph by Hillers. Courtesy of Clarence S. Jackson and Beaumont Newhall.

PORTLAND, OREGON, 1858. Lithograph by Kuchel and Dresel. The earliest recorded view of the city, taken from what is now East Portland, looking across the Willamette River.

At the farthest western limits of the nation a new section of the republic was developing at a headlong rate along the Pacific coast. From here, too, reporters sent out to scan the country in all its breadth, sent home stories that were strange and wonderful to eastern readers.

During the feverish days of 'forty-nine Paul Revere's grandson, Lieutenant Joseph Warren Revere, on a tour of military duty in California, had foretold that once the gold fever subsided, Californians would find far greater wealth by working the fertile soil of the valleys and of the coastal strip. Sixteen years later, Samuel Bowles, the distinguished editor of the *Springfield Republican,* wrote that fifty bushels of wheat to the acre was

more common in California than twenty-five in the best wheat fields of the rest of the country, and that seventy-five and eighty bushels were often gathered. In this land where there was no rain or dew to spoil the crop "there is no hot, hurrying work with planting and harvesting, as in the East," he wrote, "no dodging of showers; no lost days during the long summer. . . . A single farmer in the neighborhood of San Jose, with a twelve hundred acre farm, has this year gathered in over fifty thousand bushels of wheat." A few years later the highly specialized wheat farmer in California boasted he could bake a loaf of bread before dusk from wheat that had been standing in the field at dawn.

"I was prepared for California," wrote

WINNOWING GRAIN IN CALIFORNIA, 1872. Painting by Virgil Williams.

Collection of "The Progressive Farmer"

Bowles. "But Oregon is more of a revelation. It has rarer natural beauties, richer resources, a larger development, and a more promising future than I had learned of." Portland, Oregon's largest town, he continued, "stands sweetly on the banks of the Willamette, twelve miles before it joins the Columbia River, and one hundred and twenty miles from where the Columbia meets the Pacific Ocean. Ships and ocean steamers of highest class come readily hither; from it spreads out a wide navigation by steamboat of the Columbia and its branches, below and above; here centers a large and increasing trade." "They keep Sunday as we do in New England," Bowles added, perhaps a little nostalgically, "and as no other population this side of the Mississippi now does."

Still farther north, Bowles came to Puget Sound which he thought was "one of the water wonders of the world." "It is the great lumber market of all the Pacific Coast. Already a dozen saw-mills are located on its shores; one which we visited was three hundred and thirty-six feet long, and turns out one hundred thousand feet of lumber daily; three ships and two barks of five hundred to one thousand tons each were leading with the product direct from the mill; and the present entire export of the Sound, in prepared lumber and masts and spars, reaches nearly to one hundred millions of feet yearly, and yields at the average price of ten dollars a thousand about one million dollars."

PUGET MILL COMPANY LUMBER MILLS AT TEEKALET, WASHINGTON TERRITORY, 1856–57. Lithograph by T. Grob.
The New-York Historical Society, Bella C. Landauer Collection

THE NEW AMERICAN

After Appomattox the United States could no longer be considered an untried and venturesome experiment in government. The nation had emerged from the crucible of war tested and proven. The union conceived in liberty and dedicated to the proposition that all men are created equal had not only endured but, as Chevalier had earlier predicted, gained strength and purpose from its worst trial. And, with that supreme test endured, the dreams to which America had given rise throughout the rest of the world more than ever became a guide to action. During the next three quarters of a century thirty-three million people exchanged their lot in older countries for a new life in America. Every decade brought from abroad more than enough people to have replaced the entire population of the nation in 1776.

The American dream took on a variety of shapes and colors. For many, no doubt, it came in the words of a countryman, a relative or a neighbor who wrote home of his progress in the New World. One immigrant related that for ten years before he left for America he read all the letters reaching his village from those who had migrated. Or it might have grown from reports in one of the long list of emigrant journals published throughout western Europe. One could find the outlines of the dream in the works of the early romantic poets and novelists, or in the occasional remarks of such towering writers as Goethe and Hegel.

But for a vast number of immigrants the American dream had been drawn in rosy

The Eldest Son Bidding Farewell to his Family before Departing for America, Orsa Parish, Dalecarlia, Sweden, about 1875. Painting by S. V. Helander. Photograph courtesy of S. Artur Svensson.

Collection of the Swedish Royal Family

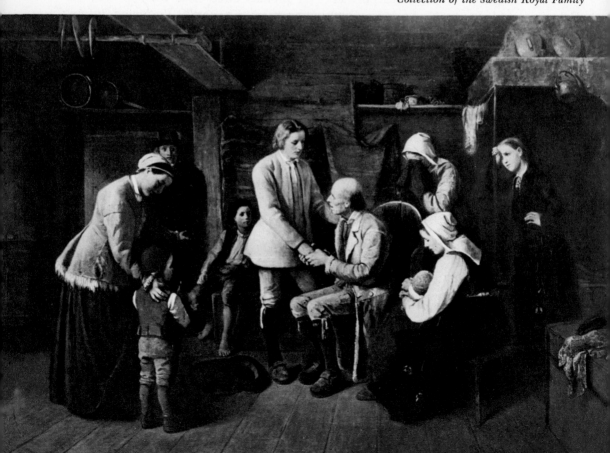

BETWEEN DECKS ON AN EMIGRANT SHIP—FEEDING TIME, 1870. Engraving by A. B. Houghton.

perspective by agents self-interested in creating and increasing a flow of humanity across the Atlantic and across the North American continent. Bent on earning "a dollar a head" the emigrant agent used his gaudy lithographs and exaggerated descriptions, as one disenchanted commentator remarked, "like a slow poison which he injected in many a peaceful and contented family." In time few villages in western Europe were without an agency to promote emigration. In 1911 a witness before the Immigration Commission stated that two steamship lines had 5000 to 6000 ticket agents in Galicia alone. The American railroad companies with land to sell and traffic to maintain had their own agents as did many of the states and territories, none of them reluctant to sell a dream for cold cash.

During the Civil War America had passed from the age of wood to the age of iron and steam. In the years that followed, the new industrialism expanded with colossal energy and dramatic speed. And from the factories and the mines went up a new and louder cry for immigrants—for labor to dig coal, man the flaming forges, and ply the needle in the garment houses, labor that could be transported more quickly and in larger masses in the new iron steamships that were plying the Atlantic. "Not since the patricians and capitalists of Rome scoured the known world for slaves—Celts, Iberians, Angles, Gauls, Saxons, Greeks, Jews, Egyptians, and Assyrians —to serve them and then disappeared themselves under a deluge of strange colors," wrote the Beards, "had the world witnessed such a deliberate overturn of a social order by masters of ceremonies. Nothing save the peculiar circumstances of the case prevented general consternation."

Up until 1880 the incoming horde of immigrants had not radically changed the racial amalgam America had achieved in 1776. Now came people of different strains from southern and eastern Europe, first in a trickle, then in a stream, and finally in a great torrent — Italians, Greeks, Croats, Czechs, Magyars, Slovaks, Poles, Hungarians, Austrians, Rumanians, Russians, and Jews. About a million of them, along with more than four million of the more familiar stock,

"The Land of Promise"; the Interior of New York's Immigration Depot at Castle Garden, 1884. Painting by Charles F. Ulrich.

came between 1881 and 1890. Two million more came in the next decade and six million—about seventy per cent of the total immigration for those years—in the first decade of this century. "During the last ten years," wrote Josiah Strong in 1891, "we have suffered a peaceful invasion by an army four times as vast as the estimated numbers of Goths and Vandals that swept over Southern Europe and overwhelmed Rome."

Many of these later-comers stayed just long enough to make the money that would enable them to return home and live in comfort. Many more came to build a brighter future in the New World. Until the 1880's, except for such passing aberrations as the Know-Nothing excitement, Americans at large had exulted that their nation was an asylum for all who chose to come to it. For the tired, the poor, and the huddled masses of the earth it was the land of promise. Let them all come, wrote Emerson: "The energy of Irish, Germans, Swedes, Poles, and Cossacks, and all the European tribes,—and of the Africans, and of the Polynesians,—will construct a new race, a new religion, a new state, a new literature, which will be as vigorous as the new Europe which came out of the smelting-pot of the Dark Ages. . . ."

The year of Emerson's death, a year before Emma Lazarus wrote her poem to be inscribed on the Statue of Liberty welcoming "the wretched refuse, the homeless, tempest-tost" peoples of the world, Congress placed the first material restriction on immigration in our national history, with the Chinese Exclusion Act. There was a growing doubt that the country, big and vigorous as it was, could safely assimilate the heterogeneous millions who stormed its gates. By 1890 New York had half as many Italians as Naples, as many Germans as Hamburg, twice as many Irish as Dublin, and two and a half times as many Jews as Warsaw. Even one-third of the people of Boston were of alien birth. Senator Lodge spoke in the Senate against the barbarian invasion and in favor of a literacy test that would exclude the most "dangerous" elements. ". . . the . . . test will bear most heavily," he said, "upon the Italians, Russians, Poles, Hungarians, Greeks, and Asiatics . . . those whose emigration to this country has begun within the last twenty years and swelled rapidly to enormous

The Library of Congress
THE LAST YANKEE; A COMMENTARY ON UNRESTRICTED IMMIGRATION. From *Leslie's Weekly*, 1888.

The A. F. Sherman Collection
THE "NEW" IMMIGRANT; A RUMANIAN SHEPHERD AT ELLIS ISLAND, N. Y., ABOUT 1900. Photograph by A. F. Sherman. Print courtesy of Alexander Alland.

proportions, races with which the English-speaking people have never hitherto assimilated, and who are most alien to the great body of the people of the United States." With others, the eminent senator felt that the menace to American destiny lay in the possible corruption or extinction of the "pure" native breed that had fused in earlier years of immigration.

The changes in the quality of our population produced by the new and different stocks which poured into the country in the decades just before and after 1900 is a matter of deep significance, but one for which there is little documentation. Between Emerson's ideal of a "real American," a human alloy to be cast from the melting pot in years yet to come, and Lodge's ideal of a pure-breed descendant of pioneering forefathers, any difference in biological vigor and efficiency would probably be hard to

THE COUNTRY SCHOOL. Painting by Winslow Homer.

The City Art Museum of St. Louis

measure. No serious exclusion of immigrants was practised until the 1920's and up until then, at least, there was no conclusive evidence that the native stock had been impaired by the infusion of strange and variant elements.

The real American, in the last analysis, was a peculiar cluster of ideals and ideas

The Library of Congress
THE STANDARDS OF AMERICA. Published by Henry F. Heiderich, 1897.

rather than a definable racial type, and the eagerness with which the typical newcomer tried to adapt himself to the American pattern of thought and outlook is an outstanding feature of the entire immigrant movement. Children (and adults) soon learned to sing of this "land of the Pilgrim's pride, land where our fathers died," with fervent voice, although they had come to America in cramped steamers centuries after the Mayflower, and although their own fathers may have died in places far from Bunker's Hill or Gettysburg. Here, as Dr. Margaret Mead has remarked, was an odd blending of the future and the past in which another man's great-grandfather became the symbol of one's grandson's future.

As Dr. Mead has also pointed out, the public schools offered the immigrant a way to turn his children into the literate and educated adults they might not become in Europe. For native-born Americans the schools provided a way of converting the little foreign invaders into safe versions of their own properly indoctrinated children. In the settlement house classrooms of the slums, as in the little red schoolhouses of the country districts, schooling in the American way of life brought the pupil some remote kinship with the founding fathers and a sense of belonging in this "sweet land of liberty." To all groups the public school promised a way of turning everyone's children into something their fathers and mothers were not. For in America, oddly, every child was expected to rise higher than his parents had done.

Immigrants who arrived before the close of land settlement had enjoyed the hope of acquiring a homestead of one hundred and sixty acres of land in the open West, which with small effort and expense they could occupy in their individual right and (often with a great deal of effort) shape into a solid inheritance. But by 1890 that ample prospect had vanished. As one inspired rhymster phrased it:

Across the plains where once there roamed
    the Indian and the Scout,
The Swede with alcoholic breath sets rows of
    cabbage out.

The A. F. Sherman Collection
INCIPIENT AMERICANS AT ELLIS ISLAND, N. Y., ABOUT 1900. Photograph by Sherman. Print courtesy of Alexander Alland.

SALUTING THE FLAG IN THE MOTT STREET INDUSTRIAL SCHOOL, NEW YORK, ABOUT 1892. Photograph by Jacob A. Riis.

The Museum of the City of New York, Jacob A. Riis Collection

The Nebraska State Historical Society

HOMESTEADERS IN NEBRASKA, 1886. The Chrisman sisters took homesteads, timber claims, and preëmption claims of 160 acres each, two or more of the girls taking turns living with the others to comply with the residence requirements of the U.S. land office. Photograph by S. D. Butcher.

For those who came later the outlook had changed. Too poor to have financed a farm in the first place, often ignorant and with little or no grasp of English, they faced the different prospect of being herded into two or three rooms—or one room—fenced in by the surrounding slums of the crowded city. Congress had long discouraged colonization by aliens in geographical units, fearful that the nation might thereby be turned into a patchwork of foreign settlements. But in these tenement colonies of the 1890's and early 1900's were just such concentrations of alien peoples, huddled together among their own kind and isolated from American influences. Every city had its ghetto, its Little Italy, its Chinatown, and other foreign sections where the awakening from the American dream was quick and rude.

Those tenements, wrote Jacob A. Riis, an immigrant himself, in 1890, "have no aesthetic resources. If any are to be brought to bear on them, they must come from the outside.

There is the common hall with doors opening softly on every landing as the strange step is heard on the stairs, the air-shaft that seems always so busy letting out foul stenches from below that it has no time to earn its name by bringing down fresh air.... In the stifling July nights, when the big barracks are like fiery furnaces, their very walls giving out absorbed heat, men and women lie in restless, sweltering rows, panting for air and sleep.... Life in the tenements in July and August spells death to an army of little ones whom the doctor's skill is powerless to save. When the white badge of mourning flutters from every second door, sleepless mothers walk the streets in the gray of the early dawn, trying to stir a cooling breeze to fan the brow of the sick baby. There is no sadder sight than this patient devotion...."

"The wonder is," Riis commented, "that they are not all corrupted, and speedily, by their surroundings. If, on the contrary, there be a steady working up, if not out of the

The Museum of the City of New York, Jacob A. Riis Collection
A "Homestead" in New York City, about 1910. Photograph probably by Jessie Tarbox Beals.

slough, the fact is a powerful argument for the optimist's belief that the world, is after all, growing better, not worse, and would go far toward disarming apprehension, were it not for the steadier growth of the sediment of the slums and its constant menace. Such an impulse toward better things there certainly is. The German rag-picker of thirty years ago, quite as low in the scale as his Italian successor, is the thrifty tradesman or prosperous farmer of today. . . . The poorest immigrant comes here with the purpose and ambition to better himself and, given half a chance, might be reasonably expected to make the most of it. To the false plea that he prefers the squalid homes in which his kind are housed there could be no better answer. The truth is, his half chance has too long been wanting, and for the bad result he has been unjustly blamed."

Aside from the work of the free schools and of such crusaders as Riis, no concerted attention was paid to Americanizing the foreign-born. Time and exposure to native conditions, it was held, would do that, as it always had. America had the correctives for the world's ills and if they were imported for treatment, so much the easier. But for the immigrant, to be wrenched from a traditional culture, however compliantly, and faced with the need of mastering some one else's way of life, could be a violent experience. "For I hardly need tell you," wrote one of them, a Rumanian more articulate than many of his fellow travelers, "that becoming an American is a spiritual adventure of the most volcanic variety. . . . To be born in one world and to grow to manhood there, to be thrust then into the midst of another with all one's racial heritage, with one's likes and dislikes, aspirations and prejudices, and to be abandoned to the task of adjusting within one's own being the clash of opposed systems of culture, tradition, and social convention— if this is not heroic tragedy, I should like to be told what it is."

The New York Public Library

A BRANCH LIBRARY READING ROOM IN A FOREIGN NEIGHBORHOOD OF NEW YORK IN THE EARLY YEARS OF THIS CENTURY.

Fortunately for those many who came with a serious desire to learn and develop new lines of thought, to better themselves, and actively to share the ideals of their adopted country, not only the public schools, day and evening, for children and for adults, but an unparalleled system of public libraries (greatly improved by the munificent gift of a Scottish immigrant, Andrew Carnegie), opened a broad democratic highway to learning and the realization of the American dream. Other institutions such as Cooper Union, founded at New York in 1859 to give practical education to the working classes without regard for race, color, or religion, continued to provide free education and in their total effect, to play an important part in shaping a uniform and progressive American civilization.

The torrential immigration of the early years of the present century excited fresh fears that America was becoming a "dumping ground" for Europe and that manifest corruption in government and disloyalty to

"A HIGHWAY TO DEMOCRACY." Meeting at Cooper Union, New York, 1903. Photograph by Byron.

The Museum of the City of New York

native ideals could be traced directly to un-
assimilable foreign elements in the population. The sentiment, according to Lord
Bryce, was least felt by those who knew the
immigrants best. Lincoln Steffens, muckrak-
ing journalist, returned from his candid re-
porting trip through the American scene
with the conclusion that the " 'foreign element' excuse" was one of the most hypocrit-
ical fictions of the time. And, in spite of the
fact that large numbers of those called to the
flag with the conscription of 1917–1918 were
foreign-born men and their sons, people with
strong surviving attachments to the hostile
countries of Europe, there were few who
placed the interest of their fatherland before
that of the United States, as Ambassador
von Bernstorff had real cause to lament.

Yet, in 1921, 1924, and 1929, policies of
rigid restriction on immigration were
adopted by Congress. After mounting from a
simmer to a furious boil, the Melting Pot was
to be allowed to cool. An era of deep significance in human history had come to an end.

The Library of Congress
"I Sympathize Deeply With You, Madame, but I
Cannot Associate With You." Drawing by Rollin
Kirby, 1923. A comment on exclusion.

New York's East Side Citizens Registering for the Draft, 1917. In this local board men of practically
every nationality registered for selective service.

The National Archives

GREAT EXPECTATIONS

The vast changes that took place in the American scene in the half century after the Civil War have been outlined in other chapters. Although the character of the Union was radically altered by that war, territorial unity had been forged into a hard, durable fact never again to be questioned. In the years that followed, railroads laced the country with new bonds of immeasurable strength. The land was settled, cleared, tilled, and mined to the uttermost boundaries of the continental nation and it was yielding far greater tribute than early explorers had envisioned in their wildest dreams. A giant industrial machine had been reared to appropriate and develop the resources that were uncovered in apparently endless depth. The people prospered—most of them—as no people had ever prospered before.

As Riis and others could point out, American prosperity was not all-inclusive and all the people did not enjoy unimpeded opportunities. Statisticians could prove that one per cent of the population owned more than fifty per cent of the country's wealth, that twelve per cent owned almost nine-tenths. Yet, despite the raw and ugly truths of their criticisms, it was also true that nowhere else in the world was the general standard of living as high as in America, nowhere else did a country's culture and economy rest upon such a broad base. And history had always accepted the sufferings of the poor, if they were not *too* annoying, as a necessary sociological alloy.

The Civil War had preserved the Union, but it was not the Federal Union of Jefferson. The "great experiment" of democracy had evolved a new national government, federal almost only in its administrative machinery, whose sovereign power increased with the passing years. A generation after the fratricidal conflict, America witnessed the twice remarkable phenomenon of a whilom Confederate officer, "Fighting Joe" Wheeler, commanding New England Yankees in an imperialistic war against Spain in Cuba and the Philippines.

For three quarters of a century—since the Treaty of Ghent in 1815—America had been preoccupied by the problems of self-development. The "splendid little war" with Spain had pushed the government well out into international currents.

There would be no return, for those currents moved with the running tide of history. But to most Americans such involvements seemed like a brief and ill-advised excursion into troubled waters. Thus, when the First World War started there was general agreement that it was no business of ours. Even after our very effective participation in that strife in Europe, there was a strong tendency to write it off as a necessary, perhaps, but certainly momentary, foreign entanglement. As the song went, it was "over over there," the

The Museum of the City of New York
"O LADY, LADY." Return to Normalcy, 1918. Drawing by Kirby.

PRESIDENT WILSON APPEALING FOR THE LEAGUE OF NATIONS AT MECHANIC'S HALL, BOSTON, FEBRUARY, 1919.

world had been made safe for democracy, and now, after another brief foray into the nettlesome disputes of the Old World, America could retreat to the tranquil isolation of the New, and from home, set a shining example for others. Convinced of its immunity and confident of its strength, long turned inward by historical necessity, and skeptical of the advantages of international co-operation, America washed its hands of Europe's perplexities and beat a hasty retreat toward "normalcy." To doughboys returning from their "great crusade" the Statue of Liberty looked sweeter than ever. "Take a good look at me, Old Girl," was a familiar remark in the American Expeditionary Forces. "If you ever see me again, you'll have to do an about face!"

Wilson pleaded that the nation could not retire from its responsibilities; that "at whatever cost of independent action" governments must act together to crush the old, war-breeding order of international politics. "The League of Nations . . .," he argued, "was the only hope for mankind. . . . Shall we or any other free people hesitate to accept

this great duty? Dare we reject it and break the heart of the world?" But his plea was in vain. And while the average American ignored the program that might have stabilized world peace, and refused the chance to assert his faith in the democratic idea, Lenin labored fruitfully.

Actually there was no possible return to normalcy and no hope of isolation. Normalcy was at best a nostalgic remembrance of things past. Life in America had never been static, and the comfortable pattern of pre-war days was outmoded by the time the troops returned from Europe. Even while the theory of isolation won adherents, America had growing economic commitments everywhere in the world which could not be separated from national policy. And, as G. K. Chesterton had warned, the world never would be made safe for democracy; democracy is a dangerous trade.

The road to normalcy led almost everywhere but to normalcy. Wilson's lofty idealism was succeeded by a stage of general cynicism and disillusionment that was anything but normal to American experience.

The Museum of the City of New York
THE SPIRIT OF PROHIBITION. Drawing by Kirby.

The spirit of self-denial and regimentation made popular by the war effort had made it possible to write the Eighteenth Amendment into the Constitution. Prohibition had a long history in this country, and at the time the Amendment was passed nearly two-thirds of the American people already lived under prohibitory laws by local option. However, a substantial bloc of citizens almost immediately regretted their heroic gesture and, with those who resented this restriction of their personal liberty, they helped usher in a period of lawlessness and corruption without precedent in our history.

The corner saloon with its welcoming swinging doors, so long a symbol of one phase of American life, was temporarily replaced by the less prominent but more picturesque speakeasy, with its peephole in the door through which could be scanned the credentials of thirsty law-breakers. "A ring at the bell. My friend has a card. We are admitted," wrote an Englishman of his visit to a New York speakeasy. "Inside it is more than ever like a boarding-house—a rather depressing one. The wallpaper is red and

A SPEAKEASY, 1929. Lithograph by J. W. Golinkin. Photograph courtesy of The Museum of the City of New York.

Collection of the Artist

International News Photo

THE ST. VALENTINE DAY MASSACRE, CHICAGO, 1929.

dingy. There is a bar. In a room of modest size a few people are dining. They are in these dim but expensive surroundings because Bacchus may be met there.

"I am in hopes that a policeman on the beat will pop in for a friendly drink, as so often happens in these places, but that touch is missing. Anyhow, I claim the privilege of paying. Three sherrys at a dollar each. Half a dollar tip. I make a remark in French. The waiter, surprisingly, takes it up. 'Ca va bien, monsieur. C'est du premier qualité.' After that one drinks with confidence. But fourteen shillings for three sherrys of very modest quality! And that is a very humdrum experience."

The "great social and economic experiment, noble in motive and far-reaching in purpose," as President Hoover described Prohibition, gradually developed into the hottest issue of the decade, ranked in importance far above unemployment and other grave national problems. Unblushing violation of the law by large numbers of otherwise respectable citizens called into service a force of highly organized professional outlaws, the bootleggers, and a group of parasiti-

cal gunmen, the hijackers who played pirate on the landward trails and contributed their special talents to the sanguinary, almost open, wars that developed between rival gangs of racketeers in one line or another of the "business."

Whether violent crimes were abnormally high during the Prohibition Era is a debatable point. But, reported one eminent criminologist, "this new style banditry . . . has created the illusion of a general crime wave. . . . The high-power motor car . . . has also given us the bandit, with his automatic gun and his easy get-away in place of the old-time footpad. Prohibition, with however much of good to its credit, has incidentally endowed us with the hip pocket flask and the machine gun warfare of rival gangs of bootleg brigands." And, whatever the causes, the murder rate in America remained far higher than in other countries. There were more killings in Chicago alone than in all England, thirty-six times as many, proportionately, in America as in Switzerland. From its revolutionary experience and from its frontier adventures, America had inherited a tradition of lawlessness.

Ewing Galloway

A Ku Klux Klan Initiation in New Jersey.

The road back to normalcy took another sharp turn in the flourishing revival of the Ku Klux Klan, which organization boasted about five million members in the early 1920's. The new Klan had little in common with the old save its determination to keep the Negro in his place. It represented rather a recurrent demonstration of the Know Nothing excitement of the 1850's, a resurgence of nativist sentiment that was hostile not only to Negroes but to other minority groups arbitrarily selected for persecution—Catholics, recently arrived immigrants of certain nationalities, Jews, and similar categories of "un-American" folk—folk, that is, who did not conform to the ideal of "native, white, Protestant" supremacy.

At its worst, Klan activity was a violent expression of the intolerance toward radicalism and toward non-conformism in general which featured the 1920's to a rare degree. That reactionary spirit found its most sensational outlet in the trial and electrocution of Nicola Sacco and Bartolomeo Vanzetti, two philosophical anarchists of foreign birth whose conviction and sentence in the face of what seemed to many liberals highly dubious evidence shocked good people throughout the world. To many thinking persons it seemed that America, once a country dedicated to political experiment, and itself a radical element in the society of nations, had become the world's most conservative power, fearful of outside influence and hostile to any suggestion of change.

In its more benign aspects, the Klan reflected the typical American's zeal to join something. Many who were ignorant of or indifferent to its sinister objectives were attracted by the Klan's freakish regalia, its cult of secrecy, and its elaborate rituals—as they might have been to any one of numberless fraternal organizations with more or less picturesque ceremonials and with various innocent social aims. As was long ago remarked, the general impersonality of democratic society demanded its compensations. The plain citizen, theoretically an exact equal of his fellow citizen, wearied of his plainness and exact equality and yearned for rites as well as rights. In the words of Arthur Schlesinger, he "hankered for the ceremonials, grandiloquent titles, and exotic costumes of a mystic brotherhood." And in a wide variety of fraternal orders he found them. More significantly, perhaps, in such fraternities the American found one more outlet for his genius for forming voluntary associations of every sort, a genius which in its broader application, bringing into interlocking memberships people from all areas of the country and of all ages, classes, and creeds, contributed one of the dominant, cohesive forces in democratic society.

A century ago Thoreau grumbled that the American had dwindled into an Odd Fellow —"one who may be known by the development of his organ of gregariousness. . . ." But it was still another point that few could suffer loneliness with such rapture as Thoreau. Isolation might be ennobling when it was voluntary. For many Americans isolation—in the forests, on the prairies, along the outer border of society—had been a bleak and sometimes fearful thing made necessary by circumstances that could not be easily changed. Against that broad and drab historic background, the eagerness with which Americans adopted, organized, and joined brotherhoods of every variety is still easier to understand.

The spectacle of a people celebrated for individualism being also a nation of joiners is less of a paradox than it seems. Individualism in America, as Professor Schlesinger points out, has not meant an individual's complete independence of his neighbor and countryman, but everyone's independence of governmental restraint. No people has ever shown such distrust of its elected officers and of collective organization in government as have Americans. The detailed character of our constitutions and the difficulty of amending them, the principle of the separation of powers, and the process of judicial review all

A MEETING OF THE INTERNATIONAL ORDER OF ODD FELLOWS, PRETTY PRAIRIE, KANSAS. Photograph by Margaret Bourke-White.

bear witness to this. On the other hand no people has more actively insisted on its right to form voluntary associations, for whatever purpose, be it business or pleasure. Limiting the power of the state, indeed, made private organization for large undertakings necessary. The success of such enterprises, in turn, automatically discouraged the growth of governmental authority.

A MAIL BOX ON THE LONELY PRAIRIE. Photograph by Marion Post Wolcott.

"Say, Doc, do me a favor. Just keep your eye on Consolidated Can Common, and if she goes bearish tell my broker to sell and get four thousand shares of P. & Q. Rails Preferred on the usual margin. Thanks."

BULL MARKET, 1927. Drawing by Carl Rose.

By permission
Copyright 1927 The New Yorker Magazine, Inc.

That such uninhibited individualism constituted the true source of America's well-being was a tradition which the 1920's used as a golden rule. After the unprecedented governmental controls made necessary by the war effort of 1917–18 the direction of American business was turned back to private management with pious zeal. Under those auspices, after a brief recession, the nation's economy again strode ahead at a quickening pace, as if to prove that the unplanned speculation and the dauntless optimism of a long pioneering past were still the best guarantees of the future. One might almost call the Bull Market of the twenties America's last frontier. Speculation and rosy optimism, in any case, rose to a crescendo of activity that looked like widespread, mounting prosperity. So it was described from the White House.

As Calvin Coolidge had tartly remarked earlier in the decade, the business of America was business. Business, it was generally agreed, was America's greatest and most characteristic achievement. Guided by their business acumen the people of this country had, after a steady upward climb since the great industrial developments during the Civil War, marched out onto an "upland of plenty." By a fairly painless savings plan and by judicious investment in solid stocks, said the chairman of the Democratic National Committee in that same manic year of 1929, anyone could and everyone should be rich. To prosper was virtually obligatory under the circumstances.

A decade before, Wilson in his first inaugural address had urged the country to take a "sober second thought" of its material well-being, to pause and count the cost of prosperity. "With riches," he said, "has come inexcusable waste. We have squandered a great part of what we might have used, and have not stopped to conserve the exceeding bounty of nature, without which our genius for enterprise would have been worthless and impotent, scorning to be careful, shamefully prodigal as well as admirably efficient." The free and wasteful opportunism of the past had ruined too much of the land—the soil and the forests as well as the mountains and streams—without heed for the future. Only a pitifully small remnant of virgin forest remained under public control and the rest was dwindling at a saddening rate.

"We have been proud of our industrial achievements," continued Wilson, "but we have not hitherto stopped thoughtfully enough to count the human cost, the cost of lives snuffed out, of energies overtaxed and broken, the fearful physical and spiritual cost to the men and women and children upon whom the dead weight and burden of it all has fallen pitilessly the years through. The groans and agony of it all had not yet reached our ears, the solemn, moving undertone of our life, coming up out of the mines and factories and out of every home where the struggle had its intimate and familiar

The Library of Congress
CUT-OVER LAND IN OREGON, 1936. Photograph by Arthur Rothstein for the Farm Security Administration.

seat . . . we were very heedless and in a hurry to be great. . . . Our work is a work of restoration." Those words sounded archaic in the golden twenties when the most respected prophets envisioned America as on a permanent high plateau of general prosperity and peace—except, perhaps, in the slums and on the tragically burdened farms of the country.

A SHARECROPPER'S CABIN, TRANSYLVANIA, LOUISIANA, 1939. Photograph by Russell Lee for the Farm Security Administration.

The Library of Congress

RETURN TO REALITY

In the dark autumn of 1929 the stock market collapsed with a thunderous crash. Suddenly, and with shocking effect, the almost mystic sanctity of American prosperity had been violated. America was unfamiliar with suffering on the scale that soon resulted. "For years," a visiting Englishwoman remarked, "it has been an article of faith with the normal American—and in this connection it makes no difference what his antecedents, or how short an American heredity he could boast—that America, somehow, was different from the rest of the world." Catastrophe and calamity, a familiar experience in the long history of European nations, was here comparatively novel and completely unexpected—unimaginable—and it left the people "outraged and baffled." The miseries of Europe were Europe's own fault. But the Great Depression in America seemed like an inexplicable prank of nature.

Three and a half years after "the great timber cut of 1929," as one writer termed the market collapse, the ghastly prank was still being perpetuated, and with cumulative effects. "Values have shrunken to fantastic levels," said President Roosevelt in his first inaugural address; "taxes have risen; our ability to pay has fallen; government of all kinds is faced by a serious curtailment of income; the means of exchange are frozen in the currents of trade; the withered leaves of industrial enterprise lie on every side; farmers find no markets for their produce; the savings of many years in thousands of families are gone.

"More important, a host of unemployed citizens face the grim problem of existence, and an equally great number toil with little return. Only a foolish optimist can deny the dark realities of the moment.

"Yet," added the new President, "our dis-

A HOUSING BARGAIN, MEMPHIS, TENNESSEE, 1940. Photograph by John Vachon for the Farm Security Administration.

tress comes from no failure of substance. . . . Plenty is at our doorstep, but a generous use of it languishes in the very sight of the supply. . . .

"If I read the temper of our people correctly, we now realize as have never realized before our interdependence on each other; that we cannot merely take but we must give as well; that if we are to go forward, we must move as a trained and loyal army willing to sacrifice for the good of a common discipline."

Grim as they were, the sufferings of the Great Depression did not dry up the mainstream of American optimism, although the current was reduced (still further reduced by the consequences of the war that followed and that totally eclipsed the depression itself). But the trials of that decade did apply a jolt that shook the relationship of Americans to their government into new and probably lasting patterns. For the moment, at least, it appeared certain that unfettered individual initiative could be dangerous and inhumane, that freedom untempered by a broad sense of public responsibility could lead to tragic inequalities, that security could not now be obtained on the old, easy terms of the past, that no purely voluntary association except the voluntary association of all the people in their government was big and strong enough to meet the largest problems, and that, as Jefferson the great individualist had himself realized, the intervention of government in the affairs of the people might not mean the destruction of individualism, but might rather provide the only means of preserving it.

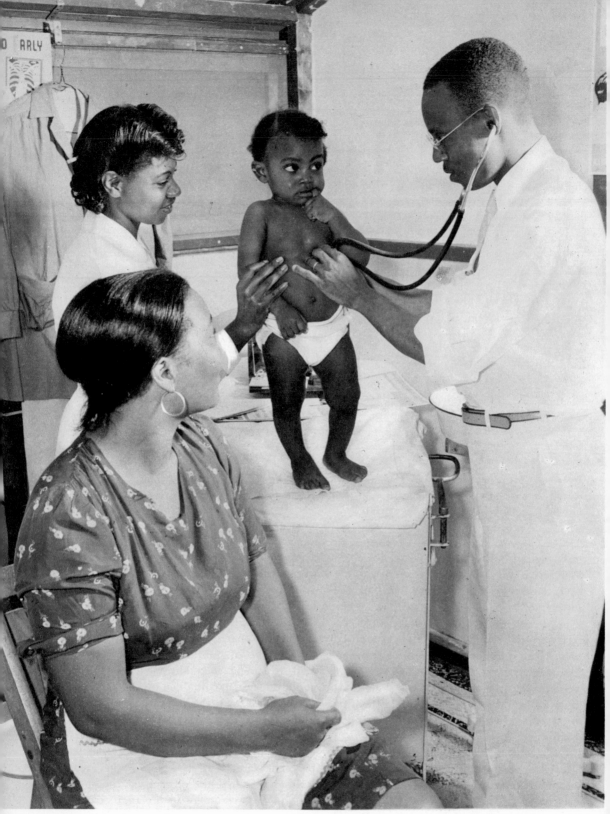

A CAMP DOCTOR AT THE FARM SECURITY ADMINISTRATION AGRICULTURAL CAMP, BRIDGETON, NEW JERSEY, 1942. Photograph by Collier for the Farm Security Administration.

In the election returns of 1932, William Allen White, the Kansas editor, descried "a new attitude in American life . . . a firm desire on the part of the American people to use government as an agency for human welfare." Although there was a traditional distrust of the "welfare state" in America the concept was novel neither in theory nor, as elsewhere told, in actual practice. Long before the New Deal, different American writers and statesmen at different times had argued that ultimately democracy could hope to redeem its pledges to mankind only by a planned use of the state for the general welfare of its citizens. The progressive nations of Europe had long since carried out many extensive reforms and plans for social betterment through governmental agencies. Indeed, to representatives from such countries many of the innovations and improvisations of the 1930's seemed more like an Old than a New Deal.

However, in America this more trusting relationship between the government and people had its first full-scale rehearsal during the depression years. New forces and new doctrines generated a dynamic spirit in the nation. America was "on its way" and, if no one was quite sure where, being on the go was in itself exhilarating. Despite the depressed times, "progress in the war against poverty," writes Allan Nevins, "made millions happier than they had been when, under Coolidge, they were told the nation had 'arrived' and could now stand still."

Historians have called the changes effected during the first two administrations of Franklin Roosevelt "the third American revolution." Popular acceptance of government as an active and helpful servant of the people instead of a mere policing agent did herald a new direction in American life. But the New Deal was in many ways only the fulfillment of programs broached with the earlier Roosevelt's Square Deal and Wilson's New Freedom. In retrospect the "normalcy" of the 1920's appears to be the aberration in our history, the progressive development of the 1930's the more traditional course.

Perhaps the most revolutionary development of the times was the general acknowledgment that unemployment, poverty, and misery were not necessarily the results of improvidence; that in a complex society equality of opportunity could not be taken for granted, it had to be contrived; and that adequate nutrition, housing, and recreational opportunities might belong among the inalienable rights of man—that without them the pursuit of happiness becomes a race on a treadmill. In purely humanitarian terms the ancient shibboleths of rugged individualism and the aloof state were called into question. "The necessary evil of government had become so necessary it had ceased to be an evil." Even those who most bitterly opposed the New Deal admitted that American life would never again be what it had been.

The Library of Congress
A County Supervisor Discussing Farm Problems with a Rehabilitation Client. Photograph by Rothstein for the Farm Security Administration.

The Library of Congress
A TOWN MEETING, WOODSTOCK, VERMONT, 1940. Photograph by Wolcott for the Farm Security Administration.

The Library of Congress
NEWSPAPERS IN ALL LANGUAGES, NEW YORK, 1943. Photograph by Marjorie Collins for the Office of War Information.

The problems of democracy are never settled. Today's developments upset yesterday's equilibrium, and never with such confusing rapidity as in very recent years. To fulfill its promises, democracy must remain susceptible to daily change and renewal, to constant and tireless adaptations to the requirements of technological advances. Not only to fulfill its promises, but to exist.

Americans have developed an almost superstitious admiration for their system of democratic government. For all its awkwardness and, at times, its almost intolerable slowness of procedure, it has served them well. In few countries—and in no other country of such size—have the liberties of the citizen been more happily reconciled with the necessary powers of society, local self-government of communities with the firm authority of the state. The "Great Voice of America" which, as Wilson said, "comes in a murmur from the hills and woods and the farms and factories and the mills rolling on and gaining volume until it comes from the homes of common men"—that voice of the people is still recognized as the fundamental authority of government. And the voice is still free, as Justice Holmes admonished that it must be, even when it expresses "opinions that we loathe and believe to be fraught with death, unless they imminently threaten immediate interference with the pressing purposes of the law."

Most of the traditional forms that have ever accompanied our civil liberty remain intact and have become invested with something close to sanctity. But the freedoms we enjoy are not purely the triumph of political genius. The land we took over from a few savages has been kind and generous to us beyond measure. During the crucial period of our development we were safely isolated from disturbance by the Atlantic Ocean—and, at other crucial times, protected by the British navy. We have, until recently, had the time to make mistakes and to correct them at leisure. As Walt Whitman reminded his countrymen almost a century ago, America has traveled roads "all even and peace-

OUTSIDE THE POLLS ON ELECTION DAY, OLNEY, MARYLAND, 1942. Photograph by Collins for the Office of War Information.

ful" and learned "from joy and prosperity only." Even after the events of the past dozen years his observation remains largely valid if one contrasts American experience with that of most of Europe and Asia.

It remains possible—and the possibility must be examined—that in our determination to preserve the inherited forms of democracy "we may overlook its substance and thwart its spirit." Our Constitution was drawn in the eighteenth century and for well over a century operated under virtually ideal conditions which no longer exist. Because it lists and defines our freedoms, the Constitution does not thereby secure those freedoms. Because we have flourished as a nation does not of necessity mean that our hallowed forms of government are those best suited to the complex conditions of today and tomorrow and the novel, complicated problems that confront us. "To revere the founding fathers," wrote the late Carl Becker, "is all

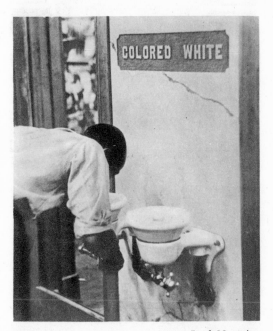

"EQUALITY OF OPPORTUNITY . . . MUST BE CONTRIVED." Photograph by Bob Leavitt.

THE PROBLEM OF FREE PEOPLE EVERYWHERE, 1942.
Photograph by John Vachon for the Office of War
Information.

WAR'S END, 1945. Photograph by Todd Webb.

very well, but it would be better if we followed their example by re-examining the fundamental human rights and the economic and political institutions best suited to secure them."

In the end democracy is not simply a political device, it is a way of life, a way of life converting the will of people into social law and order. In democracy everything depends upon the discretion and intelligence, the good faith and the sense of responsibility of ordinary people. In democracy the indispensable man is not the ruler or the law maker, but the common man.

"The nations of our time," wrote Tocqueville with his usual prescience more than a century ago, "cannot prevent the conditions of men from becoming equal, but it depends upon themselves whether the principle of equality is to lead them to servitude or freedom, to knowledge or barbarism, to prosperity or wretchedness." Since Tocqueville's day the responsibilities of democracy's citizens have grown heavier and more urgent. The equality of servitude and wretchedness has been achieved elsewhere on earth. Because she has grown rich and strong, because she is dedicated to the propositions that all men are created equal and that they are divinely endowed with the inalienable right to lead a life of freedom, because the world has shrunk and the denial of those propositions elsewhere in the contracting world threaten them at home, America has assumed responsibilities around the world. Probably no dominant nation in history has assumed international leadership at once so reluctantly and so vigorously. The problems that confront free men everywhere, and those that wish to be free, are the problems of America. Conversely, the problems that confront Americans are the problems of free people everywhere. America, "the last best hope of earth," faces a struggle in which the battles will be hard and long. It will be a struggle, not for any necessary increase of material well-being; hardly for conquest or dominion, but a struggle for the growing fulfillment of democracy.

BUILDING A HOME FOR THE UNITED NATIONS, NEW YORK, 1950. Photograph by William Vandivert.

Belgium : Home for the Electric Worker, New York, 1930. Photograph by William Vandivert

NOTES
ACKNOWLEDGMENTS
BIBLIOGRAPHY
LIST OF ARTISTS
INDEX

NOTES

SINCE there are no "superior numbers" in the text, it is necessary in each note to indicate to what portion of the text it refers. This, together with an effort to avoid monotonous repetition, has dictated the form of these notes. Page references are usually to the folio on which an annotated quotation or passage ends. Consistency has been eschewed in favor of variety. Frequently, abbreviated titles are used, since the reader can find the full title in the more formal Bibliography. Magazine articles are cited with the publication and the date — volume numbers are in the Bibliography.

Chapter I

Page

4 Friar Oderic is quoted in *Travel and Travellers in the Middle Ages*, edited by A. P. Newton, p. 149.

5 The "folk of foul stature" and the "improbable beasts" are in the same work, pp. 167 and 161.

7 A description of the map that may have been used by Columbus is given in Fite and Freeman's *A Book of Old Maps*, pp. 7-8.

Pre-Columbian explorations are discussed in W. H. Babcock's *Legendary Islands of the Atlantic*.

For the suggestiveness of the Benincasa map, see Charles de La Roncière, *La Découverte de l'Afrique au Moyen Age*, vol. III, pp. 60-63.

8 The Columbus quotation is from his "Letter to Santangel": it is given in Olson and Bourne's *The Northmen, Columbus and Cabot*, pp. 263-68.

9 Stradanus' drawing is analyzed in Baillie-Grohman's *Sport in Art*, pp. 115-45.

12 The text of Vespucci's description is given in Wilberforce Eames' article, "Description of a Wood Engraving Illustrating the South American Indians (1505)," in the *Bulletin of the New York Public Library*, September 1922, p. 759.

13 On More and the Incas, see A. E. Morgan, *Nowhere Was Somewhere*, chaps. II and III.

More's disciple is quoted on page 339 of Silvio Zavala's article, "The American Utopia of the Sixteenth Century," in the *Huntington Library Quarterly* for August 1947.

15 Germán Arciniegas (Ed.), *The Green Continent*, pp. 161-62.

19 Champlain's explanation of the "melancholy disposition" of the Indians is in his *Works,* vol. I, pp. 63-65. For his description of Mexico City, see Morris Bishop's *Champlain,* p. 19.

20 Parkman, *The Battle for North America,* pp. 257-58.

23 For Father Font see W. M. Camp, *San Francisco, Port of Gold,* p. 4.

25 Champlain on the Guadeloupe natives is found in his *Works,* vol. I, pp. 11-12.

28 On the foundation of Quebec, see Champlain's *Voyages . . . 1604–1618,* pp. 136-37. This is a volume in the *Original Narratives of Early American History* series.

29 The Champlain quotation here comes from the same pages quoted above.

Parkman's majestic quotation is in his *Pioneers of France in the New World,* pp. xxii-iii.

30 On Marquette and Jolliet, see Dorothy Anne Dondore, *The Prairie and the Making of Middle America,* pp. 11 and 14. This work is an invaluable guide to literature about the early Middle West.

30–31 Hennepin, *A New Discovery of a Vast Country in America,* the Dedication, and p. 29.

31 Adario's leftist sentiments are in Lahontan's *Suite du Voyage de l'Amérique,* p. 75.

33 The drawing by Le Bouteux is reproduced and described in an article entitled "One of the Mississippi Bubbles" in the *Newberry Library Bulletin* for September 1946.

The description of the town's foundation is in Chaville's article, "Relation du Voyage de la Louisiane," in the *Journal de la Société des Américanistes de Paris,* vol. IV (1902–3), pp. 98-143.

34 This early view of New Orleans is found in Villier's *"A History of the Foundation of New Orleans,"* pp. 237-38 in the April 1920 issue of the *Louisiana Historical Quarterly.*

36 The New Amsterdam chronicler is quoted in J. F. Jameson's *Narratives of New Netherland,* p. 210.

37 Jameson, *op. cit.,* p. 422, gives a modernized version of the description of New Amsterdam.

The early views of New Amsterdam and New York are catalogued with consummate thoroughness in Stokes' *Iconography of Manhattan Island.* For the views on this and the following pages, see vol. I, pp. 119-31 and vol. II, pp. 342-48.

40 Immaculate New Amsterdam is classically described in Mrs. Knight's *Private Journal,* pp. 67-68.

47 Hariot, *A Briefe and True Report.* Plate II. The quotation accompanies the plate.

53 The instruction to early settlers is quoted in Charles McLean Andrews' *The Colonial Period of American History,* vol. I, p. 88.

The Huguenot traveler was Durand of Dauphiné. See Gilbert Chinard's edition of *Un François en Virginie,* p. 80.

54 Rolfe's difficult marriage is described in *Life in America,* a Metropolitan Museum catalogue, p. 1. His own remarks on the situation are quoted in Lyon Tyler's *Narratives of Early Virginia,* pp. 240-41.

55 Captain John Smith is quoted in the catalogue, *Life in America,* p. 1.

57 R. C. Winthrop, *Life and Letters of John Winthrop,* vol. I, p. 310.

For William Bradford's boast see S. E. Morison's *Builders of the Bay Colony,* p. 42.

58 The anonymous pamphlet is the important *New Englands First Fruits.* This quotation is on page 12.

See the *History of the College of William and Mary,* p. 39.

For a discussion of the "Old College" at Harvard, see S. E. Morison, "A Conjectural Restoration of the 'Old College' at Harvard," in the April 1933 issue of *Old-Time New England,* the bulletin of the Society for the Preservation of New England Antiquities. The cut here is taken from the cover of that publication.

62 The anonymous Salzburger's account is quoted in Albert Bushnell Hart's *American History Told by Contemporaries,* vol. II, pp. 114-15; that of Baron von Reck in Stokes and Haskell's *American Historical Prints,* p. 25.

65 See Harry J. Carman's edition of *American Husbandry,* p. 277, on the conditions of rice culture.

The advantages of Carolina agriculture are found in *American Husbandry,* pp. 301-5, *passim.*

66 Governor Glenn's report is quoted in Frederick P. Bowes' *The Culture of Early Charleston,* p. 9.

Josiah Quincy, Jr., is quoted in the same work and on the same page.

67 Miss Anna Wells Rutledge has kindly provided information concerning Roupell's sketch.

68 *American Husbandry,* pp. 160-62, provides the data on early tobacco culture.

71 The quotation on the self-made men of Virginia is from Louis B. Wright's *The First Gentlemen of Virginia,* pp. 46-67.

American Husbandry, pp. 170 and 174.

72 The remarks on the Virginians' frivolity are in *American Husbandry,* p. 170.

Dulles, in *America Learns To Play,* p. 60, has the addiction of Washington to fox hunting.

73 The Reverend Mr. Jones is quoted in Louis B. Wright, *op. cit.,* p. 61.

Dulles *(op. cit.,* p. 62) gives the quotation on the Williamsburg theater.

74 *American Husbandry,* p. 177.

The description of a typical Virginia plantation is from Robert Beverley's *History and Present State of Virginia,* Book IV, p. 290.

Mr. William B. Marye, Corresponding Secretary of the Maryland Historical Society, has kindly supplied information on "Taylor's Mount."

75 The sophisticated servant's advertisement is quoted in E. S. Riley's *"The Ancient City,"* p. 131.

77 Bernard Faÿ, in *Franklin, the Apostle of Modern Times,* p. 112, quotes Voltaire.

Peter Kalm, *The America of 1750 . . . Peter Kalm's Travels,* vol. I, p. 33.

78 Andrew Burnaby, *Travels Through the Middle Settlements,* pp. 66-67.

The quotation on Pennsylvania's influx of Irish is from Morison and Commager, *The Growth of the American Republic,* vol. I, p. 174. These "Irish" were for the most part Ulstermen of Scottish blood.

79 The Franklin quotation is from Parton's *Life and Times of Benjamin Franklin,* vol. I, p. 312.

Burnaby, *op. cit.,* p. 61.

80 Charles Biddle is quoted in Morison and Commager, vol. I, pp. 176-77.

81 For Franklin, Parton, *op. cit.,* vol. I, pp. 450-57.

83 Sarah Kemble Knight, *The Private Journal of a Journey from Boston to New York,* pp. 66-67.

84 *Hamilton's Itinerarium,* pp. 245, 87-90.

85 The comments on Albany as a "curb" are found in A. H. Buffinton's article, "The Isolationist Policy of Colonial Massachusetts," in the *New England Quarterly* for April 1928, p. 175.

The Londoner's comments are quoted by Joseph Downs in an article, "New York Silver," in the *Bulletin of the Metropolitan Museum of Art* for June 1935, p. 130.

89 William Owen, *Narrative of American Voyages and Travels,* p. 56.

90 The classic work on the Yankee at sea is Samuel Eliot Morison's *Maritime History of Massachusetts.*

91 Captain Goelet's New York comments on the restraints of Boston are quoted in A. B. Hart's *American History Told by Contemporaries,* vol. II, pp. 61-63.

92 Hamilton, *Itinerarium*, pp. 245-46.

93–95 Many of the facts and quotations in these pages are taken from Bridenbaugh's *Cities in the Wilderness* and Kraus' *Intercolonial Aspects of American Culture on the Eve of the Revolution.*

93 Mrs. Knight's journey is described in her *Private Journal*, pp. 21 and 27-28.

94 Peter Kalm, *The America of 1750*, vol. I, p. 122.

Knight, *op. cit.*, pp. 26-27.

96 Franklin is quoted in Parton's *Life and Times*, vol. I, p. 266.

97 The quotations of the volunteers will be found in De Forest's *Louisbourg Journals*, pp. 2 and 217.

Parkman, *The Battle for North America*, pp. 454-56.

98 Voltaire is quoted in Parkman, *op. cit.*, p. 471.

99 On the Braddock defeat, see A. B. Hart, *American History Told by Contemporaries*, vol. II, pp. 366-67.

The Washington quotation under his portrait is from Sellers, *The Artist of the Revolution . . . Charles Willson Peale*, pp. 108-9.

101 Dauntless Seth Pomeroy is quoted in Parkman's *Montcalm and Wolfe*, vol. I, p. 317.

107 Parkman's classic account of the attack is, again, in *Montcalm and Wolfe*, vol. II, pp. 217-18.

The naval officer is quoted in A. B. Hart, *op. cit.*, vol. II, pp. 370-71. It is interesting to compare this with Parkman's account.

J. R. Green, *History of the English People*, vol. IV, pp. 193-94.

108 Parton, *op. cit.*, vol. I, p. 422, quotes Franklin.

The dignified protest of the Indian is quoted in Dondore, *The Prairie and the Making of Middle America*, p. 114.

110 Kalm, *op. cit.*, vol. I, p. 33.

For urban population see Bridenbaugh, *Cities in the Wilderness*, pp. 143 and 303.

112 Bridenbaugh (p. 59) also discusses the early Boston fire engines.

New York's friendly gesture is described in Michael Kraus' *Intercolonial Aspects*, pp. 59-60.

114 For early postal data, see Kraus, *op. cit.*, p. 25.

117 Cotton Mather, *The Sailours Companion and Counsellour*, p. ii.

118 Burke is quoted in George Francis Dow's *The Sailing Ships of New England*, Series Three, pp. 14-15.

119 Mrs. Edward's cosmetic wonders are described in Bridenbaugh, *op. cit.*, p. 343.

123 The Reverend Doctor Bray's prophetic remarks are from James Truslow Adams' *Provincial Society, 1690–1763*, p. 117.

125 The patriotic remarks on the Yale library are from James Birket's *Some Cursory Remarks*, pp. 36-37.

The early Princeton conveniences are described in Andrew Burnaby's *Travels*, pp. 73-74.

Philip Vickers Fithian, *Journal and Letters, 1767–1774*, p. 16.

128 Abigail Adams is quoted in E. B. Greene's *The Revolutionary Generation*, p. 419.

131 For the *London Chronicle* article, see "Impolitical Prints," p. 9.

133 All references to Revere's work and the incidents he depicted are based on Esther Forbes' *Paul Revere and the World He Lived In.*

For the Boston Tea Party, see A. B. Hart, *op. cit.*, vol. II, p. 433.

134 The lady's Adieu is given in Halsey and Cornelius, *A Handbook to the American Wing*, pp. 111-12.

137 The Salem and London *Gazettes'* accounts are quoted in Hart, *op. cit.,* vol. II, pp. 546-47 and 549.

138 *"Impolitical Prints"* gives the quotations from the disloyal Englishman and the disheartened soldier, pp. 13-14.

138, 140 The Pennsylvania newspaper is quoted in J. G. W. Dillin's *The Kentucky Rifle,* p. 83; the same work discusses hunters' shirts.

140 On British recruiting, see *"Impolitical Prints,"* p. 20.

141 Mrs. Adams' letter is given in A. B. Hart, *op. cit.,* vol. II, pp. 551-52.

The diaries of the artist Archibald Robertson were published in 1930. See p. 72 for this quotation.

142 Again, Hart quotes Abigail Adams, vol. II, pp. 552-53.

For Franklin's caustic letter, see Parton, *op. cit.,* vol. II, p. 88.

143 Washington's letters are quoted in Hart, *op. cit.,* vol. II, pp. 559-62.

144-46 The Colonial soldiers' words are in Matthews and Wecters' *Our Soldiers Speak,* pp. 30-32, 49, and 51.

146 The French volunteer is quoted on pages 169-70 of Commager and Nevins, *The Heritage of America.*

148 John Paul Jones is quoted in Hart, *op. cit.,* vol. II, p. 590.

Franklin's Autobiography, vol. II, p. 415.

149 Wood and Gabriel, in *The Winning of Freedom,* p. 256, quote the French soldier.

150-51 See Allan Forbes and P. F. Cadman's *France and New England* for this painting of Yorktown, vol. I, p. 129.

152 Hart, *op. cit.,* vol. II, p. 632, quotes Ramsay.

153 See Stokes' *Iconography,* vol. V, p. 1244, on the caption of this engraving.

Chapter II

157 *The Correspondence of Thomas Carlyle and Ralph Waldo Emerson,* vol. II, p. 177.

The immigrants who praised the liberty of life in America were John and Mary Watson, writing in 1823. See *Twenty-Four Letters from Labourers in America,* pp. 13-14.

158 The quotation at the end of this page is in Frederic Austin Ogg's *The Old Northwest,* p. 120.

161 Filson, *The Discovery, Settlement and Present State of Kentucke,* pp. 5-6. For a full discussion of Filson's map, see R. C. B. Thruston's article "Filson's History and Map of Kentucky" in the January 1934 issue of the *Filson Club Historical Quarterly,* pp. 1-38.

164 Chester Harding, *My Egotistography,* p. 36.

Byron, *Don Juan,* Canto Eight, Stanzas LXI and LXII.

165 Mrs. Morton is quoted in Dondore, *The Prairie,* p. 246.

On the high rate of early mortality among Tennesseans, see Morison and Commager, *The Growth of the American Republic,* vol. I, pp. 254-55.

167 The three passages on early Kentucky have been quoted in Seymour Dunbar's valuable *History of Travel in America,* vol. I, pp. 144-45, 166, 146.

The British traveler whose remarks and sketch are given is the anonymous author of a manuscript in the New York Public Library entitled "A Diary or Narrative by a British Subject, 1808." The author journeyed from New York City, through Albany, to the western part of New York State.

John Watson, another of whose letters is used on page 157, is quoted in *Twenty-Four Letters,* p. 12.

168 Basil Hall, *Travels in North America*, vol. I, p. 129.

170 See William Cobbett's *A Year's Residence in the United States*, vol. II, p. 323, for the excellence of American axemen.

The comments on frontier houses are in Flanagan's *America Is West*, on page 135.

171 John James Audubon, *Delineations of American Scenery and Character*, pp. 81-82.

173 On the brig *St. Clair*, see Leland D. Baldwin's *The Keelboat Age on Western Waters*, p. 168. This book and Seymour Dunbar's *History of Travel in America* have provided much of the information about western river-boating used in these pages.

174 Morris Birkbeck was the Englishman astonished at the migratory habits of the Americans. See his *Notes on a Journey in America*, pp. 31-32 and 36.

175 Tocqueville, *Democracy in America*, vol. I, pp. 295 and 296.

Watson is quoted in R. H. Brown's *Mirror for Americans*, pp. 161 and 172.

The English tourist quoted here is the same as he on page 167 — the author of the anonymous manuscript Diary.

178 Timothy Flint is quoted in C. A. and M. R. Beard's *The Rise of American Civilization*, vol. I, p. 525.

John Bach McMaster, on page 385 of volume IV of his *History*, quotes the Virginia legislative committee.

179 See Dixon Ryan Fox, *Yankees and Yorkers*, p. 191, for these verses.

Chevalier, *Society, Manners and Politics in the United States*, pp. 191 and 195.

182 The "inland flotilla" is described by John Stillman Wright in his *Letters from the West*; see Letter I.

183 Dunbar's *History of Travel*, vol. I, p. 303, gives the packet advertisement from the Cincinnati *Centinel*. On pp. 326-27 of the same work will be found the Frenchman's description of the flatboats.

184-85 In connection with the caption to Collot's map, see Stokes and Haskell, *American Historical Prints*, p. 73.

188 Mark Twain, *Life on the Mississippi*, p. 18.

189 *Mike Fink, King of Mississippi Keelboatmen*, by Walter Blair and F. J. Meine, p. 106.

191 The 1851 visitor to the Red River was F. B. Mayer. See his *With Pen and Pencil*, edited by Bertha L. Heilbron, pp. 92 and 95.

192 On the colorful visitors to St. Louis, see Greenbie, *American Saga*, p. 295.

193 Frederick Marryat, *A Diary in America*, pp. 110 and 119.

194-95 Rudolph Friederich Kurz, *Journal*, gives the author's account of his experiences at Fort Snelling.

197 Maximilian of Wied-Neuwied's account of his voyage is in his *Travels in the Interior of North America*, vol. I, p. 146.

Catlin is quoted in Everett Dick's *Vanguards of the Frontier*, p. 104.

198 The *Missouri Intelligencer* is quoted in Donald McKay Frost's article "Notes on General Ashley" in the October 1944 issue of the *Proceedings of the American Antiquarian Society*, p. 310.

199 Bernard DeVoto has written the definitive story of these summer rendezvous in *Across the Wide Missouri*. That book also has a detailed appreciation of the work of the young Baltimore artist, Miller, several of whose paintings are reproduced in this chapter.

Washington Irving, *Bonneville's Adventures*, p. 182.

The description of the fur-laden trappers is quoted in Greenbie's *American Saga*, pp. 307-8.

203 Irving, *op. cit.*, p. 27.

For the Britisher's appreciation of five-dollar beavers, see *The British Mechanic's and Labourer's Hand Book*, p. 221.

204 Captain Marcy's book is called *Thirty Years of Army Life on the Border*. See page 22.

205 Dodge, *Our Wild Indians*, p. 544.

Catlin, *North American Indians*, vol. II, p. 66.

Captain Warre's appreciation of the Blackfeet is in his *Sketches in North America*, p. 2. Warre's original sketches have been photographed for several illustrations in this chapter.

207 Catlin, *op. cit.*, vol. II, pp. 72-73.

On the Indians' lacrosse games, see Francis Blackwell Mayer's *With Pen and Pencil on the Frontier*, pp. 157 and 151-52.

210 Marryat, *A Diary in America*, p. 121.

Marcy, *op. cit.*, pp. 67-68.

The Rangers' success with revolvers is recounted in Walter Prescott Webb's *The Great Plains*, pp. 174-75.

213 Ledyard's story has been brought together by Helen Augur in *Passage to Glory*. The quotations on this page are taken *passim* from that book.

215 The discovery of the *Columbia* is from John Boit's *Log*, pp. 396-99.

217 The imperceptive Congressman is quoted in McMaster, *op. cit.*, vol. V, p. 481.

218 Greenbie's *American Saga*, pp. 344-45, quotes the *Missouri Intelligencer*.

219 The joy of the caravans on sighting Santa Fe is in Josiah Gregg's *Commerce of the Prairies*, Part I, p. 254.

Parkman, *The California and Oregon Trail*, p. 10.

221 Major Long's report is quoted in Paxson, *History of the American Frontier*, p. 216.

222-23 The quotation in the caption of Miller's scene is from Alonzo Delano's *Life on the Plains*, p. 46.

224 A good part of these pages is based on David Morris Potter's introduction to his edition of Geiger and Bryarly's Journal, which introduction gives an admirable survey of travel conditions on the Plains. For the quotation of the "bewildered traveler," see pp. 58, note, and 148.

226 Wistar, *Autobiography*, p. 101.

227 The quotation here is also from Wistar, *op. cit.*, p. 79.

229 The traveler's view of Fort Laramie is quoted in the W.P.A. Writers' Project guide to Oregon, p. 171.

Parkman, *Journals*, vol. II, pp. 440 ff.

For the Fort Laramie statistics, see McMaster's *History*, vol. VIII, p. 58, note.

230-31 The Mormon and Joel Palmer are both quoted in the W.P.A. Oregon guide, pp. 180 and 204.

231 Henry James Warre, *Sketches in North America*, p. 3.

234 The account of the rapid settlement of the Mormons at Salt Lake is in the W.P.A. guide to Utah, p. 58.

235 Mark Twain, *Roughing It*, pp. 94-95.

236 Colton, a most interesting Navy Chaplain, writes his prediction of California's appeal in his *Three Years in California*, p. 73.

238 Boggs, in *My Playhouse Was a Concord Coach*, pp. 18-19, quotes the *California Star*.

The enthusiastic description of California's gold is from Benjamin Greenleaf's *The California Almanac*, pp. 17-18.

240 Hone, *Diary*, vol. II, p. 355.

The early guidebook to the mines was entitled *The Gold Regions of California*, edited by G. G. Foster; this quotation is on pages vi-vii.

Statistics on the exodus to California are in Potter's edition of the *Trail to California*, p. 14.

242 John Woodhouse Audubon, *Illustrated Notes of an Expedition Through Mexico and California*, pp. 8-9.

243 Wistar, *op. cit.*, p. 43.

The *Tribune* correspondent was the celebrated Bayard Taylor. See his *Eldorado*, vol. I, pp. 19, 22-23, 24.

245 J. W. Audubon, *op. cit.*, discusses this route through northern Mexico.

246 Taylor, *op. cit.*, vol. I, pp. 58-59.

The bustling Sacramento is described in a quotation on page 51 of F. A. Buck's *A Yankee Trader in the Gold Rush*.

248 Borthwick, *Three Years in California*, p. 95.

248–49 *The Annals of San Francisco* by Soulé, Gihon, and Nesbit give these quotations on pages 243, 252-53, 281, 354-56.

250 The *Marysville Herald* is quoted in M. H. Boggs' *My Playhouse*, p. 61.

250–51 Rodman W. Paul, in *California Gold*, supplies much of the material on early mining and earnings. For the quotation on page 250, see that work, page 54.

The panning is described in *A Letter from a Gold Miner*, pp. 21-22. The author was named Shufelt.

252 For the passage on the necessity of hard work, see Taylor, *op. cit.*, vol. I, p. 87.

253 Francis S. Marryat, *Mountains and Molehills*, pp. 273-74.

256 The New Englander's remarks on the evils of the Forty-Niners are in *A Letter from a Gold Miner*, p. 25.

257 Alonzo Delano, *Pen-Knife Sketches*, pp. 15-16.

Harper's Weekly, in an article entitled "Mining Life in California," on page 634 of the October 3, 1857 issue, described the dances.

258 The melting pot which was California is from Bayard Taylor, *op. cit.* vol. I, p. 55.

259 Delano, *op. cit.*, p. 51.

Bayard Taylor, *op. cit.*, vol. I, pp. 209-10, 212.

261 I. J. Wistar, *Autobiography*, p. 344.

262 This Taylor passage is quoted in Everett Dick's *Vanguards of the Frontier*, p. 265.

263 Albert D. Richardson, *Beyond the Mississippi*, p. 333.

264 *Ibid*, p. 372.

Bowers is quoted in Charles Howard Shinn's *The Story of the Mine*, pp. 160-61.

270 Richardson, *op. cit.*, pp. 478-79.

272–73 On the Fort Kearny Massacre, see Jacob Piatt Dunn's *Massacres of the Mountains*, pp. 491-95.

279 Chief Joseph is quoted in Morison and Commager's *Growth of the American Republic*, vol. II, p. 83.

281 On the myriads of buffalo carcasses, see Dodge, *The Plains of the Great West*, p. 133.

288 Richardson, *op. cit.*, p. 58.

291 The description of the Klondike rush through Chilcoot Pass is quoted from Merle Colby's *A Guide to Alaska*, p. 180.

292 Thoreau, *Works*, selected and edited by H. S. Canby, p. 669.

Chapter III

298 The Englishman's plaint is quoted on page 497 of *American Husbandry*, Harry J. Carman, Editor.

Burke's description of American enterprise can be found on page 38 of Charles A. and Mary R. Beard's *A Basic History of the United States*.

299 The romantic reflections of Thoreau are found in *Walden*, p. 329.

299 For the Emerson quotation, see Ralph Waldo Emerson, *Journals* (Edward Waldo Emerson and Waldo Emerson Forbes, Editors), vol. III, p. 204.

The *Flying Cloud's* log is quoted in Robert Greenhalgh Albion's *The Rise of New York Port,* p. 360.

300 The quotation from the *Spectator* is taken from Ralph D. Paine's *The Old Merchant Marine,* pp. 24-25.

302 For Gray's clerk's letter, see Samuel Eliot Morison, *The Maritime History of Massachusetts,* p. 56.

305 Thomas W. Ward is quoted by Joseph Downs, "The American Trade with the Far East," in *The China Trade and Its Influences,* p. 15.

306 Tilden's description can be found in Colonel Lawrence Waters Jenkins' *Bryant Parrott Tilden of Salem,* p. 15.

307 Chinnery's ungallant comment is reprinted in Joseph Downs, *op. cit.,* p. 15.

308 The seal-hunting description is from Amasa Delano's *Narrative of Voyages and Travels,* p. 306.

Edmund Fanning's book is called *Voyages Round the World.* This passage is on pages 116-17.

309 The description is from Fanning, *op. cit.,* p. 420.

Delano's preference is found in his *Narrative* (cited above) on page 559.

311 The description of Salem is from Harriet Martineau, *Society in America,* vol. II, pp. 67-69.

314 John Smith is quoted in T. J. Wertenbaker, *The Puritan Oligarchy,* p. 194.

315 Ralph D. Paine, *op. cit.,* p. 77.

316 *Ibid.,* p. 104.

317 This version of Yankee Doodle is given in John Bach McMaster, *A History of the People of the United States,* vol. II, p. 384.

The two Bentley quotations are from *The Diary of William Bentley, D.D.* The first is in vol. II, p. 370; the second, vol. II, p. 319.

325 The London journal quotation is in McMaster, *op. cit.,* vol. IV, p. 90.

326 Most of the information in this section is from R. G. Albion's two books: *The Rise of New York Port* and *Square-Riggers on Schedule.* Both books are invaluable.

327 Cooper describes this scene in *Notions of the Americans,* vol. I, p. 114.

328 The Melville quotation is from *Moby-Dick,* vol. I, p. 2.

330 The first description of steerage conditions was found in Marcus Lee Hansen's *The Immigrant in American History,* pp. 39-40.

The second quotation is from Albion's *Square-Riggers on Schedule,* p. 249.

The Rise of New York Port, by Albion, gives the Dublin description on page 341.

332 The praise of American ships is in Hansen's *The Atlantic Migration,* p. 184.

333 For an account of the piracy, see Albion's, *The Rise of New York Port,* pp. 173 ff.

334 Much information on Boston's trade is derived from S. E. Morison's *The Maritime History of Massachusetts,* chap. XV.

335 Rogers' Journal is reprinted in a pamphlet edited by Ernest F. Gates.

337 Richard Henry Dana, Jr., *Two Years Before the Mast,* p. 94.

339 The chaplain was the Reverend Walter Colton, U.S.N. See his *Deck and Port,* p. 200. The less inhibited sailor was Lieutenant Henry A. Wise writing in his book, *Los Gringos,* p. 32.

341 The Melville passage is from *Moby-Dick,* vol. II, pp. 179-80.

342 Emerson is quoted in S. E. Morison, *The Maritime History of Massachusetts,* p. 315. As ever, this is a title of immense interest on this and other maritime subjects.

343 For descriptions of Hawaii in the 1860's see Rufus Anderson, *The Hawaiian Islands.*

Melville's idyllic description is found in *Typee,* pp. 168-69.

345 Melville, *Moby-Dick,* vol. I, pp. 282-83.

Browne's book is called *Etchings of a Whaling Cruise.* See page 24.

347 The *Great Britain's* log is quoted in Paine, *The Old Merchant Marine,* p. 158.

353 The description of this great day is found in Albion's *The Rise of New York Port,* p. 319.

354 The Collins effort is described in Albion's *Square-Riggers on Schedule,* pp. 265 ff.

357 The Chamber of Commerce plea is quoted in Albion's *Square-Riggers on Schedule,* p. 268.

Chapter IV

362 Bidwell and Falconer quote the *American Museum* on page 85 of their *History of Agriculture in the Northern United States.*

The description of the American frontiersman's *wanderlust* is quoted in Garet Garrett's article "A Fifty-Year Crisis in Agriculture," in the *Saturday Evening Post* of April 19, 1924, p. 3.

363 The *Prairie Farmer* is quoted in Paul H. Johnstone's article, "Old Ideals Versus New Ideas in Farm Life," *Yearbook of Agriculture, 1940,* p. 144.

The farm statistics are from Cooper, *et al., Progress of Farm Mechanization,* p. 5.

Crèvecoeur, *Sketches of Eighteenth Century America,* p. 104.

364 Statistic of tobacco shipment: E. E. Edwards, *American Agriculture,* p. 211.

365 The splendor of the plantations is quoted from Isaac Weld's *Travels,* vol. II, p. 146; their decline comes from T. J. Wertenbaker, *The Old South,* p. 119, note 1.

367 Jefferson's estimate of tobacco culture can be found in J. C. Robert's *The Tobacco Kingdom,* p. 25.

370 Washington on slavery is quoted in Edwards, *American Agriculture,* p. 209; on Mount Vernon, in *Mount Vernon . . . a Handbook,* p. 15.

371 Robert's *Tobacco Kingdom,* p. 187, on Richmond.

373 For the quotation on the influence of rice culture on slavery, see La Rochefoucauld-Liancourt, *Travels Through the United States,* vol. I, p. 622.

Negro slave owners — see A. C. Cole, *The Irrepressible Conflict,* p. 43.

374 Stine and Baker in the *Atlas of American Agriculture* give the figures for cotton production.

375 Frederick Law Olmsted, *A Journey to the Back Country,* pp. 46-48.

377 Mrs. Hall, *The Aristocratic Journey,* p. 219.

Olmsted, *The Cotton Kingdom,* vol. I, pp. 359-60.

379 James Silk Buckingham, *The Slave States of America,* vol. I, pp. 325-27.

"A Yankee" is quoted in J. H. Ingraham, *The South-West,* vol. II, pp. 84 and 86.

381 Olmsted, *The Cotton Kingdom,* vol. II, p. 68.

The more cheerful view of Fredrika Bremer is from *America of the Fifties,* p. 103.

383 Bremer, *America of the Fifties,* p. 147.

384 For wheat exports in 1800-1802, see Krout and Fox, *The Completion of Independence,* pp. 111-12.

385 Baltimore's prosperity is commented on by Tench Coxe, in *An Authentic View.*

NOTES

385 The effective hauling in Pennsylvania is in Schoepf, *Travels in the Confederation,* vol. I, p. 204.

386 The quotations on the Pennsylvania barns are from *The Pennsylvania Germans,* edited by Ralph Wood, pp. 30 and 40.

389 For the Philadelphia market, see Charles William Janson, *The Stranger in America,* p. 179.

390 Carman (Ed.) , *American Husbandry,* p. 50.

391 The Cooper quotation is from *Notions of the Americans,* vol. I, p. 60.

393 Jeremy Belknap is quoted in Schafer's *The Social History of American Agriculture,* pp. 52-53.

395 Thompson, *Independent Vermont,* p. 539.

396 Crèvecoeur, *Sketches of Eighteenth Century America,* p. 96.

Nichols, *Forty Years of American Life,* vol. I, p. 27.

398 The Secretary of Agriculture is quoted in Schafer's *Social History,* p. 159.

399 For Billings' remarks, see Wayne Caldwell Neely, *The Agricultural Fair,* p. 193.

Chevalier, *Society . . . in the United States,* pp. 115-17, *passim.*

401 On the increasing ease of transportation of New England farm produce, see Percy W. Bidwell, "The Agricultural Revolution in New England," *American Historical Review,* July 1921, p. 691.

The shift in New England produce is from Joseph Schafer's article on "Agriculture" in the *Dictionary of American History,* vol. I, p. 28.

Bushnell, *Work and Play,* pp. 376-77.

403 The 1860 statistics are found in Edwards' *American Agriculture,* p. 208.

Crèvecoeur, p. 102.

407 Dorothy Anne Dondore quotes the regional boosters on page 205 of *The Prairie and the Making of Middle America.*

Wilkey, the discouraged New Englander, speaks thus in *Western Emigration,* p. 5.

408 The German farmer is quoted by Arthur M. Schlesinger, *Paths to the Present,* p. 73.

409 The "disenchanted" German's comment is found in Dondore, *The Prairie and the Making of Middle America,* p. 301.

For the American plenty, see Marcus Lee Hansen, *The Atlantic Migration,* p. 157.

Dondore, p. 302, quotes the German novel.

For the last paragraph of this page, see Hansen, *The Immigrant in America,* pp. 71-76.

410 Joliet: Dondore, *op. cit.,* p. 22.

411 Bidwell and Falconer, *History of Agriculture,* p. 276, gives the quotation.

412 Trollope, *North America,* pp. 138 and 147.

413 Trollope, *op. cit.,* pp. 149-50.

414 The editorial is from the *Philadelphia Photographer,* August 1864, p. 126.

418 For the Dalrymple farm, see A. M. Schlesinger, *The Rise of the City,* pp. 41-42.

Cooper, *et al.,* in *Progress of Farm Mechanization,* p. 3, discuss the slowness of early harvesting.

420 See A. Whitney Griswold, *Farming and Democracy,* pp. 140-41, on the Homestead Act.

421 C. A. and M. R. Beard, *The Rise of American Civilization,* vol. II, p. 142, on Icelandic emigration.

The Nebraska salesman is quoted in Everett Dick's *The Sod-House Frontier,* p. 188.

422 The Granger quotations come from Morison and Commager's *The Growth of the American Republic,* vol. II, p. 208, and Allan Nevins' *The Emergence of Modern America,* p. 171. Hicks' summary is in *A Short History of American Democracy,* p. 459.

425 Hamlin Garland, *A Son of the Middle Border*, pp. 165-66.

427 The reassurance to the countryman is quoted in Johnstone, *Old Ideals*, pp. 160-61.

428 The uselessness of the great plains for agriculture — see Frederic Logan Paxson, "The Cow Country," in the *American Historical Review*, October 1916, p. 65.

429 Richard Henry Dana, Jr., *Two Years Before the Mast*, pp. 101-2.

430 The astonished Easterner expressed himself anonymously in *Frank Leslie's Illustrated Newspaper* on July 27, 1878, p. 350.

432 Colonel Dodge is quoted in Walter Prescott Webb, *The Great Plains*, p. 214.

433 Andy Adams, *The Log of a Cowboy*, pp. 62-64.

434 Carnegie's remarks will be found in William M. Thayer's *Marvels of the New West*, p. 538.

435 Export figures: Edwards, *American Agriculture*, p. 240.

437 The verses are quoted in Lomax, *Cowboy Songs*, p. 169.

Lake, *Wyatt Earp, Frontier Marshal*, p. vii.

439 Theodore Roosevelt, *Hunting Trips of a Ranchman*, pp. 6-7.

On cowboy costume, see Philip Ashton Rollins, *The Cowboy*, p. 103.

443–52 All these quotations are from Roosevelt, *op. cit.*, pp. 4-5, 16, 19-20.

454 Johnstone quotes the *Prairie Farmer* in *Old Ideals*, p. 127.

456–61 Carey McWilliams, in *Ill Fares the Land*, discusses the problems of the developing farm machinery, pp. 305 ff.

461 Farm statistics from U.S. Department of Agriculture, *An Historical Survey of American Agriculture*, Appendix.

462 David Lilienthal, *TVA; Democracy on the March*, p. 52.

Katherine Glover, *America Begins Again*, p. 36.

See "Dust Storms" by James C. Malin in the *Kansas Historical Quarterly*, May 1946.

464 *The Grapes of Wrath*, p. 264.

465 President Franklin D. Roosevelt is quoted in Griswold, *Farming and Democracy*, p. 15. See the same work, page 141, note 31, for this discussion.

The quotation of the share croppers' reply is from Dixon Wecter, *The Age of the Great Depression*, p. 135.

467 The transient community is described in Walter R. Goldschmidt, *Large Farms or Small*.

The farming crisis is described in Griswold, *Farming and Democracy*, chap. V.

468 For the work of the Department of Agriculture see Edwards, *American Agriculture*, pp. 246-47.

Lilienthal, *TVA; Democracy on the March*, p. 55.

470 "The Ground From Under Your Feet" by Russell Lord, *Saturday Review of Literature*, August 7, 1948, p. 34.

The Writings of Thomas Jefferson, edited by Lipscomb (Definitive Ed.), vol. XVIII, p. 278.

474 Lieutenant Joseph C. Ives, *Report Upon the Colorado River*, Part I, p. 110.

Chapter V

483 Allan Nevins (Ed.), *America Through British Eyes*, p. 415.

484 Jefferson's remarks can be found in Parrington's *Main Currents in American Thought*, vol. I, p. 347.

484 Svinin (ed. by A. Yarmolinsky), *Picturesque United States*, p. 7.

For the British report, see Victor S. Clark, *History of Manufactures*, vol. I, p. 435. This work supplied much material for the following discussion.

485 Tocqueville, *Democracy in America*, vol. II, p. 34.

Lewis Mumford, in *City Development*, p. 71, discusses enforced obsolescence.

Carl L. Becker, *Freedom and Responsibility*, p. 98.

486 Hamilton is quoted in Krout and Fox, *The Completion of Independence*, p. 104.

Crèvecoeur, *Sketches*, p. 145.

488 For the work of colonial craftsmen, see Bridenbaugh, *The Colonial Craftsman*, pp. 66-69. Here also is the quotation from Tench Coxe.

489 Tocqueville, *Democracy in America*, vol. II, chaps. 9 through 11, discusses Americans in science and the arts.

490 John Bach McMaster discusses these early attempts to organize labor in *A History of the People of the United States*, vol. III, pp. 511-13.

493 The description of Oliver Evans' grist mill is quoted in Kouwenhoven's *Made in America*, p. 44. See also, on this subject, V. S. Clark, *History of Manufactures in the United States*, vol. I, p. 179.

The prophetic description of Evans' "waggon without horses" is from a manuscript letter of Williamina Cadwalader to her aunt, Mrs. Charles Ridgely, May 29, 1797. It is quoted here through the courtesy of Miss Mabel Lloyd Ridgely.

493–94 Cotton statistics from Holland Thompson's *The Age of Invention*, in the series *The Chronicles of America*, published by the Yale University Press, pp. 48-49.

494 On the Philadelphia Water Works, John Melish, *Travels in the United States*, vol. I, p. 157.

495 The *American Citizen* is quoted in Louis C. and B. J. Hunter's *Steamboats on the Western Rivers*, p. 8.

496 On the enthusiasm for American manufactures, see *A History of the People of the United States*, by McMaster, vol. III, pp. 501-2.

498 The Kentucky legislators' plea is also in McMaster, vol. III, p. 508. For Jefferson's un-Jeffersonian remark, see his *Writings* (Monticello Ed.), vol. XIX, p. 205.

499 McMaster gives the figures for New York imports in vol. IV, p. 323.

For Webster's speech, see Claude M. Fuess, *Daniel Webster*, vol. I, p. 187.

500 The *North American Review* article is entitled "Baltimore." It is found in the issue of January 1825, p. 127.

For Tench Coxe, see Malcolm Keir, *The Epic of Industry*, in the series *The Pageant of America*, published by the Yale University Press, p. 3.

501 Chevalier, *Society, Manners and Politics*, pp. 129 and 143.

On the pre-eminence of Lowell factories, see Thompson, *The Age of Invention*, p. 96.

502 Thomas Mooney is quoted in Harold Underwood Faulkner's *Economic History of the United States*, pp. 131-32.

504 Cotton mill statistics: F. W. Wile (Ed.), *A Century of Industrial Progress*, p. 144.

Clocks: V. S. Clark, *History of Manufactures*, vol. I, p. 363.

506 Wile, *op. cit.*, p. 125, has the varied inventions of the Connecticut Yankees.

The advice to British emigrant workmen is quoted in Kouwenhoven's *Made in America*, pp. 22-23. The Committee report to Parliament in V. S. Clark's *History*, vol. III, p. 394.

507 Kouwenhoven, on page 49 of *Made in America*, quotes Miss Martineau; on page 50 of the same work occurs the passage on mass production.

508 For Captain Walker's letter and other Colt material, see Samuel Colt, *Sam. Colt's Own Record,* pp. 9-10.

509 Nasmyth's remarks are in *Eighty Years' Progress of the United States,* pp. 331-32.

512 The early description of American industry's emphasis on quantity, not quality, is quoted in Roger Burlingame's *Backgrounds of Power,* p. 159.

513-14 For many of these statistical facts, we are indebted to Clark's *History of Manufactures,* vol. I, pp. 522, 429, 142.

514 On the development of the ready-made clothing industry see *Eighty Years' Progress,* p. 309.

516 "Balloon framing": quoted in Kouwenhoven, p. 64.

517 On nails, see John Root, "The City House in the West," in *Homes in City and Country,* pp. 36-37.

"Early American Prefabrication," by Charles E. Petersen, in the *Gazette des Beaux Arts,* January 1948, pp. 37-46, and Kouwenhoven, *op. cit.,* pp. 81-82.

520 On American barter, see Clark, *History of Manufactures,* vol. I, p. 365, and for the quotation from Thomas Ashe, Roy A. Foulke, *The Sinews of American Commerce,* p. 108.

523 Clay is quoted in Wile (Ed.), *A Century of Industrial Progress,* p. xiv.

525 The popularity of American products is discussed in Clark's *History of Manufactures,* vol. I, p. 358.

526 For the popularity of Schuttler's wagons, see Cole, *The Irrepressible Conflict,* p. 24.

The Chicago booster is quoted in William T. Hutchinson's *Cyrus Hall McCormick,* pp. 207-8.

527 Burlingame, in *Backgrounds of Power,* p. 170, quotes the Chicago reporter's enthusiasm for the McCormick plant. The following paragraph is also based on this work, p. 171.

531 Tocqueville, vol. II, p. 132.

532 The British exhibits at the Crystal Palace are discussed in Christopher Hobhouse's *1851 and the Crystal Palace,* p. 73.

533 For the foreign use of American locomotives, see Clark, *History of Manufactures,* vol. I, pp. 362-63.

Nevins, *The Emergence of Modern America,* p. 396, for the exported steam shovel.

534 Clark, *op. cit.,* vol. I, p. 515, for the railroads' absorption of steel.

535 Data on Lazell, Perkins & Company are from Bishop's *A History of American Manufactures,* vol. III, pp. 488-91.

Nevins, *op. cit.,* p. 31, contrasts the ante- and post-bellum industry.

538 Exported American food is described by Nevins, *op. cit.,* pp. 365-66.

The ebullient trade journal quotes the London *Times* on the subject of the Bushman. See Clark's *History,* vol. II, p. 95.

Again, Nevins' *The Emergence of Modern America,* pp. 396-97, has been used liberally on the expansion of our industries.

Morison and Commager quote Lowell in *The Growth of the American Republic,* vol. II, p. 76.

The quotation on the Centennial Exposition is in Kouwenhoven's *Made in America,* p. 30.

543 For the nation's mineral resources, see Malcolm Keir, *The Epic of Industry,* vol. V of *The Pageant of America,* p. 4.

544 The exploitation of these deposits is discussed by Morison and Commager in *The Growth of the American Republic,* vol. II, p. 10.

545 For Pithole, see Paul H. Giddens, *Early Days of Oil,* p. 60; for the rise of Standard Oil, Ida M. Tarbell, *The Nationalizing of Business,* pp. 74-78, and the same work, pp. 84-85, for the Carnegie Corporation.

547 Thorstein Veblen, *The Instinct of Workmanship,* pp. 315-16.

549 Carnegie is quoted in Charles and Mary Beard's *The Rise of American Civilization,* vol. II, p. 175.

Arthur M. Schlesinger, in *The Rise of the City,* pp. 195-201, discusses the development of the advertising "industry."

550 Tocqueville, *Democracy in America,* vol. II, p. 161.

551 James Bryce, *The American Commonwealth,* vol. II, pp. 697 and 700.

552 On the extent of the United States Steel Corporation, see Herbert Agar, *The Price of Union,* p. 560.

552–53 Harriet Martineau, *Society in America,* vol. II, pp. 63, 61-62.

554 Theodore Roosevelt, *Autobiography,* p. 471.

R. H. Gabriel quotes Bishop Lawrence thus in *The Course of American Democratic Thought,* page 150; and Andrew Carnegie on page 152.

556 Morison and Commager quote the Governor's remarkable attribution in *The Growth of the American Republic,* vol. II, p. 254.

On the Pullman Strike, see Gabriel, *op. cit.,* p. 230.

557 On the number of strikes in the 1880's and '90's, see Morison and Commager, *op. cit.,* vol. II, p. 166. There is some difference of opinion among the authorities as to these figures, but the best estimates of the number of strikes run between 36,700 and 38,300; of the workers involved, between 6,700,000 and 9,800,000. Labor statistics before 1916 are conflicting and unreliable.

See the Beards' *Rise of American Civilization,* vol. II, pp. 241-42, on the development of labor agencies, and on the A.F.L. membership, Faulkner's *The Quest for Social Justice,* pp. 52 and 61, note 2.

Carnegie's discovery is from Ida M. Tarbell's *The Nationalizing of Business,* p. 171; mounting figures of child labor, from Schlesinger's *The Rise of the City,* p. 129.

John Spargo is quoted in Commager and Nevins, *The Heritage of America,* p. 955.

558 For the *Atlantic Monthly* quotation, see Schlesinger, *op. cit.,* p. 431.

559 The mysteries of electricity are mentioned in F. W. Wile (Ed.), *A Century of Industrial Progress,* pp. 434-35.

The awed visitor's remarks are in Hubert Howe Bancroft's *The Book of the Fair,* vol. I, p. 401.

Garland is quoted in Canfield and Wilder, *The Making of Modern America,* p. 429.

560 *The Education of Henry Adams,* p. 380.

On the harnessing of Niagara, see Malcolm Keir, *The Epic of Industry,* pp. 123 and 125.

H. G. Wells, *The Future in America,* p. 56.

V. S. Clark, *History of Manufactures,* vol. III, p. 167.

562 On Henry Ford, see Lloyd Morris, *Not So Long Ago,* pp. 332-38.

563 Stuart Chase, in *The Road We Are Traveling,* pp. 21-22, discusses the establishment of the War Industries Board.

The quotation about Hog Island is in P. W. Slosson's *The Great Crusade and After,* p. 54.

564 The discussion of standardization is based on Slosson, *op. cit.,* pp. 55 and 187.

565 For the wartime propaganda of the Creel Committee, see Morison and Commager, vol. II, pp. 475-76.

Stuart Chase, *The Road We Are Traveling,* p. 73.

566 On the astounding increase in the use of power, see Stuart Chase, *op. cit.,* pp. 61-62.

Lilienthal, *TVA; Democracy on the March,* p. 17.

For the dealing out of power, see Clark, *History of Manufactures,* vol. III, p. 356; on automobile power, Kouwenhoven, *Made in America,* p. 216.

567 V. S. Clark, *op. cit.*, vol. III, p. 356.

568 John Fritz is quoted in Kouwenhoven, *op. cit.*, p. 32.

569 Stuart Chase, *The Road We Are Traveling*, page 31, has the increase in post-war production; Slosson, on page 222 of *The Great Crusade*, Ford's boast.

Eli Whitney is quoted in Kouwenhoven, *op. cit.*, p. 41; Channing in Siegfried Giedion's *Mechanization Takes Command*, p. 127.

The strip mill is described in Burlingame's *Backgrounds of Power*, p. 231.

572–73 Dixon Wecter's *The Age of the Great Depression* (pp. 8, 1, and 81-82), is the basis for much of the material on these two pages.

573 The Stuart Chase quotation is from his *The Road We Are Traveling*, p. 75.

Carl Becker, in *Freedom and Responsibility*, p. 99, defines the American tradition.

Morison and Commager, *op. cit.*, vol. II, p. 640.

Chapter VI

3 The gentlemanly hog is found in Franklin's *Works*, vol. II, p. 470; the industrious Americans in Mrs. Hall's *Aristocratic Journey*, p. 84 and *passim*. James Silk Buckingham discusses the perpetual hurry of Americans in several places in *America, Historical, Statistic, and Descriptive*. *Vide* vol. II, p. 444 and vol. III, pp. 340-41.

4 For the utilitarian recreation of Americans, see John Woods' *Two Years' Residence . . . in the Illinois Country*, pp. 213-14, and for the harassed businessman, *The Nation* for August 7, 1873, p. 90.

6 Foster Rhea Dulles, in *America Learns To Play*, discusses the economic importance of "the amusement industry." Without Dulles' excellent book it would have been all but impossible to write this chapter.

The protest at the noisy ball players is quoted in Jennie Holliman's *American Sports*, p. 64.

For the disgraceful effects of "Foot Ball," see Bentley's *Diary*, vol. I, p. 254.

9 Stokes' *Iconography*, vol. V, p. 1085, quotes the *Royal Gazette*.

Swimming at New Lebanon is found in Holliman's *American Sports*, p. 168; the covered females in Bentley's *Diary*, vol. IV, p. 611.

10 The "fantastical manner" of dancing is described in Andrew Burnaby's *Travels*, pp. 28-29.

12 Mrs. Trollope describes the Cincinnati ball in *Domestic Manners of the Americans*, vol. I, p. 213.

13 The quotation from Hodgson is quoted in Holliman's *American Sports*, p. 101.

15 Hone's report is in his *Diary*, vol. I, p. 253, and vol. II, p. 601.

The Tocqueville quotation is in *Democracy in America*, vol. II, p. 152.

The *Salmagundi* passage is in Washington Irving's *Works*, vol. XV, pp. 361-62.

16 The Continental Congress' recommendation can be found in *The Cambridge History of American Literature*, vol. I, p. 217.

17 Royall Tyler, *The Contrast*, p. 79.

The New-York Magazine, vol. V, April 1794, p. 195, describes the Chestnut Street Theatre.

19 Tyler is quoted in Dulles' *America Learns To Play*, p. 56. The same work discusses the popularization of the theater, pp. 103-4.

20 Mrs. Trollope, *Domestic Manners*, pp. 187-88.

21 The Creek Indians' exuberance is described in Solomon Smith's *Theatrical Management in the West and South for Thirty Years,* p. 79.

22 The rough-and-tumble is from Dulles' *America Learns To Play,* pp. 74-75.

23 See Alice Felt Tyler, *Freedom's Ferment,* p. 37, for the description of the emotional revival.

24 Palmer's *Journals,* pp. 205-6.

25 Tocqueville, *Democracy in America,* vol. II, p. 106.

29 For minstrel shows see Mott, *A History of American Magazines,* vol. II, p. 196.

Fanny Kemble, *Journal,* vol. I, p. 84.

30 *Harper's Weekly,* July 11, 1857, p. 436.

32 Holmes, "The Autocrat of the Breakfast-Table," *Atlantic Monthly,* May 1858, p. 881.

The *Post* on the dependence of morality on health is quoted in Holliman's *American Sports,* pp. 145-46.

34 For horse racing, see Holliman, pp. 108-23.

35 A discussion of early trotting will be found in John Allen Krout's *Annals of American Sport,* p. 55; this book is volume XV of the invaluable *The Pageant of America,* published by the Yale University Press.

36 Pepys is quoted in *Sporting Prints and Paintings,* apropos of cut no. 9. This volume is the catalogue of an exhibition at the Metropolitan Museum of Art.

The justification of cockfighting is found in Holliman, p. 131.

37 On Jenny Lind, see Dulles, pp. 122-27.

38 Hone, *Diary,* vol. II, pp. 572-73.

40 Tyler, in *Freedom's Ferment,* p. 310, quotes Greeley.

42 Emerson, *Essays* (Second Series), p. 170.

43 *Appletons' Journal,* August 14, 1869, p. 625.

See Arthur Charles Cole, *The Irrepressible Conflict,* pp. 188-89, for skating.

44 John Smith's words are quoted in S. E. Morison's *Builders of the Bay Colony,* p. 11.

45 The English visitor is quoted in Holliman, pp. 52-53.

Nichols is quoted on page 92 of *Life in America,* a Metropolitan Museum of Art catalogue.

47 Marryat, *A Diary in America,* pp. 66-67.

Everett Dick, *The Sod-House Frontier,* pp. 378-79, quotes the Nebraska newspaper.

50 The hunter is quoted in *America Is West,* edited by J. T. Flanagan, p. 154.

51 Rollinson gives the roping story in *Wyoming Cattle Trails,* pp. 217-18.

For the champagne bath see Dulles, p. 178.

52 *Appletons' Journal,* April 3, 1869, p. 25.

53 The plea for Sabbatarian liberty is quoted from the *New York Herald* by the *Illustrated Christian Weekly,* December 5, 1874, p. 581.

55 The abandonment of New York to the dog-killers and their ilk is quoted in Albion and Pope, *The Rise of New York Port,* p. 162.

The Nation, August 7, 1873, pp. 90-91.

56 The patronizing Englishman is quoted in Cole, *The Irrepressible Conflict,* p. 188.

57 *Overland Monthly,* June 1869, p. 533. The article is entitled "Muscular Christianity by a Christian Muscleman."

Dulles, *America Learns To Play,* p. 188, for the "National Association."

The *Galaxy* here, and on page 61, is quoted in Frank Luther Mott's *A History of American Magazines,* vol. III, p. 217.

63 The praise of croquet is from the Metropolitan Museum's catalogue, *Life in America,* p. 164.

64 The first issue of *The Wheelman* was in December 1882. See p. 229.

65 *The Wheelman,* December 1882, p. 229.

Dulles discusses the bicycling craze on pp. 265-67 of *America Learns To Play,* and quotes the Census Bureau.

69 Bryce is quoted in Allan Nevins (Ed.), *American Social History as Recorded by British Travellers,* p. 547.

74 Hamlin Garland, *A Son of the Middle Border,* p. 137.

79 For the report of President Hoover's Commission, see José Luis Sert, *Can Our Cities Survive?,* p. 78.

The *Atlantic* is quoted in Dulles, p. 371.

The appreciation of Lyman Howe is quoted in Robert Grau, *The Stage in the Twentieth Century,* p. 121.

81 For censorship see Lloyd Morris, *Not So Long Ago, passim.*

82 Mark Sullivan quotes the *New York Herald* in *Our Times,* vol. III, pp. 552-53.

85 See *Our Times,* vol. I, p. 498, note, for the *Life* verses. The same work quotes Woodrow Wilson, vol. III, p. 431.

87 Hoover is quoted in Morris, *Not So Long Ago,* p. 448.

88 Stuart Chase, "Play," in *Whither Mankind,* edited by Charles A. Beard, pp. 333-34.

91 The sportswriter was John R. Tunis, in an article entitled "A Nation of Onlookers," in the *Atlantic Monthly,* August 1937. This article has been liberally used in this discussion.

93 Erwin Panofsky, "On Movies," in the *Bulletin of the Department of Art and Archaeology of Princeton University,* June 1936, p. 6.

96 Bradford is quoted in S. E. Morison, *Builders of the Bay Colony,* p. 15.

Chapter VII

102 On Cincinnati's pigs, see Max Berger, *The British Traveller in America,* p. 53.

José Luis Sert discusses the rapid growth of cities in his *Can Our Cities Survive?,* p. 201. This richly documented and profusely illustrated work is a comprehensive survey of city problems based on proposals formulated by the International Congress for Modern Architecture.

Frederick Marryat, *A Diary in America,* p. 50. The "other English observer" was Edward A. Freeman. See his *Some Impressions of the United States,* p. 215.

105 A discussion of the population of Philadelphia at the end of the eighteenth century is found in John Allen Krout and D. R. Fox's *The Completion of American Independence,* pp. 16-17. The conflicting figures found in many books are due to the inclusion or exclusion of its suburbs in estimating the inhabitants of the Quaker City.

See *Moreau de St. Méry's American Journey.*

106 Charles William Janson's book is *The Stranger in America, 1793–1806;* for this quotation, see pp. 177-78.

107 The German visitor's observations on Philadelphian frivolity are in Schoepf's *Travels in the Confederation,* vol. I, p. 380.

The contrasting picture of Philadelphia's gloom, relieved by the seductive charm of the young Quaker ladies, is in Svinin's *Picturesque United States,* p. 22.

109 Cooper, *Notions of the Americans,* vol. I, pp. 129-30.

110 The nostalgic picture of Boston boyhood is quoted in a catalogue of a special exhibition at the Metropolitan Museum entitled *Life in America,* pp. 70 and 72.

112 Schoepf, *op. cit.,* vol. I, pp. 326-27.

114 Mrs. Adams' description of the White House is from Esther Singleton's *The Story of the White House,* vol. I, pp. 11-13.

114 On early Washington, see Albert J. Beveridge's *Life of John Marshall*, vol. III, pp. 1-10.

Dickens, *American Notes*, vol. I, pp. 278-79.

118 The French general, Collot, is quoted in Stokes and Haskell, *American Historical Prints*, p. 73.

119 Michel Chevalier, *Society, Manners and Politics in the United States*, pp. 170 and 169.

Trollope, *North America*, p. 365.

120 The Reverend Mr. Zincke's appreciation of Chicago is quoted in Bessie Louise Pierce's *As Others See Chicago*, pp. 183-84.

122 The description of the Chicago fire is quoted in Commager and Nevins, *The Heritage of America*, pp. 880-81.

Edward Freeman, *Some Impressions of the United States*, p. 245.

Carl Sandburg, *Chicago Poems*, from the poem "Chicago," pp. 3-4.

123 Dana's description of San Francisco Bay is in *Two Years Before the Mast*, p. 290.

124 Samuel Bowles, *Across the Continent*, p. 292.

125 Albert D. Richardson, writing his *Beyond the Mississippi* in 1867, made this extraordinary prophecy on pages 448-49.

Will Irwin's passage is from his *The City That Was*, p. 7.

127 Baron Klinckowström is quoted in Stokes and Haskell, *op. cit.*, p. 102.

Arthur M. Schlesinger gives the passage from the *New London Gazette* on page 213 of his *Paths to the Present*.

128 Augustine E. Costello's *Our Firemen* gives much material on early fire fighting in American cities.

Basil Hall, *Travels in North America*, vol. I, pp. 19-21.

130 Alexander Marjoribanks is the English observer of the volunteer firemen. See his *Travels*, p. 433.

131 Cincinnati's Chief Engineer is quoted in David D. Dana's *The Fireman*, pp. 92-93.

132 On New York's water system, see Stokes' *Iconography*, vol. V, p. 1362.

134 The two quotations are from Hone's *Diary*, vol. II, pp. 609, 624, 625.

136 Janson, *The Stranger in America*, p. 181.

137 On General and Mrs. Washington's table manners, see Monaghan and Lowenthal, *This Was New York*, p. 113.

The passage on food spoiling in 1795 is quoted from Thomas F. De Voe's *The Market Book*, p. 373. The opening of the Fulton Market is from the same work, p. 496.

139 Basil Hall, *Travels*, vol. I, pp. 31-32.

140 Sarah M. Maury, *An Englishwoman in America*, p. 200.

141 The soda fountain as an adjunct to courtship is described in A. M. Schlesinger's *The Rise of the City*, pp. 135-36.

143 On the early refrigerator cars, see an article, "Freaks of Railroad Transportation," in the *American Railroad Journal, and Mechanics' Magazine* for June 15, 1842, p. 165, which quotes from the Boston *American Traveller*.

The exultant housewife is quoted in Schlesinger's *The Rise of the City*, p. 133.

144 Cooper, *Notions of the Americans*, vol. I, p. 302.

145 Tocqueville, *Democracy*, vol. II, p. 235.

146 Cooper, *op. cit.*, vol. I, pp. 130 and 145.

146–47 Dickens, *op. cit.*, vol. II, pp. 211-12, 215-16.

147 See Herbert Asbury's *The Gangs of New York*, pp. 7-8, on the Hot Corn girls.

149 The quotation on Chicago's rail facilities is found in Pierce's *As Others See Chicago*, p. 150.

150 Hone, *Diary,* vol. I, p. 209.

151 Tocqueville's distrust of immigrants is in his *Democracy in America,* vol. I, p. 289, note 1.

152 See Augustine E. Costello's *Our Police Protectors* on early police measures — especially chapters II and III.

James Stirling's book is *Letters from the Slave States.* This quotation is on pages 146-47.

158 On New York's omnipresent omnibuses, see Maury, *An Englishwoman in America,* pp. 176-77.

159 Broadway's confusion is in Fredrika Bremer's *America of the Fifties,* p. 2.

161 The plan for the early Elevated and other civic improvements is discussed in Stokes' *Iconography,* vol. III, pp. 699-700.

Buckingham, *America, Historical, Statistic, and Descriptive,* vol. I, p. 49.

Arthur M. Schlesinger discusses early urban street paving in *The Rise of the City,* pp. 87-89.

163 For early gas lighting see Marshall B. Davidson's article "Early American Lighting" in the *Metropolitan Museum of Art Bulletin* for Summer 1944, p. 39.

167 The indignant description of German Sabbath revels is from Matthew Hale Smith's *Sunshine and Shadow in New York,* pp. 216-17.

168 The plea for an "Underground and the Aërial Railway" is quoted in Stokes' *Iconography,* vol. V, p. 1921.

The *Harper's* article, an anonymous editorial, is entitled "More Bridges Wanted." It is in the issue of June 16, 1883, and this passage is on page 371.

170 The passage on Chicago elevators is quoted in Pierce's *As Others See Chicago,* pp. 289-90.

171 The description of early Chicago skyscraper building is in Julian Ralph's *Our Great West,* pp. 6-8.

173 Burton J. Hendrick quotes Arnold Bennett in *The Age of Big Business,* pp. 86-87.

174 Consult A. M. Schlesinger's *Rise of the City,* and Harold Underwood Faulkner's *The Quest for Social Justice* for the development of streetcars and suburbs.

On the congestion of downtown Boston, see J. F. Muirhead, *America, the Land of Contrasts,* p. 11.

177 The *Times* is quoted on page 126 of J. L. Sert's *Can Our Cities Survive?*

179 Lewis Mumford's *The Culture of Cities,* pp. 221-22, quotes Storer.

180 Lewis Gannett, *Cream Hill,* chap. I.

181 Riis' terrible indictment is found in his *How the Other Half Lives,* pp. 43-44, 46.

182 *Independent Magazine,* November 7, 1907, pp. 1092-93. The article is by William Frederick Dix and is entitled "Conquerors of the Road."

183 The anguished English visitor is quoted in Pierce, *op. cit.,* p. 467.

185 Frederick Gutheim, "Greenbelt Revisited," in the *Magazine of Art* for January 1947, p. 18.

186 See Sert, *op. cit.,* p. 40, for the housing problem of New York.

188 Sert also quotes the Congress for Modern Architecture's report on page 95 of *Can Our Cities Survive?*

Chapter VIII

195 The inaccurate prognostication of the Dean of Gloucester is quoted in John Fiske's *The Critical Period of American History, 1783–1789,* p. 58.

For Washington's warning, see A. B. Hulbert, *The Paths of Inland Commerce,* p. 9.

Albert J. Beveridge gives the Madison quo-

195 tation in his *Life of John Marshall,* vol. I, pp. 284-85.

196 Calhoun's famous phrase is quoted by Morison and Commager in *The Growth of the American Republic,* vol. I, p. 439.

Tocqueville is quoted in Louis C. and B. J. Hunter's *Steamboats on the Western Rivers,* p. 28.

197 The "exuberant prophet" is quoted in B. A. Botkin's *A Treasury of American Folklore,* pp. 284-85.

Mark Twain, *Life on the Mississippi,* p. 475.

199 Seymour Dunbar, in *A History of Travel in America,* vol. I, p. 191, has the quotation on the Baltimore roads. Much of the material in this chapter is based on this voluminous account of early travel.

Jefferson's letter and the Grigsby quotation are both from Beveridge's *Marshall,* vol. I, pp. 259-60.

201 On the famous Charles River bridge, see the *New-York Magazine* for September 1795. The article entitled "Description of Charles River Bridge" is on page 513.

202 Robert Sutcliff, *Travels in Some Parts of North America,* pp. 69-70.

The lament on bad roads is quoted in Beveridge, *op. cit.,* vol. I, p. 257, note 4.

203 On the Lancaster Turnpike, see Ralph H. Brown, *Mirror for Americans,* p. 272, note 15.

Wheaton J. Lane's *From Indian Trail to Iron Horse,* page 144, gives the figure on turnpikes before 1801, and on page 146, the quotation of the critics.

204 Beveridge, *op. cit.,* vol. I, p. 255, quotes the Baltimore–New York traveler.

Moreau de St. Méry's American Journey, pp. 96-97.

205 Brissot de Warville's book is *New Travels in the United States.* This passage is on pages 112-13 of volume I.

The English visitor is quoted in Commager and Nevins, *The Heritage of America,* p. 261.

206 Svinin's praise of our bridges is in his *Picturesque United States,* p. 15.

For our inland ocean-going ships, see Leland D. Baldwin's *The Keelboat Age,* chap. VII.

211 Baldwin's book also has the Conestoga wagons at Pittsburgh, p. 184. See also Wheaton J. Lane's *From Indian Trail to Iron Horse,* pp. 134-35.

On the fleet-scudding wagons, see John Bach McMaster, *A History of the People of the United States,* vol. IV, pp. 219-21.

212 In the *Journal of Economic and Business History* for February 1931, appears Oliver Wendell Holmes' article on "Levi Pease, the Father of New England Stage-Coaching." On page 263, he quotes the *American Traveller.*

213 Cooper, *Notions of the Americans,* vol. I, p. 65.

The Duke is quoted by McMaster, *op. cit.,* vol. II, p. 563, note.

214 McMaster, in the same work, vol. III, p. 472, discusses the high cost of American transportation.

215 The verses are given in Alvin F. Harlow's *Old Towpaths,* p. 118.

217 Washington, *Writings,* vol. X, pp. 408-9.

218 Harlow, *op. cit.,* p. 66, has the statistics on early use of the Erie Canal. For further matter on the significance of the Erie trade, see Seymour Dunbar's *A History of Travel,* vol. III, p. 832, note 1.

221 Frederick Marryat, *A Diary in America,* pp. 47-48.

223 Martineau, *Society in America,* vol. I, pp. 232-33.

224 The best general account of the steamboat's early development is James Thomas Flexner's *Steamboats Come True.*

224 *New-York Mirror,* November 28 and December 5, 1840, article, "A Few Thoughts on All This Steaming," by T. S. Fay.

226 Svinin, *Picturesque United States,* pp. 9-10.

On the increasing popularity of the Hudson River boats see Albion and Pope, *The Rise of New York Port,* p. 162.

228 Fredrika Bremer, *The Homes of the New World,* vol. I, pp. 48-49.

231 The *New World,* the *South America,* and their Hudson contemporaries are discussed in Albion and Pope, *op. cit.,* pp. 157 ff.

232 Mark Twain, *Life on the Mississippi,* pp. 1-2.

234 The *Cincinnati Gazette* is quoted in Hunter's *Steamboats on the Western Rivers,* p. 4.

C. H. Ambler gives the Schoolcraft quotation on page 134 of *A History of Transportation in the Ohio Valley.*

236 Francis Blackwell Mayer, *With Pen and Pencil on the Frontier,* pp. 73-74.

237 On steamboat arrivals at Cincinnati, see Hunter, *op. cit.,* p. 645.

Wessen's undated manuscript letter is in the collection of the Historical and Philosophical Society of Ohio.

238 On the Red River carts see William J. Petersen's *Steamboating on the Upper Mississippi,* pp. 163-64.

239 For the remarkable statement in the last sentence of this page, see W. J. Petersen's article, "Steamboating on Western Waters," in the *Dictionary of American History,* vol. V, p. 179.

240 The 1868 log is given in Everett Dick's *Vanguards of the Frontier,* p. 174.

241 The unhappy plight of the gentlemen deprived of female company is in Kurz's *Journal,* p. 8.

Mark Twain, *Life on the Mississippi,* p. 66.

242 *Ibid.,* p. 322.

244 Evans' prophecy is given in Dunbar, *A History of Travel,* vol. III, pp. 887-88.

245 Dunbar, *op. cit.,* vol. III, p. 918, has the quotation on the horse railroads.

Evans is quoted in the same work, vol. III, pp. 886-87.

247 "Third Street Hall" in *Atkinson's Casket* for September 1834, p. 385.

249 The 1830 newspaper is quoted by Dunbar, *op. cit.,* vol. III, p. 938.

250 *Plank Roads* is the short title of the comprehensive report of an Ithaca, N.Y., Committee of 1848.

251, 252 The Dickens quotations are from *American Notes,* vol. I, pp. 146-47.

253 Anthony Trollope, *North America,* p. 112.

The indignant protest against a lack of "delicate consideration" for the sex is from a letter to the editor of the *New York Graphic,* January 6, 1874, p. 435. The letter is entitled "Promiscuous Sleeping-Cars," and is signed "Mrs. R. C. M."

254 J. G. Kohl, *Travels,* vol. II, pp. 165-67.

255 Roebling is quoted in John A. Kouwenhoven's *Made in America,* p. 59.

The "somewhat fatuous philosopher" was Henry Hudson Holly — see his *Holly's Country Seats,* p. 169.

256 The comments on our people's "locomotive propensities" are from the article "Third Street Hall" in *Atkinson's Casket* for September, 1834, p. 385.

257 On the 1849 St. Louis convention, see John Bach McMaster's *History,* vol. VII, pp. 582-83.

Thoreau, *Walden,* pp. 128-29 of vol. II in his *Writings.*

258 Albert D. Richardson, *Beyond the Mississippi,* p. 331.

Mark Twain writes thus on the Pony Express in *Roughing It,* vol. I, p. 54.

260 On the commander of the camel corps, see Stephen Bonsal's *Edward Fitzgerald Beale,* pp. 203 and 205-6.

261 Horace Greeley is quoted in Everett Dick's *Vanguards of the Frontier,* p. 344.

The other quotation on prairie freighting is from the same work, p. 345.

262 The description of the Via Mala is in Paxson's *History of the American Frontier,* p. 464.

263 Mark Twain, *Roughing It,* vol. I, pp. 23-24.

The journalist was Albert D. Richardson. See his *Beyond the Mississippi,* pp. 367 and 369.

265 The *Weekly West* is quoted in Root and Hickman's article "Pike's Peak Express Companies" in the *Kansas Historical Quarterly,* February 1946, p. 53.

Mark Twain, *Roughing It,* vol. I, p. 52.

266 The eclipse of the Pony Express is in Root and Hickman's article, cited above, p. 69.

268 Samuel Bowles, *Across the Continent,* pp. 255-56.

General Dodge is quoted by Commager and Nevins in *The Heritage of America,* pp. 833-34.

269 Anthony Trollope, *North America,* pp. 441-42.

271 The rush tempo of construction on the railroad is from E. L. Sabin, *Building the Pacific Railway,* p. 158.

A. D. Richardson, *Beyond the Mississippi,* p. 567.

273 Elsworth is described in an article, "A Trip to the End of the Union Pacific in 1868," in the August 1944 issue of the *Kansas Historical Quarterly,* p. 198.

274 General Dodge: See Commager and Nevins, *op. cit.,* p. 837.

Bret Harte, "What the Engines Said."

275 Frederic Logan Paxson, *History of the American Frontier,* p. 501.

276 Mark Twain, *Life on the Mississippi,* p. 194.

277 R. L. Stevenson, *Across the Plains,* pp. 48-50.

279 The report of President Hoover's commission is quoted in David L. Cohn's *Combustion on Wheels,* p. 24.

The automobiling statistics of 1949 were supplied by the Public Roads Administration.

The clerical recognition of the bicycle's permanence is from *The Wheelman* for December 1882. The article is "Clergymen and the Bicycle" by A. O. Downs, on page 218.

281, 282 The *Vogue* article, as well as the Senator from Texas, is quoted in D. L. Cohn, *op. cit.,* pp. 9 and 64.

283 On the early use of railway maps in motoring see F. L. Paxson, "The Highway Movement," in the *American Historical Review* for January 1946.

284 Henry Ford is quoted by Roger Burlingame in *Backgrounds of Power,* p. 294.

285 On the 1918 military convoy, see Paxson's "Highway Movement," cited above, p. 244.

289 The surprised housewife is quoted by Lloyd Morris in *Not So Long Ago,* p. 381.

290 On the number of bus passengers, see Dixon Wecter, *The Age of the Great Depression,* p. 226.

291 Truck drivers: Lloyd Morris, *op. cit.,* p. 396.

297 ff Jeremiah Milbank, Jr., *The First Century of Flight in America,* p. 15, has this quotation of Jeffries and is the source of much of the information and many of the quotations in the pages immediately following.

299 The *Journal* is quoted in Frank Luther Mott's *A History of American Magazines, 1741–1850,* pp. 467-68.

303 The Exquisite's song is from *Peabody's Parlour Journal* for March 15, 1834.

307 The enthusiasm aroused by the 1910 aviation meet is described in an unidentified Los Angeles newspaper for January 15, 1910.

308 On Lindbergh's tour of the United States, see P. W. Slosson, *The Great Crusade and After*, p. 403.

Chapter IX

315 Denis Brogan, in *The American Character*, p. xix, gives Adams' disquieting experience.

Turgot is quoted in Morison and Commager's *The Growth of the American Republic*, vol. I, p. 320.

For the pessimistic prognostication of the French diplomat, see John C. Ranney's article "The Bases of American Federalism" on page 3 of the January 1946 issue of the *William and Mary Quarterly*.

316 Patrick Henry's remark is quoted in Beveridge's *Marshall*, vol. I, p. 406.

Rush's summary of the Revolution is quoted by Herbert Agar in his *The Price of Union*, pp. 36-37.

318 Again, for Patrick Henry, see Beveridge, *op. cit.*, vol. I, p. 388.

320 Washington, *Writings*, vol. XI, p. 385.

For John Adams' remark, see Parrington's *Main Currents*, vol. I, p. 316.

Jefferson's letter to Abigail Adams is in Ford's edition of his *Writings*, vol. IV, p. 370.

321 Mrs. Adams' tart comment on Jefferson is in *New Letters of Abigail Adams*, edited by Stewart Mitchell, p. 147; her fears of disunion are in the same work, p. 83.

322 For conflicting evidence as to the acts and intentions of the Virginia Republicans in 1799, see A. J. Beveridge, *The Life of John Marshall*, vol. II, pp. 381-408 and Andrew C. McLaughlin, *A Constitutional History of the United States*, pp. 272-81.

John Bach McMaster quotes the *Courant* in his *History*, vol. II, p. 495, note.

Jefferson: see the Definitive Edition of his *Writings*, vol. X, p. 410.

323 The *Columbian Centinel* is quoted in Krout and Fox, *The Completion of Independence*, p. 202.

On the Hartford Convention see *The Proceedings of a Convention of Delegates*, p. 3 and *passim*.

325 Tocqueville, *Democracy in America*, vol. II, p. 277.

Washington on the militia system is quoted by Beveridge, *op. cit.*, vol. I, p. 84, and on the needs of military education, in Slosson's *The American Spirit in Education*, p. 99.

327 Beveridge, *Life of John Marshall*, vol. IV, pp. 470-71.

See McMaster, *op. cit.*, vol. VII, pp. 162 ff. for the expanding franchise.

Tocqueville, *op. cit.*, vol. I, p. 55.

329 Tocqueville, vol. I, p. 204.

330 Quincy is quoted in E. B. White's *The Wild Flag*, p. 100.

331 On the Jackson inauguration, see Morison and Commager, *op. cit.*, vol. I, p. 471.

Alice Felt Tyler, in *Freedom's Ferment*, p. 22, quotes the candidate.

332 Carl L. Becker, *Freedom and Responsibility*, p. 17.

Hone, *Diary*, vol. I, p. 506.

334 See McMaster's *History*, vol. VI, chap. LXIX, for the 1840 campaign.

335 Agar, *The Price of Union,* p. 689. This work gives a thorough and understanding discussion of American political practice.

336 Two excellent books on the history and problems of immigration, from which much of the material in the following pages has been drawn, are Marcus Lee Hansen's *The Atlantic Migration* and *The Immigrant in American History.*

338 Bryce, *The American Commonwealth,* vol. II, chap. CXI.

Crèvecoeur, *Sketches of Eighteenth Century America,* p. 154.

Bryce, *op. cit.,* vol. II, p. 874.

340 Pastorius' condemnation of slavery is in Arthur D. Graeff's article, "American History Visualized in Pennsylvania German Almanacs," in the *American-German Review* for February 1940, p. 12.

341 Svinin, *Picturesque United States,* edited by Yarmolinsky, p. 23.

342 For statistics of early religious affiliations, see A. F. Tyler, *Freedom's Ferment,* p. 361.

On the intensely interesting John Carroll, see R. J. Purcell's article on him in the *Dictionary of American Biography,* vol. III, pp. 526-28.

343 See E. E. Slosson's *The American Spirit in Education,* pp. 195-96, for the work of Fathers Badin and Nerinckx.

Thomas Low Nichols is quoted in Alice Felt Tyler, *op. cit.,* p. 362.

344 On the French immigrants, aristocratic and humble, see Hansen's *The Atlantic Migration,* pp. 58, 63, and 91-92.

345 Tyler, in *Freedom's Ferment,* discusses the New Harmony experiment extensively.

346 Once more, Hansen's *Atlantic Migration* is the source on the German influx. See also McMaster, vol. VII, p. 222, for the British remark on the "poor wretches."

347 The German's classification of his fellow travelers is quoted in Samuel P. Orth's *Our Foreigners,* pp. 133-34, note 1.

349 The likening of the wave of immigration to the Gothic invasions is in A. C. Cole's *The Irrepressible Conflict,* p. 120.

Irish population statistics: Morison and Commager, vol. I, p. 500.

351 Arthur M. Schlesinger, *New Viewpoints in American History,* p. 3.

352 Governor Berkeley is quoted in Slosson's *American Spirit,* p. 81.

353 Alice Felt Tyler, in *Freedom's Ferment,* discusses the opposition to tax-supported education.

Slosson's *American Spirit* considers the rise of "higher education" in the West.

355 Emerson's remark in the caption is from *The Conduct of Life,* p. 142.

356 See Tyler, *op. cit.,* p. 243, for the Yale professor.

Morison and Commager, *op. cit.,* vol. I, p. 512.

On labor's sentiments anent universal free education and for statistics, see Carl Russell Fish, *The Rise of the Common Man,* pp. 212 and 226.

357 Tyler quotes the educator's important query in *Freedom's Ferment,* p. 233.

The Englishman's remarks on our educated citizens are in Allan Nevins' *America Through British Eyes,* p. 253.

See the Metropolitan Museum catalogue, *Life in America,* p. 164, for the quotation on the newsboys.

358 Emerson, *Society and Solitude,* p. 24.

359 Hone, *Diary,* pp. 515, 573, and 516.

360 John Eliot is quoted in Tyler, *op. cit.,* p. 229, and Abigail Adams in the same work, p. 429.

363 The Indiana Constitution is quoted in Becker's *Freedom and Responsibility,* p. 44.

Huxley's view is discussed in Slosson, *The American Spirit,* p. 165.

364 Michel Chevalier, *Society, Manners and Politics,* pp. 309-10.

British Mechanic's . . . Hand Book, p. 96.

366 Fredrika Bremer, *America of the Fifties,* p. 93.

368 Chevalier, *op. cit.,* pp. 305-6.

George Washington's plight is discussed on page 96 of *This Was New York,* by Frank Monaghan and Marvin Lowenthal.

369 Mrs. Trollope, *Domestic Manners of the Americans,* vol. II, p. 75.

370 Francis Higginson is quoted in *America Is West,* edited by John T. Flanagan, p. 627.

For Leatherstocking as the epitome of the American man see Ralph Henry Gabriel, *The Course of American Democratic Thought,* pp. 20-21.

372 Hegel is quoted in the *Literary History of the United States,* vol. I, p. 214.

373 On the crusaders of the first half of the last century, see Alice Felt Tyler, *Freedom's Ferment.*

Emerson is so quoted in Morison and Commager's *Growth of the American Republic,* vol. I, pp. 524-25.

376 The discussion of women's rights has relied heavily on Tyler, *op. cit.,* chap. XVI.

377 *Literary History of the United States* quotes Lincoln to Mrs. Stowe on page 563.

378 On Adams' prophecy, see Agar, *op. cit.,* p. 354.

379 The Louisiana editor who saw the threat of slavery to independent workers is quoted in A. M. Schlesinger's *Paths to the Present,* p. 62.

Chevalier, *op. cit.,* pp. 394-95.

380 Ulrich B. Phillips quotes the Boston clergyman in *Life and Labor in the Old South,* p. 214, note 4.

Whittier, "Ichabod."

383 A. B. Hart has Brown's statement in his *American History Told by Contemporaries,* vol. IV, pp. 148-50.

Thoreau, *Works,* selected and edited by H. S. Canby, p. 845.

384 The Charleston lady was Mary Boykin Chesnut. The quotation is from her *Diary from Dixie,* p. 39.

385 Walt Whitman, *Writings,* vol. IV, p. 29.

386 Denis W. Brogan, *The American Character,* p. 164.

Whitman is quoted in R. H. Gabriel's *The Course of Democratic Thought,* p. 127.

For an interesting account of the numbers in Washington's armies, see Samuel Eliot Morison, *The Oxford History of the United States,* vol. II, pp. 177-83.

Marjorie Barstow Greenbie quotes the superlatives of the Civil War in her *American Saga,* p. 489.

387 See Canby's *Walt Whitman,* pp. 216 and 221, for the poet's letters.

388 Brogan, *op. cit.,* p. 18.

389 Tocqueville: See *Literary History of the United States,* vol. I, p. 213.

390 Lincoln's letter, and the comment on his leadership, are quoted in Agar, *op. cit.,* pp. 424-25 and 434.

Cole, *The Irrepressible Conflict,* pp. 403-4, gives the Southerner's opinion on slave soldiers.

391 Gabriel's summary is on page 119 of his *Course of American Democratic Thought.*

392 The Northern traveler is quoted in Commager and Nevins, *The Heritage of America,* p. 808.

393 Grady's remark is from Morison and Commager, *op. cit.,* vol. II, p. 23.

Edward King, in his *The Great South,* p. 54, describes the bustling Cotton Exchange at New Orleans.

394 For the Englishman's estimate of the North, see Roger Burlingame, *Backgrounds of Power*, pp. 183-84.

395 The optimistic prophet of the West is Albert D. Richardson, in his *Beyond the Mississippi*, p. ii.

396 Richardson's book quoted also on the previous page is only one of a long file of reports on the West that were published in the decades after the Civil War.

397 *The Education of Henry Adams*, p. 312.

400 Major John Wesley Powell's book was entitled *First Through the Grand Canyon*. This quotation is on page 48. Ralph Henry Gabriel, in his *The Course of American Democratic Thought*, discusses Powell on pages 168-72.

403 Samuel Bowles, *Across the Continent*, pp. 169 and 182-83.

405 For the Galicia agents, see Agar, *op. cit.*, pp. 560-61.

Charles A. and Mary R. Beard, *The Rise of American Civilization*, vol. II, p. 247.

406 Strong is quoted in Arthur M. Schlesinger's *Paths to the Present*, p. 64.

Emerson: See Gabriel's *The Course of American Democratic Thought*, p. 45.

407 On the foreign-born population of the cities, see Schlesinger, *The Rise of the City*, pp. 72-73.

Senator Lodge is quoted in Louis M. Hacker's *The Shaping of the American Tradition*, vol. II, p. 843.

408 Margaret Mead, *And Keep Your Powder Dry*, p. 50.

409 The rhyme is in Brogan's *The American Character*, p. 23.

410–11 The Riis quotations are from his *How the Other Half Lives*, pp. 163-64, 166, and 23-24.

411 The Rumanian immigrant is quoted in Greenbie's *American Saga*, pp. 623-24.

413 Steffens is quoted in Hacker, *op. cit.*, vol. II, p. 928.

414 Morison and Commager, in their *Growth of the American Republic*, vol. II, p. 362, give the statisticians' findings.

For "Fighting Joe" Wheeler, see Gabriel, *op. cit.*, p. 132.

415 The returning doughboys are quoted in Dixon Wecter's *When Johnny Comes Marching Home*, p. 298.

For Wilson's plea, see Hacker, *op. cit.*, vol. II, pp. 1009-10.

416 On prohibition under local option, consult Harold Underwood Faulkner, *The Quest for Social Justice*, p. 227.

417 The Englishman's experience in the speakeasy is in Nevins' *America Through British Eyes*, pp. 433-34.

Preston William Slosson, in *The Great Crusade*, pp. 97-98 and 96, analyzes the crime wave.

419 A. M. Schlesinger, *Paths to the Present*, p. 38. See this work *passim* for the foundation of these paragraphs.

421 Woodrow Wilson, *Selected Addresses*, edited by A. B. Hart, pp. 2-3.

422 On the belief in a unique America, see Nevins, *op. cit.*, p. 446.

423 President F. D. Roosevelt is quoted in Hacker, *op. cit.*, pp. 1148-49.

425 See Dixon Wecter's *The Age of the Great Depression*, p. 54, for W. A. White's comment.

Allan Nevins in *Literary History of the United States*, vol. II, p. 1259.

426 On the kindness of our land and our dependence on others, see Charles Wright Ferguson, *A Little Democracy*, pp. 27-28.

428 Carl Becker, *Freedom and Responsibility*, p. 78.

Tocqueville, *Democracy in America*, vol. II, p. 334.

ACKNOWLEDGMENT

GRATEFUL ACKNOWLEDGMENT is made to Alfred A. Knopf, Inc., for permission to quote from Germán Arciniegas, The Green Continent; to Harper & Brothers for permission to quote from The Autobiography of Isaac Jones Wistar and from Mark Twain's Roughing It and Life on the Mississippi; to Houghton Mifflin Company for permission to quote from Andy Adams, The Log of a Cowboy; to Henry Holt and Company, Inc., for permission to quote from Carl Sandburg's Chicago Poems, and to The Macmillan Company for permission to quote from The Bitter Cry of the Children by John Spargo and A Son of the Middle Border by Hamlin Garland.

BIBLIOGRAPHY

Adams, Abigail Smith, *New Letters of Abigail Adams, 1788–1801*. Ed. by Stewart Mitchell. Boston, 1947.

Adams, Andy, *The Log of a Cowboy*. Boston, 1903.

Adams, Henry, *The Education of Henry Adams*. Boston, 1930.

Adams, James Truslow, *Provincial Society, 1690–1763*. New York, 1927. In *A History of American Life*, III.

Agar, Herbert, *The Price of Union*. Boston, 1950.

Albion, Robert Greenhalgh, *Square-Riggers on Schedule*. Princeton, 1938.

Albion, Robert Greenhalgh, and J. B. Pope, *The Rise of New York Port*. New York, 1939.

Ambler, Charles Henry, *A History of Transportation in the Ohio Valley*. Glendale, Calif., 1932.

Anderson, Rufus, *The Hawaiian Islands*. New York, 1864.

Andrews, Charles McLean, *The Colonial Period of American History*. New Haven, 1934–38.

Arciniegas, Germán, ed., *The Green Continent*. New York, 1944.

Asbury, Herbert, *The Gangs of New York*. New York, 1928.

Audubon, John James, *Delineations of American Scenery and Character*. New York, 1926.

Audubon, John Woodhouse, *Illustrated Notes of an Expedition Through Mexico and California*. Reprinted in the *Magazine of History*, XI (Extra Number 41), 1916.

Augur, Helen, *Passage to Glory: John Ledyard's America*. New York, 1946.

Babcock, William H., *Legendary Islands of the Atlantic*. New York, 1922.

Baillie-Grohman, William A., *Sport in Art*. [London, 1919.]

Baker, O. E. *See* O. C. Stine.

Baldwin, Leland D., *The Keelboat Age on Western Waters*. Pittsburgh, 1941.

"Baltimore," *North American Review*, XX (Jan. 1825).

Bancroft, Hubert Howe, *The Book of the Fair*. Chicago, 1893.

Barton, Glen T. *See* Martin R. Cooper.

Beard, Charles A. and Mary R., *A Basic History of the United States*. New York, 1944.

—— *The Rise of American Civilization*. New York, 1927–42.

Becker, Carl L., *Freedom and Responsibility in the American Way of Life*. New York, 1945.

Bentley, William, *Diary*. Salem, Mass., 1905–14.

Berger, Max, *The British Traveller in America, 1836–1860*. New York, 1943.

Beveridge, Albert J., *The Life of John Marshall*. Boston, 1916–19.

Beverley, Robert, *The History and Present State of Virginia*. Ed. by Louis B. Wright. Chapel Hill, N.C., 1947.

Bidwell, Percy Wells, "The Agricultural Revolution in New England," *American Historical Review*, XXVI (July 1921).

Bidwell, Percy Wells, and J. L. Falconer, *History of Agriculture in the Northern United States*. Washington, 1925. Carnegie Institute Pub. No. 358.

Birkbeck, Morris, *Notes on a Journey in America*. London, 1818.

Birket, James, *Some Cursory Remarks*. New Haven, 1916.

Bishop, J. Leander, *A History of American Manufactures from 1608 to 1860*. Philadelphia, 1868.

Bishop, Morris, *Champlain*. New York, 1948.

Blair, Walter, and F. J. Meine, *Mike Fink, King of Mississippi Keelboatmen*. New York, 1933.

Boggs, Mae Hélène Bacon, comp., *My Playhouse Was a Concord Coach*. Oakland, Calif., 1942.

Boit, John, *John Boit's Log of the Second Voyage of the "Columbia."* Ed. by Frederic W. Howay. In the *Massachusetts Historical Society Collections*, LXXIX (1941), *Voyages of the "Columbia."*

Bonsal, Stephen, *Edward Fitzgerald Beale*. New York, 1912.

Borthwick, J. D., *Three Years in California*. Edinburgh, 1857.

Botkin, Benjamin A., ed., *A Treasury of American Folklore*. New York, 1944.

Bourne, E. G. *See* J. E. Olson.

Bowes, Frederick P., *The Culture of Early Charleston*. Chapel Hill, N.C., 1942.

Bowles, Samuel, *Across the Continent*. Springfield, Mass., 1865.

Bremer, Fredrika, *America of the Fifties: Letters of Fredrika Bremer*. Ed. by Adolph B. Benson. New York, 1924.

—— *The Homes of the New World*. Tr. by Mary Howitt. New York, 1853.

Bridenbaugh, Carl, *Cities in the Wilderness*. New York, 1938.

—— *The Colonial Craftsman*. New York, 1950.

Brissot de Warville, Jacques Pierre, *New Travels in the United States*. [London, 1794.]

The British Mechanic's and Labourer's Hand Book. London, 1840.

Brodell, Albert P. *See* Martin R. Cooper.

Brogan, Denis W., *The American Character*. New York, 1944.

Brown, Ralph H., *Mirror for Americans*. New York, 1943.

Browne, John Ross, *Etchings of a Whaling Cruise*. New York, 1846.

Bryarly, Wakeman. *See* David Morris Potter.

Bryce, James, *The American Commonwealth*. New York, 1910.

Buck, Franklin A., *A Yankee Trader in the Gold Rush . . . Letters of Franklin A. Buck*. Comp. by Katherine A. White. Boston, 1930.

Buckingham, James Silk, *America, Historical, Statistic, and Descriptive*. London [1841].

—— *The Slave States of America*. London [1842?].

Buffinton, A. H., "The Isolationist Policy of Colonial Massachusetts," *New England Quarterly*, I (April 1928).

Burlingame, Roger, *Backgrounds of Power*. London and New York, 1949.

Burnaby, Andrew, *Travels Through the Middle Settlements in North America in . . . 1759 and 1760*. London, 1798.

Bushnell, Horace, *Work and Play*. New York, 1864.

Butler, Frances Anne. *See* Frances Anne Kemble.

Byron, George Gordon, Lord, *The Complete Poetical Works*. Boston, 1933. (Cambridge Ed.)

Cadman, Paul F. *See* Allan Forbes.

The Cambridge History of American Literature. Ed. by W. P. Trent, John Erskine, S. P. Sherman, and Carl Van Doren. New York, 1917–21.

Camp, William Martin, *San Francisco, Port of Gold*. Garden City, N.Y., 1947.

Canby, Henry Seidel, *Walt Whitman*. Boston, 1943.

Canfield, Leon H., and H. B. Wilder, *The Making of Modern America*. Boston, 1950.

Carlyle, Thomas, and Ralph Waldo Emerson, *The Correspondence of Thomas Carlyle and Ralph Waldo Emerson, 1834–1872*. Boston, 1883.

Carman, Harry J., ed., *American Husbandry*. New York, 1939.

Catlin, George, *North American Indians, Being Letters and Notes on Their Manners, Customs, and Conditions*. London [193–?].

Champlain, Samuel de. *Voyages . . . 1604–1618*. Ed. by W. L. Grant. New York, 1907. In *Original Narratives of Early American History*.

—— *Works*. H. P. Biggar, gen. ed. Toronto, 1922–36.

Chase, Stuart, "Play," in *Whither Mankind*. Ed. by Charles A. Beard. New York, 1928.

—— *The Road We Are Traveling, 1914–1942*. New York, 1942.

Chaville, Franquet de, "Relation du Voyage de la Louisiane," *Journal de la Société des Américanistes de Paris*, IV (1902–3).

Chesnut, Mary Boykin, *A Diary from Dixie*. Ed. by Ben Ames Williams. Boston, 1949.

Chevalier, Michel, *Society, Manners and Politics in the United States*. Boston, 1839.

Chinard, Gilbert, ed., *Un Français en Virginie . . . après l'Edition . . . 1687*. Paris, 1932.

Clark, Victor S., *History of Manufactures in the United States*. New York, 1929.

Clemens, Samuel Langhorne, *Life on the Mississippi*. New York, 1917.

—— *Roughing It*. New York, 1913.

Cobbett, William, *A Year's Residence in the United States*. London, 1819.

Cohn, David L., *Combustion on Wheels.* Boston, 1944.

Colby, Merle, *A Guide to Alaska.* New York, 1941. In the American Guide Series.

Cole, Arthur Charles, *The Irrepressible Conflict.* New York, 1934. In *A History of American Life,* VII.

Colt, Samuel, *Sam. Colt's Own Record.* Hartford, Conn., 1949.

Colton, Walter, *Deck and Port.* New York, 1850.

—— *Three Years in California.* New York, 1852.

Commager, Henry Steele, and Allan Nevins, eds., *The Heritage of America.* Boston, 1939.

Commager, Henry Steele. *See also* Samuel Eliot Morison.

Cooper, James Fenimore, *Notions of the Americans.* Philadelphia, 1828.

Cooper, Martin R., G. T. Barton, and A. P. Brodell, *Progress of Farm Mechanization.* Washington, 1947. U.S. Dept. of Agriculture, Misc. Pub. No. 630 (Oct.).

Cornelius, Charles O. *See* R. T. Haines Halsey.

Costello, Augustine E., *Our Firemen.* New York, 1887.

—— *Our Police Protectors.* New York, 1885.

Coxe, Tench, *An Authentic View of the Progress of . . . Pennsylvania.* [Philadelphia, 1799.]

Crèvecoeur, St. John de, *Sketches of Eighteenth Century America.* Ed. by H. L. Bourdin, R. H. Gabriel, and S. T. Williams. New Haven, 1925.

Dana, David D., *The Fireman.* Boston, 1858.

Dana, Richard Henry, Jr., *Two Years Before the Mast.* Boston, 1929.

Davidson, Marshall B., "Early American Lighting," *Metropolitan Museum of Art Bulletin,* III (Summer 1944).

De Forest, Louis Effingham, ed., *Louisbourg Journals, 1745.* New York, 1932.

Delano, Alonzo, *Life on the Plains.* Auburn, N.Y., 1854.

—— *Pen-Knife Sketches.* Sacramento, Calif., 1853.

Delano, Amasa, *Narrative of Voyages and Travels.* Boston, 1817.

"Description of Charles River Bridge," *New-York Magazine,* VI (Sept. 1795).

"Description of the New Theatre, Philadelphia," *New-York Magazine,* V (April 1794).

De Voe, Thomas F., *The Market Book.* New York, 1862.

DeVoto, Bernard, *Across the Wide Missouri.* Boston, 1947.

"A Diary or Narrative by a British Subject, 1808." Anonymous manuscript in the New York Public Library.

Dick, Everett, *The Sod-House Frontier.* New York, 1937.

—— *Vanguards of the Frontier.* New York, 1941.

Dickens, Charles, *American Notes.* London, 1842.

Dillin, John G. W., *The Kentucky Rifle.* Washington, 1924.

Dix, William Frederick, "Conquerors of the Road," *Independent,* LXIII (Nov. 7, 1907).

Dodge, Richard Irving, *Our Wild Indians.* Hartford, Conn., 1882.

—— *The Plains of the Great West.* New York, 1877.

Dondore, Dorothy Anne, *The Prairie and the Making of Middle America.* Cedar Rapids, Iowa, 1926.

Dow, George Francis, *The Sailing Ships of New England* (Series Three). Salem, Mass., 1928.

Downs, A. O., "Clergymen and the Bicycle," *Wheelman,* I (Dec. 1882).

Downs, Joseph, "The American Trade with the Far East," in *The China Trade and Its Influences* (Catalogue of a Special Exhibition at the Metropolitan Museum of Art). New York, 1941.

—— "New York Silver," *Bulletin of the Metropolitan Museum of Art,* XXX (June 1935).

Dulles, Rhea Foster, *America Learns To Play.* New York, 1940.

Dunbar, Seymour, *A History of Travel in America.* Indianapolis, 1915.

Dunn, Jacob Piatt, Jr., *Massacres of the Mountains.* New York, 1886.

Eames, Wilberforce, "Description of a Wood Engraving Illustrating the South American Indians (1505)," *Bulletin of the New York Public Library,* XXVI (Sept. 1922).

Edwards, Everett E., *American Agriculture—The First 300 Years.* Washington, 1941. U.S. Dept. of Agriculture Yearbook Separate No. 1783. In *An Historical Survey of Agriculture.*

Eighty Years' Progress of the United States . . . by Eminent Literary Men. Hartford, Conn., 1868.

Emerson, Ralph Waldo, *The Conduct of Life.* Boston, 1922. In *Complete Works,* VI. (Centenary Ed.)

—— *Essays* (Second Series). Boston, 1903–4. In *Complete Works,* III. (Centenary Ed.)

—— *Journals.* Ed. by Edward Waldo Emerson and Waldo Emerson Forbes. Boston, 1909–14.

—— *Society and Solitude.* Boston, 1912. In *Complete Works,* VII. (Centenary Ed.)

—— *See also* Thomas Carlyle.

Falconer, John L. *See* Percy Wells Bidwell.

Fanning, Edmund, *Voyages Round the World.* New York, 1833.

Faulkner, Harold Underwood, *Economic History of the United States*. New York, 1928.

—— *The Quest for Social Justice*. New York, 1931. In *A History of American Life*, XI.

Faÿ, Bernard, *Franklin, the Apostle of Modern Times*. Boston, 1929.

Fay, Theodore S., "A Few Thoughts on All This Steaming." *New-York Mirror*, XVIII (Nov. 28 and Dec. 5, 1840).

Federal Writers' Project. *See* W.P.A.

Ferguson, Charles Wright, *A Little Democracy Is a Dangerous Thing*. New York, 1948.

Filson, John, *The Discovery, Settlement and Present State of Kentucke*. Wilmington, Del., 1784.

Fish, Carl Russell, *The Rise of the Common Man, 1830–1850*. New York, 1927. In *A History of American Life*, VI.

Fiske, John, *The Critical Period of American History, 1783–1789*. Boston, 1916.

Fite, Emerson D., and Archibald Freeman, eds., *A Book of Old Maps*. Cambridge, Mass., 1926.

Fithian, Philip Vickers, *Journal and Letters, 1767–1774*. Ed. by John Rogers Williams. Princeton, 1900.

Flanagan, John T., ed., *America Is West*. Minneapolis, 1945.

Flexner, James Thomas, *Steamboats Come True*. New York, 1944.

Forbes, Allan, and P. F. Cadman, *France and New England*. Boston, 1925–29.

Forbes, Esther, *Paul Revere and the World He Lived In*. Boston, 1942.

Foster, G. G., ed., *The Gold Regions of California*. New York, 1848.

Foulke, Roy A., *The Sinews of American Commerce*. New York, 1941.

Fox, Dixon Ryan, *Yankees and Yorkers*. New York, 1940.

—— *See also* John Allen Krout.

Franklin, Benjamin, *The Life of Benjamin Franklin, Written by Himself*. Ed. by John Bigelow. Philadelphia, 1874.

—— *Works*. Ed. by Jared Sparks. Boston, 1836–40.

"Freaks of Railroad Transportation," *American Railroad Journal, and Mechanics' Magazine*, n.s., VIII (June 15, 1842).

Freeman, Archibald. *See* Emerson D. Fite.

Freeman, Edward A., *Some Impressions of the United States*. New York, 1883.

Frost, Donald McKay, "Notes on General Ashley," *Proceedings of the American Antiquarian Society*, LIV, Pt. 2 (Oct. 1944).

Fuess, Claude Moore, *Daniel Webster*. Boston, 1930.

Gabriel, Ralph Henry, *The Course of American Democratic Thought*. New York, 1943.

—— *See also* William Wood.

Gannett, Lewis, *Cream Hill*. New York, 1949.

Garland, Hamlin, *A Son of the Middle Border*. New York, 1928.

Garrett, Garet, "A Fifty-Year Crisis in Agriculture," *Saturday Evening Post*, CXCVI (April 19, 1924).

Geiger, Vincent. *See* David Morris Potter.

Giddens, Paul H., *Early Days of Oil*. Princeton, 1948.

Giedion, Siegfried, *Mechanization Takes Command*. New York, 1948.

Gihon, John H., M.D. *See* Frank Soulé.

Glover, Katherine, *America Begins Again*. New York, 1939.

Goldschmidt, Walter R., *Large Farms or Small: The Social Side* (mimeographed). A paper prepared for the Annual Meeting of the Western Farm Economic Association, June 28, 1944.

Graeff, Arthur D., "American History Visualized in Pennsylvania German Almanacs," *American-German Review*, VI (Feb. 1940).

Grau, Robert, *The Stage in the Twentieth Century*. New York, 1912.

Green, John Richard, *History of the English People*. London, 1879–81.

Greenbie, Marjorie Barstow, *American Saga*. New York, 1939.

Greene, Evarts Boutell, *The Revolutionary Generation*. New York, 1943. In *A History of American Life*, IV.

Greenleaf, Benjamin, *The California Almanac for 1849*. San Marino, Calif., 1942.

Gregg, Josiah, *Commerce of the Prairies*. Cleveland, 1905. In *Early Western Travels*, ed. by R. G. Thwaites, XIX-XX.

Griswold, Alfred Whitney, *Farming and Democracy*. New York, 1948.

Gutheim, Frederick, "Greenbelt Revisited," *Magazine of Art*, XL (Jan. 1947).

Hacker, Louis Morton, *The Shaping of the American Tradition*. New York, 1947.

Hall, Basil, *Travels in North America*. Edinburgh, 1829.

Hall, Margaret Hunter (Mrs. Basil Hall), *The Aristocratic Journey . . . Letters . . . 1827–1828*. Ed. by Una Pope-Hennessy. New York, 1931.

Halsey, R. T. Haines, and C. O. Cornelius, *A Handbook of the American Wing* (Metropolitan Museum of Art), New York, 1924.

Hamilton, Dr. Alexander, *Hamilton's Itinerarium*. Ed. by Albert Bushnell Hart. St. Louis, 1907.

Hansen, Marcus Lee, *The Atlantic Migration, 1607–1860.* Cambridge, Mass., 1940.

—— *The Immigrant in American History.* Cambridge, Mass., 1940.

Harding, Chester, *My Egotistography.* Cambridge, Mass., 1866.

Hariot (Harriot), Thomas, *A Briefe and True Report . . . of Virginia . . . a Reproduction of the Edition Printed at Frankfort in 1590 at the Expense of Theodore de Bry.* Ed. by W. Harry Rylands. Manchester, Eng., 1888.

Harlow, Alvin F., *Old Towpaths.* New York, 1926.

Hart, Albert Bushnell, ed., *American History Told by Contemporaries.* New York, 1897–1929.

Harte, Bret, *The Complete Poetical Works.* Boston, 1912. (Cabinet Ed.)

Hartford Convention, *The Proceedings of a Convention of Delegates.* Boston, 1815.

Haskell, Daniel C. *See* I. N. Phelps Stokes.

Hendrick, Burton J., *The Age of Big Business.* New Haven, 1919. In *The Chronicles of America,* XXXIX, Yale University Press.

Hennepin, Louis, *A New Discovery of a Vast Country in America.* London, 1698.

Hickman, Russell K. *See* George A. Root.

Hicks, John D., *A Short History of American Democracy.* Boston, 1943.

Hobhouse, Christopher, *1851 and the Crystal Palace.* London, 1937.

Holliman, Jennie, *American Sports (1785–1835).* Durham, N.C., 1931.

Holly, Henry Hudson, *Holly's Country Seats.* New York, 1863.

Holmes, Oliver Wendell, "The Autocrat of the Breakfast-Table," *Atlantic Monthly,* I (May 1858).

Holmes, Oliver Wendell, "Levi Pease, the Father of New England Stage-Coaching," *Journal of Economic and Business History,* III (Feb. 1931).

"Home Exercises," *Harper's Weekly,* I (July 11, 1857).

Hone, Philip, *Diary.* Ed. by Allan Nevins. New York, 1927.

Hulbert, Archer B., *The Paths of Inland Commerce.* New Haven, 1920. In *The Chronicles of America,* XXI, Yale University Press.

Hunter, Louis C., and Beatrice J., *Steamboats on the Western Rivers.* Cambridge, Mass., 1949.

Hutchinson, William T., *Cyrus Hall McCormick.* New York, 1930.

"Impolitical Prints"; an Exhibition of Contemporary English Cartoons Relating to the American Revolution (New York Public Library; intro. by R. T. Haines Halsey). New York, 1939.

Ingraham, J. H., *The South-West.* New York, 1835.

Irving, Washington, *Bonneville's Adventures.* New York, 1849. In *Works,* X.

Irving, Washington, William Irving, and J. K. Paulding, *Salmagundi.* Philadelphia, 1873. In Washington Irving, *Works,* XV.

Irwin, William Henry (Will), *The City That Was.* New York, 1906.

Ives, Joseph C., *Report Upon the Colorado River.* Washington, 1861. House of Representatives Exec. Doc. No. 90, 36th Congress, 1st Session.

Jameson, J. Franklin, ed., *Narratives of New Netherland.* New York, 1909. In *Original Narratives of Early American History.*

Janson, Charles William, *The Stranger in America, 1793–1806.* London, 1807.

Jefferson, Thomas, *Writings.* Ed. by Paul Leicester Ford. New York, 1892–99.

—— *Writings.* Ed. by A. A. Lipscomb. Washington, 1903–5. (Monticello Ed.)

—— *Writings.* Ed. by A. A. Lipscomb. Washington, 1905. (Definitive Ed.)

Jenkins, Lawrence Waters, *Bryant Parrott Tilden of Salem.* Princeton, 1944. (A Newcomen Address.)

[Johnson, Robert] *Nova Britannia.* London, 1609.

Johnstone, Paul H., "Old Ideals Versus New Ideas in Farm Life," *Yearbook of Agriculture, 1940.* Washington, 1941. Yearbook of the U.S. Dept. of Agriculture, entitled *Farmers in a Changing World.*

Kalm, Peter, *The America of 1750; Peter Kalm's Travels in North America.* Ed. by Adolph B. Benson. New York, 1937.

Keir, John Malcolm (Malcolm), *The Epic of Industry.* New Haven, 1926. In *The Pageant of America,* V, Yale University Press.

Kemble, Frances Anne (Butler), *Journal.* Philadelphia, 1835.

King, Edward, *The Great South.* Hartford, Conn., 1875.

Knight, Sarah Kemble, *The Private Journal of a Journey from Boston to New York . . . 1704.* Albany, N.Y., 1865.

Kohl, J. G., *Travels in Canada, and Through the States of New York and Pennsylvania.* London, 1861.

Kouwenhoven, John A., *Made in America.* Garden City, N.Y., 1948.

Kraus, Michael, *Intercolonial Aspects of American Culture on the Eve of the Revolution.* New York, 1928.

Krout, John Allen, *Annals of American Sport.* New Haven, 1929. In *The Pageant of America*, XV, Yale University Press.

Krout, John Allen, and D. R. Fox, *The Completion of Independence.* New York, 1944. In *A History of American Life,* V.

Kurz, Rudolph Friederich, *Journal.* Tr. by Myrtis Jarrell. Ed. by J. N. B. Hewitt. Washington, 1937. Smithsonian Institution, Bureau of American Ethnology Bulletin 115.

Lahontan, Louis Armand, Baron de, *Suite du Voyage de l'Amérique.* Amsterdam, 1728.

Lake, Stuart N., *Wyatt Earp, Frontier Marshal.* Boston, 1931.

Lane, Wheaton J., *From Indian Trail to Iron Horse.* Princeton, 1939.

La Rochefoucauld-Liancourt, François, Duc de, *Travels Through the United States.* London, 1799.

La Roncière, Charles de, *La Découverte de l'Afrique au Moyen Age.* Cairo, 1924–27.

A Letter from a Gold Miner (1850). Intro. by Robert Glass Cleland. San Marino, Calif., 1944.

Life in America; a Special Loan Exhibition of Paintings (Metropolitan Museum of Art). New York, 1939.

Lilienthal, David, *TVA; Democracy on the March.* New York, 1944.

Literary History of the United States. Ed. by R. E. Spiller, E. W. Thorp, T. H. Johnson, H. S. Canby, and Associates. New York, 1948.

Lomax, John Avery and Alan, *Cowboy Songs.* New York, 1938.

Lord, Russell, "The Ground From Under Your Feet," *Saturday Review of Literature,* XXXI (Aug. 7, 1948).

Lowenthal, Marvin. *See* Frank Monaghan.

McLaughlin, Andrew C., *A Constitutional History of the United States.* New York, 1936.

McMaster, John Bach, *A History of the People of the United States.* New York, 1883–1913.

McWilliams, Carey, *Ill Fares the Land.* Boston, 1942.

Malin, James C., "Dust Storms," *Kansas Historical Quarterly,* XIV (May 1946).

Marcy, Randolph B., *Thirty Years of Army Life on the Border.* New York, 1866.

Marjoribanks, Alexander, *Travels in South and North America.* London, 1853.

Marryat, Francis Samuel (Frank), *Mountains and Molehills.* London, 1855.

Marryat, Frederick, *A Diary in America.* New York, 1839.

Martineau, Harriet, *Society in America.* New York, 1837.

Mather, Cotton, *The Sailours Companion and Counsellour.* Boston, 1709.

Matthews, William, and Dixon Wecter, *Our Soldiers Speak, 1775–1918.* Boston, 1943.

Maury, Sarah Mytton, *An Englishwoman in America.* London, 1848.

Maximilian, Prince of Wied-Neuwied. *See* Wied-Neuwied, Maximilian, Prince of.

Mayer, Francis Blackwell, *With Pen and Pencil on the Frontier in 1851; the Diary and Sketches of Frank Blackwell Mayer.* Ed. by Bertha L. Heilbron. St. Paul, 1932.

Mead, Margaret, *And Keep Your Powder Dry.* New York, 1942.

Meine, Franklin J. *See* Walter Blair.

Melish, John, *Travels in the United States.* Philadelphia, 1812.

Melville, Herman, *Moby-Dick.* London, 1922. In *Works,* VII-VIII. (Standard Ed.)

—— *Typee.* London, 1922. In *Works,* I. (Standard Ed.)

Milbank, Jeremiah, Jr., *The First Century of Flight in America.* Princeton, 1943.

"Mining Life in California," *Harper's Weekly,* I (Oct. 3, 1857).

Monaghan, Frank, and Marvin Lowenthal, *This Was New York.* Garden City, N.Y., 1943.

"More Bridges Wanted," *Harper's Weekly,* XXVII (June 16, 1883).

Moreau de Saint-Méry, Médéric Louis Elie, *Moreau de St. Méry's American Journey.* Tr. and ed. by Kenneth Roberts and Anna M. Roberts. Garden City, N.Y., 1947.

Morgan, Arthur Ernest, *Nowhere Was Somewhere.* Chapel Hill, N.C., 1946.

Morison, Samuel Eliot, *Builders of the Bay Colony.* Boston, 1930.

—— "A Conjectural Restoration of the 'Old College' at Harvard," *Old-Time New England,* XXIII (April 1933).

—— *The Maritime History of Massachusetts.* Boston, 1921.

—— *The Oxford History of the United States.* London, 1928.

Morison, Samuel Eliot, and H. S. Commager, *The Growth of the American Republic.* New York, 1942.

Morris, Lloyd R., *Not So Long Ago.* New York, 1949.

Mott, Frank Luther, *A History of American Magazines.* Cambridge, Mass., 1938.

—— *A History of American Magazines, 1741–1850.* New York, 1930.

Mount Vernon . . . a Handbook. Mt. Vernon, Va., 1947.

Muirhead, James Fullarton, *America, the Land of Contrasts.* London and New York, 1902.

468

Mumford, Lewis, *City Development.* New York, 1945.

—— *The Culture of Cities.* New York, 1938.

"Muscular Christianity by a Christian Muscleman," *Overland Monthly,* II (June 1869).

Neely, Wayne Caldwell, *The Agricultural Fair.* New York, 1935. In *Columbia University Studies in the History of American Agriculture,* II.

Nesbit (Nisbit), James. *See* Frank Soulé.

Nevins, Allan, ed., *America Through British Eyes.* New York, 1948.

—— ed., *American Social History as Recorded by British Travellers.* New York, 1923.

—— *The Emergence of Modern America.* New York, 1927. In *A History of American Life,* VIII.

—— *See also* Henry Steele Commager.

New Englands First Fruits. London, 1643.

Newton, Arthur Percival, ed., *Travel and Travellers in the Middle Ages.* London, 1926.

Nichols, Thomas L., *Forty Years of American Life.* London, 1864.

Ogg, Frederic Austin, *The Old Northwest.* New Haven, 1920. In *The Chronicles of America,* XIX, Yale University Press.

Old-Time New England, XXIII (April 1933).

Olmsted, Frederick Law, *The Cotton Kingdom.* New York, 1861.

—— *A Journey in the Back Country.* New York, 1860.

Olson, J. E., and E. G. Bourne, eds., *The Northmen, Columbus and Cabot.* New York, 1906. In *Original Narratives of Early American History.*

"One of the Mississippi Bubbles," *Newberry Library Bulletin,* No. 5 (Sept. 1946).

Orth, Samuel Peter, *Our Foreigners.* New Haven, 1920. In *The Chronicles of America,* XXXV, Yale University Press.

Owen, William, *Narrative of American Voyages and Travels.* Ed. by Victor Hugo Paltsits. New York, 1942.

Paine, Ralph D., *The Old Merchant Marine.* New Haven, 1920.

Palmer, John, *Journals of Travels in the United States.* London, 1818.

Panofsky, Erwin, "On Movies," *Bulletin of the Department of Art and Archaeology of Princeton University,* June 1936.

Parkman, Francis, Jr., *The Battle for North America.* Ed. by John Tebbel from the Works of Francis Parkman. Garden City, N.Y., 1948.

—— *The California and Oregon Trail.* New York, 1849.

—— *Journals.* Ed. by Mason Wade. New York, 1947.

—— *Montcalm and Wolfe.* Boston, 1910.

—— *Pioneers of France in the New World.* Boston, 1910.

Parrington, Vernon Louis, *Main Currents in American Thought.* New York, 1927–30.

Parton, James, *Life and Times of Benjamin Franklin.* New York, 1864.

Paul, Rodman W., *California Gold.* Cambridge, Mass., 1947.

Paulding, James Kirke. *See* Washington Irving.

Paxson, Frederic Logan, "The Cow Country," *American Historical Review,* XXII (Oct. 1916).

—— "The Highway Movement, 1916–1935," *American Historical Review,* LI (Jan. 1946).

—— *History of the American Frontier, 1763–1893.* Boston, 1924.

Peabody's Parlour Journal, I (Mar. 15, 1834).

Petersen, Charles E., "Early American Prefabrication," *Gazette des Beaux Arts,* XXXIII (Jan. 1948).

Petersen, William J., *Steamboating on the Upper Mississippi.* Iowa City, Iowa, 1937.

—— "Steamboating on Western Waters," *Dictionary of American History.* New York, 1946.

Philadelphia Photographer, I (Aug. 1864), editorial.

Phillips, Ulrich Bonnell, *Life and Labor in the Old South.* Boston, 1929.

"Picnic Excursions," *Appletons' Journal,* I (Aug. 14, 1869).

Pierce, Bessie Louise, ed., *As Others See Chicago.* Chicago, 1933.

Plank Roads. The Report of the Committee, Appointed at a Meeting of the Citizens of Ithaca [New York] . . . *Held February 10th, 1848.* [n.p., 1849?]

Pope, Jennie Barnes. *See* Robert Greenhalgh Albion.

Potter, David Morris, ed., *Trail to California. The Overland Journal of Vincent Geiger and Wakeman Bryarly.* New Haven, 1945.

Powell, John Wesley, *First Through the Grand Canyon.* Ed. by Horace Kephart. New York, 1915.

"Promiscuous Sleeping-Cars," *New York Graphic,* III (Jan. 6, 1874).

Purcell, Richard J., "John Carroll," *Dictionary of American Biography.* New York, 1928–37.

"Raising Supplies of Meat for Foreign Markets," *Frank Leslie's Illustrated Newspaper,* XLVI (July 27, 1878).

Ralph, Julian, *Our Great West.* New York, 1893.

LIFE IN AMERICA

Ranney, John C., "The Bases of American Federalism," *William and Mary Quarterly*, III (Jan. 1946).

Richardson, Albert D., *Beyond the Mississippi*. Hartford, Conn., 1867.

Riis, Jacob A., *How the Other Half Lives*. New York, 1890.

Riley, Elihu Samuel, *"The Ancient City."* Annapolis, Md., 1887.

Robert, Joseph Clarke, *The Tobacco Kingdom*. Durham, N.C., 1938.

Robertson, Archibald, *Archibald Robertson . . . Diaries and Sketches in America, 1762–1780*. Ed. by Harry Miller Lydenberg. New York, 1930.

Rochefoucauld-Liancourt, Duke of. *See* La Rochefoucauld-Liancourt, François, Duc de.

Rogers, James A., *Journal*. Ed. by Ernest F. Gates. New Bedford, Mass., n.d. Reprinted in a pamphlet by the Reynolds Printing Co.

Rollins, Philip Ashton, *The Cowboy*. New York, 1922.

Rollinson, John K., *Wyoming Cattle Trails*. Caldwell, Idaho, 1948.

Roncière, Charles de la. *See* La Roncière, Charles de.

Roosevelt, Theodore, *Autobiography*. New York, 1920.

—— *Hunting Trips of a Ranchman*. New York, 1885.

Root, George A., and R. K. Hickman, "Pike's Peak Express Companies," *Kansas Historical Quarterly*, XIV (Feb. 1946).

Root, John W., "The City House in the West," in *Homes in City and Country*. New York, 1893.

Sabin, Edwin L., *Building the Pacific Railway*. Philadelphia, 1919.

"A Sacred Concert," *Illustrated Christian Weekly*, IV (Dec. 5, 1874).

Sandburg, Carl, *Chicago Poems*. New York, 1916.

Schafer, Joseph, "Agriculture," *Dictionary of American History*. New York, 1946.

—— *The Social History of American Agriculture*. New York, 1936.

Schlesinger, Arthur M., *New Viewpoints in American History*. New York, 1922.

—— *Paths to the Present*. New York, 1949.

—— *The Rise of the City*. New York, 1933. In *A History of American Life*, X.

Schoepf, Johann David, *Travels in the Confederation*. Tr. and ed. by Alfred J. Morrison. Philadelphia, 1911.

Scudder, John L., "The Pulpit and the Wheel," *Wheelman*, I (Oct. 1882).

Sellers, Charles Coleman, *The Artist of the Revolution . . . Charles Willson Peale*. Hebron, Conn., 1939.

Sert, José Luis, *Can Our Cities Survive?* Cambridge, Mass., 1942.

Shinn, Charles Howard, *The Story of the Mine*. New York, 1896.

Singleton, Esther, *The Story of the White House*. New York, 1907.

Slosson, Edwin E., *The American Spirit in Education*. New Haven, 1921. In *The Chronicles of America*, XXXIII, Yale University Press.

Slosson, Preston William, *The Great Crusade and After*. New York, 1930. In *A History of American Life*, XII.

Smith, Matthew Hale, *Sunshine and Shadow in New York*. Hartford, Conn., 1868.

Smith, Solomon, *Theatrical Management in the West and South for Thirty Years*. New York, 1868.

Soulé, Frank, J. H. Gihon, M.D., and James Nesbit (Nisbit), *The Annals of San Francisco*. New York, 1855.

Sporting Prints and Paintings (Catalogue of a Special Exhibition at the Metropolitan Museum of Art). New York, 1937.

Steinbeck, John, *The Grapes of Wrath*. New York, 1939.

Stevenson, Robert Louis, *Across the Plains*. New York, 1892.

Stine, O. C., and O. E. Baker, "Cotton," in *Atlas of American Agriculture*. *Advance Sheet No. 4* (Section A of Part 5). Washington, 1918. U.S. Dept. of Agriculture.

Stirling, James, *Letters from the Slave States*. London, 1857.

Stokes, I. N. Phelps, *The Iconography of Manhattan Island*. New York, 1915–28.

Stokes, I. N. Phelps, and D. C. Haskell, *American Historical Prints*. New York, 1932.

Sullivan, Mark, *Our Times*. New York, 1926–35.

"Sunday Riding," *Wheelman*, I (Dec. 1882).

Sutcliff, Robert, *Travels in Some Parts of North America . . . 1804, 1805, & 1806*. Philadelphia, 1812.

Svinin, Pavel Petrovich, *Picturesque United States . . . a Memoir on Paul Svinin . . . by Avrahm Yarmolinsky*. New York, 1930.

"Table-Talk," *Appletons' Journal*, I (April 3, 1869).

Tarbell, Ida M., *The Nationalizing of Business*. New York, 1936. In *A History of American Life*, IX.

Taylor, Bayard, *Eldorado*. New York, 1850.

Thayer, William M., *Marvels of the New West*. Norwich, Conn., 1887.

470

"Third Street Hall," *Atkinson's Casket* (Sept. 1834).

Thompson, Charles Miner, *Independent Vermont*. Boston, 1942.

Thompson, Holland, *The Age of Invention*. New Haven, 1921. In *The Chronicles of America*, XXXVII, Yale University Press.

Thoreau, Henry David, *Walden*. Boston, 1906. In *Writings*, II. (Walden Ed.)

—— *The Works of Thoreau*. Selected and ed. by Henry Seidel Canby. Boston, 1946.

Thruston, R. C. Ballard, "Filson's History and Map of Kentucky," *Filson Club Historical Quarterly*, VIII (Jan. 1934).

Tocqueville, Alexis de, *Democracy in America*. Ed. by Phillips Bradley. New York, 1945.

"A Trip to the End of the Union Pacific in 1868," *Kansas Historical Quarterly*, XIII (Aug. 1944).

Trollope, Anthony, *North America*. New York, 1862.

Trollope, Frances M., *Domestic Manners of the Americans*. London, 1832.

Tunis, John R., "A Nation of Onlookers?" *Atlantic Monthly*, CLX (Aug. 1937).

Twain, Mark. *See* Samuel Langhorne Clemens.

Twenty-Four Letters from Labourers in America to Their Friends in England. London, 1829.

Tyler, Alice Felt, *Freedom's Ferment*. Minneapolis, 1944.

Tyler, Lyon G., ed., *Narratives of Early Virginia, 1606–1625*. New York, 1907. In *Original Narratives of Early American History*.

Tyler, Royall, *The Contrast*. Philadelphia, 1790.

U.S. Department of Agriculture, *An Historical Survey of American Agriculture*. Washington, 1941. Yearbook Separate No. 1783, a reprint from the 1940 Yearbook.

"Vacations," *Nation*, XVII (Aug. 7, 1873), editorial.

Veblen, Thorstein, *The Instinct of Workmanship*. New York, 1922.

Villiers, Marc, Baron de, "A History of the Foundation of New Orleans" (tr. by Warrington Dawson), *Louisiana Historical Quarterly*, III (April 1920).

W.P.A. (Works Progress Administration, Federal Writers' Project), *The Oregon Trail*. New York, 1939. In the American Guide Series.

—— *Utah: A Guide to the State*. New York, 1941. In the American Guide Series.

Warre, Henry James, *Sketches in North America and the Oregon Territory*. [London, 1848.]

Washington, George, *Writings*. Ed. by W. C. Ford. New York, 1889–93.

Webb, Walter Prescott, *The Great Plains*. Boston, 1931.

Wecter, Dixon, *The Age of the Great Depression*. New York, 1948.

—— *When Johnny Comes Marching Home*. Boston, 1944.

—— *See also* William Matthews.

Weld, Isaac, Jr., *Travels Through the States of North America*. London, 1807.

Wells, H. G., *The Future in America*. New York, 1906.

Wertenbaker, Thomas Jefferson, *The Old South*. New York, 1942.

—— *The Puritan Oligarchy*. New York, 1947.

Wessen, Charles, Undated manuscript letter at the Historical and Philosophical Society of Ohio.

White, E. B., *The Wild Flag*. Boston, 1946.

Whitman, Walt, *Complete Writings*. Ed. by R. M. Bucke, T. B. Harned, and H. L. Traubel. New York, 1902. (Camden Ed.)

Whittier, John Greenleaf, *The Complete Poetical Works*. Boston, 1894. (Cambridge Ed.)

Wied-Neuwied, Maximilian, Prince of, *Travels in the Interior of North America*. Cleveland, 1905. In *Early Western Travels*, ed. by R. G. Thwaites, XXII–XXIV.

Wilder, Howard B. *See* Leon H. Canfield.

Wile, Frederic William, ed., *A Century of Industrial Progress*. Garden City, N.Y., 1928.

Wilkey, Walter (Ebenezer Deming), *Western Emigration*. New York, 1839.

William and Mary College, *The History of the College of William and Mary*. Richmond, Va., 1874.

Wilson, Woodrow, *Selected Addresses and Public Papers*. Ed. by Albert Bushnell Hart. New York, 1918. (Modern Lib. Ed.)

Winthrop, Robert C., *Life and Letters of John Winthrop*. Boston, 1864.

Wise, Henry Augustus. *Los Gringos*. New York, 1849.

Wistar, Isaac Jones, *Autobiography*. Philadelphia, 1937.

Wood, Ralph, ed., *The Pennsylvanian Germans*. Princeton, 1942.

Wood, William, and R. H. Gabriel, *The Winning of Freedom*. New Haven, 1927. In *The Pageant of America*, VI, Yale University Press.

Woods, John, *Two Years' Residence . . . in the Illinois Country*. London, 1822.

Wright, John Stillman, *Letters from the West*. Salem, Mass., 1819.

Wright, Louis B., *The First Gentlemen of Virginia*. San Marino, Calif., 1940.

Yarmolinsky, Avrahm. *See* Pavel Petrovich Svinin.

Zavala, Silvio, "The American Utopia of the Sixteenth Century," *Huntington Library Quarterly*, X (Aug. 1947).

LIST OF ARTISTS

473

INDEX

INDEX

and by-products, 140-43; canning industry, 143

Football, ii, 6, 69, 88-91

Forbes, John, i, 174

Ford, Henry, i, 507, 562, 569; ii, 85; quoted on mass production, ii, 284

Ford Motor Company, ii, 284-85

Forests, clearing of, i, 168, 170; protection of, 471

Forrester, Frank, cited on American hunters and fishermen, ii, 38

Forts, trading, i, 193-97, 228-29, 230

Forty-niners, i, 198. *See also* Gold rush

Fourierists, ii, 345

Fourth of July, celebration of, ii, 40-41

Fox, Captain, i, 299

Fox sisters, ii, 37, 373

France, claims in New World, i, 20, 24-34; threat of, to American colonies, 96-99; loss of Canada, 101-8; in American Revolution, 148-49; shipping war with, 314-17; in eastern Pacific, 339

Francis I, King of France, i, 24

Frank Leslie's Magazine, quoted on grain threshing, i, 417

Franklin, Benjamin, i, 128, 213, 288; on need for colonial union, i, 59; on American colonies, 59; on Germans in Pennsylvania, 78-79; on conflict in Pennsylvania, 80-81; on danger from French and Indians, 96; works for colonial union, 98, 101, 108; Postmaster General, 114; "Pennsylvanian Fire-Places," 119; breadth of interests, 121; on reading in Colonies, 123; letter to Strahan, 142; on British in Philadelphia, 148; on French aid in Revolution, 148; on westward migration, 157; on bow and arrow, 210; on farming, 361; on work in America, ii, 3; on daylight saving time, 162; on rivers and canals, 214; on balloon, 298; on American government, 316

Fraternal orders, ii, 419

Frederick the Great, i, 144; cited on United States, ii, 315

Freedom, doctrine of, in United States, ii, 315-17, 318-23; religious, 336-43; of children, 369

Freeman, Edward A., quoted on Chicago, ii, 122

Freight rates, ii, 214, 218

Freighting business, western, ii, 260-61

Frémont, Lieutenant John Charles, i, 233

French and Indian Wars, i, 98, 101-8

Frenchmen, immigration of, ii, 344-45, 348

Frick, Henry Clay, i, 545

Frigates, American, i, 317

Fritz, John, i, 568

Frog Pond, Boston, ii, 134

Frolics, ii, 4

Frontier, expansion and disappearance of, i, 157-59, 161, 292, 453

Fugitive Slave Act, ii, 380-82

Fulton, Robert, i, 495; ii, 224, 232

Fulton Market, New York, ii, 137

Fundamental Constitutions of Carolina, i, 65

Fur seals, in China trade, i, 308-9

Fur trade, i, 85, 190-91, 192, 193, 198-203, 214, 215, 216, 217, 337

Gabriel, Ralph Henry, cited on Civil War, ii, 391

Gage, General Thomas, i, 138

Galaxy, quoted on baseball, ii, 57, 61

Gallatin, Albert, quoted on communications, ii, 198; on federal union, 278, 279

Gallipolis, Ohio, i, 177

Games, early interest in, ii, 6-9. *See also* Play, Recreation, Sports *and individual games by name*

Gaming, ii, 16

Gangs, ii, 147, 151

Gannett, Lewis, cited, ii, 180

Garland, Hamlin, i, 426, 427; quoted on Grange and County Fair, i, 424-25; on Chicago World's Fair, 559; on circus, ii, 74

Garrison, William Lloyd, ii, 380

Garrisons, frontier, i, 193-97

Gaslight, ii, 162-63

Gaspé, i, 24

Gates, General Horatio, i, 144; ii, 206

Gazette, Cincinnati, quoted on steamboat, ii, 234

Gazette, London, quoted on fighting at Concord, i, 137

Gazette, New York, quoted on Fulton Market, ii, 137

Gazette, Salem, quoted on Battle of Lexington, i, 136

General Pickering, privateer, i, 300

Genesee Valley, New York, i, 175, 361-62, 384, 405, 406

George, Fort, i, 217

George, Henry, i, 461

George, Lake, i, 101

George II, King of England, i, 63

George III, King of England, i, 130, 149, 161

Georgetown College, ii, 342

Georgia, settlement and growth, i, 59, 60-63; secession, ii, 384

Germans, in Pennsylvania, i, 77, 78, 385-86; use of leisure, ii, 38; militia companies and lodges, 40; immigration of, 167, 346-48; in South America, 346

Geronimo, i, 158

Ghent, Treaty of (1815), ii, 324

Gila River, i, 245

Girdling, process of, i, 168

Gladstone, William Ewart, quoted on American Constitution, ii, 316

INDEX

Labor, organization of, i, 490, 553-54; skilled, early demand for, 492; dignity of, 502; strikes, 556-57; growing power of, 557; child, 557

Labor-saving devices, penchant for, i, 493

La Charette, i, 216

Lachine Rapids, i, 25

Lacrosse, i, 207

Ladies' Billiard Messenger, The, ii, 31

Lady Washington, sloop, i, 214

Lafayette, Marquis de, i, 332

Laffite, Jean, ii, 117

Lahontan, Baron de, quoted on Indians, i, 31

Land, boom of 1870's and '80's, i, 421. *See also* Agriculture, West

Land laws, American, i, 420

Landholding, in England and America, i, 56-57

Langley, Samuel, i, 559; ii, 304

Laramie, Fort, i, 228-29, 244, 272

La Rochefoucauld-Liancourt, Duke of, ii, 105; quoted on Charleston, i, 373; on balls in Philadelphia, ii, 107; on American inns, 213

La Salle, Robert Cavelier, Sieur de, i, 20, 24, 30, 32; quoted on prairies, i, 410

Latin America, i, 9; trade with, i, 334, 339; wars of independence, 333, 339; Germans in, ii, 346

Latrobe, Benjamin Henry, ii, 112, 132

Laudonnière, René de, i, 25

Law, John, i, 32-34

Lawrence, Bishop William, quoted on godliness and riches, i, 554

Lawrence, Kansas, ii, 382

Lazarus, Emma, ii, 406

Lazell, Perkins & Company, i, 534-35

Leadville, Colorado, i, 263; ii, 38

League of American Wheelmen, ii, 279

League of Nations, ii, 415

Leatherstocking, Cooper's portrayal of, i, 201; ii, 370-72

Leavenworth, Fort, i, 261

Leavenworth, Kansas, ii, 260

Le Boeuf, Fort, i, 98

Le Bouteux, Jean Baptiste Michel, i, 32-33

Lectures. *See* Lyceum movement

Ledyard, John, i, 213-14

Lee, Richard Henry, cited on time and distance as obstacles to federal union, ii, 200

Lee, Robert E., i, 71; ii, 383, 386, 391

Lee, William, ii, 140-41

Leipzig, i, 198, 203

Leisure, need for, ii, 4-5; early status of, 15; employment of, 78-79

L'Enfant, Major Pierre, ii, 113

Lenin, Nikolai, ii, 415

Leslie's Illustrated Newspaper, quoted on prize fighting, ii, 33

Leslie's Weekly, quoted on railway, ii, 259

"Letter to Santangel, The," i, 7-8

Lewis, Meriwether, i, 192, 216-17, 474

Lewis and Clark expedition, i, 53

Lexington, Battle of, i, 136-38

Liberty. *See* Freedom

Libraries, in colonial America, i, 122-25

Library Company of Philadelphia, i, 123

Life, quoted, ii, 85

Lighthouse, first, at Boston, i, 93

Lighting, of cities, ii, 162-63, 174

Lightning, clipper, i, 347

Liguest, Pierre Laclède, i, 192

Lilienthal, David, quoted on soil destruction, i, 462; on public need, 468, 470; on T.V.A., 566

Lima, Peru, i, 15

Lincoln, Abraham, ii, 385; on Egypt of the West, i, 289; on slavery, 383; Homestead Act, 420; on western prairies, 542; applauds "Dixie," ii, 29; study of German, 347; first inaugural address, 383-84; on Union and slavery, 390; second inaugural address, 391

Lincoln Highway, ii, 283

Lind, Jenny, ii, 36-37

Lindbergh, Charles A., ii, 308

Lisa, Manuel, i, 192, 217

Little Big Horn, Battle of the, i, 275-76

Little Turtle, i, 172, 173

Livingston family, i, 87

Locke, John, i, 65, 121

Lockport, New York, ii, 220

Locomotives, American, in Europe, i, 533

Lodge, Henry Cabot, quoted on menace of immigration, ii, 407

London, influence of, on colonial culture, i, 121; growth of, ii, 102

Long, Major Stephen H., i, 221, 283

Long Branch, New Jersey, ii, 55

Long Island Sound, ii, 226

Longfellow, Henry Wadsworth, i, 332

Lord, Russell, quoted on American land, i, 470

Los Angeles, i, 22; ii, 127, 190

Louis XVI, King of France, ii, 344

Louis Philippe, King of France, ii, 105, 213, 344

Louisbourg, Cape Breton, i, 96-97, 98, 104

Louisiana, French in, i, 20, 32-34; New Orleans described, 378-79; sugar production, 379; secession, ii, 384

Louisiana Purchase, i, 158, 190, 221

Louisville, Kentucky, ii, 167

Lowe, T. S. C., ii, 301

Lowell, Francis Cabot, i, 501

Lowell, James Russell, ii, 134; cited on American malpractice, i, 538

Lowell, Massachusetts, early industrial community, i, 500-502, 504, 520

Lower California, i, 22

Lower Creek Indians, i, 62

Lumber, for sailing vessels, i, 351

Lutherans, i, 60-62, 80; ii, 339

INDEX

INDEX

Yerba Buena, i, 237. *See also* San Francisco
York engine, ii, 246
Yorktown, siege of, i, 149
Young, Brigham, i, 233, 235

Yukon, i, 291

Zincke, Reverend Foster Barham, quoted on Chicago, ii, 120